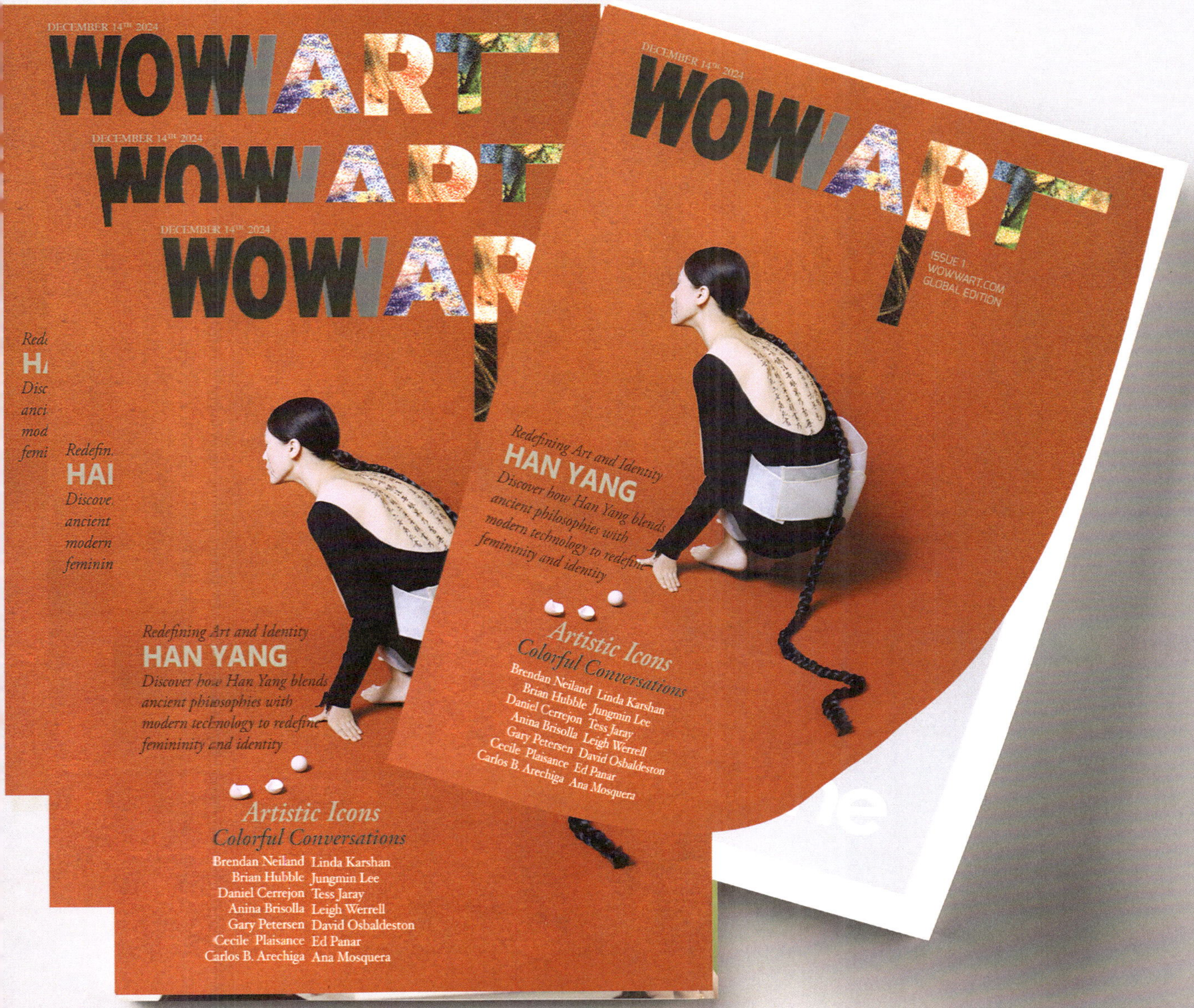

Dive
Into a
Great
Journey

Ready to
share
your
story?
https://entrepreneurprime.co.uk
editor@entrepreneurprime.co.uk

entrepreneur prime
Empowers Globally

Builds global branding, reaching over 190 countries and thousands of platforms

A good book
will keep you
fascinated
for days.
A good bookshop
for your
whole life.
Waterstones
WOWwART II 5

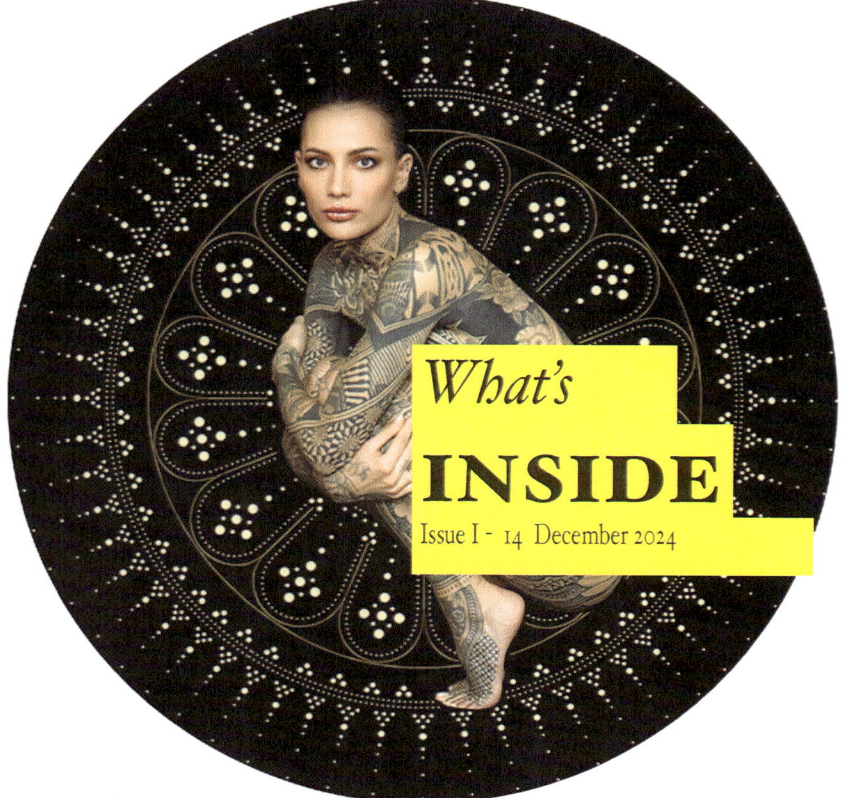

16 CECILE PLAISANCE

Plaisance redefines Barbie, transforming her into a symbol of strength and rebellion in the fight for women's rights

What's
INSIDE
Issue I - 14 December 2024

Cover
Redefining Art and Identity

18 HAN YANG

Discover how Han Yang blends ancient philosophies with modern technology to redefine femininity and identity

Han Yang explores metaphysical nothingness and posthumanism, blending ancient and modern elements to challenge traditional gender narratives and redefine identity through her innovative art and photography.

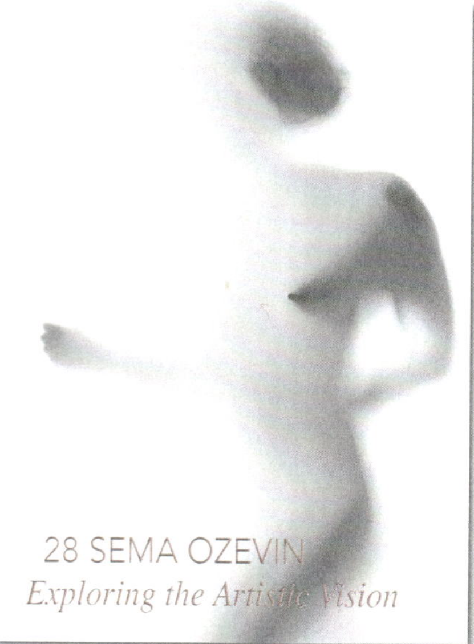

28 SEMA OZEVIN
Exploring the Artistic Vision

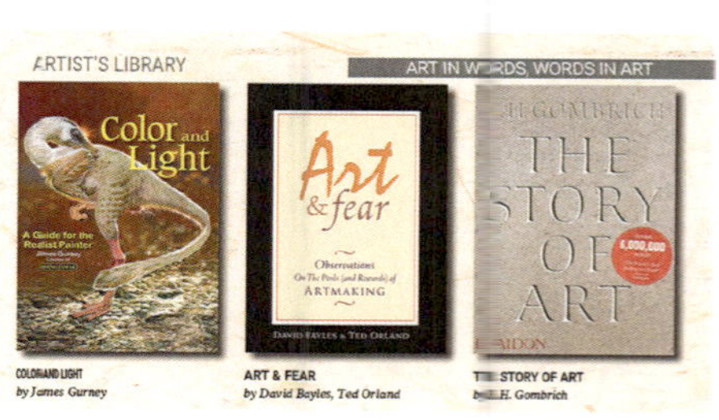

eMag

PUBLISHER: WOWwARt, A Subsidiary of NewYox Media Group. 200 Suite 134-146 Curtain Road, EC2A 3AR London, United Kingdom
t: +44 79 3847 8420 editor@wowwart.com II http://wowwart.com
EDITORIAL: Roberto Pandozzi, Editor-in-Chief, Olivia.Lee, Managing Editor, Noah Davis, Sam.Taylor, Ayla Walker Content Editors
Reporters: Jack Wilson, Jenny Taylor , J. Evans, Amy Browm CONTRIBUTOS: Claudine D. Reyes, Z. Roberst, Adrian T.

From the Editor's Desk

Welcome to the inaugural issue of WOW-wART, your premier source for exploring the vibrant world of the art industry. We are thrilled to embark on this journey with you, as we delve into the diverse talents and stories of artists, photographers, curators, and all those who contribute to the rich tapestry of creative expression. Through in-depth interviews, insightful articles, and stunning visuals, our aim is to celebrate the passion and innovation that drive the art community, inspiring you to appreciate and engage with art in all its forms.

Here's why being part of WOWwART is a game-changer for artists and creators alike:

Tangible Credibility and Prestige

Being featured in a printed magazine is a testament to an artist's dedication to quality and higher standards. Unlike the transient nature of online content, print offers a sense of permanence and credibility.

Global Reach and Timeless Presence

WOWwART defies the odds in the publishing world by maintaining a robust presence in print across 190 countries and over 40,000 retailers and platforms, including giants like Amazon, Barnes & Noble, Walmart, Blackwells, and Waterstones. Unlike traditional monthly or bimonthly publications, WOWwART issues are available indefinitely, ensuring that your feature remains accessible and relevant for years to come. This timeless availability enhances your global reach and keeps your work in the spotlight long after the initial publication.

Enhanced SEO and Marketing Performance

One of the standout features of WOWwART is its strategic use of METADATA, which significantly boosts an artist's SEO and marketing performance.

Exclusive and High-Quality Features

WOWwART is selective, featuring only 20 to 24 artists per issue. This exclusivity ensures that each artist receives a personalized editorial introduction and praise, creating a promotional tool that can be leveraged in marketing efforts.

Integration with Digital Channels

While the digital landscape offers numerous opportunities for reaching audiences, WOWwART complements these efforts by providing a tangible, high-quality platform that enhances digital marketing strategies. The magazine serves as a powerful tool for social media and Google Ads campaigns, offering a unique blend of traditional and modern marketing techniques that maximize your reach and impact.

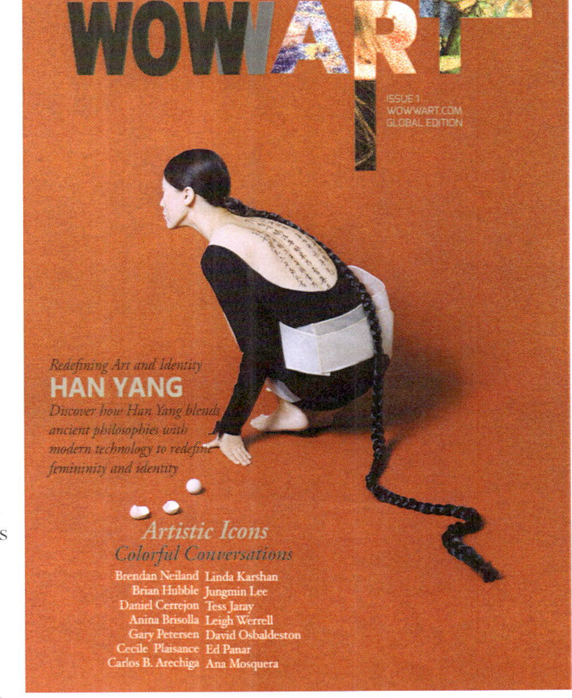

Being featured in WOWwART magazine is not just about being in print; it's about leveraging a prestigious platform that offers global reach, enhanced SEO, exclusive features, and unparalleled credibility. For artists looking to make a lasting impression and expand their audience, WOWwART is an invaluable ally in the ever-evolving world of publishing.

Thank you for joining us on this exciting journey. We look forward to sharing the incredible stories and works of art that will inspire and captivate you.

R. Pazdozzi
Editor-In-Chief

ART FAVORITES

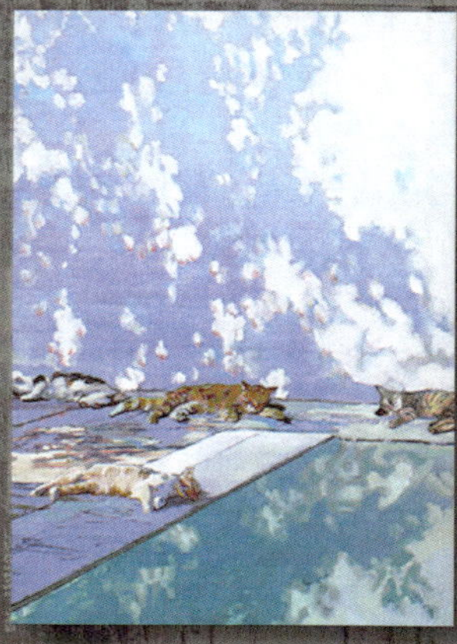

Greek Kitty's #4 (2024)
TIMOTHY A. MATTHEWS
Oil painting on Canvas
Size: 40.64 x 55.88cm
$899
https://bit.ly/48U8SiX

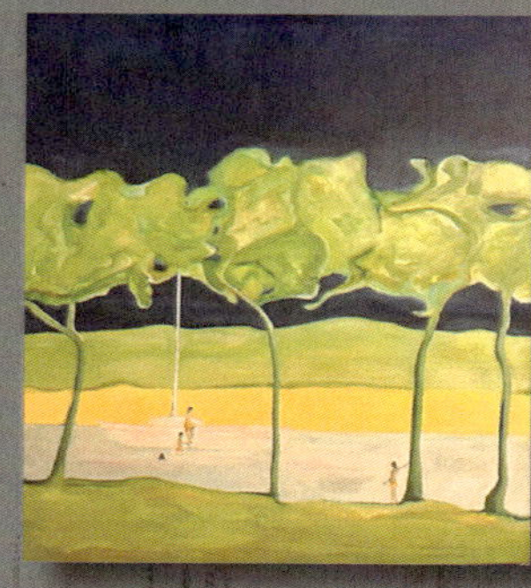

Swimming in the Uruguay River (2024)
ROMUALD M MUSIOLIK
Oil painting on Canvas
Size: 100 x 120 x 2cm
$399
https://bit.ly/4fxjbMn

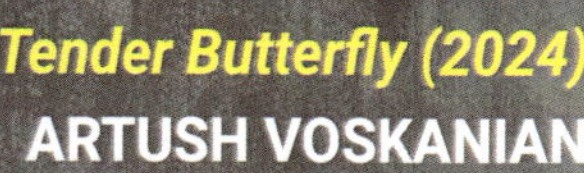

Tender Butterfly (2024)
ARTUSH VOSKANIAN
Oil painting on Canvas
Size: 60 x 80 x 2cm (unframed)
$3,230.74

https://bit.ly/3AMRq33

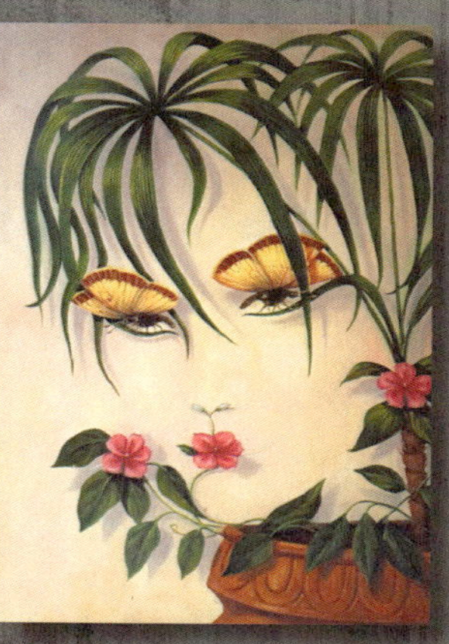

Vik Muniz
Brazilian, b. 1961
Digital chromogenic print (c-print)
Image: 44.5 x 25.5 in. (113.03 x 64.77 cm.)
$7.000

https://bit.ly/48R4eiI

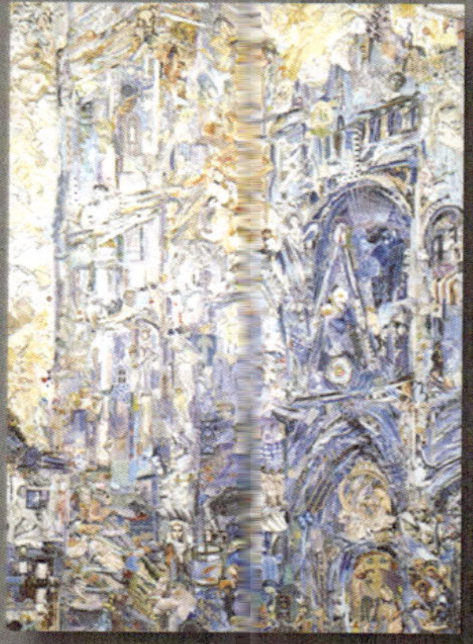

Miami Beach Hut (2022)
EMMA LOIZIDES
Oil painting on Canvas
Size: 90 x 122 x 5cm (framed)
$640.85

https://bit.ly/3Z6kewK

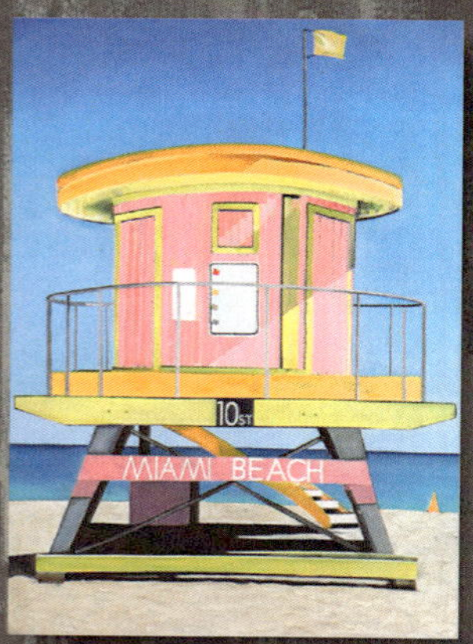

Seascape (2024)
DMITRY OLEYN
Oil painting on Canvas
Size: 40 x 50 x 2cm (unframed)
$2,441.91

https://bit.ly/4eC5Dxf

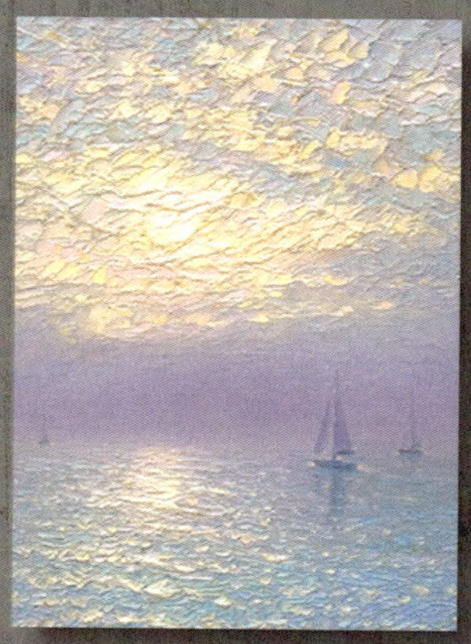

Nude VII (2021)
ALEXANDER TITORENKOV
Oil painting on Canvas
Size: 60 x 90 x 2cm (unframed)
$4,900

https://bit.ly/3Z7zr0x

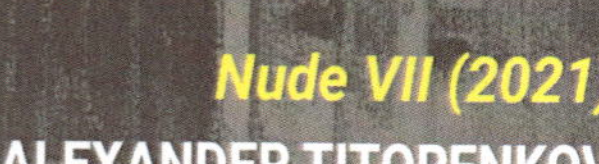

Ballet Dancer CDLXVII (2023)
REME JR.
Watercolour on Paper
Size: 24.5 x 34 x 1cm (unframed)
$237.12

https://bit.ly/4foL74O

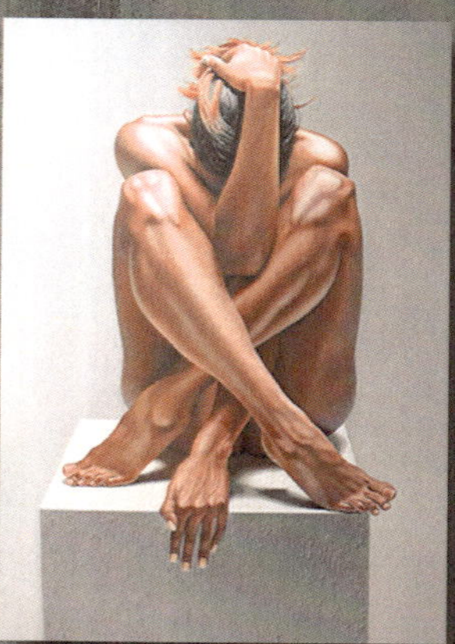

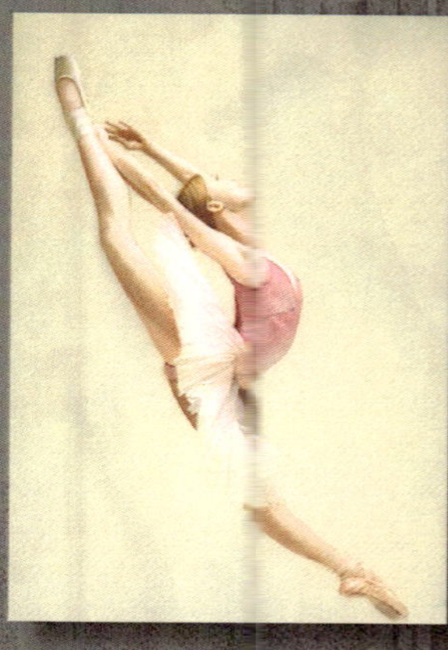

ART FAVORITES

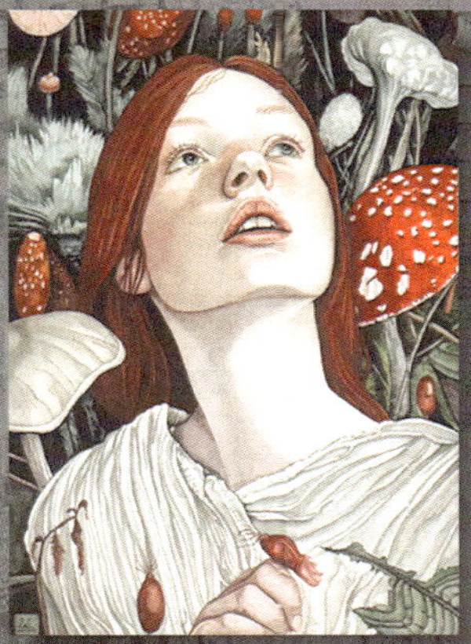

I Hear You Calling (2024)
LISA LENNON
Watercolour on Paper
One of a kind artwork
Size: 24 x 33 x 0.1cm (unframed)
$820.29

https://bit.ly/3YYwlLk

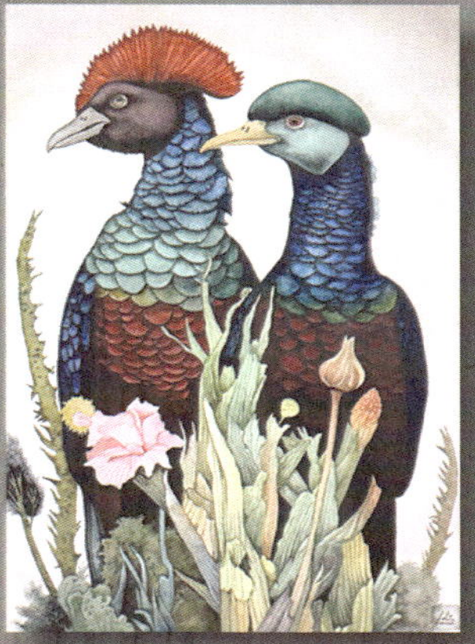

Red and Blue Crested Birds (2024)
LISA LENNON
Watercolour on Paper
Size: 29 x 42 x 0.1cm (unframed)
$692.12

https://bit.ly/3Z6OyHH

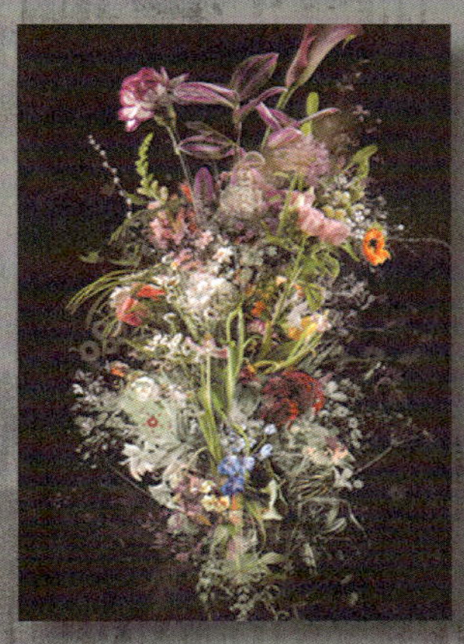

Bouquet Cinquante (2022)
TEIS ALBERS
Mixed-media painting on Canvas
One of a kind artwork
Size: 80 x 120 x 4cm
$2,601.17

https://bit.ly/3ObT3KF

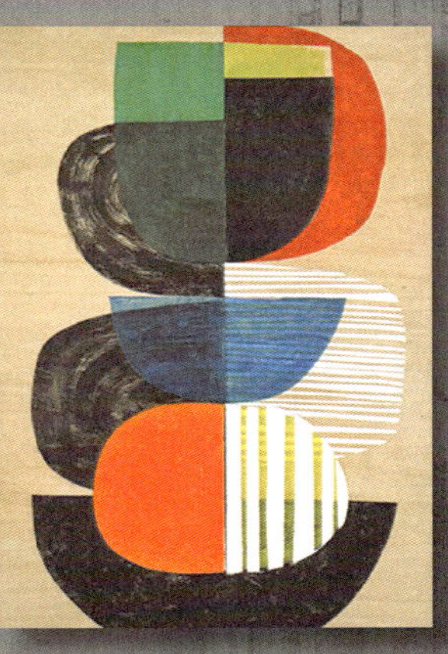

Setting Sail for Ithaca
DOMENICA BROCKMAN
Mixed-media painting on Panel / Board / MDF
Size: 60.96 x 91.44 x 1.91cm (unframed)
$1,400

https://bit.ly/4hSfFxC

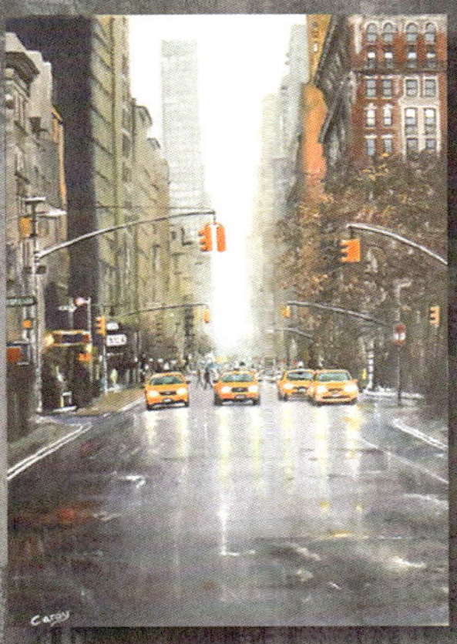

New York (2023)
DARREN CAREY
Mixed-media painting on Paper
Size: 28 x 38cm (unframed)
$442.19

https://bit.ly/4hOerDr

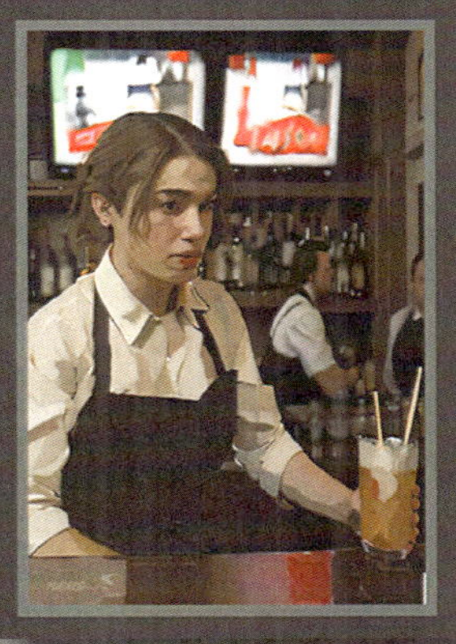

THE BARMAID V (2024)
JOE MCHARG
Mixed-media painting on Panel / Board / MDF
Size: 77.47 x 107.95 x 0.76cm (unframed)
$790

https://bit.ly/4fGkRCO

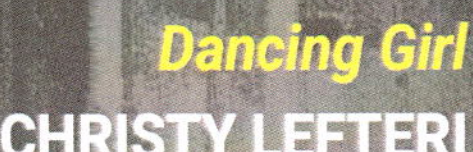

Dancing Girl
CHRISTY LEFTERI
Canvas Art
Rolled Canvas/Frameless
$218

https://bit.ly/4eARbGd

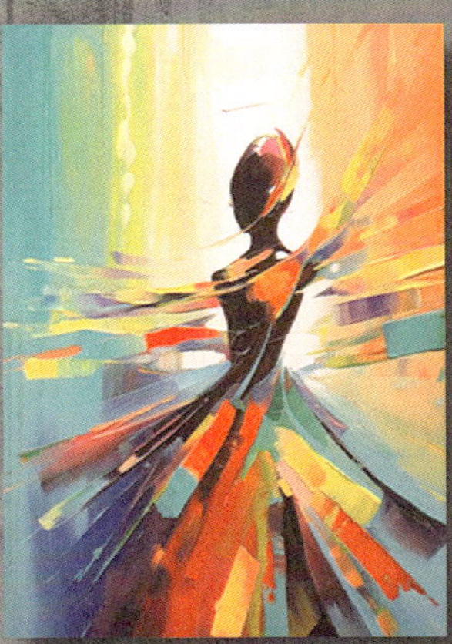

Geometric Abstract
ROLPH SCARLETT
Frame Included
$50,742.92

https://bit.ly/48UsF1v

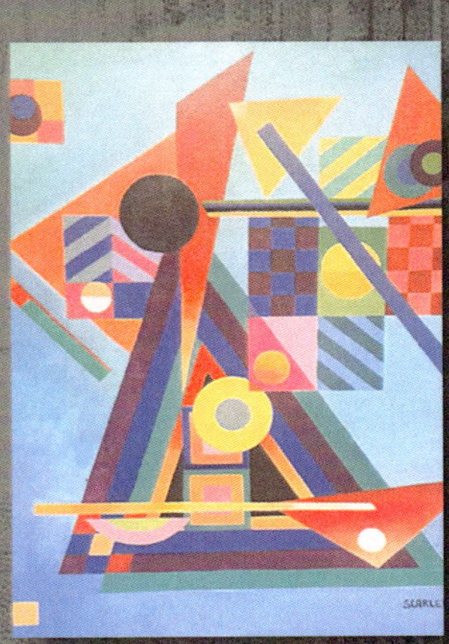

Brendan Neiland reflects on his artistic evolution, from peaceful landscapes to bustling cities, and shares how urban reflections, vibrant colors, and dynamic architecture became the heart of his creative expression.

BRENDAN NEILAND

The Power Of Modern Metropolitan Life As A Muse

as told to Archie Preston

Brendan Neiland's work captures the essence of urban life in a way few others can, transforming everyday cityscapes into vibrant, reflective wonders. Known for his fascination with architectural forms, mirrored surfaces, and the dynamic pulsating energy of metropolitan settings, Neiland invites viewers to see cities as multi-layered compositions of light, colour, and structure. His art draws you in, reflecting the compelling contrast of grand scale and intricate detail, capturing the dichotomy of intimacy within enormity that defines city life. Through decades of dedication, his works have become iconic portrayals of the modern urban experience, reflecting his unique ability to blend meticulous technical skill with an emotional depth that resonates universally.

Neiland shares insights into his creative journey—from his formative years in East Anglia and Birmingham to his lifelong captivation with cities around the globe. His story unveils how the stark transition from pastoral landscapes to urban vitality shaped his artistic vision, instilling a fascination with the scale, dynamism, and vibrancy of urban environments. Neiland's commitment to capturing the energy of city life, often through countless hours spent observing, walking, and photographing, becomes the foundation

"Brendan Neiland in his studio, where his passion for urban reflections and architectural forms takes shape on canvas."

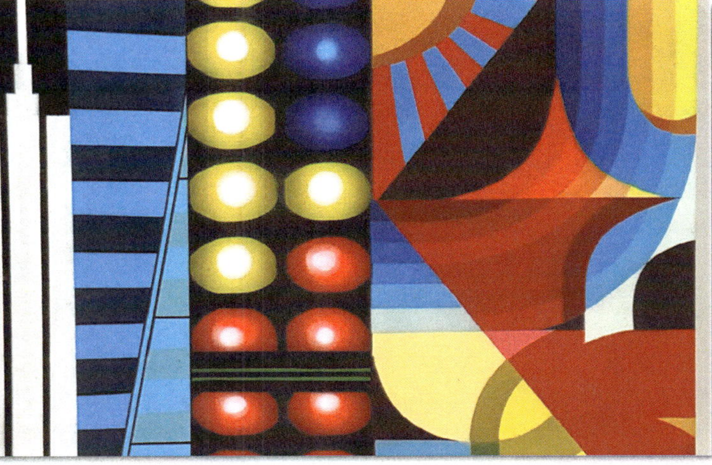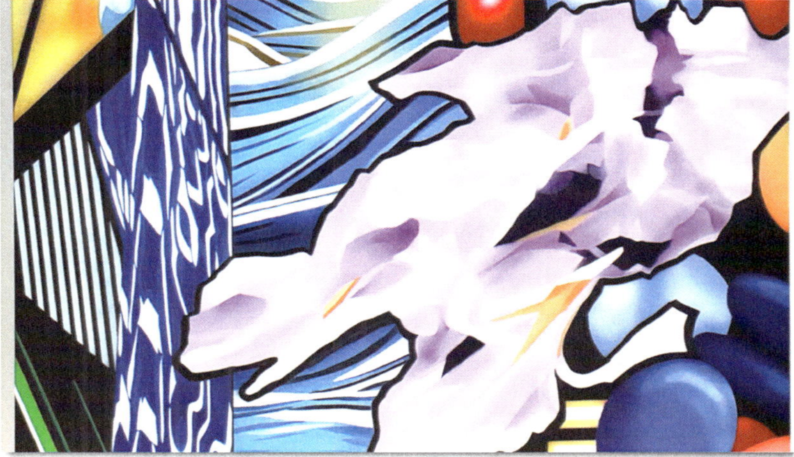

Brendan Neiland's vibrant abstract composition invites viewers into a dynamic exploration of urban life, where bold colors and geometric patterns reflect the pulsating energy of cityscapes. Each section of the painting captures the intricate interplay of light and structure, embodying Neiland's fascination with the modern metropolis and his journey from the serene landscapes of East Anglia to the vibrant streets of Birmingham and beyond.

of his art—a dedication to portraying the allure of modernity in all its raw and polished forms.

How has your background and education influenced your approach to painting and printmaking?

I lived in East Anglia until I was fourteen, peaceful, blissful, huge skies with lush flat meadows. And then I moved to Birmingham.

Amazing, all embracing. From Constable to Fernand Leger.

This altered my life, I felt exhilarated. it was so exciting to live in a place so vibrant...

Everything, the size, activity, noise, the shops and factories, it was so vital and I loved it.

I attended St. Phillip's a Catholic school run by the Oratorians. I went from there to the White Fathers seminary in the depths of Ireland. Here I spent a highly organised and disciplined two years studying philosophy and preparing for the priesthood. The Father Superior encouraged me in my art, painting and creating. Through dyed sawdust, I created huge heads of saints which were destroyed by the processions on feast days.

I did however miss the world and left Ireland to join Birmingham Art School Strangely the change was not anywhere as extreme as I had anticipated,

to be a priest or an artist both demand complete dedication and commitment.

I spent some months in various factories making colour studies of the huge iron ingots being smelted and turned into beautiful parts for ships and cars.

In 1996 I was accepted inti the painting school of the RCA. An extraordinary and very formative environment, led by Carel Weight with Peter Blake, Dick Smith and Jim Dine.

Your art often reflects themes of modern metropolitan existence. What aspects of urban life do you find most inspiring or challenging?

The City became my subject matter. Starting with machine parts, then cars, the environment reflected in the car bodies and finally the buildings of the city.

Since Birmingham I have lived in and visited cities worldwide

My first visit to New York City in the early seventies shocked and stunned me. It was exhilarating. I have made a pilgrimage every year since.

Exhibitions and commissions and desire have taken me, amongst others, to Singapore, Hong Kong, Shanghai, Central America and many cities within Europe The strangest experience being Las Vegas, pure theatre, no night or day pure enticement.

I walk and walk looking listening and soaking up the atmosphere.

I always have a camera. The photographs provide a reminder

and a visual support in the studio but it is the walking and being totally immersed in the environment that is primarily important.

At first the city buildings provided my inspiration with the reflections of the sky and the traffic. Gradually the advertisements with their powerful colour, the displays in the shop windows, the extraordinary crowds within the city centres the multitude of languages feed into the paintings. City centres are incredibly enticing, the displays and the advertisements are huge catalysts and ever present in our daily lives

How do you balance the intimate and grand elements in your artwork, and what do you hope viewers take away from this contrast?

I want the excitement and awe that I feel to be present in my paintings

The architecture and all of the other elements that make up the city strive for a certain perfection through form material and colour to win over the approbation of us all

A way of life is being displayed, one that is so rich and desirable

I immerse myself in it. I Love it and it provides my inspiration

Brendan Neiland's mastery lies in his ability to capture the beauty, complexity, and vibrancy of urban life with profound emotional resonance.

Artist Brian Hubble blends fine detail with surreal, expressive imagery, using image-transfer techniques to create pieces that explore the relationship between images, performance, and the unexpected. His work invites contemplation through poetic contrasts.

BRIAN HUBBLE

A Dialogue Through Drawing

Using a Range of Materials

Editor's Desk

Brian Hubble's artistic journey reads as a tapestry woven from his explorations across continents, styles, and mediums. Rooted in the diverse energy of Brooklyn, New York, for over two decades, Hubble's work carries a deeply reflective quality, channeling experiences from his stints in Italy and Chicago. His art has graced respected spaces like the Museum of Contemporary Art in Chicago and MoMA PS1, while his unique interpretations have been highlighted in the New York Times, Taschen Books, and Print Magazine. Hubble's artistry invites viewers into his meditative creative space, where images blend and transform, balancing meticulous detail with bold, surreal contrast.

An artist with a dedication to defying convention, Hubble's work radiates both intimacy and complexity. He navigates striking contrasts—fine detail meets cartoon simplicity, historical iconography mingles with the everyday, and his pieces explore the relationship between images, performance, and dialogue through drawing, balanced by innovation. Hubble's distinctive image-transfer techniques and reverence for process elevate each piece, cultivating a "dreamy uneasiness" that lingers in the viewer's mind. Here, in this exclusive WOWwArt Magazine interview, Hubble shares insights into his world of contradictions, process, and performance—revealing an artist as thoughtful as his creations are unforgettable.

Can you describe how your early experiences with drawing have shaped your current artistic practice?

My earliest memory is of my mother patiently teaching me to draw a spider web when I was five. That experience sparked my curiosity and inspired me to try drawing something

> I believe contradictions play a crucial role in dreams—an idea I keep in mind when merging original and classical imagery."

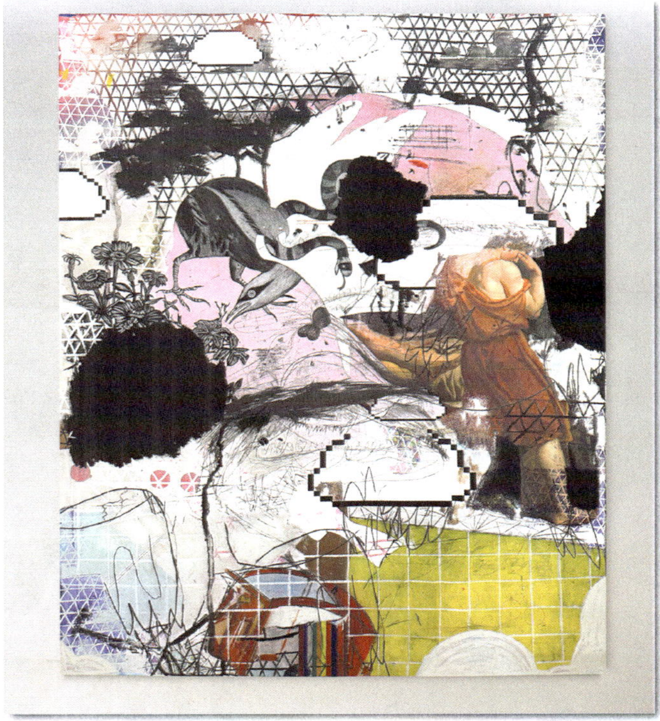

more complex, like our family pets or a face. Once I explored those subjects, I felt the need to return to something more immediate, which often manifested as hasty scribbles or crayon markings. These impulsive drawings held as much significance for me as the "harder" pieces. Years later, as an art student, this ebb and flow became a driving force in my work. I was always interested in creating artworks that serve as a rebuttal to those that came before, both in timing and content. I still work this way today.

You mention the use of image transfers in your work. How has this technique evolved over time, and what does it add to your creative process?

As a longtime admirer of Robert Rauschenberg's work, I have always been fascinated by the various techniques for creating image transfers. My version is quick and inexpensive. I print on silicone coated release paper—typically discarded after peeling off envelope labels or stickers. Its surface has just enough coating to retain the printed image yet pliable enough for an effective transfer onto clean paper. I photograph the most successful transfers and refine them as single images in post-production software before integrating them into an overall composition. This method is repeated for every element of a piece until it is nearly exhausted into completion. At this point, an ultraviolet print of the composition is made onto a large sheet of canvas. I work on top of the print with graphite, colored pencils, oil, and pastels. I intentionally leave select areas in their UV print form, exposing colorful yet disquieting backgrounds. This multi-step process allows me to slowly manipulate volume and stillness within the piece.

Your drawings exhibit a blend of laborious detailing and cartoon flatness. How do you navigate this balance, and what do you hope to convey through these contrasts?

Deciding whether to make a detailed drawing or something quicker depends on the subject at hand, and how previous pieces were created. My next concern is the interaction between each drawing and the surrounding images. I'm constantly tweaking because, for me, one of the joys of being an artist is form discovery. I hope that the forms in my work poetically mingle with tension. I want to share the weary yet hopeful, meditative space I fall into while creating them.

You discuss creating a sense of "dreamy uneasiness" in your work. What specific techniques do you employ to achieve this effect?

I believe contradictions play a crucial role in dreams—an idea I keep in mind when merging original and classical imagery. I collage appropriated art historical figures such as cherubs and charmers, with curious animals and saturated flowers. I assign both familiar and surprising surfaces to the images I draw and paint. For instance, multiple layers of colored pencils can render skin with the translucent quality of marble. Graphite lends drawings of filing cabinets the chill of cold metal, while a combination of materials imparts a warm patina to wood. Illogical yet nuanced scenes feature recurring elements like orbs, rainbows, and patterned landscapes, which blur the line between representation and abstraction.

Your exhibition on Andy Kaufman explores the intersection of art and performance. How do you see your own work reflecting or challenging traditional notions of performance art?

We may someday need to have a separate interview about my time with Andy Kaufman and the exhibition I organized at the Museum of the Moving Image! I spent 16 years studying everything in Andy's world and cherish the friendship I developed with his family during that time in my life. While I experimented with performance art in graduate school, I have since transitioned to a hermetic studio practice. Although I wouldn't say there's a direct line from performance art to the paintings and drawings I'm making now, I like to think that a bit of Andy's spirit is woven into them from time to time.

What role do you believe nostalgia plays in your art, particularly when you incorporate drawings from 20 years ago with your current work?

Incorporating work I made in the past with newer pieces has led to unexpected breakthroughs. When reviewing my previous works, I don't feel a sense of the past or longing for what once was. At the time of making them, I probably didn't fully grasp how they might function down the road. I may have felt they were complete, but perhaps I was mistaken—I'm not entirely sure. I'm interested in introducing them to recent images to hopefully produce something surprising and genuine as a result. Many of these experiments fail, of course, but I suppose the idea is to fail a bit less with each attempt.

Crafting Dreams and Dualities in Modern Art

DANIEL CERREJON

A Dialogue Through Drawing

Using a Range of materials

Editor's Desk

> The knots are made by tying one after another in a compulsive manner until the rope can no longer be folded."

Daniel Cerrejon is a visionary artist whose work challenges the boundaries between the tangible and the abstract, the personal and the universal. With a career that spans continents and artistic disciplines, Cerrejon has cultivated a practice that is as intellectually rigorous as it is emotionally resonant. His art delves into the intersections of data, objects, and the human body, transforming cold, statistical abstractions into visceral, poetic forms. From his CORPUS series, which reimagines bodily measurements as intricate knots imbued with warmth and humanity, to his exploration of proxemics and relational distances, Cerrejon's work invites viewers to reconsider the ways in which we perceive ourselves and the spaces we inhabit. His ability to balance the technical with the corporeal, the conceptual with the sensory, marks him as a singular voice in contemporary art.

In this exclusive interview for WOWwART Magazine, Cerrejon offers a rare glimpse into his creative process and the philosophies that underpin his practice. From his early studies in Madrid and New York to his time at the Whitney Independent Study Program, he reflects on the cultural and intellectual influences that have shaped his journey. Through his thoughtful responses, Cerrejon unpacks the layers of meaning in his work, revealing how he transforms data into art and abstraction into intimacy. This conversation is a testament to his profound ability to bridge the gap between the empirical and the emotional, creating art that not only engages the mind but also resonates deeply with the soul.

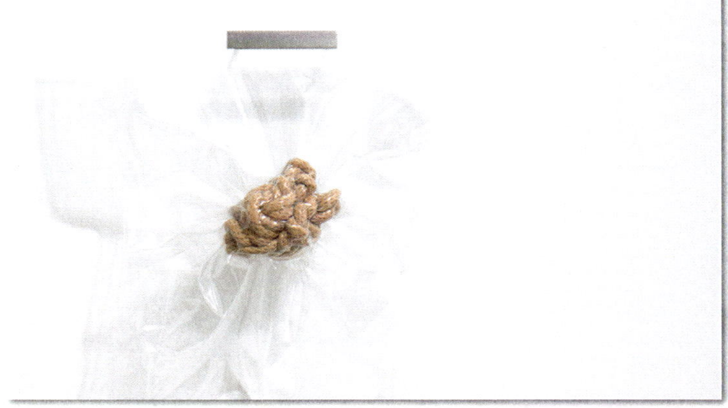

In the CORPUS series, what significance do the knots and flesh-like tones hold in relation to the "cold" statistical language used in the titles?

Each piece in the CORPUS series consists of various components. To answer your question, we can focus on four: the knots, color, titles, and bodily measurements. I appreciate how you frame your question in terms of 'coldness.' To me, two of these components are 'cold'—the measurements and color—while the other two, the knots and titles, feel 'warm.' By 'cold,' I mean purely conceptual elements lacking traditional artistry. The measurements represent body data, while the color comes from covering the knots with makeup in a shade that approximates the average skin tone of the American population at the time the works were made. Each piece in the CORPUS series reflects 'the average American person,' as indicated by the titles.

The two elements I consider 'warm,' as opposed to the 'cold' ones, are the knots and titles. Each title in this series combines various standard bodily measurements, arranged in a poetic way. The rules for these poetic titles vary for each piece. Sometimes, the poetry lies in the sound and rhythm of the words, while other times, it emerges from the sequential meaning of specific measurements. An example title from this series is From One Hand to the Other, whilst Each Holds the Other, of the Average American Person.

The last of the four elements we're discussing is the knot, which I described as a 'warm' element in this temperature analogy. Each knot is made by cutting a rope to the length specified in the title and tying it into a continuous knot without a beginning or end. The process of knotting is arbitrary and emotional, created by tying one knot after another in a compulsive manner until the rope can no longer be folded.

Your work brings a visceral, almost tangible presence to abstract measurements. How do you balance the contrast between the technical and the corporeal in your art?

My artwork is the embodiment of data, often related to our bodies, into physical objects. This process involves a back-and-forth between a scientific approach—an empirical method of acquiring knowledge —and an artistic approach, which is more intuitive in solving and understanding a situation. As we discussed, some works begin with a system of bodily measurements. These measurements transform into language, which is articulated in a specific way, and this language, in turn, influences the form of the work. This form is then received by the viewer, shifting their perception of themselves. It is in this final stage, when the work is perceived, that I would describe the experience as visceral. Not only because some pieces resemble guts or internal organs, evoking raw, physical sensations, but also because the perception of objects appeals to physical sensations rather than logical reasoning. I believe this sensory engagement shapes how we understand ourselves. It's not just in artworks; all the objects around us play a role in shaping our self-perception.

Could you share more about your exploration of proxemics in your work? How do you approach representing human relational distances through sculpture?

Proxemics is the study of how people use space and distance in communication, and how these distances can convey meanings,

emotions, and social dynamics. In my work, I explore these 'empty distances'—the spaces between people interacting—and transform them into objects. The resulting objects serve as index of an absence.

How does the concept of "average" influence your art, particularly in terms of bodily metrics and flesh tones, and what commentary are you hoping to make on standardization?

I became interested in the concept of the average because it transforms something universal into something particular. The data tables I use in my work are already the result of averaging—data taken from a large group of people within a specific segment of the population, with the average presented as a universal. In my work, I often reverse this process, calculating the average of various universal data points to produce a singular value, which then becomes an art object. The average calculation explores the relationship between the universal and the particular, or the collective and the individual.

By using this averaging method, I break the typical logic of data extraction. While averaging is normally part of data analysis, in my work it serves no practical purpose other than to create art.

For viewers of your work, what emotions or reactions do you hope to evoke as they encounter the embodied and recontextualized measurements in your sculptures?

As I mentioned before, more than emotions or reactions, I'm interested in art and the act of making because of how our surroundings influence our perception of ourselves. Making art is a way for me to engage with the constellation of things around us.

Redefining Boundaries in Art and Space

Anina Brisolla discusses her innovative art practice, exploring themes of privatization, environmental politics, and digitality through layered works that challenge societal structures and humanity's relationship with space and materiality.

ANINA BRISOLLA

Exploring the intersections of digitality, materiality, and humanity's impact on nature and the cosmos

Editor's Desk

Anina Brisolla is a visionary artist whose work challenges the boundaries of medium, material, and meaning. Based in Berlin and the Oderbruch, her practice spans digital painting, collage, video, and installation, creating a rich tapestry of thought-provoking explorations. Brisolla's art delves into the intersections of privatization, power structures, and humanity's relationship with nature and space, offering a critical lens on the visual language of institutions and the societal shifts brought about by digitality. Her creations are as conceptually profound as they are visually striking, embodying a delicate balance between fragility and structure, the digital and the tangible, the real and the imagined.

In this exclusive interview for WOWwART Magazine, Brisolla takes us behind the scenes of her creative process, offering insights into her recent series such as "Prospect," "fabrics," and "value systems." From her intricate 3D pen sculptures to her layered explorations of space privatization and environmental politics, Brisolla's work invites us to question the systems that shape our world—and the worlds we may one day inhabit. Join us as we delve into the mind of an artist whose practice is as multifaceted as the themes she so eloquently interrogates.

In your series 'Prospect', you explore the concept of space as a new frontier for privatization. What inspired you to address this theme through NASA and ESA imagery?

I was looking at one image that was all over the news back then, entitled ‚New earth-like planet found'.

> **The transfer between digital and analogue media has characterized my work for a long time.**

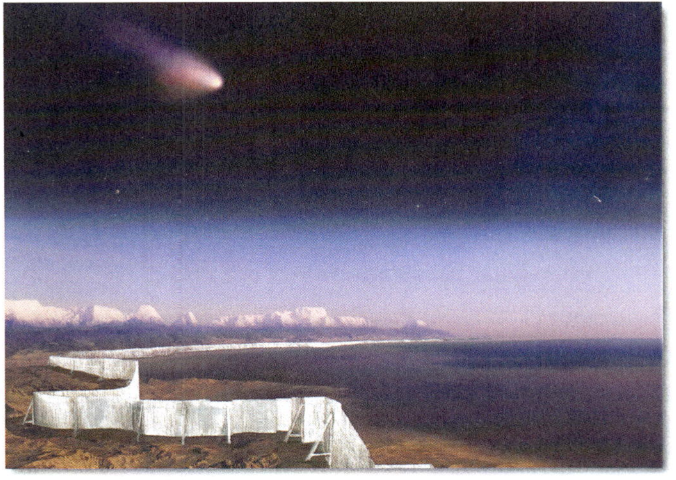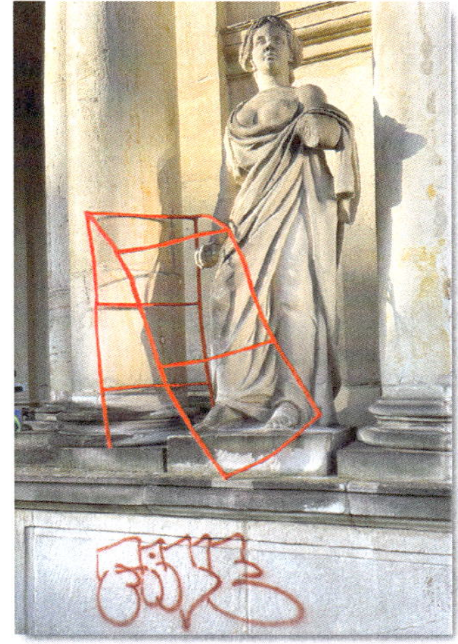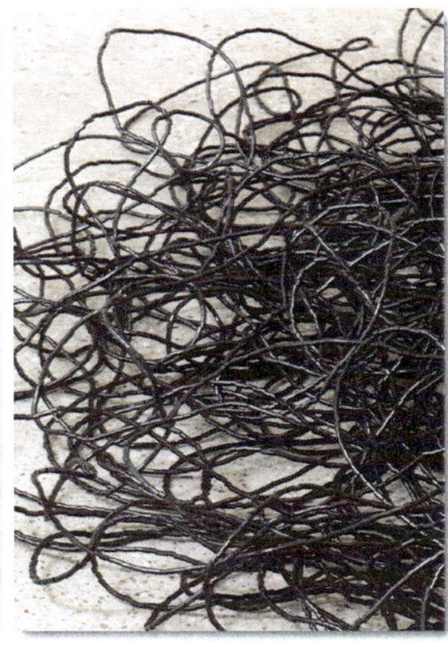

Anina Brisolla's captivating creations are a testament to her extraordinary talent and vision. Her work masterfully bridges the realms of art and technology, evoking deep emotions and sparking meaningful conversations. Each piece reflects her dedication to pushing boundaries, making her a true inspiration in the contemporary art world.

The image made me wonder what this would imply. So I printed it and started drawing directly onto the print. The image had a dark romanticism about it, almost like some sort of

> Anina Brisolla's art is a profound fusion of intellect and creativity, offering bold critiques of societal and environmental paradigms.

heavy-metal cover-artwork. That triggered me. As I continued the 'prospect' serie, I started to work with a program similar to Google Earth, but in space. This allowed me to explore space and 'take pictures' of sceneries stars, exoplanets, etc.

How do you view the intersection between environmental politics and space exploration in your work, particularly with the concept of space enclosures?

I consider fencing off an area to be an ancient cultural technique. In this we visibly separated ourselves from nature and in doing so, we have placed ourselves above nature.

What will we humans do after having destroyed this world? We fly to another planet and colonize it. And what is the first thing we do there?

We stake out land, put up fences and take possession. This is already happening now. Not literally like in my drawings, but the race to be the first has long since begun. And even though there are regulations and acts like for example the 'Outer Space Treaty' from 1967, the economic interests are a strong engine to fuel this „New Space Economy" Space is already full of junk. Wherever men will go, a line of left behinds shows our appearance.

Could you describe the specific process you follow to achieve the final layered look in your pieces, especially when working with large-scale images that you draw over?

For the 'prospect' series, I worked from real models. This means that the fences and walls I drew there all have a real place in the world. My work is often preceded by intensive research and I like to use images that are anchored in the collective consciousness.

For 'prospect' for example I collected a lot of material of border fences and walls. I found it interesting to pursue questions of materiality onto another planet, so I decided for a way of drawing that is both realistic and painterly somehow and you get an idea of what the thing is made of. As the imagery often has some 'kitschy' aspect to it, this creates an interesting tension.

Shifting between different media, from video to installation, seems to be a key aspect of your work. What influences your decision to choose one medium over another for specific projects?

A new project usually arises from direct involvement with a specific topic, reading or watching a documentary for example. I have always been interested in how digitalization affects society. And at the same time, the transfer between digital and analogue media is an idea that has characterized my work for a long time. For me, it therefore seems just logical to include the choice of working material in the conceptual process with every new project.

Sometimes I work with a kind of 'reverse engineering' and that also determines the final result.

Some of my work of recent years deals with the process of 3D printing in this analytical way. I replaced the mechanics of the print head, which is calculated and controlled by the computer, with the movement of my hand along predetermined lines of movement.

Could you explain the significance of the 40,000-bead installation '8 Milliarden' in your SMAC exhibition and how it complements the other works?

'8 Milliarden' - 8 billion - corresponds to the current population of the world. In my exhibition called 'space mining' at SMAC I created work along three timelines: past – present – future.

'8 Milliarden' is thus to be seen as the present. I wanted to see the world's population manifested and at the same time know for myself how big this pile would be. There is an addition to the title: M 1:200.000. This is the scale in which the work is carried out. So one pearl corresponds to the population of a middle sized city such as Kassel here in Germany or i.e. Norwich in the UK.

'space mining' denotes the concept of mining raw materials in space. Optimistic scientists predict that in twenty years' time, it will likely be possible to apply those techniques. Globalization has mapped the world anew and revealed the finitude of raw materials. The quest for resources has always inspired the human spirit - and attempts to pursue them have had a lasting impact on human history. This is where I started my artistic reflection on the topic, questioning the motives of the actors involved. I conceived this model of the present in order to use it as a starting point for these considerations.

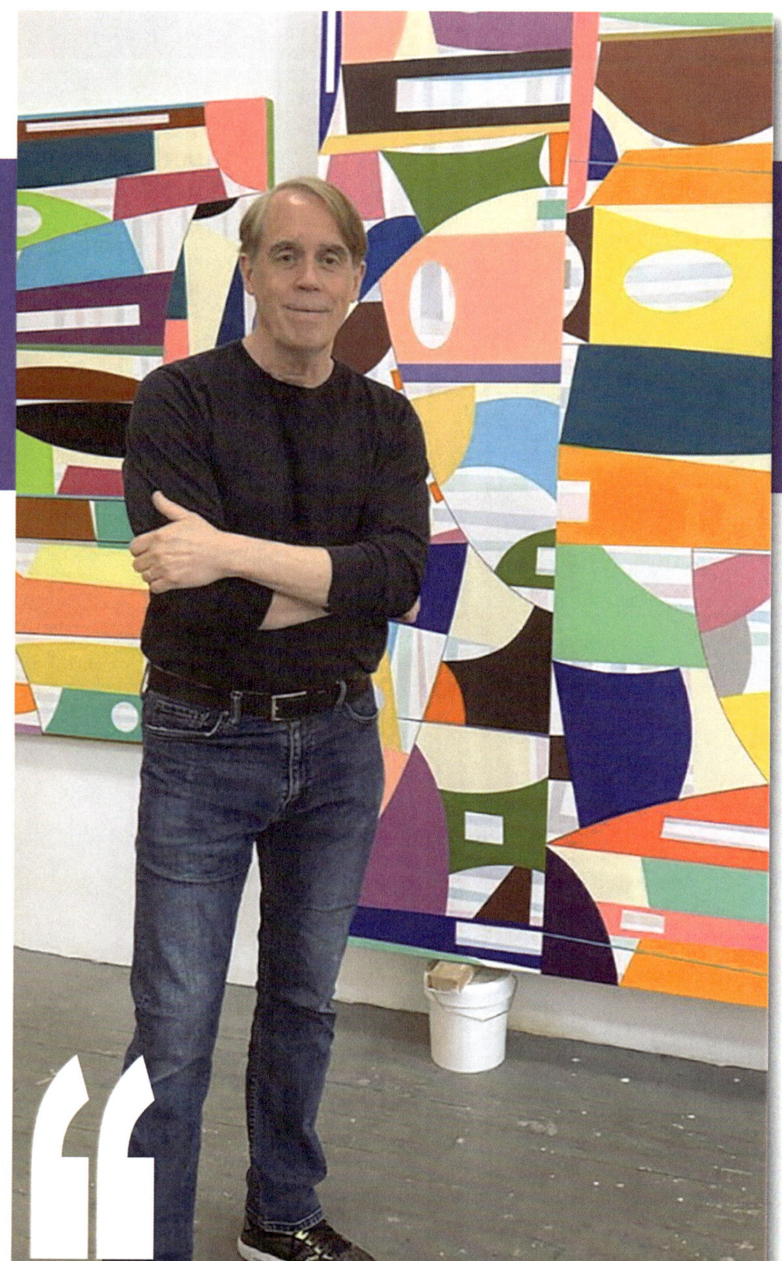

The luxury of time at both residencies allowed me to explore new avenues in my work, free from the usual day-to-day distractions"

Gary Petersen explores his journey from Staten Island to international acclaim, reflecting on how residencies, awards, and solo shows have shaped his bold, vibrant approach to abstraction and his evolving color palette.

GARY PETERSEN

An inside look at Petersen's creative process and inspirations

Editor's Desk

Gary Petersen's work radiates an extraordinary sense of colour, shape, and rhythm, breathing life into geometric abstraction with a style that is both playful and profound. Over the years, he has established a unique visual language, characterized by bold compositions and vibrant palettes that defy the confines of the canvas, inviting viewers to delve into layered meanings and emotional resonances. His ability to balance precision with spontaneity results in paintings that seem to vibrate with movement, a testament to his mastery of form and hue. Petersen's work not only captures the eye but also elicits an immersive experience—one that has earned him a well-deserved place in prestigious collections and institutions worldwide, including the Jewish Museum and the Dallas Museum of Art. From his studios in Brooklyn and Hoboken, he continues to push the boundaries of abstraction, bridging contemporary sensibilities with timeless artistic inquiries.

Petersen reflects on the influences that shaped his journey, from his Staten Island upbringing to his unexpected turn from animal science to art during his college years. He shares insights into his creative process, shaped by transformative residencies and international exhibitions, and discusses the profound impact of awards like the Barnett and Annalee Newman Foundation Grant. Join us as Petersen offers a rare glimpse into his inspirations, challenges, and hopes for the lasting impact of his art.

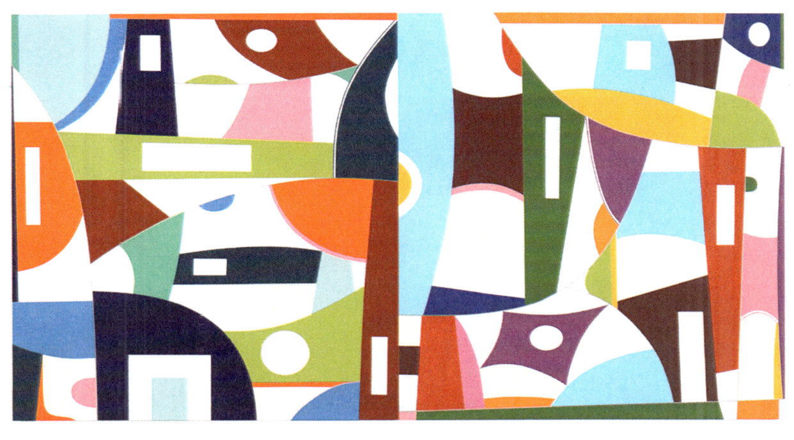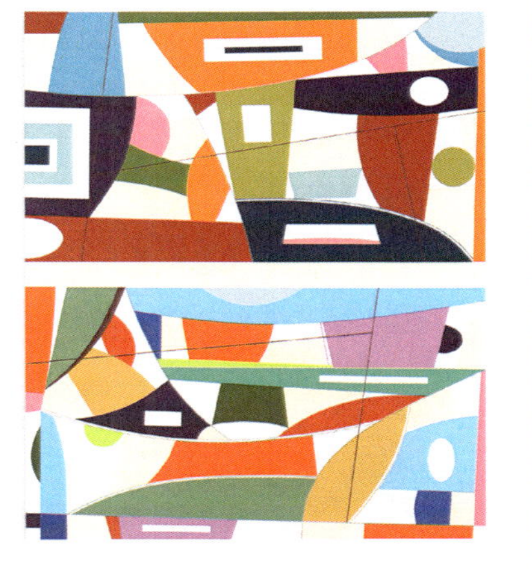

Gary Petersen's mastery of color and form infuses geometric abstraction with emotional depth, inviting viewers to experience art as connection.

How did growing up in Staten Island and studying at Pennsylvania State University influence your artistic development and approach to painting?

Staten Island is one of the five boroughs that make up New York City, and I grew up there in a lower-middle-class household. My parents did not have a college education, and I attended Catholic schools without any art classes. While I always had an interest in art and biology, as a first-generation college student, I felt pressure to become something rather than simply study something. When I was accepted to Pennsylvania State University, I chose to major in Animal Science, thinking I wanted to become a veterinarian. At that time, it never even crossed my mind to study art. But in my junior year, I took an art class as an elective and fell in love with it. I also began to socialize with some of the graduate art students and realized that this was what I truly wanted to pursue. I wanted to become an artist.

You have received several prestigious residencies, including at MacDowell and the Bogliasco Foundation in Italy. How have these experiences shaped your creative process?

The wonderful thing about artist residencies is twofold: you meet creatives outside your own field, and you're given the gift of time and space. The luxury of time at both residencies allowed me to explore new avenues in my work, free from the usual day-to-day distractions. At Bogliasco in particular, the Ligurian light and vibrant colors of the Italian cityscape inspired me to push my color palette even further.

What was it like being awarded The Barnett and Annalee Newman Foundation Grant in 2020, and how has this recognition impacted your career?

It was a complete surprise. After decades of work, it's wonderful to be recognized and validated for all the effort you put in. The award gave me the freedom to focus on my studio practice without financial worries, and, additionally, the Foundation purchased one of my paintings and donated it to the Jewish Museum in New York as part of the Newman Foundation collection. This prestigious collection includes many well-known artists, and it's such an honour to be a part of it.

You've exhibited your work internationally, from New York to Munich. How does your approach differ when preparing for solo exhibitions versus group exhibitions?

In group shows, you have limited control; the curator or art dealer installs the pieces and decides which works to include. With solo shows, however, I think more intentionally about how my work will interact with the space where it will be displayed. Since I'm always working in my studio, the gallerist often visits, and together we select the paintings for the show. We discuss which pieces work well in conversation with each other. When I know about a solo show well in advance, I also consider the sizes I want to paint and how they'll function within that specific space.

Many prominent publications have reviewed your work over the years. How do you feel about the role of art criticism in your career and the reception of your paintings?

I generally enjoy reading reviews of my work, as they often offer insights that give me new perspectives to consider. It's especially gratifying to read thoughtful criticism, such as John Yau's reviews of my work. He is both articulate and insightful about painting, and he can explain my work far better than I ever could.

Your work is featured in both private and public collections, including the Dallas Museum of Art and The Jewish Museum. What do you hope viewers take away from your paintings when they see them in these different contexts?

First, it's an honour to be included in these permanent collections. I hope my work captures the viewer's eye, drawing them in to look, connect, reflect, and perhaps experience a bit of joy. The Dallas Museum holds an earlier work compared to the piece at The Jewish Museum, but both are part of their contemporary collections, so the contexts are similar. My hope is that these works resonate with viewers about our present world and remain relevant for generations to come.

The Birth of Metaphorical Realism

Vladimir Kush, founder of Metaphorical Realism, blends imagination and realism to create art that celebrates life, nature, and metaphor, inspiring audiences worldwide with his unique and positive vision of surrealism.

Vladimir Kush Redefines Surrealism with Metaphorical Realism, Blending Imagination and Nature in a Visionary Artistic Journey

Vladimir Kush is a renowned contemporary artist and the founder of "Metaphorical Realism," a unique artistic style that blends realism with metaphorical imagination. His works, displayed in galleries worldwide and in his own "Kush Fine Art" galleries, invite viewers to explore hidden connections between seemingly unrelated elements, offering a fresh perspective on the world.

Kush describes Metaphorical Realism as the art of discovering hidden likenesses between objects and connecting them in unexpected yet harmonious ways. Unlike traditional surrealism, which often distorts reality, his style emphasizes the internal similarities between realistic objects, creating a romantic and imaginative view of the world. For Kush, the goal is to reflect life through metaphor, finding parallels for every aspect of existence.

Metaphor, for Kush, is more than a linguistic tool—it is a way of understanding and communicating. Through metaphor, he stimulates the subconscious, awakening the viewer's imagination. He likens this process to Plato's concept of the "cave," where human souls retain core ideas of the world. Kush's art serves as a catalyst for this subconscious recollection, allowing viewers to see the familiar in a new light. "Imagination is more important than knowledge," he emphasizes, as imagination creates connections between seemingly unrelated elements.

Kush's journey from a struggling artist to an internationally acclaimed visionary is a story of perseverance. Growing up in Moscow, he was deeply influenced by classical art, literature, and the cultural values of his family. His father, a mathematician and poet, played a pivotal role in shaping his artistic sensibilities. In 1990, Kush made the bold decision to stay in the United States, embarking on a challenging path of self-discovery. From drawing portraits on the beaches of Santa Monica to establishing his own galleries, Kush's journey is a testament to his relentless pursuit of his vision.

The 1990s were a formative period for Kush, marked by relentless effort and the search for his unique style. By 1998, his hard work bore fruit, and he emerged as the founder of Metaphorical Realism. Iconic works like *Wind*, *Fauna in La Mancha*, *Bound for Distant Shores*, and *Music of the Woods* became defining examples of his method, laying the foundation for his artistic legacy.

Kush's creativity extends beyond painting. He has ventured into sculpture, jewelry, and even interactive apps for children, translating his artistic concepts across various mediums. "Sculptures and jewelry allow me to add another dimension to my ideas," he explains. This versatility demonstrates the universality of metaphor, proving that it can exist not only in words and paintings but also in three-dimensional forms.

While Kush cites Salvador Dali as an influence, his artistic journey was shaped by a diverse range of inspirations. His father, despite being a mathematician, was his first teacher, nurturing his love for art from an early age. Kush's artistic evolution began with Renaissance art, transitioned through Impressionism, and eventually found its voice in Surrealism. However, it was the French artist Claude Verlinde who had the greatest impact on his work.

Kush's approach to Surrealism diverges from the darker tones of Dali's era, which were shaped by war and crisis. Instead, Kush introduces a fresh, positive perspective, harmonizing his art with nature and celebrating the beauty of the world. "For the first time in art history, I have introduced a positive side of Surrealism," he says, highlighting the originality of his vision.

Kush's art has been showcased in prestigious galleries and exhibitions worldwide, from South Korea to Russia and the United States. Despite his international acclaim, Kush believes that inspiration comes from within. "If there is inner emptiness, the whole world cannot fill it," he asserts. His art transcends cultural boundaries, inviting viewers from all walks of life to see the world through the mirror of metaphor.

Vladimir Kush's contributions to contemporary art are profound and enduring. As the pioneer of Metaphorical Realism, he has redefined the way we perceive and connect with the world. His art, rich in imagination and cultural depth, serves as a bridge between the material and the metaphorical, the real and the surreal. Through his paintings, sculptures, and other creative endeavors, Kush continues to inspire audiences worldwide, reminding us of the beauty and interconnectedness of life.

Vladimir Kush is a masterful artist whose visionary works redefine surrealism, inspiring awe with their depth, imagination, and beauty.

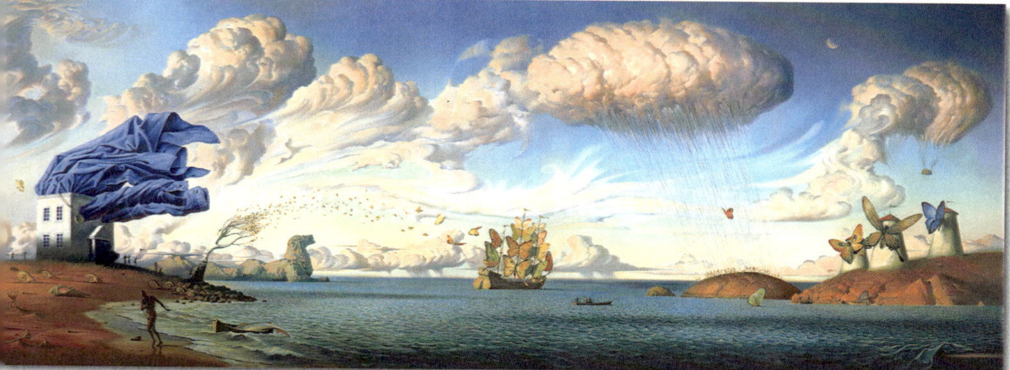

" *Imagination is more important than knowledge.*"

Vladimir Kush

Art as a Bridge Between Personal and Public Narratives

Danica Dakić discusses how the Bosnian War influenced her art, exploring themes of identity, collectivity, and the tension between personal and public narratives through innovative media.

Danica Dakić, a visionary artist whose work has been profoundly shaped by her experiences during the Bosnian War and the siege of Sarajevo, continues to captivate audiences with her exploration of identity, collectivity, and the interplay between personal and public narratives. An interview conducted with the artist for Mosaic Digest delves into the transformative impact of these experiences on her artistic vision and practice.

The war in Bosnia and the subsequent isolation from her homeland marked a pivotal shift in Dakić's artistic journey. During this period, she grappled with the meaning and function of art, leading her to explore new themes, media, and methods. Her installation "Blaues Auge" (1996) exemplifies this shift, addressing the disconnection between personal experience and media narratives. By collaging thousands of newspaper photos and headlines on transparent foil, Dakić created a powerful visual barrier that symbolized the opacity of media representations during times of conflict. This work, and others like it, reflect her ongoing artistic engagement with the tension between personal and public narratives.

Dakić's video installation "Grand Organ" (2010), commissioned for the Touched exhibition at St. George's Hall in Liverpool, further exemplifies her innovative approach to art. Inspired by the hall's majestic organ and neoclassical architecture, the installation explores themes of justice, performance, and music. By transforming the boys' choir into an organ with human pipe voices, composer Bojan Vuletić's sound design highlights the interplay between the legal system and spectacle. The involvement of local choirs, including the Liverpool Signing Choir and the "Sparrows" of Sparrow Hall, underscores Dakić's focus on polyphony and childhood, creating a narrative that examines power dynamics and community.

Throughout her career, Dakić has experimented with various mediums, from painting to video, sound, and text. Her choice of medium is driven by the narrative or message she wishes to convey, with each medium offering a unique way to experience her images. As an "image maker," Dakić believes in the power of images to communicate complex ideas and emotions that transcend traditional media boundaries.

Dakić's work is deeply informed by historical and social contexts, particularly in relation to identity and collectivity. While her personal experiences of war and displacement influence her exploration of these themes, her art speaks to universal experiences of mobility, migration, and living in multiple languages and cultures. Her work invites viewers to reflect on the perception of the global present and the role of the individual within larger societal structures.

The tension between individuality and collectivity is a recurring theme in Dakić's art, as seen in the allegorical references to music and law in "Grand Organ." She explores this tension on visual, acoustic, performative, and emotional levels, offering a nuanced perspective on the individual's place within society. Her art challenges viewers to consider the complexities of identity and the interconnectedness of personal and collective experiences.

Danica Dakić's artistic journey is a testament to her resilience and creativity in the face of adversity. Her work continues to inspire and provoke thought, offering a powerful commentary on the human condition and the ever-evolving narratives that shape our world. Through her innovative use of media and exploration of profound themes, Dakić has established herself as a leading voice in contemporary art, captivating audiences with her ability to transform personal experiences into universal narratives.

> **Dakić's experiences during the Bosnian War reshaped her artistic vision, leading to new themes and media explorations.**

Danica Dakić is a visionary artist whose profound insights and creativity transform personal experiences into universal narratives.

> **"** *"The war had a strong influence on my life and my art."*

Danica Dakić

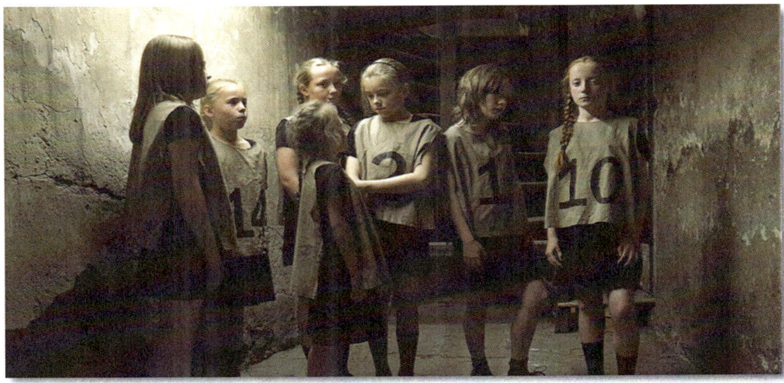

Barbie as a Feminist Icon
CECILE PLAISANCE'S BOLD VISION

Cecile Plaisance discusses her artistic journey, using Barbie and lenticular prints to address feminism, female autonomy, and societal constraints, challenging traditional roles and celebrating women's freedom of expression.

Plaisance redefines Barbie, transforming her into a symbol of strength and rebellion in the fight for women's rights

as told to Archie Preston

Cecile Plaisance's artistry is an unapologetic celebration of femininity, freedom, and provocative expression. With a career that began in the European financial markets before transitioning to photography, Plaisance's work boldly explores themes of gender, societal expectations, and religious constraints. She is known for her imaginative use of Barbie dolls as a medium, transforming the iconic figure into a symbol of female autonomy and challenging the viewer's perception of beauty and identity. Her distinct visual style combines playful imagery with serious commentary, asking us to reflect on the constructs that shape women's lives.

Plaisance's photographs resonate far beyond their immediate appeal. Through her series such as "Fuck the Rules" and her thought-provoking lenticular prints, she weaves a narrative of rebellion and empowerment. Her artistic voice pushes boundaries, inviting dialogue on the roles women occupy in society. With influences from luminaries like Helmut Newton and Ellen von Unwerth, Plaisance's work is simultaneously bold and thoughtful, elevating the conversation about femininity while presenting beauty, humour, and defiance in a unique and captivating form. Her images, often a blend of the provocative and profound, challenge societal norms and open the door for women to embrace their freedoms unapologetically.

How did your background in economics and finance influence your artistic journey, if at all?

My economic and financial background has not influenced my work as a photographer. On the other hand, even as a little girl, I collected magazine photos/images that I found beautiful. Mostly photos of women. I like to transcend the beauty of women. I'm fascinated by beauty.

When I left the world of finance, I moved on completely, not knowing where this new adventure would take me. And here I am!

What drove you to transition from photographing travel scenes and objects to focusing on Barbie dolls as subjects?

I've always had a camera at hand, especially since the birth of my children, whom I've obviously bombarded with photos! We've been lucky enough to travel a lot as a family, so I have photo reports of all our adventures.

When I went to photography school in 2008, we had to hold regular exhibitions with set themes. In 3rd and final year, the theme was free. I did a tribute to Helmut Newton, my mentor. I was looking for models who would be willing to stand in front of my camera, but nothing came of it. That's when the Barbie came to the fore... there were lots of them in my house... it was both a nod to my childhood (I played Barbie a lot) and a humorous way of dealing with feminists! Because who could be more feminist than Helmut Newton and his femmes fatales! And what consumer object could be more reviled than the Barbie....

I'm a feminist who asks women to play with everything that's possible in femininity.

How do you balance the playful and provocative aspects of your Barbie images while conveying deeper messages about femininity and women's rights?

What I just told you... Although the battle for gender equality is far from over, women must not abandon their femininity. The right to dress as they please, to wear make-up and lingerie... in short, to feel beautiful, should not be seen as a provocation to men. These are rights we have acquired, and we are free to use them or not. That's why my Barbie, with her ultra-feminine shape, allows me to deliver an even stronger message. I don't accept that laws dictated by men, particularly religious laws, should prevent our freedom of movement. My photos, like those of Femen, are indeed provocative. But the more provocative they are, the more my message gets out. Long live freedom for women.

Can you expand on the decision to undress Barbies in your work, and how it connects to broader statements about female autonomy?

As mentioned, the more provocative I am in my work, the more my message gets out. I undress my Barbies or Mannequins, to show that in a free world, the Woman (the Barbie) has the right to choose whether she wants to show her body or not. In the 21st century, the religious laws in force in certain countries hinder women's freedom, making them invisible, submissive, and dependent. This is no longer acceptable.

How has your process evolved now that you're working with human models, and how does it differ from working with Barbies?

It's still the same work with the same idea, that of defending women's freedom. The difference is that now, the models I work with fully support my project. The exchange is always fruitful and collaborative. Some women go even further than I do. I'm thinking of Marisa Papen, with whom I've worked on several series, and who pushes the idea to the point of living naked (as far as that's possible). I love working with women, the exchange is much more nourishing than with my Barbies!

What is the significance of your use of lenticular prints in your work, and how do you think it enhances the viewer's experience?

I've always worked in diptychs. With a before photo and an after photo: dressed / undressed... When I discovered this medium: lenticular, I knew right away that it was my medium, it's a "car stopper". It allows me to deliver my message in a more playful but also more conspicuous way. When people see my work, whether they like it or not, they stop. They move in front of the photo, they try to understand... it's also a bit reminiscent of our childhood, with double decimeters or placemats bought in souvenir stores.

Here is one of my famous work: Fuck the Rules. It shows a women in Burqa : undressed with a cigarette in her mouth and almost nude with written on her breast: Fuck the Rules. I think it is very explicit.

The second one, with the same model says in French: and God created Woman! It is also a very famous Film with Brigitte Bardot from Director: Roger Vadim in 1956!

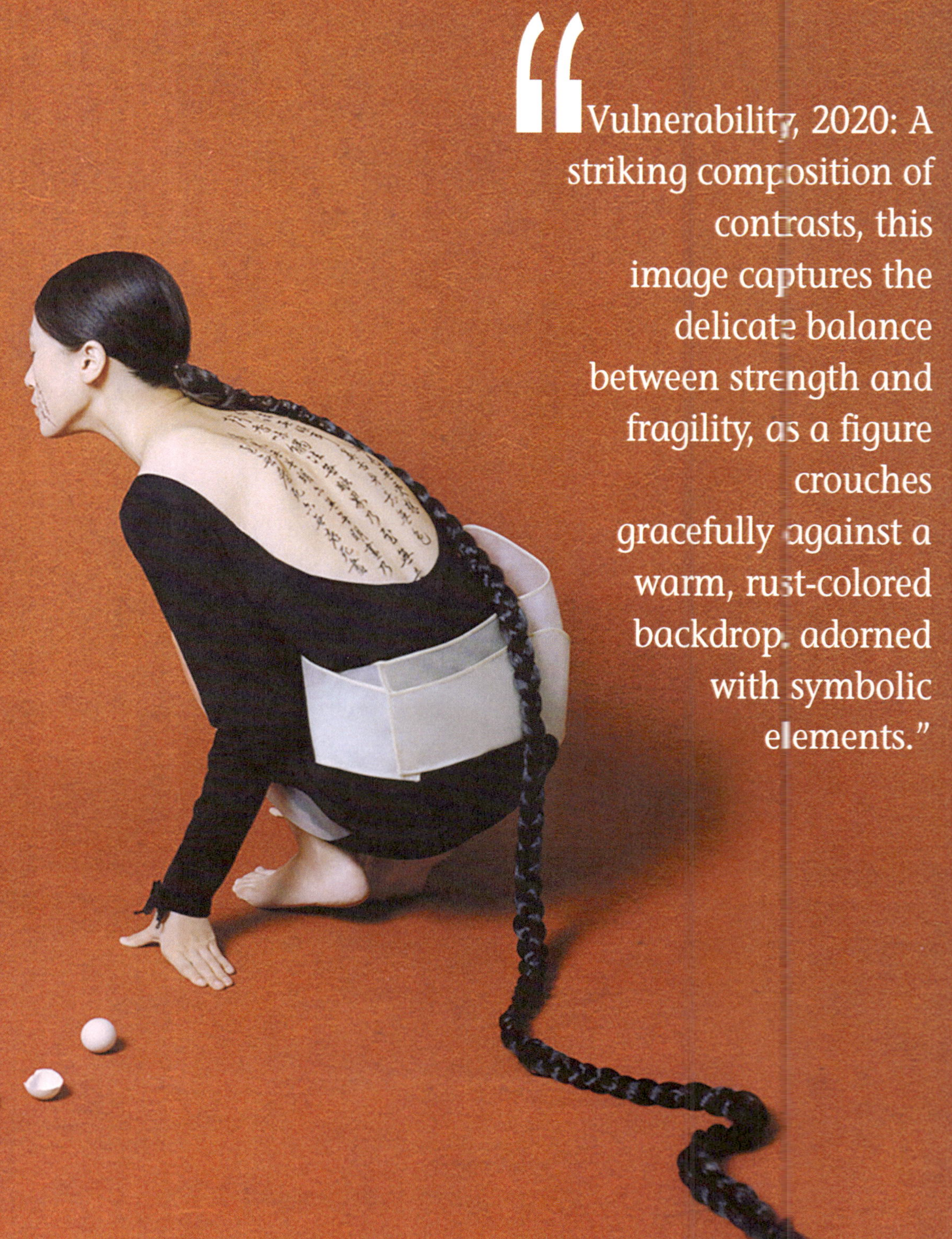

"Vulnerability, 2020: A striking composition of contrasts, this image captures the delicate balance between strength and fragility, as a figure crouches gracefully against a warm, rust-colored backdrop, adorned with symbolic elements."

Redefining Art and Identity

HAN YANG

Discover how Han Yang blends ancient philosophies with modern technology to redefine femininity and identity

as told to Archie Preston

Han Yang, a visionary artist and fine art photographer, graces the cover of WOW-wART magazine this month, bringing with her a profound exploration of art that challenges the very fabric of traditional aesthetics. Her work is a testament to the power of art to transcend boundaries and redefine norms, as she delves into the metaphysical realm of nothingness—a concept that has not only fueled her intellectual curiosity but also formed the foundation of her groundbreaking dissertations.

Han Yang's artistic journey is a harmonious blend of empirical life experiences and the timeless principles of Buddhist philosophy, expressed through a diverse array of multimedia forms. Her unique ability to visually articulate metaphysical nothingness is a hallmark of her innovative spirit, echoing the essence of ancient Zen paintings while simultaneously pushing the envelope of contemporary art.

In her photography, Han Yang masterfully intertwines themes of femininity, the human body, and technology with oriental metaphors, challenging and expanding traditional gender narratives. By integrating elements of Chinese culture with futuristic imagery, she reimagines femininity as powerful and autonomous, creating a visual dialogue that transcends cultural boundaries and redefines identity in a modern context.

Her research on posthumanism further enriches her artistic practice, allowing her to explore identity and gender through a nonhuman lens. By merging human and mechanical elements, Han Yang dissolves conventional boundaries, promoting a vision of identity that is fluid, interconnected, and liberated from traditional constraints.

Han Yang's creative process is a journey into the psychological depths of her subjects, capturing their inner worlds with a delicate balance of abstract and surreal elements. Her work navigates the intersection of commercial fashion photography and personal conceptual exploration, seamlessly blending artistic expression with market demands.

Recognized with prestigious accolades such as the SONY Young Photographer Award and the World's Top 10 Women Photographers Contest, Han Yang's career is a testament to her relentless pursuit of innovation and boundary-pushing artistry. As she continues her PhD at King's College London, her academic research and visual art practice intertwine, drawing inspiration from posthumanist and gender studies to create visual narratives that challenge and inspire.

Han Yang's work is not just art; it is a profound exploration of identity, technology, and the human condition, inviting us all to see the world through a lens of infinite possibilities.

Your work often intertwines themes of femininity, the human body, and technology with oriental metaphors. How do you use these metaphors to challenge or enhance traditional narratives of gender in your photography?

Han Yang explores metaphysical nothingness and posthumanism, blending ancient and modern elements to challenge traditional gender narratives and redefine identity through her innovative art and photography.

Continued *on page 26* 

COVER DIALOGUE

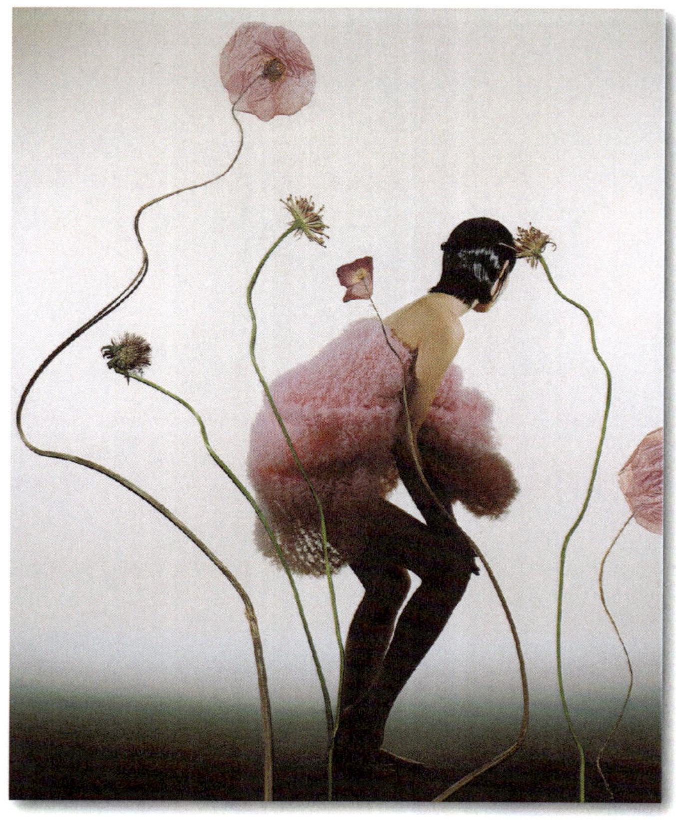

PAPAVER ROSES

A whimsical dreamscape unfolds as a figure in a fluffy pink garment interacts with oversized flowers, creating an ethereal atmosphere that blurs the line between fashion and nature.

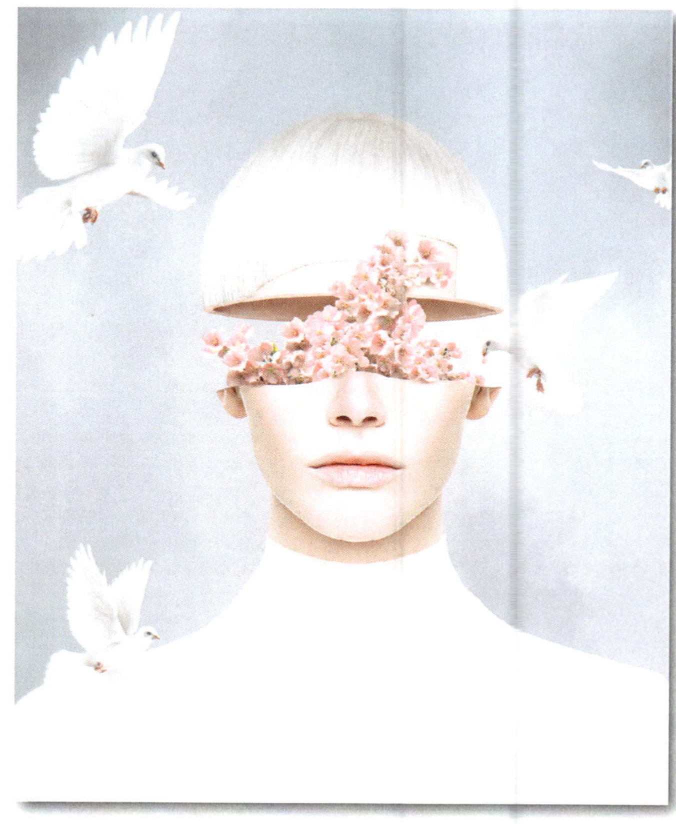

INVISIBLE, 2020

An evocative exploration of presence and absence, 'Invisible, 2020' captures the essence of what is seen and unseen, inviting viewers to ponder the hidden layers of reality.

In my photography, I use oriental metaphors to challenge and expand traditional gender narratives by incorporating elements of Chinese culture into contemporary representations of femininity. I often draw on cultural symbols like ancient Chinese script, mythical creatures, and traditional garments, which embody strength, transformation, and resilience. These symbols serve as a foundation for reinterpreting femininity in a modern context.

By combining these symbols with futuristic and technological imagery, I aim to portray women as powerful and autonomous, moving away from conventional passive depictions. Technology, in my work, symbolizes evolution—indicating that gender and identity are not static, but rather fluid and ever-changing. The juxtaposition of ancient and modern elements creates a visual conversation that not only transcends cultural boundaries but also redefines femininity in a way that harmonizes tradition with progress.

You're currently conducting research on posthumanism, particularly exploring gender through a nonhuman perspective in photography. How does **this research inform your artistic practice, and how do you envision posthuman concepts reshaping our understanding of identity and gender in art?**

My research on posthumanism informs my artistic practice by allowing me to challenge conventional notions of identity and gender. Posthumanism extends the concept of the "self" beyond human limitations, embracing the influence of technology, artificial intelligence, and the environment on identity formation. In my photography, I often merge human bodies with mechanical or abstract elements, dissolving the boundaries of gender and biological traits. This exploration of nonhuman perspectives highlights gender as fluid and evolving, rather than binary or fixed. I envision posthuman concepts reshaping art by promoting identities that are hybrid, interconnected, and no longer defined by traditional physical or social constraints, allowing for more inclusive and expansive representations of the self.

Your photography combines abstract and surreal elements with rich, delicate emotions. Can you walk us through your creative process and how you capture the psychological depth and inner

Han Yang is a visionary artist whose work transcends boundaries, redefining identity and challenging traditional narratives with profound innovation.

world of the characters you portray?

My creative process begins with understanding the emotional core of the concept or subject I'm working with. I spend time reflecting on the psychological nuances I want to evoke, whether it's vulnerability, strength, or transformation. From there, I incorporate abstract and surreal elements to create a visual language that mirrors these emotions without being bound by realism. I often use lighting, color, and unconventional angles to suggest an altered or dream-like reality, allowing the viewer to step into the internal world of the character. During the shoot, I work closely with the model, encouraging them to channel specific emotions, which helps bring out a raw, authentic expression. The delicate balance between surreal imagery and emotional depth is where I believe the psychological richness of my work emerges.

As both an artist and a fine art photographer, how do you navigate the balance between fashion photography's commercial aspects and your more personal, conceptual explorations of gender and the human body?

Navigating between the commercial nature of fashion photography and my personal conceptual work requires a constant balancing act. In fashion photography, the visual language often needs to align with brand identity and market trends, which can sometimes feel limiting.

However, I see this as an opportunity to bring my own voice into commercial projects by subtly weaving in themes of gender fluidity and the human body's complexities. When working on personal projects, I have the freedom to fully explore these concepts without constraints, diving deeper into abstract interpretations of identity and embodiment. I strive to find intersections where the artistic and commercial worlds can coexist, creating images that not only fulfil commercial needs but also provoke thought and emotion, allowing both worlds to inform and enrich each other.

You've been recognized with prestigious awards like the SONY Young Photographer Award and the World's Top 10 Women Photographers Contest. How have these accolades influenced your career, and what role do you see awards playing in the development of your artistic voice?

Receiving awards such as the SONY Young Photographer Award and recognition in the World's Top 10 Women Photographers Contest has greatly influenced my exploration of gender, identity, creativity, and technology. These accolades have given me the platform to delve deeper into these themes, allowing me to continue challenging traditional narratives around gender and identity through my work. They have affirmed my artistic direction and opened new pathways for creative collaborations where I can further merge technology with the human form. While awards are not the only validation, they play an important role in providing the space and recognition to push boundaries and experiment more freely, encouraging me to expand my exploration of posthumanism, fluidity, and innovation in both photography and art.

As you pursue your PhD at King's College London, how do you integrate your academic research with your visual art practice? Are there any particular philosophical or theoretical concepts that have recently inspired your work?

My PhD research has deeply informed and enriched my visual art practice. I explore the intersections of posthumanism, gender studies, and identity, drawing heavily from theoretical frameworks that challenge human-centric perspectives. Concepts such as Donna Haraway's cyborg theory and Rosi Braidotti's posthuman subjectivity have particularly inspired me to think beyond traditional representations of the body. These ideas resonate in my photography, where I often merge organic and mechanical elements to represent fluidity in identity and gender. The academic environment allows me to critically engage with these philosophical discourses and translate them into visual narratives. My research also helps me push the boundaries of how technology, the human form, and identity interact, making both my scholarly and artistic work extensions of each other.●

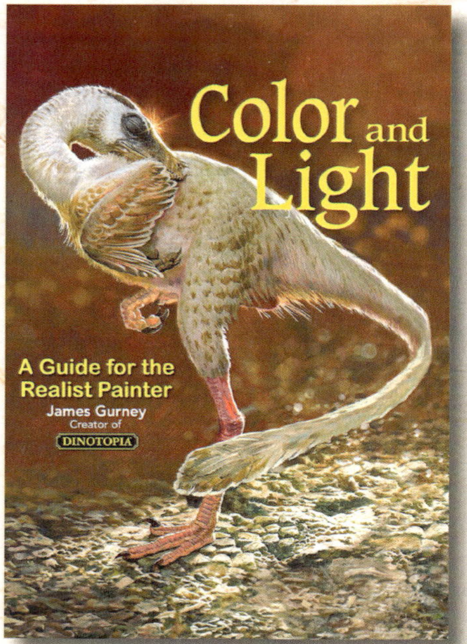

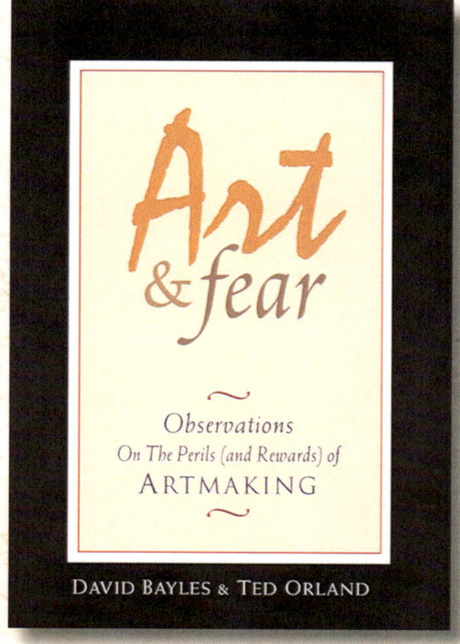

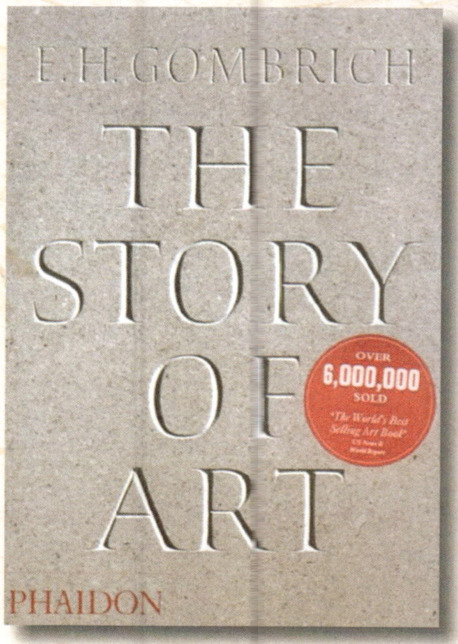

COLOR AND LIGHT

by James Gurney

ART & FEAR

by David Bayles, Ted Orland

THE STORY OF ART

by E.H. Gombrich

This is an essential addition to any serious artist's library, particularly those focused on realistic painting. It's not just a book to read once, but a resource to consult repeatedly as you develop your understanding of color and light in art. Whether you're a beginner seeking to build a strong foundation or an experienced artist looking to refine your knowledge, this book delivers exceptional value..

"Color and Light" is an exceptional resource that stands as one of the most comprehensive and practical guides available for artists seeking to master these fundamental aspects of painting. Gurney, known for his Dinotopia series, brings his extensive experience and methodical approach to demystifying what are often considered the most challenging elements of realistic painting.

What makes this book particularly valuable is Gurney's ability to bridge the gap between scientific principles and artistic application. Rather than merely presenting abstract theories, he grounds each concept in practical examples, often illustrated through his own stunning artwork. The book's approach is systematic yet accessible, making complex concepts digestible for artists at all skill levels.

The content is thoughtfully organized, progressing from basic principles to more advanced concepts. Gurney's examination of how historical masters handled color and light adds depth to the technical instruction, while his scientific explanations of color properties and light behavior provide crucial foundational knowledge. The inclusion of a glossary, pigment index, and bibliography makes this an even more valuable reference tool.

One of the book's greatest strengths is its visual presentation. The abundant illustrations and examples directly demonstrate the principles being discussed, making it easier to understand and apply the concepts. Gurney's own artwork serves as both inspiration and practical demonstration of the techniques he describes.

While the book is incredibly detailed, it remains engaging throughout, thanks to Gurney's clear writing style and logical presentation. The only potential drawback might be that some beginners might find certain technical sections overwhelming at first, though these same sections make the book valuable as a reference to return to as one's skills develop.

This book is essential reading for any artist, whether beginning or experienced, who has ever struggled with creative blocks, self-doubt, or the fear of making art. It's not a book that will teach you how to make art, but rather how to navigate the emotional landscape of being an artist. Its enduring popularity and word-of-mouth success speak to how deeply it resonates with its intended audience. Keep it close at hand for those moments when the artistic journey feels particularly challenging.

"Art & Fear" is a refreshingly honest and deeply insightful exploration of the psychological challenges that artists face in their creative journey. Unlike many art books that focus on technique or theory, this slim volume delves into the emotional and mental aspects of being an artist – the doubts, fears, and internal struggles that often go unaddressed in formal art education.

What makes this book particularly powerful is its authenticity. Written by working artists who understand the daily challenges of creating art, Bayles and Orland speak with a voice that resonates with genuine experience rather than theoretical pontification. Their approach is both compassionate and practical, acknowledging the very real fears that can paralyze artists while providing thoughtful perspectives on moving past them.

The book's greatest strength lies in its demystification of the artistic process. By challenging the notion of genius and focusing instead on the "ordinary art" made by ordinary people, the authors make artmaking feel more accessible and less intimidating. Their discussion of perfectionism, self-doubt, and creative blocks is particularly valuable, offering insights that feel like conversations with understanding mentors.

The writing style is concise and contemplative, with each chapter offering memorable observations that artists can return to whenever they need encouragement. The authors manage to be both philosophical and practical, weaving together personal anecdotes with broader insights about the nature of creativity and artistic development.

While some readers might wish for more specific solutions or exercises, the book's power lies in its ability to normalize the struggles of artistic creation and provide a framework for understanding and moving through creative challenges.

Recommended for both art novices seeking a solid foundation in art history and experienced enthusiasts looking for a well-structured refresher. This book truly deserves its reputation as the definitive introduction to art history.

"The Story of Art" stands as a masterful introduction to the vast world of art history, maintaining its relevance and authority even decades after its first publication. Gombrich's approach is nothing short of remarkable – he manages to distill centuries of artistic development into a narrative that feels both comprehensive and intimate.

What sets this book apart is Gombrich's exceptional ability to communicate complex artistic concepts in accessible language. Rather than drowning readers in academic jargon, he guides them through art history as if telling a fascinating story to a friend. His writing style is engaging and conversational, making even the most intricate artistic movements comprehensible to newcomers while remaining insightful enough for seasoned art enthusiasts.

The 1995 edition's improvements are significant. The addition of full-color illustrations throughout the book, including six fold-outs, brings the artwork to life in a way that previous editions couldn't match. The strategic placement of images alongside relevant text creates a seamless reading experience, allowing readers to immediately connect visual examples with the concepts being discussed.

While the book excels as a comprehensive overview, it's worth noting that it tends to favor Western art traditions, which might leave readers wanting more coverage of non-Western art forms. However, this limitation doesn't diminish its value as an introductory text.

The updated bibliographies and redrawn maps and charts make this edition particularly valuable for serious students of art history, while the clear organization and readable prose make it equally suitable for casual readers.

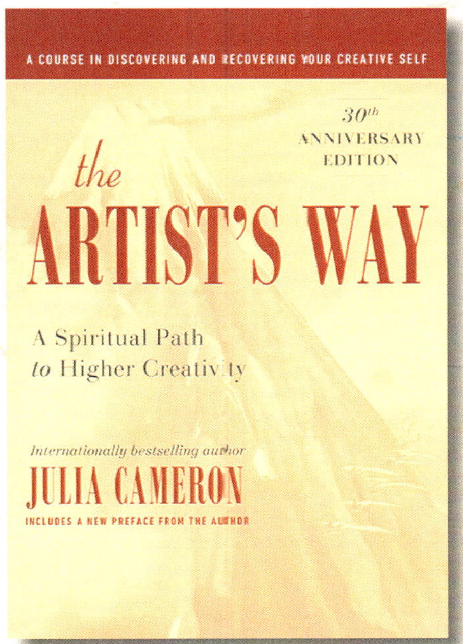

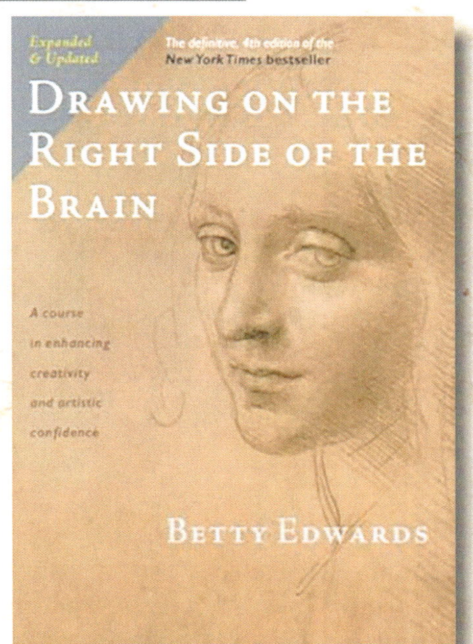

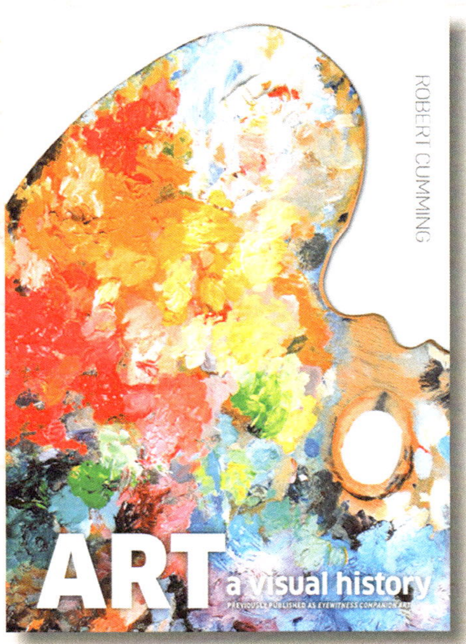

THE ARTIST'S WAY

by Julia Cameron

It is more than just a self-help book: it's a comprehensive creative recovery program that has stood the test of time.

"The Artist's Way" is a transformative and influential work that has rightfully earned its place as a cornerstone text in creative self-development. Now in its 30th anniversary edition, this book continues to resonate with artists, writers, and creative individuals across all disciplines, proving its timeless relevance.

At the heart of Cameron's approach are two fundamental tools: Morning Pages and Artist Dates. The Morning Pages practice - three pages of stream-of-consciousness writing done first thing each morning - is deceptively simple yet profoundly effective in clearing mental blocks and accessing deeper creativity. The Artist Date concept, which involves setting aside weekly time for solo creative exploration, helps nurture the inner artist in practical, enjoyable ways.

What sets this book apart is its comprehensive, structured approach to creative recovery. Cameron has crafted a 12-week program that systematically addresses various aspects of creative blocks, from dealing with criticism to managing time. The exercises and activities, while numerous, are thoughtfully designed to build upon each other, creating a journey of self-discovery and artistic renewal

The writing style is compassionate and accessible, avoiding both new-age vagueness and clinical sterility. Cameron writes with the understanding of someone who has personally navigated creative struggles, making the guidance feel authentic and tested. The inclusion of real-life examples and testimonials helps readers connect with the material and see practical applications.

Minor criticisms might include the book's length and intensity - the 12-week program requires significant time commitment and emotional investment. Some readers might find certain exercises repetitive or the spiritual undertones too pronounced for their taste.

DRAWING ON THE RIGHT SIDE OF THE BRAIN

by Betty Edwards

A must-have resource for anyone serious about learning to draw or understanding the connection between brain function and artistic expression.

"Drawing on the Right Side of the Brain" remains a groundbreaking and transformative guide for anyone interested in developing their artistic abilities. Betty Edwards' approach is revolutionary in how it breaks down the mental barriers that often prevent people from drawing effectively.

Strengths:

- The book's methodology is based on solid neuroscience, explaining how engaging the right hemisphere of the brain can dramatically improve drawing skills

- Excellent progression of exercises that build upon each other logically

- Clear, detailed instructions accompanied by before-and-after examples that demonstrate dramatic improvement

- The updated research on brain plasticity adds scientific credibility to the methods

- New sections on childhood development and creativity provide valuable context for parents and educators

Minor drawbacks:

- Some exercises may feel time-consuming for busy learners

- Initial concepts can seem abstract to practically-minded readers

- Requires dedicated practice time to see results

The 4th edition successfully modernizes this classic text while maintaining its core principles. Whether you're a complete beginner who "can't draw a straight line" or an experienced artist looking to improve your observational skills, this book provides a structured approach to developing drawing ability.

The most remarkable aspect is how it teaches you to truly see what you're drawing, rather than relying on symbolic representations. This shift in perception is valuable not just for art, but for developing overall creative thinking and problem-solving skills.

ART, A VISUAL HISTORY

by Robert Cumming

An essential addition to any art lover's library, combining visual splendor with scholarly insight in DK's signature accessible style.

DK's "Art: A Visual History" stands as a masterful compilation that brings the vast world of art history into stunning focus. This second edition continues to uphold DK's reputation for excellence in visual education while offering readers an accessible entry into the complex world of art appreciation.

The book's greatest triumph lies in its ability to balance scholarly depth with approachable presentation. Through its pages, readers journey from prehistoric art to contemporary works, experiencing the evolution of human creativity through crisp, high-quality reproductions and enlightening commentary. The selection of over 650 artists provides a comprehensive overview without becoming overwhelming, while the in-depth analysis of 22 masterpieces offers valuable insights into the nuances of artistic interpretation.

What truly sets this volume apart is its thoughtful organization and visual clarity. Each era and movement is contextualized within its historical period, helping readers understand not just what they're seeing, but why it matters. The book excels at explaining technical aspects of art creation while maintaining reader engagement through compelling storytelling and visual presentation.

The writing strikes an ideal balance between academic rigor and accessibility. Art terminology is clearly explained, making complex concepts digestible for newcomers while providing enough depth to satisfy more knowledgeable readers. The critical analyses are particularly enlightening, offering fresh perspectives on both famous and lesser-known works.

While the focus primarily remains on Western art, which might be limiting for some readers, the depth of coverage within this scope is impressive. The updated edition brings fresh insights and improved visual presentations that make it even more valuable as both a reference work and an educational tool.

For anyone seeking to understand the grand narrative of art history or looking to develop a more nuanced appreciation of visual art, this book proves an invaluable resource. It's more than just a coffee table book: it's a comprehensive guide that invites repeated consultation and rewards careful study.

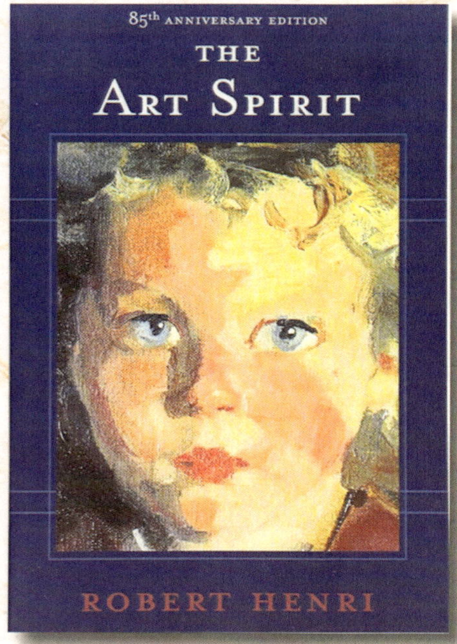

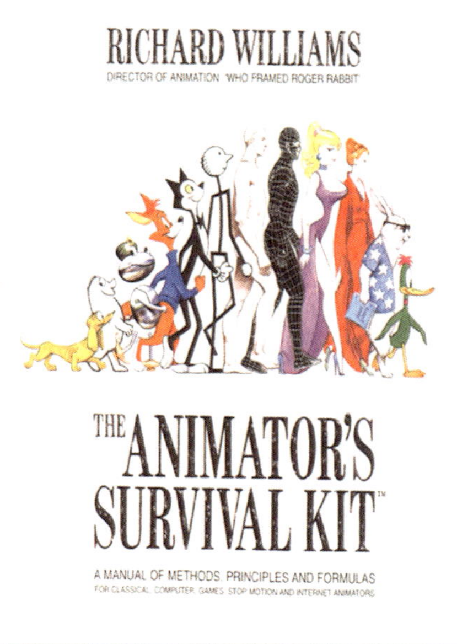

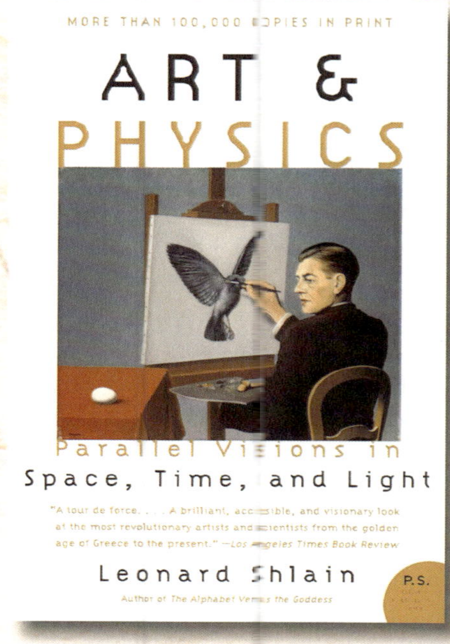

THE ART SPIRIT
by Robert Henry

A masterpiece of art philosophy that continues to inspire and illuminate the creative path for each new generation of artists and art lovers.

"The Art Spirit" stands as a timeless testament to the profound relationship between art and the human experience. First published in 1923, Henri's collected wisdom continues to resonate with remarkable clarity and relevance nearly a century later.

This book transcends the typical boundaries of an art instruction manual. While it certainly contains valuable technical guidance, its true power lies in Henri's philosophical approach to art and creativity. His words speak not just to painters or traditional artists, but to anyone seeking to understand the creative impulse and its role in human expression.

Henri's writing style is both intimate and universal, reading like a conversation with a wise mentor who understands both the technical challenges and spiritual struggles of artistic creation. His insights emerge from decades of experience both as a practicing artist and an influential teacher, offering readers a unique blend of practical advice and profound reflection.

What makes this work particularly special is its emphasis on the democratization of art. Henri firmly believed that artistic expression belongs to everyone, not just a select few. This revolutionary perspective challenged the elitism often associated with fine art, making his teachings accessible and relevant to creators at all levels.

The book's structure, composed of collected notes and observations, allows readers to digest its wisdom in manageable portions while maintaining a coherent philosophical thread throughout. Each section offers fresh insights that build upon previous ideas, creating a comprehensive vision of what it means to live an artistic life.

This enduring work deserves its place as a foundational text in any artist's library, offering both practical guidance and spiritual sustenance for the creative journey.

THE ANIMATOR'S SURVIVAL KIT
by Richard Williams

An essential resource that has rightfully earned its place as the animation industry's bible.

Richard Williams' comprehensive guide stands as the definitive text for animation professionals and enthusiasts alike. This masterwork, drawing from Williams' half-century of experience and expertise, including his groundbreaking work on "Who Framed Roger Rabbit?", delivers an unparalleled educational experience in animation fundamentals.

The book's greatest strength lies in its universal applicability. While animation technology continues to evolve rapidly, Williams focuses on the timeless principles that underpin all forms of animation, whether traditional hand-drawn, computer-generated, stop-motion, or digital. These fundamental concepts are presented with remarkable clarity through hundreds of meticulously crafted illustrations and examples.

Williams' teaching approach is both systematic and engaging. He breaks down complex movements into digestible components, explaining not just the "how" but also the crucial "why" behind each principle. His emphasis on understanding natural movement and translating it into convincing animation is particularly valuable, helping readers develop an eye for authentic motion.

The book excels in its treatment of timing and spacing, two critical elements of animation that often prove challenging for beginners. Williams provides detailed breakdowns of walks, runs, jumps, and other common actions, offering invaluable formulas and methods that have become industry standards.

The organization is logical and progressive, building from basic principles to more complex concepts. The abundant illustrations and clear explanations make even the most intricate techniques accessible to dedicated learners. The book's format allows readers to return repeatedly, discovering new insights with each review.

One particularly valuable aspect is the book's emphasis on observation and analysis. Williams teaches readers not just to animate, but to see and understand movement in a new way, developing the crucial observational skills that distinguish great animators.

Though primarily focused on character animation, the principles presented are applicable across all animation disciplines. The book's enduring relevance in an era of rapid technological change testifies to the fundamental nature of its teachings.

ART & PHYSICS
by Leonard Shlain

A brilliant fusion of art and science, revealing stunning parallels between creative vision and physics throughout human history.

"Art & Physics: Parallel Visions in Space, Time, and Light" is a fascinating exploration of the unexpected connections between artistic innovation and scientific discovery. Leonard Shlain masterfully weaves together seemingly disparate threads of human creativity and scientific understanding, revealing how artists have often intuited fundamental physical concepts before scientists formally discovered them.

The book's most compelling argument lies in its careful documentation of historical parallels, such as how Monet and Cezanne's revolutionary approaches to perspective and light preceded Einstein's groundbreaking theories. Shlain's writing style is accessible and engaging, making complex physics concepts digestible while maintaining the wonder of artistic expression.

While some connections might seem stretched, the overall thesis is convincingly presented through well-researched examples and thoughtful analysis. The author's background as a surgeon brings a unique perspective to this interdisciplinary exploration, offering fresh insights into how different forms of human understanding intersect.

Particularly noteworthy is the book's examination of how both artists and physicists grapple with representing the unrepresentable — whether it's quantum mechanics or abstract expressionism. The inclusion of illustrations helps readers visualize these parallel developments.

Though occasionally the narrative can become dense with information, the reward for careful reading is a deeper appreciation of both fields. This book is essential reading for anyone interested in the intersection of art and science, offering a compelling argument for the unity of human creative and analytical endeavors.

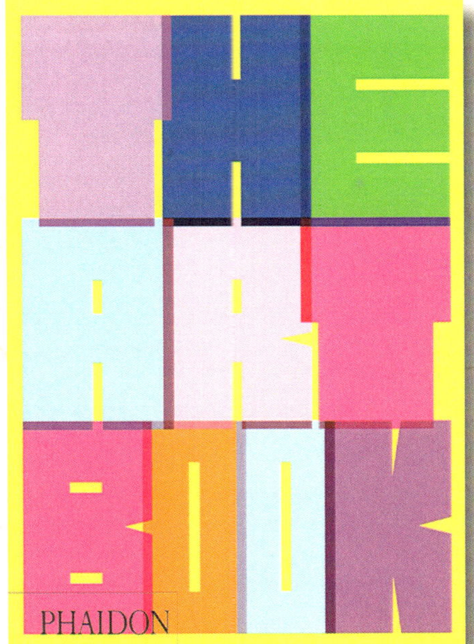

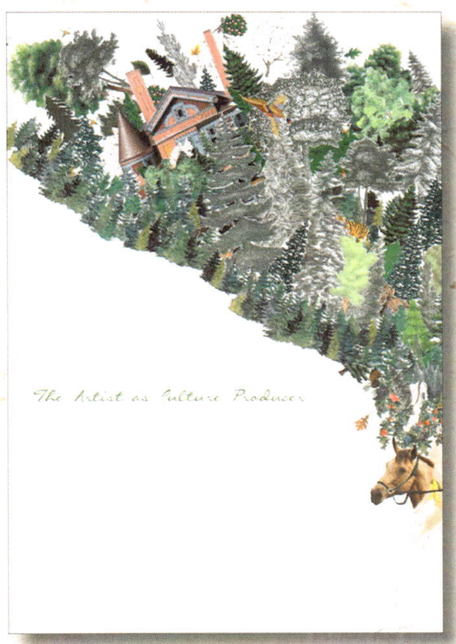

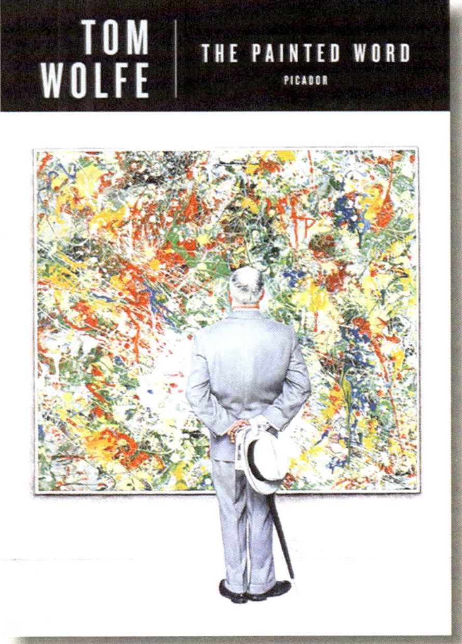

THE ART BOOK

by by Phaidon Editors

The Art Book dazzles with 600+ masterpieces, brilliantly connecting centuries of human creativity through stunning visuals and insightful commentary.

A comprehensive and beautifully curated journey through art history, The Art Book (2020 Edition) stands as an essential reference for both art enthusiasts and newcomers. This revised edition brilliantly expands its scope by including previously overlooked artists and contemporary masters, making it more inclusive and representative of diverse artistic voices.

The book's unique A-Z format breaks free from traditional chronological constraints, creating unexpected and enlightening juxtapositions that spark fresh perspectives on artistic expression across centuries. Each entry pairs a significant artwork with concise, illuminating text that provides context and insight without overwhelming the reader.

The addition of 40 new works, including pieces by influential artists like Hilma af Klint, Kerry James Marshall, and Zanele Muholi, demonstrates Phaidon's commitment to addressing historical oversights and embracing contemporary developments in the art world.

This accessible yet authoritative volume serves as both a valuable reference tool and a source of inspiration. Its thoughtful curation and high-quality reproductions make it an indispensable resource for anyone interested in understanding the breadth and depth of artistic achievement throughout history.

The only minor drawback might be that some readers could prefer a more traditional chronological arrangement, but the alphabetical format succeeds in making art history more approachable and engaging.

HE ARTIST AS CULTURE PRODUCER

by Sharon Louden

A must-read for anyone interested in the real-world intersection of art and community impact.

This illuminating collection of 40 essays offers a vital perspective on how contemporary artists navigate and influence the world beyond their studios. Editor Sharon Louden has assembled a diverse chorus of voices that effectively challenges the stereotype of the isolated artist, instead revealing how creative professionals actively shape our cultural and economic landscape.

The strength of this book lies in its real-world testimonies - by turns practical, inspiring, and refreshingly honest. Artists share their experiences working in education, non-profit sectors, and corporate environments, demonstrating how artistic practice can create meaningful social and economic impact. These aren't just success stories; they're roadmaps for sustainability in the arts.

Particularly valuable is the book's focus on artists as entrepreneurs and community leaders. The essays provide concrete examples of how artists can expand their practice while contributing to society's well-being. For art students, established artists, or anyone interested in the intersection of creativity and community, this book offers both practical guidance and inspiration.

Following the success of Louden's first volume, this sequel further enriches the conversation about sustaining creative lives in the contemporary world. With its accessible writing and diverse perspectives, "The Artist as Culture Producer" is an essential read for understanding the evolving role of artists in today's society.

THE PAINTED WORD

by Robert Cumming

A witty, provocative read that challenges conventional wisdom about modern art, though it sometimes sacrifices nuance for the sake of its argument. Essential reading for anyone interested in art criticism, even if you end up disagreeing with Wolfe's conclusions.

Tom Wolfe's scathing critique of modern art and its theoretical underpinnings is as entertaining as it is controversial. Written with his trademark wit and flamboyant style, this slim volume delivers a powerful punch at the art world's pretensions and the critics who, according to Wolfe, have hijacked modern art with their theories.

Published originally in 1975, "The Painted Word" remains remarkably relevant today. Wolfe argues that modern art has become less about visual experience and more about the theories explaining it - to the point where the art itself is merely an illustration of the theory. He traces this development through Abstract Expressionism, Pop Art, Minimalism, and Conceptual Art, skewering sacred cows along the way with gleeful precision.

The book's strength lies in Wolfe's razor-sharp observations and his ability to make complex art-world dynamics accessible through humor and satire. His description of how a small circle of New York critics essentially dictated what constituted "important" art is both hilarious and unsettling.

However, readers should approach this book understanding it's more polemic than balanced criticism. While Wolfe's arguments are compelling, his take is decidedly one-sided and some might find his dismissal of certain artistic movements overly harsh.

Redefining the American Dream

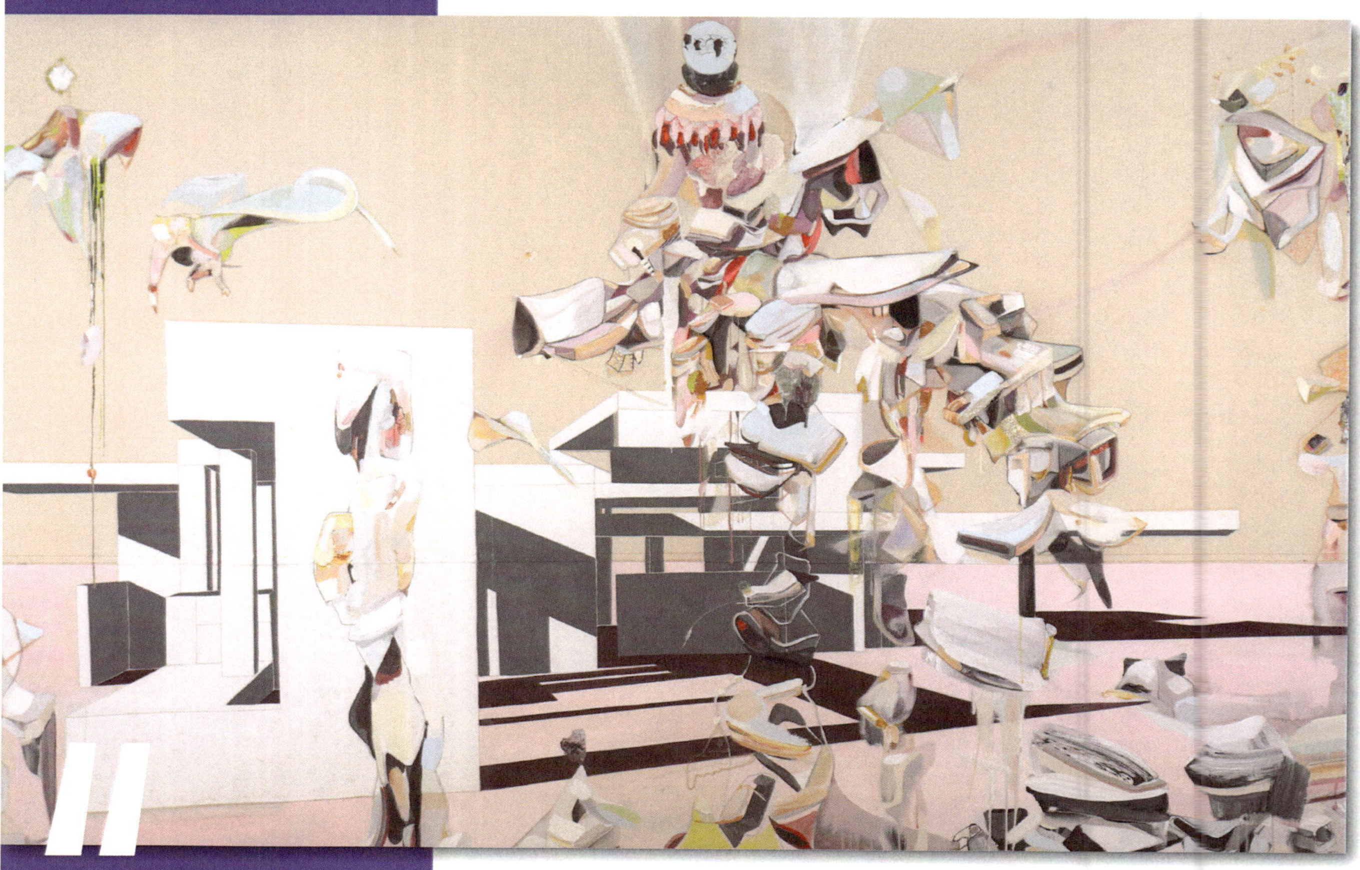

CARLOS BELTRAN ARECHIGA

An exploration of aspiration and exclusion through evocative visuals that challenge traditional narratives of success and belonging

Carlos Beltran Arechiga discusses the themes of existential ambiguity, identity, and social structures in his art, inviting viewers to reflect on their own experiences.

Carlos Beltran Arechiga, a visionary artist deeply attuned to themes of identity, cultural nuance, and environmental interconnectedness, stands at the forefront of contemporary art with a style that blends figuration and abstraction in a dynamic, thought-provoking manner. His work delves into the spaces "in-between," inviting viewers to consider the complex layers of existence, belonging, and the structures that shape human experience. As both a painter and an immigrant, Arechiga's compositions resonate with the richness of his personal journey, bridging the diverse worlds he inhabits through vibrant, intricate visual narratives. His canvases serve as both personal explorations and universal reflections, often incorporating textures and materials—like worn construction tarps—imbued with history and memory. By weaving together organic and geometric forms, Arechiga constructs layered commentaries on balance, conflict, and harmony within a world defined by both its aspirations and its exclusions.

Arechiga offers insights into the core elements that drive his artistic vision: existential ambiguity, the interplay between abstract and representational elements, and the evocative tension that defines his signature style. His exploration of social structures, environmental justice, and cultural dissonance comes to life in his responses, unveiling an artistic process grounded in empathy, resilience, and a relentless quest for understanding. Readers are invited into a rare and intimate conversation that reveals not only the depth of Arechiga's artistry but also his unwavering commitment to crafting spaces for introspection and collective dialogue.

How do you define existential ambiguity in your work, and how does it influence your artistic process?

Existential ambiguity is a central theme in my paintings, expressed through a deliberate formal and aesthetic in-betweenness. I create the background using representational structures that establish the context and mood of each piece. This approach encourages viewers to bypass the need for literal interpretation or understanding, inviting them instead to engage with the work on a deeper, more visceral level—similar to the way one might connect with the beauty and complexity of nature.

My exploration of subjects that strive for balance, without adhering to any single extreme, is deeply rooted in my personal experiences as an immigrant living in Los Angeles. This unique position has shaped my navigation through a rich tapestry of cultures, languages, and identities. In my work, I reflect the complexities of existing between these various influences, highlighting the nuances of representation and the quest for a harmonious sense of self amidst the contradictions. Through this lens, my paintings become a space for contemplation and emotional resonance, inviting viewers to reflect on their own experiences of ambiguity and balance in a multifaceted world

Can you explain the significance of the tension between figuration and abstraction in your art? How do you balance these elements in your creations?

Tension plays a crucial role in my work, as I aim for the paintings to create a dynamic push and pull that challenges the viewer's comfort

level in their interpretation. The structures within my pieces are intentionally designed from multiple perspectives, allowing them to accommodate a variety of organic anthropomorphic forms that resonate with natural structures. This interplay suggests a sense of fluid freedom, yet it exists within the confines of sleek, hard-edged elements that may either complement or contradict these organic shapes.

This tension is not only thematic but also formal, reflected in my compositional choices. I often incorporate marks and textures left on the fabric from its previous uses, particularly with construction tarps that have served in projects involving the undocumented immigrant community. These remnants add layers of meaning and history to the work, creating a dialogue between the past and present. By blending these elements, I invite viewers to confront their own perceptions of comfort and discomfort, challenging them to engage with the complexities of identity, labor, and existence in a world that is often at odds with itself.

What specific resources and opportunities do you seek to address through your exploration of tangible and intangible structures in your work?

I delve into the concept of structures to emphasize the significance of observation and thoughtful consideration. This exploration encompasses both societal frameworks—such as the policies and infrastructures that dictate access, representation, education, and investment—and the natural structures that face degradation, particularly in the context of environmental justice.

For instance, when examining societal structures, I reflect on how policies can create barriers or gateways for marginalized communities. Consider the impact of educational institutions: they can either empower individuals or reinforce existing inequities, depending on their resources and accessibility. Similarly, infrastructure projects can determine the flow of investment into specific neighbourhoods, shaping economic opportunities and community development.

On the other hand, I also focus on the decline of natural structures, such as ecosystems under threat from pollution and climate change. This decline often disproportionately affects certain sectors of the community, raising urgent questions about environmental justice. For example, low-income neighbourhoods may bear the brunt of industrial waste or lack access to clean green spaces, revealing the intersection of social and environmental issues.

By examining these structures, I aim to foster a deeper awareness of how they influence our lives and the world around us. This dual perspective encourages viewers to engage critically with both the systems that govern us and the natural environments we inhabit, ultimately prompting a more nuanced understanding of their interconnectedness.

How do the recurring edifices in your paintings represent the traditional "American Dream," and what message are you trying to convey by disrupting this imagery with abstract markings?

The visual language I employ in designing the structures of my paintings draws inspiration from sleek mid-century modern archetypes, which were integral to the mass deployment of advertising campaigns that promised a better life. However, it's important to recognize that this promise often served only a select segment of society, typically defined by ethnicity and socioeconomic status.

By echoing these aesthetic forms, I aim to critique the underlying narratives that have historically marginalized certain groups while privileging others. This juxtaposition invites viewers to reflect on the complexities of aspiration and exclusion embedded within these structures.

Disrupting the status quo has always been a catalyst for change throughout human history. It is through challenging established norms and conventions that societies can evolve and progress. In my work, I seek to engage with this idea, encouraging viewers to question not only the visual elements before them but also the broader societal frameworks they represent. By

doing so, I hope to inspire a dialogue about the possibilities for a more inclusive future—one where the promises of better living conditions and opportunities are accessible to all, regardless of their background.

In what ways do you believe your art challenges preconceived notions of a "Promised Land"? Can you provide examples from your work?

In my work, I challenge the concept of the "promised land" through subtle and often understated means, which may not be immediately apparent to the viewer. As previously mentioned, many of my paintings are created on fabrics that carry the memory of the construction trade. This choice is significant because it highlights the often-overlooked contributions of workers who inhabit the shadows—those who are invisible and underrepresented despite their critical role in building the cities we inhabit.

These workers, often immigrants, face systemic barriers that deny them access to representation and recognition. By using materials that reflect their labour, I aim to bring their experiences and struggles into the foreground, prompting viewers to confront the disparity between the promise of prosperity and the reality faced by many.

This approach serves as a reminder of the complex layers of societal narratives surrounding labour and belonging. It invites viewers to engage with the notion of the Promised Land not just as an idealized vision but as a nuanced reality that includes both aspiration and exclusion. In doing so, I hope to foster a deeper understanding of the interconnectedness of our lives and the importance of acknowledging all contributors to our society.

How do you hope viewers will respond to the dynamic visual experience you create through the interplay of gestural markings and structures in your art?

When it comes to my audience's response, my goal is to establish formal and conceptual frameworks that provide just enough context to create a space for reflection and interpretation, regardless of the viewer's background. I aspire for my paintings to act as mirrors, inviting viewers to engage personally with the work and to contribute to its meaning through their own experiences and perspectives.

I believe that the true success of a painting lies in its ability to evoke a change in the viewer, even if only momentarily, in their mind or heart. These fleeting moments of connection can serve as powerful catalysts for change, igniting thoughts and emotions that linger long after the initial viewing. I see these small triggers as significant, as they can influence one's daily life and perceptions, ultimately fostering a broader awareness and deeper understanding of our shared human experiences. By encouraging this introspection, I hope to inspire a dialogue that extends beyond the artwork itself, prompting ongoing reflection and engagement with the world.

Redefining Creativity With Rhythm, Structure, And Transitional Space

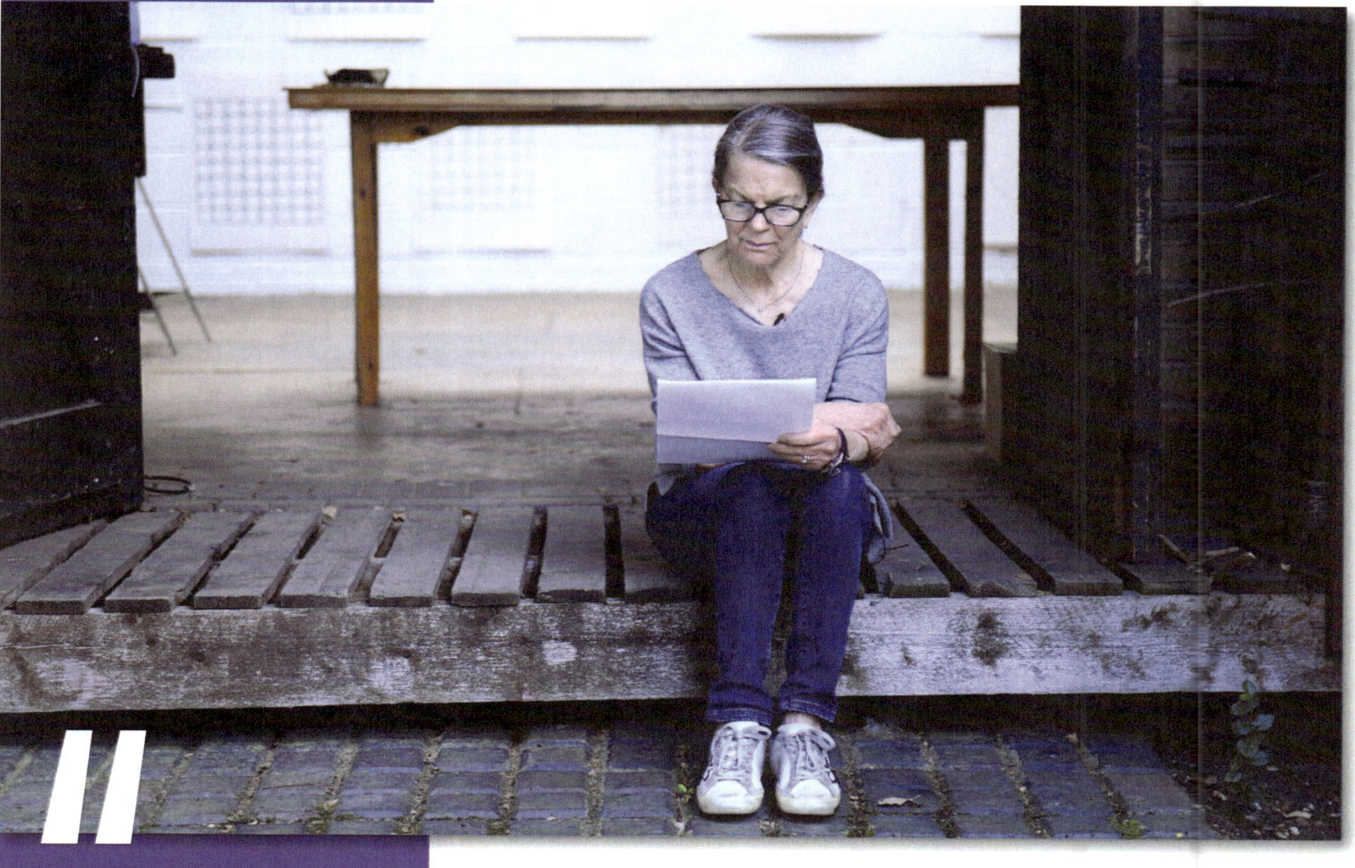

Exploring How Linda Karshan Merges Psychological Theories With Artistic Expression To Create Works Of Profound Depth

Linda Karshan discusses the influence of psychology on her art, her rhythmic approach to creation, and how her unique methods invite viewers to engage with the essence of creativity.

LINDA KARSHAN

We delve into the profound artistic journey of a true innovator whose works transcend traditional boundaries. Linda Karshan, an artist of exceptional depth and insight, merges the realms of psychology and art in a manner that resonates with both intellect and emotion. With a foundation built on her education at esteemed institutions such as the Sorbonne and the Slade School of Art, Karshan has cultivated a unique approach that reflects her extensive studies and experiences.

Her oeuvre, characterized by intricate drawings, prints, and artists' books, embodies a delicate balance between structure and organic expression. Karshan's exploration of transitional space and creative play, influenced by the psychological theories of D.W. Winnicott, reveals an artist deeply engaged in the process of self-discovery and artistic expression. Her works invite viewers into a dialogue about the nature of creativity itself, challenging us to reconsider the boundaries of artistic practice. With exhibitions in prestigious museums and collections around the globe, including the British Museum and the Metropolitan Museum of Art, Karshan continues to inspire and captivate audiences with her evocative, rhythmically structured creations. This conversation offers a rare glimpse into her artistic philosophy and the dynamic interplay between movement, thought, and expression that define her work.

How did your studies in psychology and Plato's theory of numerical order influence your performance-based artistic method?

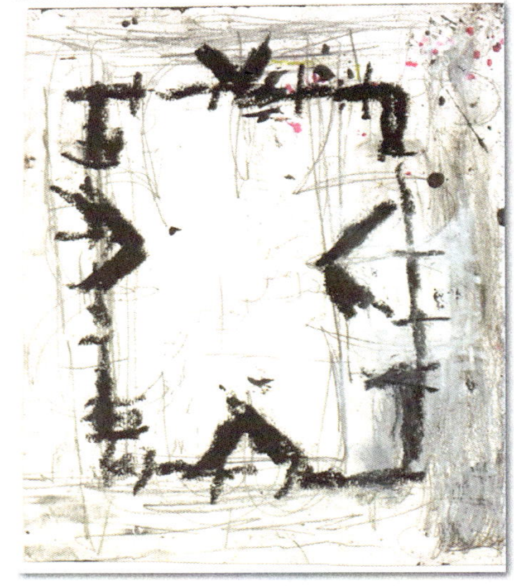

In my work it's never a case of influence but of affinity.

My studies in psychology focused on Donald Winnicott, whose theories of transitional space and transitional phenomena are key to my artistic practice. Winnicott's theories gave me ballast, even courage, to stay in pace and place throughout the making of an artwork.

He wrote about creative play. It's a precarious place that hovers between the unconscious and consciousness. He said it was here and only here that anything original gets made, and so it is. Every drawing of mine comes through transitional space. Otherwise

> Linda Karshan is a visionary artist whose profound exploration of transitional space and creative play resonates deeply, inspiring viewers and fellow creators alike.

it would be manufactured.

Plato found me.

I had made a suite of prints which became an artist's book, Time, Being; le temps, lui.

I asked my friend, the philosopher David Wiggins, to write an accompanying text. After inspecting the prints for thirty minutes, he said 'Ah, there is no need. The text exists. He sent me the passage from Plato's Timeus, on the creation of time.

As Mara Gerety wrote, 'she moves her body through each space.. marking out Plato's perfect numerical ordering of the universe.'

Can you describe the role that your concept "inner choreography" plays in the creation of your prints and drawings?

It is key. That inner choreography IS the moving figure assigned to me. It determines every drawing, on paper or in space. I can

count on it, literally and figuratively, and I do. It sounds like this:

1-2-3-4-5-6-7-8 turn

1-2-3-4-5-6-7-8 turn

It's what my body does, guided by my mind. It first appeared in the drawing I call my Self-Portrait. Crucially, the day it appeared I saw Quad, the teleplay by Samuel Beckett. It was as if I were watching my drawing performed on stage. Beckett remains the artist with whom I feel the closest affinity.

In 1994, you transitioned to a more structured, rhythmic approach in your art-making. What prompted this shift from expressive compositions to performance-based, iterative works?

The appearance of the moving figure, with its numbers, rhythm and direction to turn the sheet. When it came into being, I recognized it for what it was. Thanks to Winnicott I knew not to get in the way; not to impinge. Once this small, iconic drawing was done, I pinned it to the wall, caught my breath, and knew I could begin.

So it wasn't a transition I planned, but one that appeared. I immediately saw its significance. Yes, it is more structured, and it is rhythmic, but it is in the same breath organic.

How do the physical movements, such as turning the paper counter-clockwise and counting increments of time, contribute to the geometric patterns and grids in your work?

Two important things to say here. Perhaps my most original jotting goes like this: man marks himself vertically, it is the Earth that turns. That's how we make the grid, that's why we make the grid.

And so I have to turn the sheet. It's directive. I have no choice.

I do not make the line that you read as horizontal. It's another vertical line. And I never confuse my horizontals and my verticals.

So turning the sheet is absolutely key, and while I never thought that I make grids, of

course that's what they are. Horizontal and vertical lines, but they come into being as a result of the turn.

Your MA thesis explored D. W. Winnicott's theories of transitional space and creativity. How do these psychological concepts continue to shape your artistic practice today?

My thesis was called Play, Creativity, and the Birth of the Self. I believe in those things now more than ever. These ideas are at the heart of every drawing I make. They started with Winnicott, but developed through my artistic practice.

It's worth reiterating that Winnicott's ideas on transitional space are key to the artistic side of my work.

The other key is my Bauhaus training, in which I was taught to build a drawing, to cross those corners. The drawing should not fall apart when I get up close.

But Winnicott's insistence on creative space - it is here and only here that anything original gets made - is essential.

You've exhibited in major galleries and museums across Europe and the U.S. How do you feel your work has been received in these different cultural contexts?

That's a great question. There is a predisposition in certain cultural milieu, where my work can be seen and felt, because it's close to the experience of the viewer. It's in understanding this that I often think of another passage, Plotinus, another Friend of Time:

'The mind sheds radiance on the objects of sense, out of its own store.'

If a culture has in its store my figure—that moving figure assigned to me—my work is immediately recognized. It's heartwarming for me to exhibit in those places.

Dreams and Found Materials

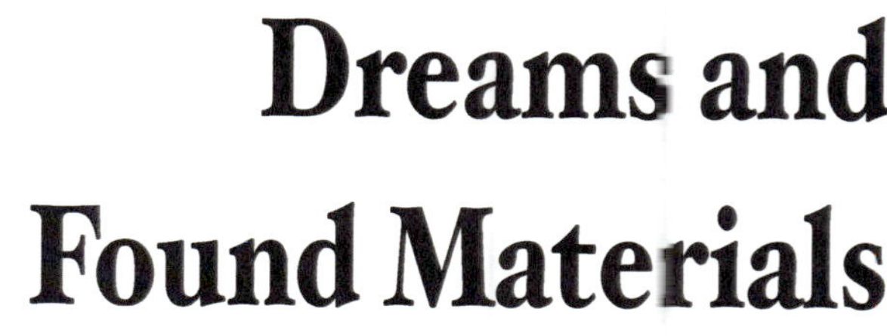

Discovering the imaginative process behind Lee's unique, tactile creations

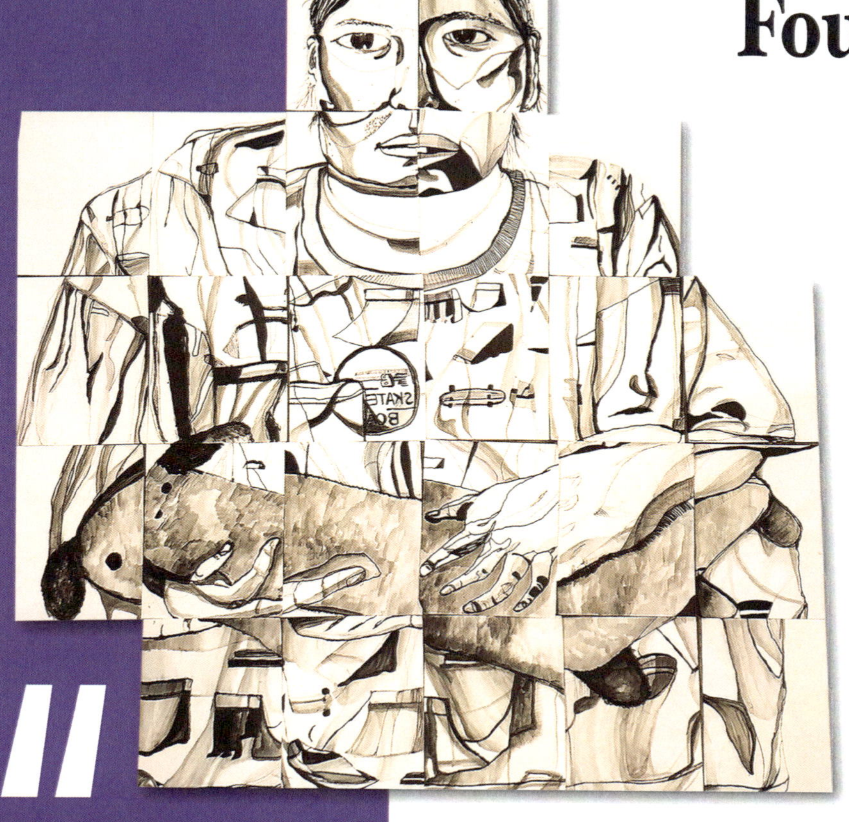

> "Drawing, painting and sculpting makes me remember what I enjoyed, when I felt a strong emotion, which lets me slow down in my present life."

JUNGMIN LEE

Jungmin Lee's art, inspired by childhood, dreams, and cultural heritage, blends personal and collective memory through mixed media, creating intimate, miniature worlds that celebrate family, tradition, and the timeless warmth of nostalgia.

Jungmin Lee's art transports us to a world rich with nostalgia, dreams, and the tactile warmth of memory. This talented South Korean artist and designer, a graduate with distinction from the ArtCenter College of Design, blends storytelling with a love for found and mixed media to create intricate, evocative pieces. Her works invite viewers into intimate moments of family gatherings, childhood explorations, and even dreamscapes—transforming everyday materials into portals to the past. Lee's creativity is steeped in the heritage of her culture, tracing her roots through memories of her grandparents' home, traditional rituals, and cherished heirlooms, reimagined into vivid visual narratives.

Throughout her work, Lee demonstrates a profound ability to weave together personal and collective memory. Her piece Cabinet, a layered collage of stamps, stickers, and pages from her mother's notebooks, powerfully bridges her own life and history with a broader cultural experience. With each brushstroke and piece of found material, she crafts a miniature world where fragments of her heritage live on. It is through these meticulously crafted "miniatures" that Lee explores themes of belonging, identity, and emotional resilience. In this exclusive interview, WOWwArt Magazine delves into the inspirations, creative process, and unique perspectives that make Jungmin Lee's art both intensely personal and universally resonant.

Can you describe how your childhood experiences in South Korea influence your artistic themes and subjects?

Jungmin Lee, an accomplished artist from Incheon, South Korea, finds inspiration in the whimsical realms of childhood, dreams, and family. A graduate with distinction from ArtCenter College of Design, her work beautifully blends found and mixed media, storytelling from cherished memories, and the tactile creation of 3D objects. Her art is a vivid tapestry of imagination and heartfelt narratives.

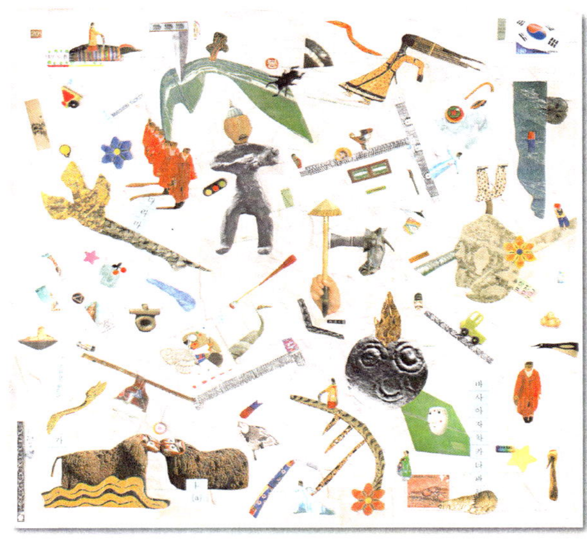

Jungmin Lee captivates audiences with her profound storytelling, transforming ordinary objects into extraordinary visual narratives that resonate with universal human warmth.

When I was young, my family liked to go on trips to visit big, old trees, such as the 800 year old Ginkgo tree in Jangsudong, Incheon, South Korea. In the beginning, I didn't know why we were going to see trees. But as time went by, these trips became my memory points to spiritually go back as the place of family gathering. This nostalgic warmth is also connected to my grandparents and visiting their home. I appreciate their time to cook delicious foods like Ramyun, soybean paste soup, seasoned spinach, and more. I remember when my grandparents brought small dogs to home on a cold winter evening. I remember when my family prepared food and visited the parents of my grandparents at the cemetery, covered with snow. These moments are living inside of me, and art helps to bring me the forgotten past. Because I am now far away from my grandparents, this childhood feels like a dream. Drawing, painting and sculpting makes me remember what I enjoyed, when I felt a strong emotion, which lets me slow down in my present life, and rethink why I want to study art.

What role do dreams play in your creative process, and how do you incorporate them into your work?

Dreams to me are uncertain, blurry, weird so it gives me open possibilities to experiment. It can be changed during the thinking process, or sometimes the new pieces of another dream come up after sleep. Memory is changing and they are fantastical. Anything can happen so I appreciate that dream gives me free ground to start from. It represents to me less pressure and motivates me to switch the storyline, draw without a plan, combine found materials, or maybe erase and restart.

How do you use mixed media in your artwork, and what materials do you find most inspiring?

I like to travel in my house to collect, find new materials, such as trash, recycle bins or old boxes in the garage. One day, I start with one object, then maybe the next day, I cut it out. Another day, I might paint over, or look over the magazine to find the image. I think I make it in the process with less plan, and I like to practice these experiments with different types and scales of the media. These days, I am also interested in learning more about watercolor and brush. I enjoy playing with water and unexpectedness with where the inks would go and share its feelings.

Can you explain your concept of a "miniature world" in your paintings and how it reflects collective and individual dynamics?

I think the practice of thinking about a "miniature" helps me to observe the world in a simple way or to view from a far away. The making process is also like playing with a toy or going back to when I was young. Inside of the miniature world, the creatures and houses seemed to feel safe and open a way to start an adventure. Miniature drawings or objects become able to hold in hands, move around, or invite me to make my own world. I think this process of creating a small environment gives a coziness and warmth to my mind, and I hope this feeling could help to share the playful spirits and healing aspects of art.

How do cultural backgrounds and customs shape the characters and narratives in your art?

From my memories in Korea, the traditional foods and ancestral rites with my family come to my mind. Often, my family members and their personality became my starting point to sketch the unknown creatures or my imaginary friend characters. In another moment, grandparents become the main characters who show me the steps of Jesa, Korean ancestral rituals, or as the biographed figure by interviewing with them. The folk tales and traditional music in Korea help me to learn where I come from, teach me new languages that were used in the past, or how ancestors lived their lives.

What psychological observations do you hope to convey through the interactions between collective power and individual power in your work?

To me, collective power guides me the sympathy that can be made with wider people, and individual power as the departure from the personal memory. My work can begin with my personal backgrounds or interactions within myself. But my bigger hope is to observe the influences of childhood to adulthood and the conflicted minds of people, which I like to try sharing this diverse human emotions in art so that one can feel connected or belong. I hope my work can help more people to dream and imagine, especially to feel free in their state of mind.

Innovative Techniques in Light Painting unblemished moment

SEMA ÖZEVİN

Multi-Award Winning Photo and Video Artist

Exploring the Artistic Vision

Sema Özevin, an acclaimed artist, blends photography and video art, exploring memory and storytelling through innovative techniques, while navigating the challenges of the digital art landscape.

Editor's Desk , London

Sema Özevin has made a significant mark in the realms of photography and video art since 1996, producing works that resonate on international platforms. Her projects, including the Choronotope series, Womans Aura, Kinesthetic, Cosmos, Cocoon, Paradoxical Loop, Space, Parallel Universe, and Ouroboros Loop, showcase a diverse range of styles—fictional, experimental, figurative, and abstract. Özevin's ability to intertwine abstract time with concrete space is a hallmark of her artistry, often employing experimental techniques that involve image manipulation, deconstruction, and form distortion.

> "I describe the subject with a special technical and aesthetic photographic language that I have created with my perspective on life and art."
>
> – Sema Özevin

In addition to her artistic endeavors, Özevin has contributed to industrial documentaries, starting with her project on the Pişmaniye dessert, which highlights local labor through the stories of various industries. Her work in corporate communication and sustainable brand communication complements her teaching role at several universities, where she imparts her knowledge in the field of art. Her portfolio can be explored further at semozevin.com.

Beyond photography, Özevin is actively engaged in video art, documentary short films, and feature films, serving as both director and cinematographer. Her notable works include the short films "Babam`a," "Davut Dedem," and "Pişmaniye," as well as her cinematography in the feature film "Shelter." She also produces video clips for Amselcom Music Production in Berlin, with her video works available on her YouTube channel, Sema Özevin Art TV.

Özevin's academic background is impressive: she graduated at the top of her class from Kocaeli University's Faculty of Fine Arts, specializing in Photography, and later completed her master's degree at Gazi University, focusing on video art's paradoxes and cycles. Currently, she is pursuing her doctorate in Radio, Television, and Cinema.

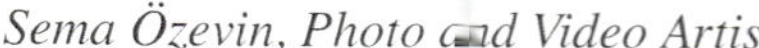

Sema Özevin, Photo and Video Artist

Her artistic journey
has garnered her over 350
awards in various national
and international competitions,
including prestigious titles from
the International Photographic Art
Federation in France. These accolades
have significantly enhanced her recognition on global platforms.

Özevin's innovative approach to light painting—a technique involving long exposure
with a flashlight—has redefined experimental
photography. This unique style gained attention
when it was featured in major Turkish news outlets
during her solo exhibition.

When discussing her visual language, Özevin emphasizes the importance of memory in storytelling. She
believes that photography transcends mere representation,
serving as a medium for conveying complex narratives.
Her projects often stem from personal experiences,
societal issues, and artistic inspirations, leading to a
meticulous planning process that includes research,
storyboarding, and technical considerations.

Influenced by renowned photographers like Annie
Leibovitz, Steve McCurry, and Cindy Sherman,
Özevin draws from a rich tapestry of artistic styles.
However, she faces challenges in the digital age,
particularly regarding the reproducibility of her
work and the complexities of marketing art. Despite
these hurdles, she remains committed to maintaining the integrity of her editions and ensuring that
her works are presented with care.

Özevin's storytelling approach is deeply
embedded in her projects, where each image is
part of a larger narrative. She prefers to create
series that interconnect, allowing viewers to
engage with the work on a personal level.
Her technical preferences include professional camera bodies and   a
variety of lenses, alongside a commitment to
using advanced editing tools like Photos-
hop and Lightroom to refine her images.

As she continues to explore new projects in photography, video, and installation
art, Özevin remains dedicated to her journey
of learning and growth. Through her work
with Portfolio Art Space, she fosters sustainable art communication and provides guidance to
emerging artists.

Sema Özevin's contributions to the art world are
commendable, showcasing her as a multifaceted artist
who seamlessly blends technical skill with profound
storytelling. Her ability to navigate the complexities of
contemporary art while remaining true to her vision is a
testament to her talent and dedication. As she continues
to evolve, her work promises to inspire and challenge
audiences, making her a significant figure in the landscape
of modern photography and video art.

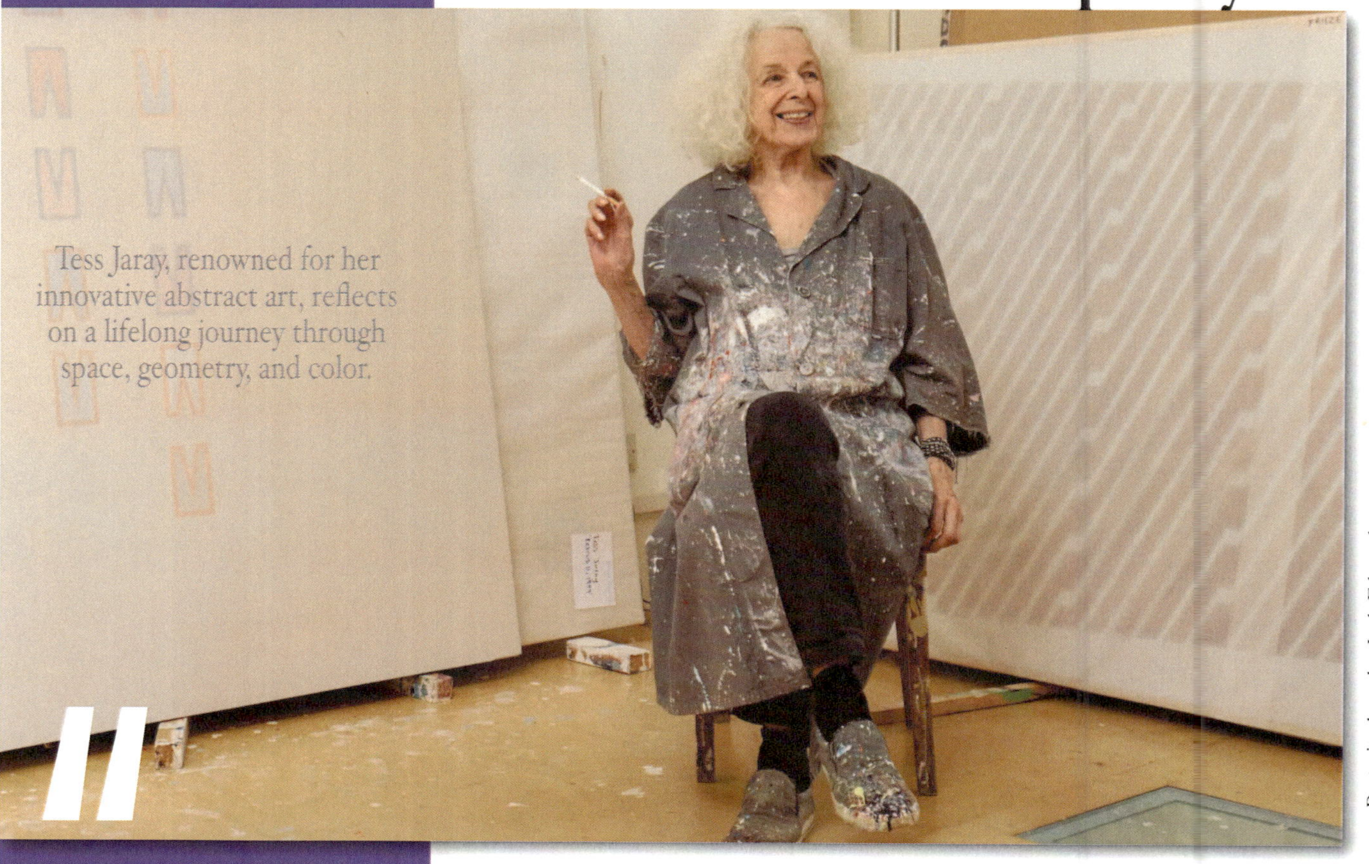

Tess Jaray, renowned for her innovative abstract art, reflects on a lifelong journey through space, geometry, and color.

Portrait photo by Jack Edwards

> "It's not in any way deliberate that when I'm painting I set out to create space. It's all part of a process."

TESS JARAY

How Tess Jaray's paintings create profound illusions of architectural depth and beauty

In this interview, Tess Jaray reflects on her journey as an artist, her architectural inspirations, and the challenges she faced as a pioneering female lecturer at the Slade School of Art.

Tess Jaray is a force within the landscape of contemporary abstract art, with a career that spans over six decades of innovation and boundary-pushing. Born in Vienna in 1937 and arriving in the United Kingdom as a young child during the upheaval of WWII, Jaray's work is a profound blend of personal history and creative exploration. Her early studies at the prestigious Saint Martin's School of Art and the Slade School of Fine Art laid the foundation for a practice that transcends categorization, skillfully interweaving elements of Op Art, Minimalism, and Colour Field painting. Her role as the first female lecturer at the Slade School marked a groundbreaking moment for women in art education and paved the way for generations of artists to follow. With public commissions that have redefined

spaces across the UK—from Birmingham's Centenary Square to London's Victoria Station—Jaray's contributions to art and architecture are enduring and transformative.

Jaray's paintings create an atmosphere that feels at once solid and ethereal, a reflection of her unique approach to space and form. Utilizing vibrant color palettes and geometric motifs inspired by Italian Renaissance and Middle Eastern architecture, her compositions explore how repetition and isolation of forms can evoke the essence of architectural space without directly depicting it. Her work invites viewers to step into a world where structural lines and bold hues suggest something deeper—an unspoken connection between art and the built environment. Held in renowned collections worldwide, including the Tate, the Centre Pompidou, and the Victoria and Albert Museum, Jaray's art is celebrated for its sophistication, its complexity, and its ability to

Tess Jaray, a pioneering figure in contemporary abstract art, blends vibrant colors and geometric forms to create immersive spaces that reflect her unique artistic journey and architectural influences. Her work invites viewers to explore the intricate relationship between art and the built environment, showcasing her innovative spirit and commitment to redefining abstract art.

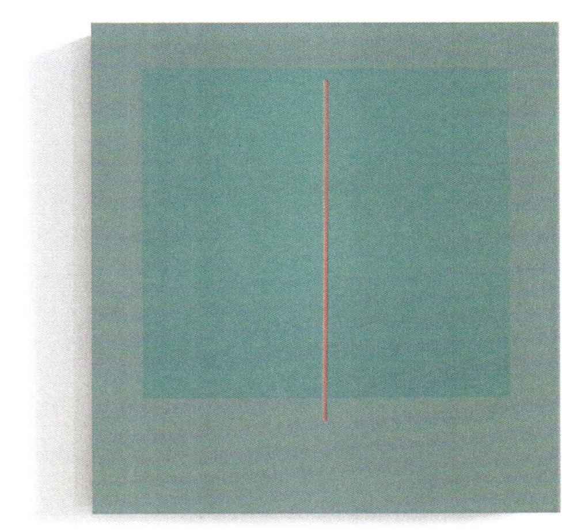

continually reshape our perceptions of abstract art.

How has your background as a Jewish refugee from Austria influenced your artistic perspective and the themes present in your work?

I rejected it. It was so 'foreign' and I wanted to be a nice English girl. My parents saw themselves

> Tess Jaray's compositions create expansive spaces through precise geometric forms and vivid colors, echoing the architectural influences that shape her art.

as 'becoming English'. They loved everything English. We came to England in 1938, the year after I was born, so I knew little about life in Austria except through my mother who was a great storyteller. She loved talking about her family and her early years. German wasn't spoken at home as a matter of principle. My parents' English was already good and they were well-versed in the English culture of their time.

My father was a chemical engineer who was able to escape to England because he had an industrial connection in Worcestershire. I grew up in rural Worcestershire. We kept goats, chickens and pigs and my best friend was a farmers daughter. I took all that for granted and I still miss it but simultaneously I wanted to get away from it because I wanted to be an artist and thought that artists were of the city.

It is only as I've grown older that I've discovered my wider cultural heritage and explored the musical and visual culture of Europe in my work.

Can you describe your process of using geometric forms and color to create the perception of space in your paintings?

It's not in any way deliberate that when I'm painting I set out to create space. It's all part of a process. It's more that without space there never seemed to be anything there. I'm not sure if that applies to other artists' work but at least to mine it does. In itself a straight edge is not a particularly interesting thing so you have to use it to create space and make it interesting.

In what ways do you think your work interacts with or challenges the conventions of minimalism and Op Art?

When pushing non-figurative work beyond new boundaries you are always in the process in some ways of reduction and there is only so far that can go. The visual language is a limited language and the visual non-figurative language is even more limited. I think if I had realised that as a young artist I might have avoided it but it did seem at the time to be the right thing to aim for…to say as much as possible with as little as possible.

You've mentioned the importance of architectural influences in your art; how do you translate the experience of architecture onto a canvas?

It's more a question of creating spaces that have a certain expression and form than a direct expression. It's a question of looking at how the space works. You're trying to reach something that you sense is there but you don't quite know what it is. I think this happened organically, architecture has always been part of my vocabulary as an artist. It opened the world, as it meant that you looked at architecture as well as the space it was in and the space it was contributing. Architecture, to me, seems to be the essential nature of art - how things relate together. Much like in architecture where the architect must consider making something that relates to what is around it. In painting one must consider how to paint something new in a context that's full of work that's 500 years old.

What role does teaching play in your artistic practice, and how has your experience as the first female art teacher at the Slade School of Art shaped your work?

It's always good practice to be forced to identify with students or other artists, and I was lucky to teach at the Slade where the calibre of students has always been very high. Some of my closest friends were originally my students. You can develop very close friendships with younger artists particularly if you are facing similar difficulties in your work.

When I went to teach at the Slade in 1968 I was the first female teacher there. I actually got the job because I was talking to one of the teachers, William Townsend, at a party and he said "Oh you must come in and do a days teaching." I said "Yes, I'd love to" and then I woke up the next morning and I remembered that William Coldstream had said 'as long as I am professor here, no woman will set foot over the threshold and teach."

So I rang William Townsend and said "I can't possibly come in with Bill having said that" and he said "Oh, don't take any notice of that." And so I came in for a days teaching and then a few more and a few more and amazingly I've heard the odd complaint that there are too many women teaching there now and I think that's a terribly good sign. Although, things have improved greatly for women artists, overall it was an advantage if you were a man, particularly a White, Western man.

As you continue to innovate in your practice, what new geometric forms are you exploring, and what do you hope to express through them?

I'm not interested in new geometric forms - I don't think that's possible. It's a question of looking at what the extant forms can do and perhaps haven't yet been used for. The marks themselves tell me how to proceed.

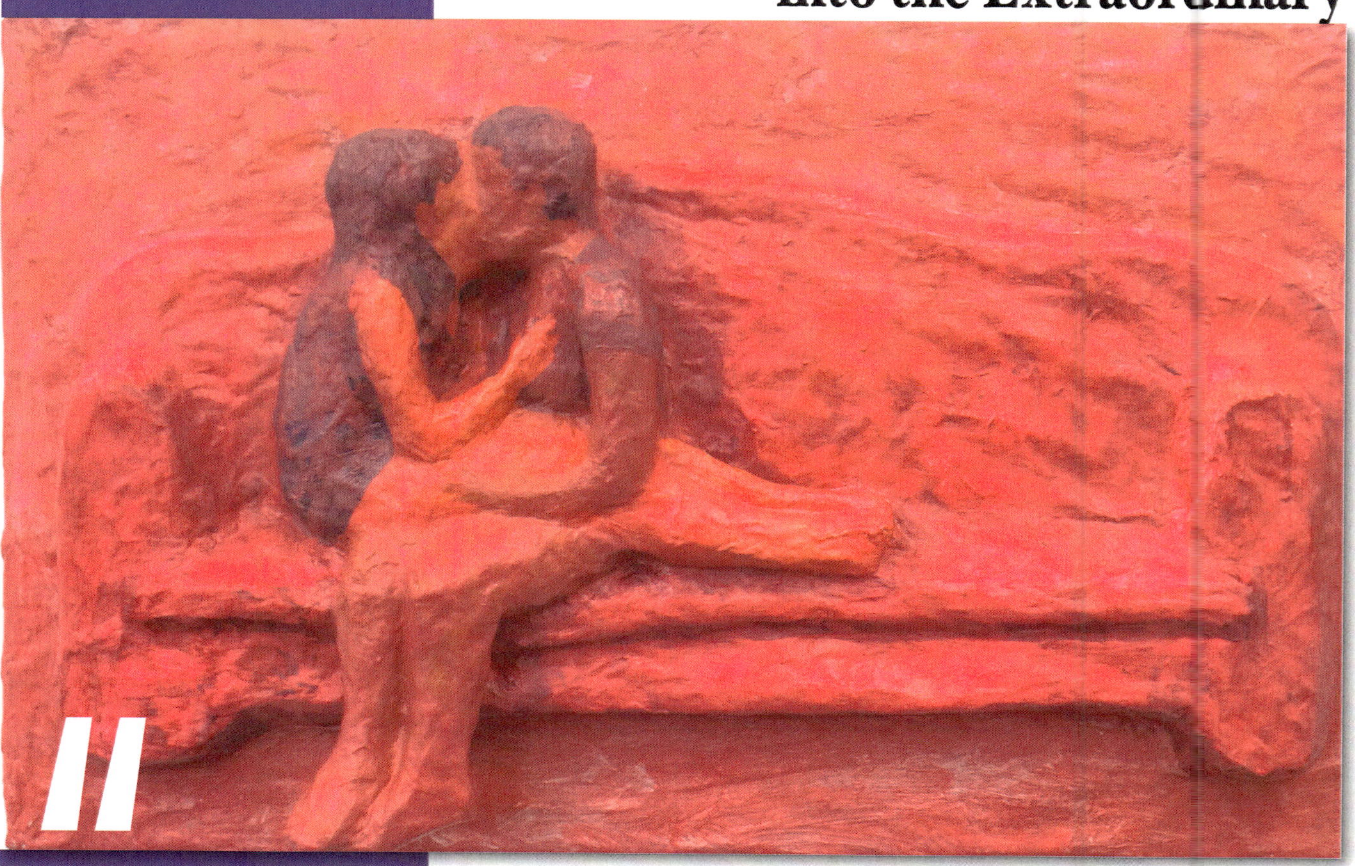

LEIGH WERRELL

Exploring emotion, ambiguity, and connection through painting and sculpture

Leigh Werrell discusses her artistic process, the emotional depth of her work, and how themes of ambiguity and connection shape her paintings and three-dimensional creations.

Leigh Werrell's art invites viewers into a world where the ordinary transforms into the extraordinary, where the familiar is imbued with mystery, and where emotion is rendered in vivid, tactile form. Her work, spanning painting and three-dimensional creations, is deeply personal yet universally resonant, exploring themes of mental discord, nostalgia, and the unease of the unknown. Through her masterful use of color, luminescence, and texture, Werrell crafts narratives that are as much about what is hidden as what is revealed, encouraging viewers to bring their own interpretations to her evocative scenes. Her ability to balance ambiguity with emotional clarity makes her work both compelling and profoundly human.

A graduate of the Pennsylvania Academy of the Fine Arts and represented by Cross McCleaf Gallery, Werrell has established herself as a significant voice in contemporary art. Her work has been featured in exhibitions at esteemed institutions such as the Woodmere Art Museum, Cerulean Arts Gallery, and Bowery Gallery, among others. Her recent explorations into papier-mâché relief and sculptural elements demonstrate her fearless experimentation and commitment to pushing the boundaries of her practice. Leigh Werrell's art is a testament to her ability to find beauty and meaning in the overlooked and the mundane, transforming them into poignant reflections of the human experience.

How did your experience during the pandemic influence the themes and subjects in your recent work?

Because my work is informed by my everyday experiences, the sense of openness, commu-

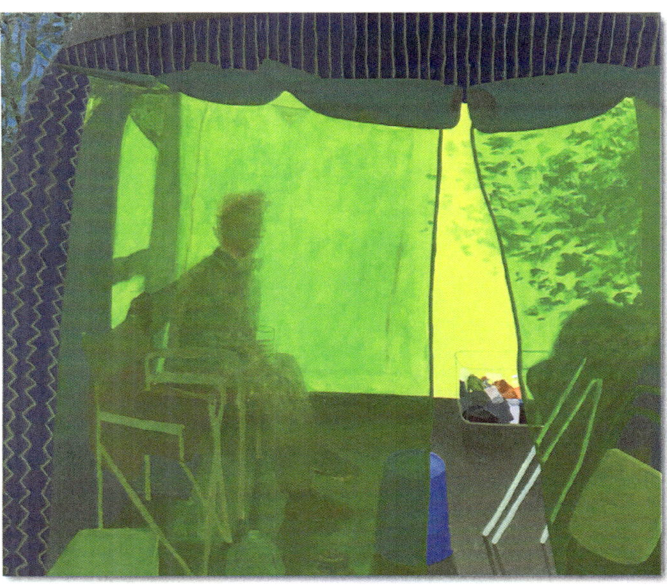

nity and gathering in my pre-pandemic work turned to a feeling of solitude and uneasiness after 2019. In my 2022 exhibition, my work was pervaded by a yearning for human connection – searching for it out of windows, peeking into neighbors' homes and the storefronts and restaurants that used to be so easy to enter. Happily, I have started to incorporate a more social lifestyle into my more recent work.

Can you talk about how you use color, luminescence, and translucency to evoke emotion and invite viewer interpretation?

I use color in the same way that films and television shows use filters to establish specific moods. I usually do a wash of one color that I choose intuitively to fill the panel before drafting.

The quality of tonal shifts impacts the mood of a painting. A highly contrasting detail in a painting may intonate strength or power, whereas a softer shift may show gentleness or tranquility. For example, I'm currently working on a tonally dark painting of myself nursing my child in the middle of the night, and the edges of each object and figure will be fuzzy and indeterminate. However, other work includes intense neon lights or the glare of a nighttime window, details that deliver a more frenetic and energizing experience.

Often, I think of translucency as a way to obscure a narrative, to allow the viewer to find familiarity by bringing their own interpretation to the scene. I find windows especially enticing, as they hold a separate world hostage behind silent glass panels or brightly lit signs.

What role does ambiguity play in your work, and why do you think it is essential for creating an empathetic connection with viewers?

Ambiguity draws people in and allows them to see a story that includes their own experience. Often, I use shallow tonal shifts, blurry edges, sanding, and overglazing to allow viewers to interpret what they see in their own way. My process includes taking pictures of dark places with undefinable objects. These photographs serve as starting points as I expand on what I believe to exist, using tidbits from my known world, but also creating forms which have no reality beyond the painted world. This tension creates a mystery that is enticing and emotionally stimulating, and the imprecision of this process gives my work more emotion and character.

How do three-dimensional works and classical stone relief sculpture influence the way you structure and present your scenes?

My recent papier-mâché work was inspired by work I saw in Vermont at the Bread and Puppet Theater, including some by Peter Schumann, who had taken inspiration from classical bas-relief sculptures to make a more raw and primitive version of them. I am most interested in the way that the medium allows for some loss of control within the making process. In 2018 I started experimenting with incorporating 3D elements into my paintings by bringing objects and figures out of the surface. Color is still important to these works; however, they are often more monochrome, to allow the sculptural components to speak for themselves. The sculpture, "Tent," explores pandemic isolation by illustrating that there is no way in or out of the structure, and no way to reach the party inside.

In what ways do you hope your art encourages viewers to see themselves or others in new perspectives?

I believe the greatest joy one can get from a piece of art, a novel, or music is feeling seen, connecting emotionally, and finding similarities between one's own experience and the story within the piece. I hope that by making work that speaks to my own life, my viewpoint, and what moves me, a viewer can feel a connection and a mutuality that inspires deeper contemplation of the themes and sentiments of the work. I think viewers, especially right now, need something to help them recognize the beauty held within conventionally unattractive or mundane scenes.

How do you approach balancing familiar emotions with elements of the unexpected in your pieces?

Many of my scenes may appear as everyday trivialities at first, but I find the parts that interest me and emphasize them with tone and color, and enhance or restructure elements in order to accentuate them. For example, in 2018 I was captivated by a food truck across from the Eiffel Tower, from which was emanating a beautiful luminescence. It had a certain character that I brought out by emphasizing the eerie light and obscuring or leaving out the smaller details that took away from that brilliance.

Bridging Worlds Through Color and Canvas

Catherine Chambers creates art that explores identity and culture through Ethiopian influences, combining oil paintings and icon series to tell universal stories about human connection and social dynamics.

Catherine Chambers weaves cultural narratives and personal stories into powerful artistic expressions that transcend geographical boundaries

In the vibrant intersection of cultural narratives and personal storytelling, Catherine Chambers emerges as a masterful chronicler of our times. Her art, deeply rooted in human connection and cross-cultural understanding, offers a fresh perspective on identity, belonging, and the threads that bind our global community.

Through her studio in London, Chambers crafts powerful visual narratives that challenge our preconceptions about culture and identity. Her work, particularly influenced by her profound connection to Ethiopia, serves as a testament to the universality of human experience – a theme that resonates throughout her diverse portfolio.

"People the world over perform the same basic activities to support their lives," Chambers reflects, discussing her observations from years of working between continents. *"My Ethiopian friends do exactly, in the setting of their environment and culture, as I do in mine."*

Working in two distinct styles – figurative oil paintings and acrylic icon series – Chambers has developed a unique visual language that speaks to both personal and universal truths. Her oil paintings capture intimate moments laden with symbolic weight, while her triptych-format icons draw inspiration from Ethiopian Orthodox Christian tradition to tell contemporary stories.

One of her most striking pieces, *"Lying,"* currently exhibited at the National Portrait Gallery, exemplifies her ability to weave complex social commentary into seemingly simple scenes. The painting depicts a man asleep in a football shirt, touching upon themes of global consumerism and accessibility in ways that transcend geographical boundaries.

Chambers' work often challenges viewers' preconceptions, sometimes leading to surprising interpretations. She recalls an incident where a London viewer insisted that playing cards couldn't exist in Lalibela, Ethiopia – the very location where the referenced cards were purchased. Such moments of misconception fuel her creative drive to bridge cultural gaps through art.

The artist's appreciation for historical masters, particularly William Hogarth, influences her approach to social commentary. Like Hogarth's famous series *"A Rake's Progress,"* Chambers' work often follows narrative sequences that explore the consequences of human actions and decisions, particularly in cross-cultural contexts.

In an era of increasing global connectivity, Chambers' art serves as a crucial reminder of our shared humanity. Through her careful observation and masterful execution, she creates works that not only please the eye but also challenge the mind, inviting viewers to question their own assumptions about culture, identity, and human connection.

As we continue to navigate an increasingly interconnected world, Catherine Chambers' art stands as a beacon of understanding, reminding us that beneath our surface differences lie universal experiences that bind us all together. Her work isn't just about observing culture – it's about building bridges between worlds, one canvas at a time.

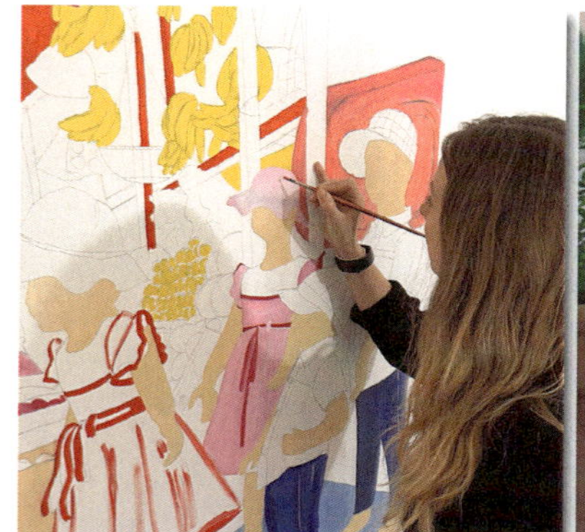

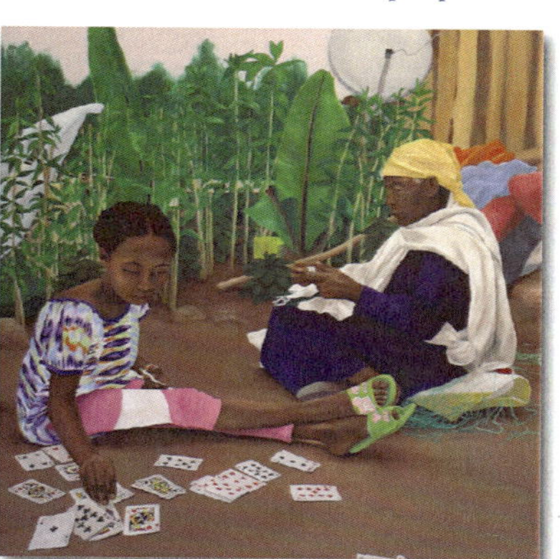

People the world over perform the same basic activities to support their lives. My Ethiopian friends do exactly, in the setting of their environment and culture, as I do in mine."

Catherine Chambers

The Paper Whisperer

I n exclusive interview with Mosaic Digest magazine, now shared with WOWvART readers, paper artist Clare Pentlow reveals the intricate world of her unique artistic expression, where mathematics meets creativity in the most delicate of mediums.

During her Surface Pattern Design studies at University in Swansea, Wales, Clare discovered an unexpected love affair with paper that would define her artistic career. What started as a simple university project has blossomed into a distinctive artistic style characterized by her signature "fluffy-like" texture that continues to captivate audiences worldwide.

"Paper has always been my constant companion," Clare shares with Mosaic Digest. *"From folding train tickets in my pocket as a child to creating complex artistic pieces today, it's been an evolving relationship."* Her work, which now graces private collections across Europe and America, demonstrates the extraordinary potential of this humble medium.

Clare's impressive portfolio includes collaborations with luxury brands like Hermès and Lexus, and her recent appointment as an associate at the Royal Birmingham Society of Artists marks a significant milestone in her career. Working from her studio at Holyhead Studios in Coventry, she continues to push the boundaries of paper art while maintaining a strong connection to community engagement through workshops.

The artist's unique approach combines precision with organic forms, influenced by her fascination with mathematics and natural patterns. "Looking at nature under a microscope, from pollen to diatoms in water, provides endless inspiration," she explains. Her work particularly shines in its interaction with light and shadow, creating pieces that seem to dance with their environment.

What sets Clare's work apart is her methodical experimentation with paper's limitations. *"I'm constantly asking questions of the paper - how small can I cut, how many layers can I add?"* This scientific approach to artistic creation has resulted in groundbreaking techniques that challenge our perception of paper as a medium.

Despite working with prestigious brands and achieving international recognition, Clare remains committed to sharing her passion with others. "I hope people realize that paper can be more than just a surface to write on," she reflects. "It's about rediscovering the joy of creating something with your hands, away from screens and digital devices."

As paper art experiences a renaissance similar to the recent resurgence of traditional crafts like crochet and knitting, Clare stands at the forefront of this movement, proving that sometimes the most ordinary materials can yield the most extraordinary results.

For more information about Clare's workshops and upcoming exhibitions, visit her studio at Holyhead Studios, Coventry, or follow her journey on social media.

A Journey Through Texture and Light Transforms Ordinary Paper into Extraordinary Art

"Delicate Cellular Forms" - A mesmerizing arrangement of white paper sculptures by Clare Pentlow showcases her signature spiky formations, each piece meticulously crafted to capture light and shadow while evoking microscopic natural structures.

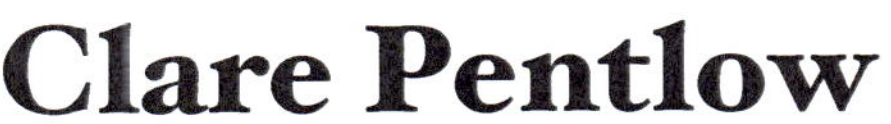

Clare Pentlow

Paper is something I've grown up with, it's something I've continually played around with."

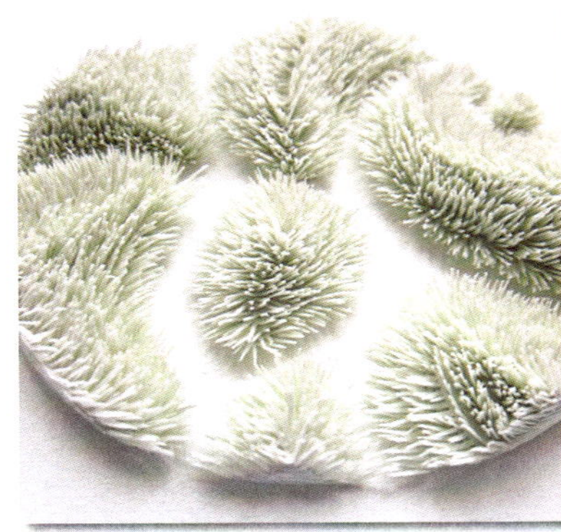

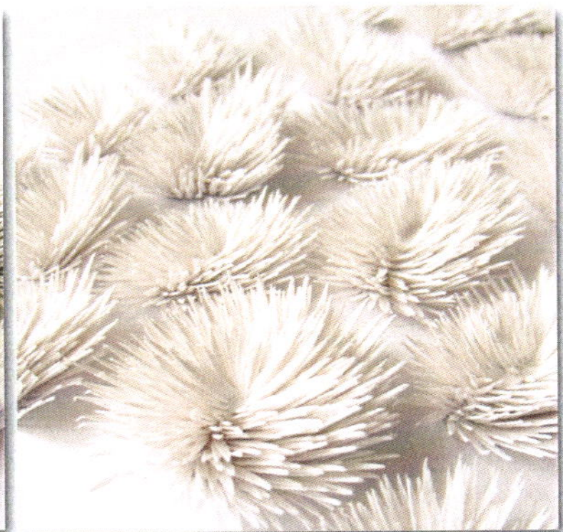

Exploring the Creative Process

Janet Hennessey Dilenschneider discusses her creative process, influences, and the themes of hope and tranquility in her art, emphasizing the importance of evolving and addressing societal issues.

Janet Hennessey Dilenschneider draws inspiration from her surroundings and global events to create impactful art

Janet Hennessey Dilenschneider, a celebrated artist known for her expressionist style infused with impressionist influences, has captivated audiences worldwide with her vibrant and emotive paintings. Her latest exhibition, "Come To The Light," is a testament to her ability to convey hope and tranquility through art. In an interview conducted for Mosaic Digest, Dilenschneider shared insights into her creative process, influences, and the profound messages she aims to communicate through her work.

Dilenschneider's surroundings in Connecticut, coupled with global events, significantly impact her artistic expression. Her painting "Come To The Light" exemplifies her desire to offer peace and solace to a troubled world, providing inspiration and hope. A memorable sunrise witnessed from her window became the catalyst for this exhibition, leading her to create paintings that capture the ethereal beauty of light and sun, elements that resonate deeply with many and hold spiritual significance for some.

A pivotal moment in Dilenschneider's artistic journey occurred at the age of 16 when she encountered renowned artist Roy Lichtenstein. Initially rejected from a juried show, she was later awarded first place in Watercolor, thanks to Lichtenstein's encouragement. This experience, along with the support of a teacher who urged her to pursue art, set her on a path of artistic exploration. Her first solo show in Paris in 2013 marked a significant milestone, leading to numerous exhibitions worldwide.

Dilenschneider's expressionist style, influenced by impressionism, is characterized by free brushstrokes and vibrant colors. She aims to evoke emotions in viewers, allowing them to feel the passion and joy she experiences while painting. Her use of "simultaneous contrast," a technique borrowed from the Impressionists, creates a dynamic interplay of colors that "sing" together, adding excitement and depth to her work.

As an artist, Dilenschneider feels a personal obligation to give something meaningful to her viewers. Her paintings invite participation, encouraging viewers to find a sense of renewal and spiritual connection. She believes art can be healing and motivational, offering a respite from the chaos of the world.

In her creative process, Dilenschneider allows her "creative brain" to take over, interpreting colors and designs in unique ways. Experiences like her drive through Provence, where she was inspired by the enchanting landscapes, influence her work, resulting in paintings that capture the essence of the scenes she encounters.

Looking ahead, Dilenschneider is excited to explore new techniques and themes. She is particularly drawn to the shapes of clouds and the "misting out" of landscape scenes, aiming to capture the magical and atmospheric qualities of these subjects. Her commitment to evolving as an artist is evident in her desire to challenge her artistry and reach new heights.

Dilenschneider's passion for art was nurtured by her mother and sister, whose influence shaped her artistic style and career. She continues to apply lessons learned from them, such as the importance of contrast in both art and life.

In addition to creating beautiful art, Dilenschneider believes artists have a responsibility to comment on societal issues, such as ecology and global warming. She balances conveying these messages with creating art that provides peace and beauty, encouraging viewers to appreciate nature and develop an awareness of ecological issues.

For emerging artists, Dilenschneider advises "beating their own drum" and observing the world around them. She emphasizes the importance of learning from others while finding one's unique voice. By immersing themselves in art and allowing their "creative brain" to guide them, young artists can discover the joy and passion that define their work.

Janet Hennessey Dilenschneider's art is a beacon of light in a world often overshadowed by darkness. Her ability to inspire and uplift through her paintings is a testament to her talent and dedication to her craft. As she continues to explore new themes and techniques, her work will undoubtedly continue to resonate with audiences, offering hope and beauty to all who encounter it.

Janet Hennessey Dilenschneider is a visionary artist whose passion and dedication illuminate the art world with profound beauty.

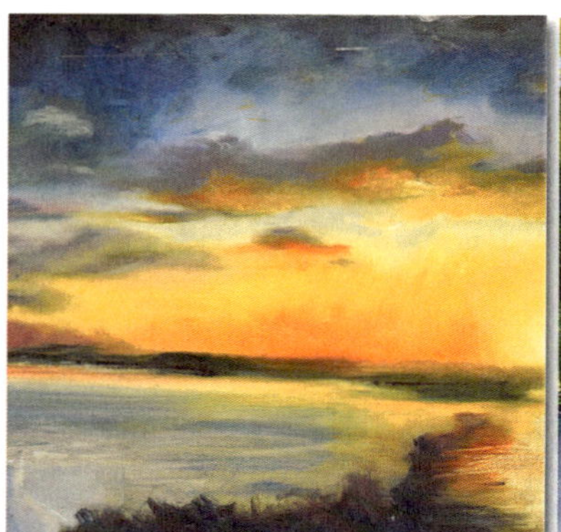
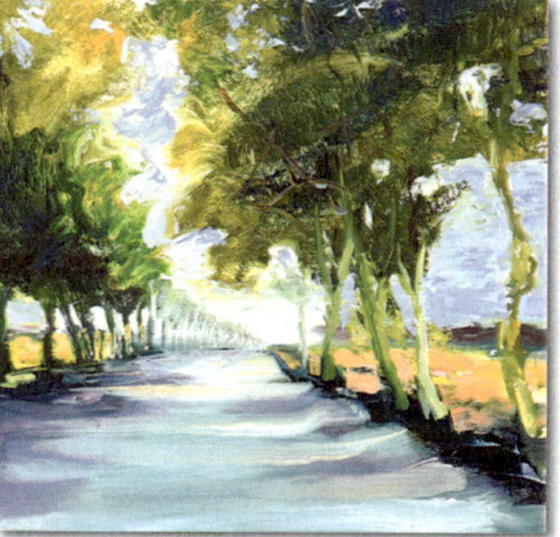

> *Art can be healing and motivational if we allow it to be."*

Janet Hennessey Dilenschneider

A Journey of Art, Identity, and Connection

Sofia Ruiz, a Costa Rican artist, explores identity and memory through painting and printmaking, drawing from personal experiences and international residencies to create universally resonant and introspective art.

Sofia Ruiz, a distinguished Latin American artist hailing from San José, Costa Rica, has captivated audiences worldwide with her evocative and introspective works. Her journey into the art world began at the tender age of 16, a path shaped by personal experiences and a profound sense of longing for connection. In an interview conducted for Mosaic Digest, Ruiz shared insights into her artistic evolution, revealing how her early life experiences and academic pursuits have influenced her creative vision.

Ruiz's artistic journey was sparked by her childhood experiences, where drawing became a refuge during challenging times. Her father, often absent due to work, provided her with small notebooks and a pen to occupy her time while visiting her mother, who suffered from temporary amnesia. This period of isolation and the absence of childhood photographs deeply influenced Ruiz, driving her to explore themes of memory, identity, and psychoanalysis in her art. Her work serves as a visual diary, a healing process that continues to evolve, reflecting her quest for belonging and understanding.

In 2007, Ruiz graduated with a major in Painting and Printmaking from the School of Fine Arts in Costa Rica. These two mediums, though distinct, complement each other in her work. Printmaking, with its intricate techniques and materials, allows for careful layering of ideas, while painting offers spontaneity and raw expression. This dynamic interplay between structure and freedom is central to Ruiz's creative process, enabling her to explore complex themes with both precision and intuition.

Ruiz's artistic journey has taken her across the globe, participating in international residencies from the USA to South Korea. These experiences have enriched her understanding of art's role in diverse cultural contexts, encouraging her to experiment and blend technology with traditional printmaking. Engaging with artists from various backgrounds has broadened her perspective, allowing her to view her work through different cultural lenses and infusing her art with a global sensibility.

With over 35 exhibitions worldwide and numerous accolades, including the prestigious Best Overseas Artist Prize at the Women in Art Prize in London, Ruiz's career is marked by significant milestones. Her first solo exhibition was a pivotal moment, offering both excitement and vulnerability. Each opportunity to showcase her work, whether in a small gallery or a renowned museum, is a testament to her talent and perseverance. These experiences have bolstered her confidence, inspiring her to continue creating even in challenging times.

Beyond her artistic practice, Ruiz holds a Master's in Education, a background that profoundly influences her engagement with art. Teaching has honed her ability to simplify complex ideas, a skill that translates into her art, making intricate concepts like identity more relatable to viewers. Both teaching and creating are avenues for understanding and sharing ideas, allowing Ruiz to express them in a clearer, more accessible manner.

Through her art, Ruiz invites viewers to embark on a journey of introspection. Her exploration of themes such as fragmentation, identity, and memory encourages audiences to delve into their emotional layers, fostering a deeper understanding of their own experiences. Her work resonates universally, transcending cultural boundaries and highlighting the duality of identity—how we define ourselves versus how others perceive us. This universal theme of connection and introspection is at the heart of Ruiz's artistic vision, leaving a lasting impact on all who encounter her work.

Sofia Ruiz's art is a testament to her remarkable talent and dedication, a celebration of her journey from a young girl in Costa Rica to an internationally acclaimed artist. Her works continue to inspire and connect, offering a profound exploration of the human experience.

Exploring the profound themes of memory and identity, Sofia Ruiz's art transcends cultural boundaries and invites introspection.

Sofia Ruiz is a visionary artist whose profound exploration of identity and memory captivates and inspires audiences worldwide.

> *Winning the Best Overseas Artist Prize at the Women in Art Prize in London was another important moment."*

Sofia Ruiz

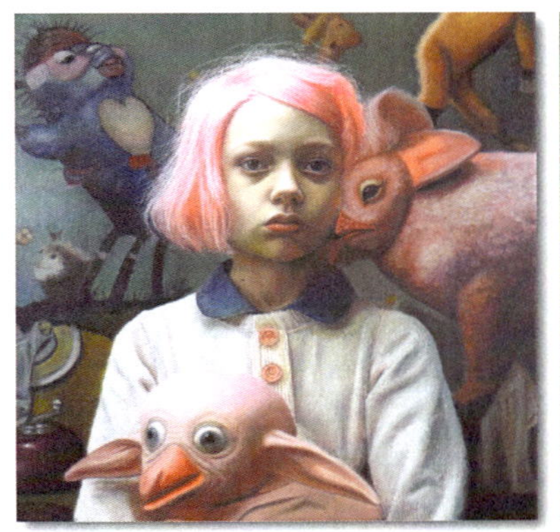
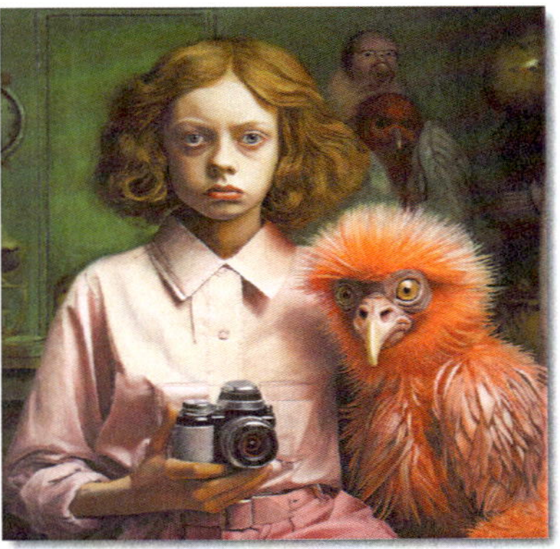

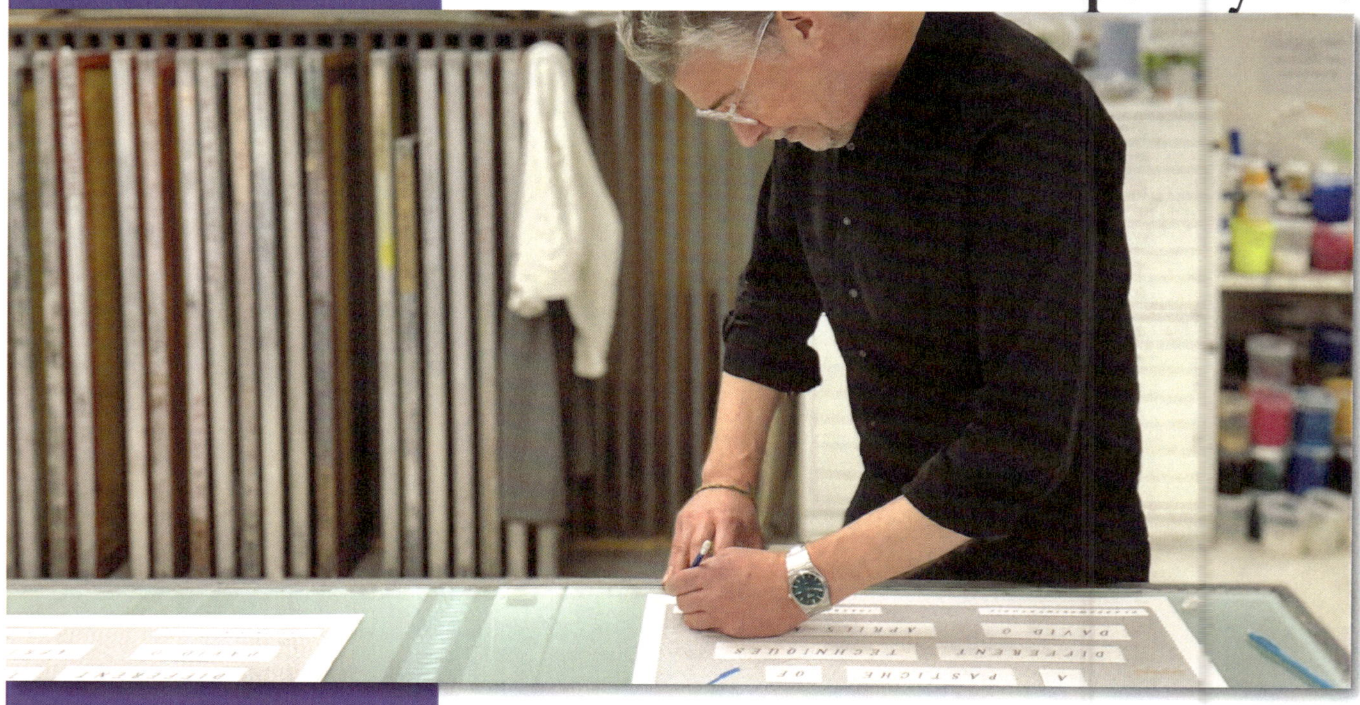

> **"Drawing is the basis of everything I do. It is like a hidden language that operates directly out of the nervous system."**

DAVID OSBALDESTON

David explores the dynamic interplay of images and words through his innovative collage and printmaking techniques

David Osbaldeston discusses his artistic process, the significance of scale in his work, and the themes of identity and value in his upcoming publication.

David Osbaldeston, whose innovative approach to collage and printmaking invites viewers to reconsider the boundaries between words and images. Osbaldeston's work stands as a testament to the power of visual storytelling, marrying the spontaneity of collage with the meticulous craftsmanship of intaglio etching. Through his dynamic use of scale and material, he challenges traditional notions of value, class, and identity, creating a dialogue that resonates deeply with contemporary audiences.

Osbaldeston's artistic practice embodies a unique synthesis of historical influences and modern techniques, as he navigates the intricate relationships between disparate elements. His belief that drawing is a hidden language that operates from within the nervous system permeates his work, revealing the layered complexities of identity and perception. With a keen eye for the interplay of forms, he transforms the act of making into a form of social commentary, inviting us to reflect on our own positions within the fabric of society. In this exclusive interview, Osbaldeston shares insights into his creative process, the significance of scale, and the motivations behind his upcoming publication, "A Pastiche of Different Techniques." Prepare to be inspired by an artist whose work is as thought-provoking as it is visually stunning.

How does collage serve as a medium for exploring the relationships between images and words in your work?

It's a way to put images together. Words are images. My interest in collage deals simply with the re-arrangement of separate realities.

It is a form of open play, so I think with my hands as much as my head. I'm always prepared

David Osbaldeston's innovative approach and mastery of collage reveal profound insights into identity and perception, captivating audiences with every piece.

for the collages to not work out, but the ones that do often end up as large-scale intaglio etchings. I don't enjoy making things difficult, but the paradox between the spontaneity of collage and the slowness of etching creates a tension that becomes an essential part of the message. The priority is in making the right word and image work together. It's the same with the 'word prop' series I have been making on prepared linen which are screen prints.

Can you discuss the significance of scale in your artwork, particularly regarding your artist's books versus your large-scale etchings?

I discovered a long time ago that I like to work at opposite ends of scale. Sometimes an idea will be best suited to the modest scale of an artist's book where it makes more sense for the work and the reader to be in sync.

Other times when I embark on a large etching, I find myself obsessing over how an image occupies space almost like a piece of sculpture. For my first solo show I made a composite etching to fit the surface area of a billboard where the intimacy of it on such a scale invited a closer form of visual reading.

What role does drawing play in your artistic process, and how does it inform the other media you engage with?

Drawing is the basis of everything I do. It is like a hidden language that operates directly out of the nervous system as an interaction. Each time I begin something, a different challenge always presents itself, but it always comes through drawing. I consider drawing as something other than simply making pictorial observations.

You mention a desire to challenge perceptions of value, class, and identity. How do these themes manifest in your work?

Fine art practice is generally rooted in perceptions and realities of remoteness and exclusivity. I like to work with opposites of process. Etching is thought of as a substitute for painting. Screen printing evolved from an industrial process, and so on... The irony is I don't see myself as a printmaker, but much of my interest stems from a desire to satirise the assumptions of what an art object might be which is probably a very bourgeoise idea in itself.

I'm not attempting to identify as a working-class artist, but I understand it. Like many others, my mother came to post-war England from rural Ireland with no qualifications and held it together for most her working life as a carer and hospital cleaner. After lots of jobs my dad worked for a while as a librarian in F.E but due to mental health issues decided to opt out in his forties. We had no money. Growing up I was acutely aware of how that feels, and it never leaves you.

What motivated you to create the upcoming book "A Pastiche of Different Techniques," and what can audiences expect from it?

The book charts the development of studio work I've made over the last two years for solo exhibitions at Glasgow Print Studio and Moon Grove in Manchester. I'm drawn to the idea of it extending their life and it will be an artist's book in the sense that it has a two-colour screen-printed dustjacket. The book will be published in early 2025 and tell the story of the work's development with images of recent etchings, screen prints on linen, and collaged paintings each made in series.

As you describe it. In what ways do you aim to create a porous relationship between your studio practice and the outside world through your exhibitions and publications?

I've come to think of what I make as 'flat sculpture' which is a way to describe how images and words are pushed together to make a compressed form. An artwork that slots through a letter box is still a very seductive idea, just as it can be when a work is made to be sited on a wall. But it's always material.

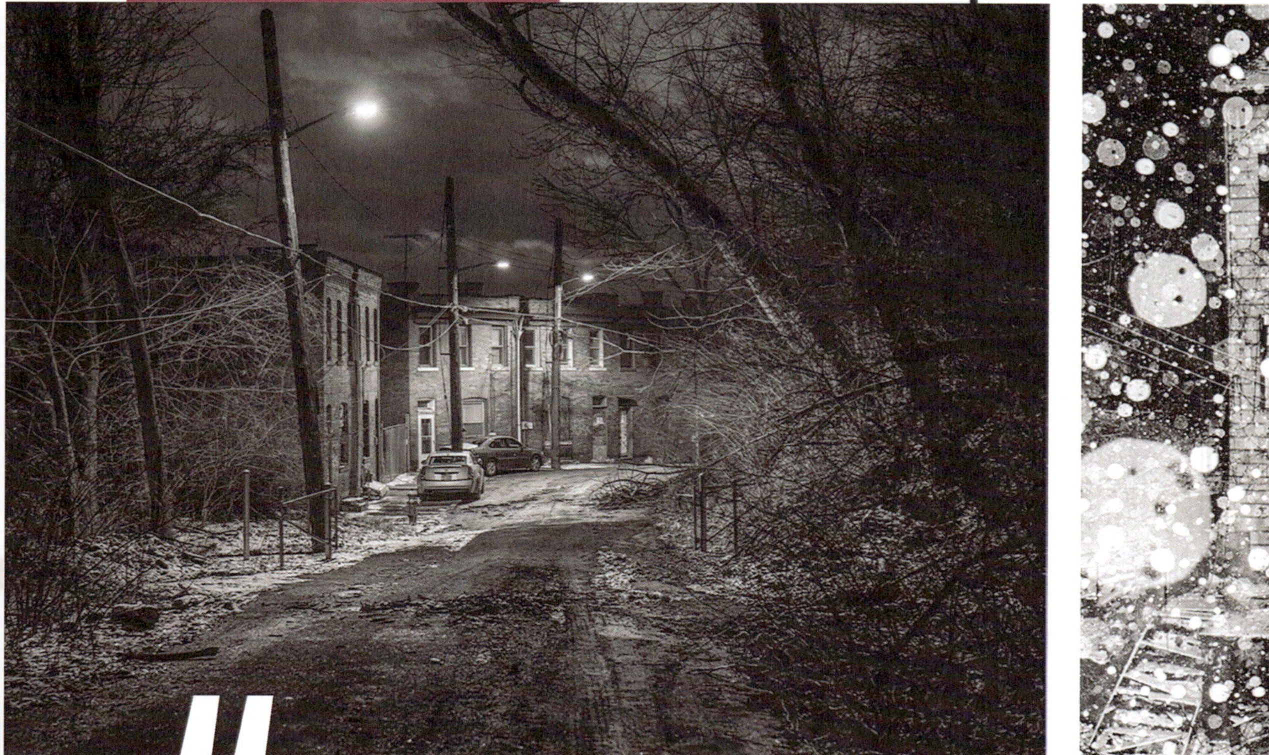

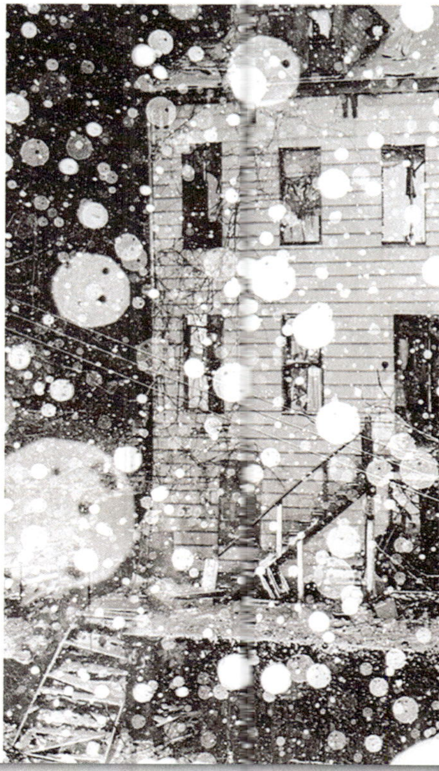

Photography is an excellent tool to learn how to notice and to appreciate your everyday environment and these everyday mysteries more fully.

ED PANAR

Ed Panar on the Power of Visual Storytelling

Carlos Beltran Arechiga discusses the themes of existential ambiguity, identity, and social structures in his art, inviting viewers to reflect on their own experiences.

Ed Panar's artistic journey is a profound exploration of the often-overlooked beauty in everyday surroundings, captured with a sense of wonder and meticulous observation. His approach to photography reveals a fascination with the ordinary as he navigates his environment by foot, bicycle, and public transport. Panar's work has a unique way of transforming familiar landscapes and commonplace moments into scenes that evoke a deep, meditative curiosity about our surroundings. His images invite viewers to pause and reconsider what may initially seem mundane, revealing layers of meaning through subtle compositions and nuanced contrasts. Celebrated for his photobooks—such as Winter Nights, Walking and In the Vicinity—he has become a seminal figure in contemporary photography, consistently pushing the boundaries of visual storytelling.

Panar offers an intimate look into the philosophy and process behind his work. He discusses his early inspirations, his commitment to exploring the world close to home, and the vital role of photobooks in his creative practice. His latest endeavors, including co-founding the project space Spaces Corners in Pittsburgh, underscore his dedication to fostering a community centered around photographic art. With an eye for detail and a respect for the subtle, Panar reminds us that beauty is not only found in the extraordinary but in the quiet, overlooked corners of our daily lives.

What initially drew you to photography during your high school years, and how did it shape your approach to capturing everyday moments?

I was drawn to photograph as an amateur like anyone else, to remember things and to 'capture memories'. I was under the impression that it could easily and effortlessly copy and capture

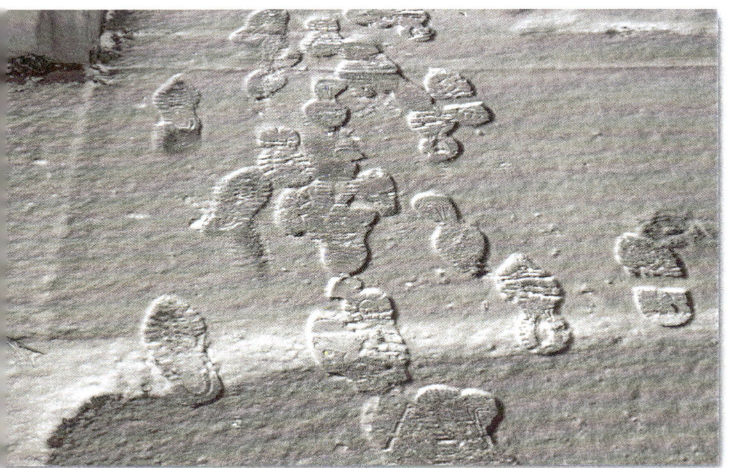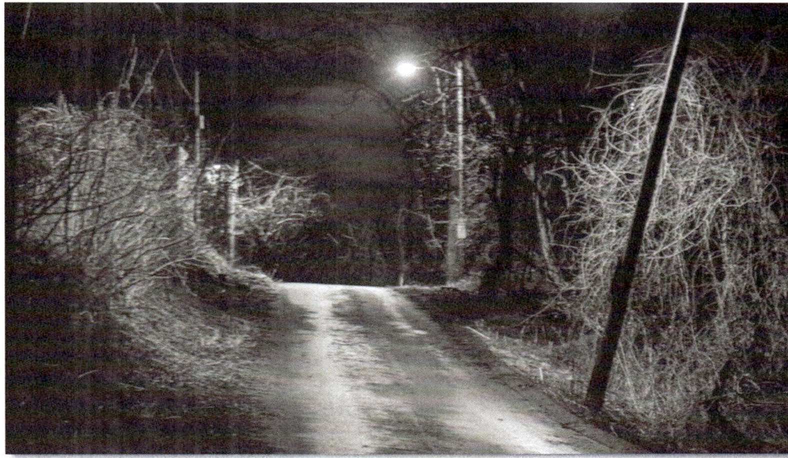

reality, preserve our memories and seemingly freeze time and space. Of course I was being optimistic and it wasn't quite that simple, but those kinds of dreams and delights about photography captivated me then and continues to fascinate me. Noticing the sometimes shocking rift between a lived moment and the resulting photographs from that moment made me aware of the unexpected power of the accidental and the unplanned in photography so I still look back at my earliest photographs for inspiration and reminders of that feeling.

Much of your work focuses on exploring your

surroundings through walking, biking, and public transport. How do these modes of travel influence the way you see and photograph your environment?

I grew up in a walkable neighborhood and town so it's just how I learned to get around and to see the world. I still haven't managed to get my license, so part of this has always been based on practicality as well. I also really enjoy biking around town, since it helps to get to even more places and cover ground at my own pace. I'll often bike to a certain area and walk around as well, so it is not uncommon that I am doing both or all three when I'm roaming with my camara. Almost all of my work is made in publicly accessible spaces and that feels important. I used to dream of going to far away places to make beautiful photographs, but at some point I realized that just because some places are deemed 'photogenic' or worthy of postcards, why just those certain places? Of course what seems 'ordinary and everyday' to one person might be the most strange and unimagined reality to someone else so I try to remember this as well.

Your body of work emphasizes the beauty in the mundane. How do you approach finding meaning or value in ordinary, everyday scenes?

I think it comes down to a lot of different things, like being open and curious, and part of it is simply seeing things around you for the deep and fundamental mysteries that they actually are. I don't really believe the world itself could ever be mundane, it's more of an external label applied that is more reflective of momentary laziness, inattention or inability to connect with our surroundings than anything intrinsic or fundamental to a place or object itself. It's a common error to mistake one's feelings about something for the thing itself, and for me photography is an excellent tool to learn how to notice and to appreciate your everyday environment and these everyday mysteries more fully, so for me at least it has helped.

Could you share some insights into the process of creating your photobooks? What role do these books play in your overall artistic expression?

Photobooks and bookmaking are central to my practice for many reasons. I share the belief that photobooks are one of the most ideal formats to experience groups of photographs together. I am very interested in the notion of how photographs interact and bounce off of each other, and the book form is one of the most interesting and intimate formats that allows this action to take place. I tend to favor the 'project' and work with large sets of images. For me the process of making a book usually happens after collecting photographs over the course of several years and becomes a way to tie together multiple threads and hopefully make new discoveries as well. So the possibilities of creating a series or set of sequences, the overall edit, and how the images are placed onto pages and spreads is an exciting - if daunting - way to imagine a sprawling body of work being distilled to a relatively tiny selection of images. And hopefully somehow in the end it says and does more than you could have imagined while making the individual photographs.

How has your perspective on photography evolved from your first published monograph Golden Palms in 2007 to your more recent work like Winter Nights, Walking?

In all categories I believe my work has grown and improved since then, but also contains a consistency of interest which I tend to sum up as an interest in cities and the built environment and how photographs of a place can work together to reflect something about the experience of simply wandering through a city or town. Each of my photobooks takes a certain location or observed phenomena of the built environment and reconfigures them in a condensed and meditative fashion. In all of my books one goal is always to allow room for the viewer to wander along at their own pace, make their own discoveries and to be able to make their own connections. I am still very interested in the book as a set of combined possibilities that is activated by the reader and can feel a little different each time you open it up, so in that way I think of them as collaborative experiences as well. My early experience of living in Los Angeles certainly changed my idea of what a city could be forever and my latest book Winter Nights, Walking reflects my getting to know my current hometown of Pittsburgh over the past ten winters or so..

What inspired you to co-found Spaces Corners, and how does the project space contribute to your artistic community in Pittsburgh?

Melissa Catanese and I have been collaborating since we met in graduate school at the Cranbrook Academy of Art in Bloomfield Hills, Michigan about 20 years ago. It was through photo books that we learned so much about what was possible with photography and so our love of photobooks continued and expanded when we moved to Pittsburgh in 2011 and started Spaces Corners. It was a way to share our love of photobooks in a new way, not just as artists making books which was a nice change of perspective. We arrived after living in New York for several years and felt that Pittsburgh could afford us the opportunity to pursue our own endeavors at our own pace. We are very lucky to live in a beautiful city that is still somewhat affordable and feels like it is full of possibilities yet unrealized. There is a small but very active and enthusiastic photography community here that we're proud to be a part of. Best of all, Pittsburgh is simply a gem of a city to wander and photograph in so I don't think I will ever tire of that either.

The Symphony of Space and Light

Ezra Masch discusses his innovative fusion of sculpture and music, his approach to immersive installations, adapting works for diverse venues, and the essential role of audience interaction in experiencing art.

Ezra Masch on the Intersection of Music, Art, and Audience Engagement

Ezra Masch stands out as a visionary artist whose work transcends traditional boundaries, seamlessly blending sound, light, and space into immersive environments that feel both alive and transformative. His multimedia installations do more than fill a space: they reshape it, allowing audiences to experience sound as a physical, visible force and light as a pulsing, rhythmic presence. Drawing from his dual backgrounds in sculpture and music, Masch's signature project, "VOLUMES", exemplifies his unique vision. Through live percussion and custom-designed light structures, each installation pulses and resonates in sync with the performance, creating an atmosphere where sound and sight merge. Masch's work invites viewers into a world where art isn't just observed—it's experienced viscerally.

This exclusive interview offers an intimate glimpse into Masch's creative journey, where he reveals the deep connections between his musical and sculptural practices and how they shape his approach to installation art. Reflecting on the impact of his time at the Skowhegan School of Painting and Sculpture, he shares insights on adapting his work for varied spaces—from major museums to experimental project venues. Masch's reflections on audience interaction reveal his installations as collaborative experiences that dissolve traditional barriers between artist and audience, performer and space.

How does your background in both sculpture and music influence your approach to creating immersive multimedia installations?

I think a lot about overlapping concepts in music and visual art. When it comes to both sculpture and music there's always a compositional structure at play. It could be the way that multiple parts come together to form a whole, or the use of a series of chance operations within a set of parameters. Time-based and object-based composition have some obvious differences, but there are a lot of interesting parallels too. In my work, I really like creating spaces where 3-dimensional structures and temporal structures intersect.

Can you describe a particular installation that you feel best captures the fusion of sonic and visual elements in your work?

My ongoing project VOLUMES uses live sound from percussion instruments to activate a series of immersive light installations. With each installation, I transform a new exhibition space into an interactive audio-visual instrument. It's always evolving. The latest one was in Austin, TX last month and it featured performances by 6 different musicians. Each artist explored the connection between sound, light, and space in their own unique way.

How has your time at the Skowhegan School of Painting and Sculpture shaped your artistic practice?

Skowhegan opened me up to different ways of thinking. There were so many artists coming from different places, and doing different things. It was an atmosphere of complete freedom, and it inspired me to change course with my art. Instead of continuing with the trajectory of my sculpture practice, I started to lean into my love of music. I brought my drum set there and formed a band with a few of the other residents. I began making drawings based on musical scores. These were some of my first attempts at merging sound and image. It definitely marked a turning point in my artistic practice.

Your work has been exhibited in a wide range of venues, from museums to project spaces. How do you adapt your installations to different environments?

The layout is always based on the proportions of the built environment. I use the height, length, and width of each space to determine a ratio that defines the arrangement of lights. It's a way of connecting the instrument and the architecture. But my installations also adapt to different spaces in terms of public programming. Larger institutions are able to facilitate community engagement initiatives like open calls and educational programs, whereas independent venues function more like pop-up performances. One feels like an exhibition while the other feels like a rock concert, but I really enjoy aspects of both.

How do you see the relationship between audience interaction and the success of your installations?

The audience can literally see the performer's ideas taking shape all around them. And this profoundly impacts their perception of sound. For performers and audiences alike, I think it transforms the way that we both create and experience music. My installations are most successful when the distinctions between performer, audience, instrument, and space become blurred.

What role do you believe sound plays in enhancing the emotional or conceptual impact of your visual art?

Sound (and especially music) makes us experience emotions in a way that is impossible to fully understand. My method of visualizing sound is based on a mathematical system in which measurements of frequency and amplitude are represented using coordinates in a 3-dimensional grid. So my work combines an approach that is methodical and cerebral with an expression that is very mysterious and visceral. It kind of exists in these two worlds at once.

Ezra Masch, an interdisciplinary artist, brings light and sound together to create unique, immersive experiences that engage and transform audiences.

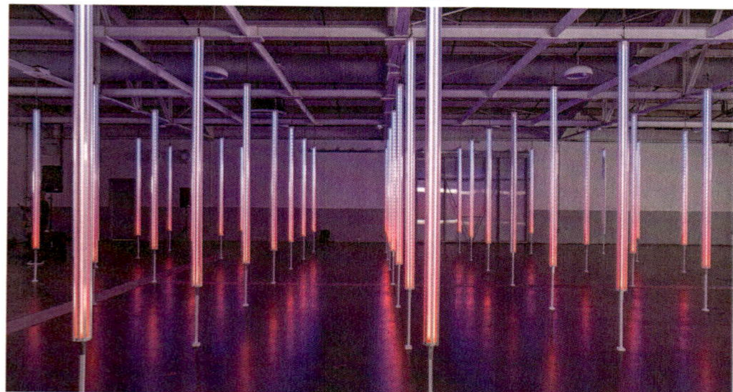

"Sound (and especially music) makes us experience emotions in a way that is impossible to fully understand. My method of visualizing sound is based on a mathematical system in which measurements of frequency and amplitude are represented using coordinates in a 3-dimensional grid."

Ezra Masch

Shortness of Breath Not Going Away?

Ask Your Doctor for a Blood Test

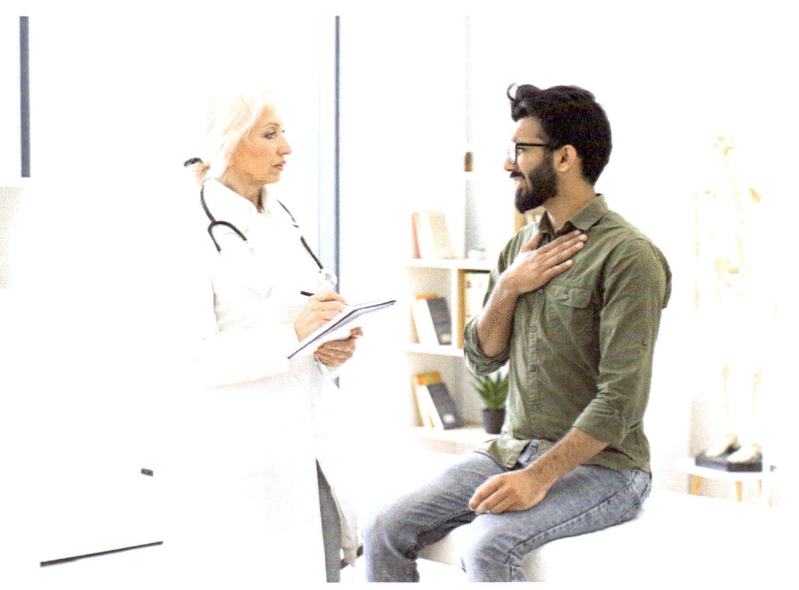

Pulmonary alveolar proteinosis (PAP) is a rare lung disease often misdiagnosed due to symptom similarities with other conditions. The American Lung Association's campaign aims to improve aPAP awareness and diagnosis.

Pulmonary alveolar proteinosis (PAP) is an ultra-rare lung disease with approximately 3,600 diagnosed cases in the United States. Unfortunately, some people are potentially living with the disease without knowing it, as it is often misdiagnosed.

That is why the American Lung Association, with support from Savara Inc., is launching a new educational campaign to help healthcare providers and patients better recognize the signs and symptoms of autoimmune pulmonary alveolar proteinosis, (aPAP), the most common form of the disease. As part of the campaign, they are sharing these fast facts:

What is aPAP? This disease is characterized by the abnormal buildup of surfactant in the air sacs of the lungs, which can make breathing difficult. The buildup is due to an inability to clear the surfactant. Occurring in both males and females, aPAP is often diagnosed between the ages of 30 and 60.

What are its symptoms? Some people who are living with aPAP may not show symptoms initially, while others may have progressive shortness of breath. Additional symptoms include chronic cough, fatigue, unintentional weight loss and chest pain.

Why is aPAP commonly misdiagnosed? Since aPAP is so rare, and because symptoms are similar to other more common lung diseases, it is often misdiagnosed. Common misdiagnoses include both acute and chronic lung diseases such as pneumonia and asthma.

How is aPAP diagnosed? If you are diagnosed with another lung disease and the treatment is not effective, your doctor may recommend a chest CT scan. If you have an abnormal chest scan with unresolved lung symptoms, you should also talk to your healthcare provider about getting a free, simple blood test called aPAP ClearPath, which measures the level of the GM-CSF antibodies in your blood to determine if you have the disease.

How is aPAP treated? Currently, there is no cure for aPAP and no FDA-approved therapies; however, symptoms can be managed. The most common treatment is whole lung lavage, (WLL) also called "lung washing." WLL washes out the built-up surfactant from the lungs, allowing you to breathe more easily. This treatment often needs to be repeated, as it doesn't address the underlying cause of the disease.

Managing aPAP well means seeing a specialist who is familiar with this rare lung disease and going to all of your regularly scheduled healthcare appointments.

To learn more, visit www.Lung.org/PAP

Without treatment, this progressive disease can increase the risk of infection and lead to respiratory failure that may become life threatening. Don't wait. Talk to your doctor if your respiratory symptoms are not being managed with current treatments.

Weaving Cultural Narratives Through Art

Cecile Chong's art reflects her multicultural heritage, engaging with urban spaces and exploring identity, while emphasizing social justice and interconnectedness through innovative use of materials and site-specific installations.

Cecile Chong's multicultural background profoundly influences her layered artistic expressions.

Cecile Chong's artistry is a vibrant tapestry woven from her rich cultural heritage and profound understanding of identity. Born in Ecuador to Chinese parents and raised across the diverse landscapes of Quito and Macau, Chong has settled in New York City, where her experiences continue to inform her innovative approach to multimedia art. She masterfully intertwines painting, sculpture, installation, and public art, creating works that resonate with the complexities of layered identities and histories. Her installations, such as the poignant "EL DORADO – The New Forty Niners", reflect not only her artistic vision but also her commitment to engaging with the cultural nuances of urban spaces. Through her art, she fosters a dialogue about belonging, migration, and social justice, urging audiences to recognize the interconnectedness of humanity.

Chong's artistic practice is characterized by a remarkable ability to layer materials—ranging from volcanic ash and natural seeds to found objects— each symbolizing distinct cultural narratives. Her installations invite viewers to explore their own connections to the themes of heritage and belonging, making her work both personal and universally relevant. Her exhibitions have graced esteemed venues and institutions, solidifying her place in the contemporary art world. As a member of various artist communities and organizations, Chong's contributions extend beyond her own practice, fostering collaboration and dialogue among diverse artists.

In an interview conducted for Mosaic Digest, Chong elaborates on how her multicultural background influences her art. She describes the act of layering in her work as a reflection of her multiple identities, representing the complex interplay of traditions, languages, and experiences from moving across cultures. Her materials, whether natural elements like volcanic ash from Ecuador or found objects such as beads and circuit board materials, act as symbols of these layered histories. By layering, she sets up a juxtaposition and dialogue between these entities, much like the figures in her paintings.

Chong's public installations, like "EL DORADO – The New Forty Niners", engage with the diverse cultural contexts of urban spaces. She ensures each installation resonates with the specific cultural context of New York City's five boroughs. The sculptures of guaguas, a symbol of common humanity, allow her to create site-specific works that pay tribute to the 49% of NYC households that speak a language other than English. Each installation is tailored to connect with the unique historical context and character of its site, from maritime history in Staten Island to the UN sustainability goals in Dag Hammarskjöld Plaza.

Her "Strainger Series" presents a challenge in balancing personal heritage with broader, universal themes. Using kitchen strainers as masks, Chong explores identity and perception, symbolizing the filtering of experiences. The beaded image of a guagua on each strainer reflects the nurturing aspect of culture, blending personal heritage with broader ideas of belonging and otherness. This series connects her narrative with global discussions on identity.

Chong's extensive participation in artist residencies shapes her creative process over time. She immerses herself in the immediate landscape, sourcing materials directly from the grounds to create site-specific installations. These materials become central to her work, allowing her to create installations that resonate with both the environment and broader themes of commonality in the human condition, migration, and environmental concerns.

Social justice is a recurring theme in Chong's work. She believes that recognizing our shared humanity is essential to building a just and inclusive society. Her work celebrates the contributions of immigrant communities and challenges viewers to perceive nature as an extension of themselves, emphasizing that justice is only achievable when we embrace our equality with each other and the world around us.

Cecile Chong's work is a testament to the power of art to bridge cultural divides and foster a deeper understanding of our shared human experience. Her ability to weave together diverse materials and narratives into cohesive, thought-provoking pieces makes her a standout figure in contemporary art.

Chong's art masterfully layers diverse materials and narratives, creating thought-provoking pieces that resonate with universal themes of belonging and humanity.

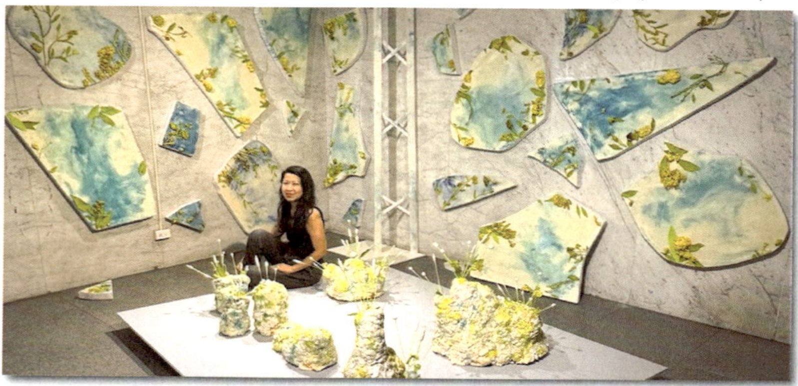

> *Justice and equality require acknowledging that our differences do not make us separate but rather enrich the collective experience."*

Cecile Chong

Alexander Deschamps discusses his artistic journey, blending playful imagery with serious themes, and his commitment to community-based art through ventures like Vandeavors Fine Art Services and Neighbors Gallery.

Alexander Deschamps, a Miami-born visual artist, has become a vibrant force in New York's art scene, celebrated for his unique blend of creativity and community engagement. Based in Greenpoint, Brooklyn, Deschamps has developed a distinctive visual language that combines elements of cartoons, signage, and pop culture with serious themes, creating art that is both playful and thought-provoking. His work often explores complex issues such as consumerism and environmental decay, using a colorful palette to draw viewers in before challenging them with deeper messages.

Deschamps' journey in the arts began at New York University, where he graduated with a Bachelor of Fine Arts in 2009. Reflecting on his time at NYU, Deschamps describes it as a formative period that provided a creative haven amidst the bustling city. Despite the distractions of youth, he honed his skills and developed an artistic style that balances comedy and tragedy, using familiar cartoon imagery to engage audiences and provoke thought.

In 2012, Deschamps founded Vandeavors Fine Art Services, a company that has become integral to New York's art community, supporting galleries, collectors, and artists with logistical expertise. This venture not only sustains his artistic practice but also deepens his understanding of the art world, influencing his own work by emphasizing the importance of craftsmanship and presentation.

Deschamps' commitment to community and noncommercial art is most evident in his latest venture, Neighbors Gallery. Founded in 2023 with his partner and neighbors, Neighbors began as a shared space in Chinatown, showcasing underrepresented and outsider art. The gallery quickly gained a reputation for its innovative exhibitions, such as a show dedicated to T-shirts and another featuring Department of Sanitation workers. When the lease ended, Deschamps transformed Neighbors into a roving pop-up gallery, continuing its mission to celebrate unconventional voices and foster community through art.

In an interview conducted for Mosaic Digest, Deschamps shared insights into his artistic process and vision for Neighbors Gallery. He emphasized the importance of relatability in his work, using tangible imagery to engage viewers and spark discussion. By incorporating elements of pop culture and politics, Deschamps creates art that resonates with audiences, encouraging them to question and explore the themes presented.

Deschamps' dedication to showcasing noncommercial art at Neighbors Gallery reflects his belief in the transformative power of art as a force for social and cultural dialogue. By prioritizing artistic expression over financial gain, he has created a platform that values creativity and community over commercial success. This approach not only enriches New York's art scene but also provides opportunities for artists from diverse backgrounds to be seen and heard.

Through his work and initiatives, Alexander Deschamps continues to redefine what it means to be an artist in today's world. His vibrant visual language and commitment to community-based art have made him a vital figure in New York's cultural landscape, inspiring others to embrace creativity and collaboration. As Neighbors Gallery evolves, Deschamps remains dedicated to supporting and celebrating the beauty of unconventional art, ensuring that diverse voices have a place in the broader art community.

Exploring the dynamic blend of creativity and community in Deschamps' unique visual language and artistic ventures

> " *When a gallery is unbound by financial concerns, the art is usually better and more interesting.*"

Alexander Deschamps

Alexander Deschamps is a visionary artist whose dynamic creativity and community focus enrich New York's vibrant cultural landscape.

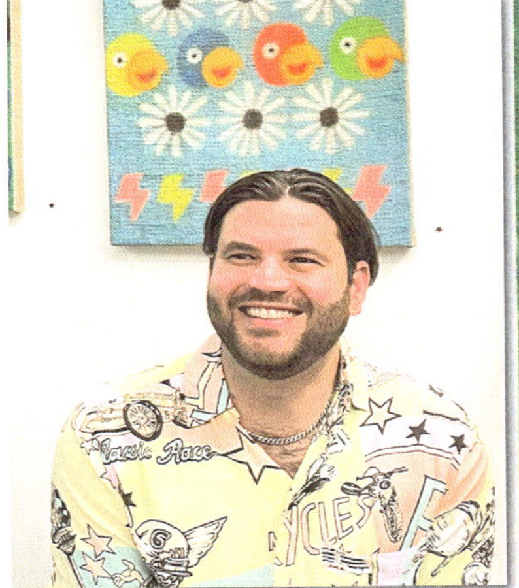

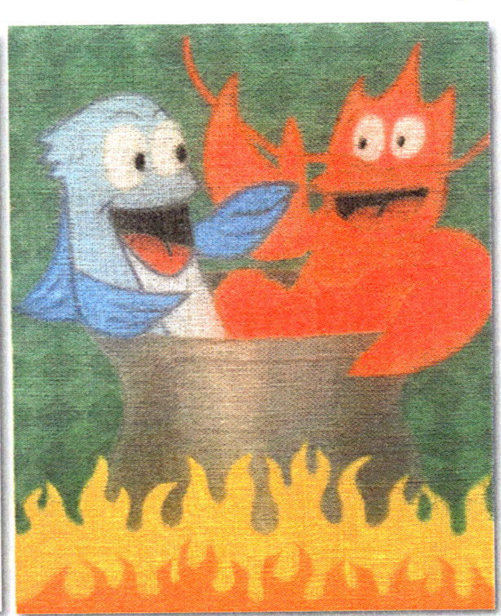

Capturing the Extraordinary in the Everyday

Rachael Blakey, a visionary photographer, transforms ordinary moments into extraordinary narratives, exploring time and environment, with her acclaimed work recognized by prestigious outlets like National Geographic and the BBC.

From pencil drawings to photography, Rachael Blakey's journey is a testament to her artistic vision and dedication

Rachael Blakey, a visionary photographer originally from the United Kingdom, has made a remarkable journey to Canada, where her profound love for art and exceptional talent have flourished. Her work transcends the ordinary, transforming everyday moments into extraordinary visual narratives that reveal hidden beauty. An interview conducted with the artist for Mosaic Digest highlights her unique perspective and dedication to her craft, which have earned her accolades from prestigious outlets such as National Geographic, the BBC, CBC, and Canon (UK) Ltd.

Rachael's artistic journey began with pencil drawings, a foundation that deeply influences her approach to photography. Her ability to see the world differently, honed through years of drawing, allows her to use her camera as a paintbrush, creating images that evoke emotion and thought. Her acclaimed photograph "Eye Drops," recognized by National Geographic, exemplifies her fascination with the macro world and her talent for revealing what is often hidden from the human eye. This photograph, a play on words, captures eyes reflected in water drops placed on a metal spring and now hangs in the IWK Hospital specialist eye clinic in Halifax, Nova Scotia.

Rachael describes her photography as an exploration of time and its relationship with the environment. She captures fleeting moments that will never happen again, preserving them for eternity. This sense of temporality is particularly important in her portrait work, where she captures emotions and expressions that are unique to each moment. Her dedication to capturing these ephemeral moments makes her a true artist and a remarkable storyteller.

The recognition Rachael has received from prestigious outlets has significantly shaped her career and artistic growth. Exhibiting her work in Manhattan, New York, was a dream come true, boosting her confidence as a photographer. Despite her success, Rachael remains self-critical, always striving to push her creative boundaries and explore new ideas.

As a specialist in Creative Fine Art Photography, Rachael finds inspiration in balancing creativity with technical precision. This balance requires patience and a willingness to experiment, as seen in her series "Through a Rainy Window." This series captures street photography through rain-soaked windows, playing with light, reflections, and the intrinsic nature of everyday life. The challenge of working in such an environment only fuels Rachael's passion and drive.

Rachael's journey is not without its challenges. Living with arthritis in both her hands and feet, she has become even more driven and passionate about her photography. This determination is evident in her work, which continues to captivate audiences and inspire fellow artists.

Rachael Blakey's photography is a celebration of the fleeting nature of time, capturing moments that will never happen again and preserving them for eternity. Her dedication to her craft and her continuous pursuit of creative excellence make her a true artist and a remarkable storyteller. Her work can be explored further on her website, www.rachaelskyphotography.com, and her Instagram, @rachaelb321. Through her lens, Rachael invites us to see the world differently, to appreciate the beauty in the ordinary, and to cherish the moments that define our lives.

Rachael Blakey is a visionary artist whose dedication and unique perspective transform the ordinary into extraordinary visual narratives.

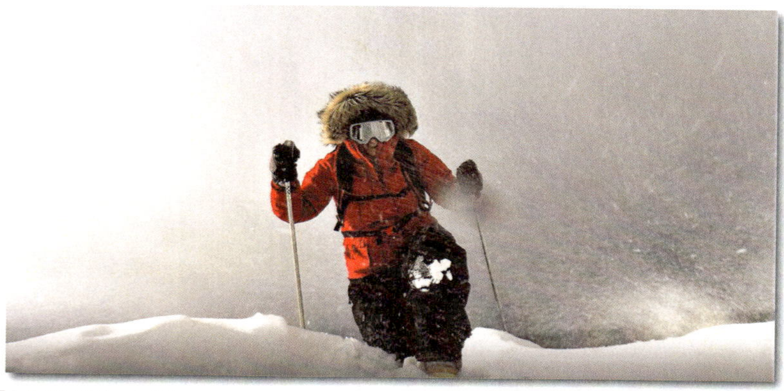

> *I found the relationship between drawing and photography have a strong connection."*

Rachael Blakey

Capturing Emotion and Nature Through Art

Yana Barabash discusses her artistic journey, the influence of the Isle of Wight, her creative process, and her life coaching philosophy focused on joy and living in the moment.

Yana Barabash is a visionary artist whose work transcends the boundaries of traditional painting, capturing the essence of human emotion and the beauty of the natural world. Born in Odessa, Yana's artistic journey began at a young age, and her passion for art has only deepened over the years. Her unique ability to convey complex emotions through her portraits and genre compositions has earned her a well-deserved reputation in the art world. Yana's dedication to her craft is evident in her multi-layered paintings, which invite viewers to explore the intricate details and textures that define her style. Her work is a testament to her belief in the transformative power of art, offering a glimpse into her dreams and the world as she sees it.

In an exclusive interview conducted for Mosaic Digest Magazine, Yana Barabash opens up about her artistic journey, the influences that have shaped her work, and the profound impact of her move to the Isle of Wight. She shares insights into her creative process, revealing how she balances traditional techniques with modern technology to bring her visions to life. Yana also discusses her approach to life coaching, offering a unique perspective on finding joy and fulfillment in the present moment. Her story is one of resilience, passion, and an unwavering commitment to sharing beauty with the world. Join us as we delve into the mind of this extraordinary artist and explore the inspirations behind her captivating works.

The Isle of Wight has profoundly influenced Yana's artistic style and the themes she explores in her paintings. The island's serene landscapes provided a much-needed sense of peace and safety during a time of significant life changes. The stunning natural beauty of the Isle of Wight inspired Yana to paint seascapes, a subject she had not explored extensively before, despite her upbringing in Odessa, a city by the sea. The island's quiet, slow pace allows her to reflect and find inspiration, resulting in a more measured and thoughtful approach to her art.

Yana's creative process involves creating multi-layered paintings that achieve depth and detail through the use of both acrylics and oils. She begins with acrylics, often applied in a watercolor style, to quickly establish the foundation of her work. This is followed by the application of oils to add the final details and depth. This technique not only speeds up the drying process but also allows Yana to experiment with textures and color schemes, enhancing the richness of her paintings.

The Isle of Wight is home to many hidden gems that inspire Yana's recent works. She captures the quintessential English vibe through her art, showcasing the island's old, beautiful walls, cottages, roses, moss, and lush greenery. The tides, moss-covered boulders, crabs, slopes, seagulls, and unique coastal features serve as sources of inspiration, allowing Yana to convey the incredible variety of textures and details that define her style.

Balancing traditional techniques with modern technology is an integral part of Yana's creative process. While traveling, she uses a tablet to sketch ideas quickly and effectively, capturing the essence of her experiences. However, she always transfers her best ideas to canvas, valuing the tactile experience of creating something physical with her own hands. This approach allows her to experiment with textures and colors, ultimately enhancing the depth and detail of her work.

Yana's approach to life coaching is rooted in her personal experiences and the lessons learned from living through challenging times. She emphasizes the importance of understanding what brings happiness and joy, both for oneself and others. The war has taught her to live in the moment, appreciate what she has, and find joy in everyday life. Her recent visit to Odessa reinforced this perspective, as she observed people enjoying life to the fullest despite the circumstances. Yana's life coaching philosophy encourages others to embrace this mindset, focusing on the present and finding fulfillment in the simple pleasures of life.

Yana Barabash's art and life philosophy are a testament to her resilience, passion, and commitment to sharing beauty with the world. Her work continues to inspire and captivate audiences, offering a glimpse into her dreams and the world as she sees it.

Yana Barabash's art transcends traditional boundaries, capturing human emotion and natural beauty

Yana Barabash is a visionary artist whose passion and dedication to her craft inspire and captivate audiences worldwide.

> **"** *Painting is what saved me from falling into a deep depression."*

Yana Barabash

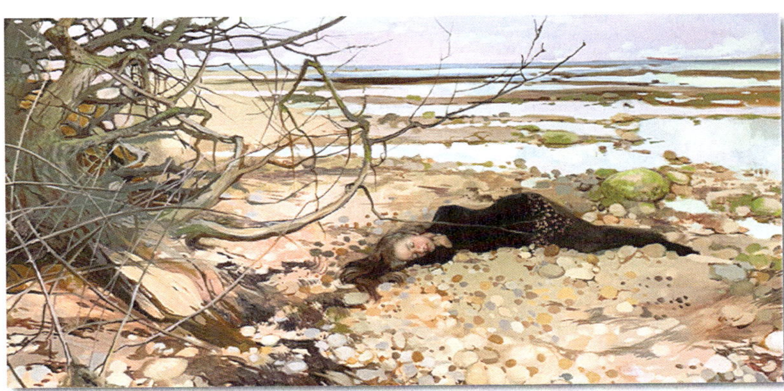

The Poetry of Space and Memory

Hannah Collins, Turner Prize nominee and acclaimed artist, creates powerful visual narratives through photography, film, and text, exploring cultural histories while bridging personal and universal human experiences.

A Visual Journey Through Time and Culture Shapes Modern Art's Landscape

Masterful storyteller and visual poet Hannah Collins stands at the forefront of contemporary art, crafting profound narratives through photography, film, and text. Her distinguished career, spanning four decades, demonstrates an exceptional ability to capture the intersection of history, memory, and human experience.

Collins' large-scale, black-and-white photographs first captivated audiences in the 1980s, earning her a Turner Prize nomination in 1993. Her subsequent evolution as an artist has garnered international acclaim, culminating in the prestigious Spectrum Prize in 2015. The artist's work continues to resonate with growing audiences worldwide, speaking to both personal and universal truths.

"The decision over which medium to use often makes itself," Collins explains, discussing her creative process. Her project "The Fragile Feast," created with chef Ferran Adria, exemplifies this intuitive approach, combining precision photography with thoughtful essays about food's relationship with the natural world.

Living between London, Barcelona, and Almeria has profoundly shaped Collins' artistic vision. The desert landscape of Almeria, where she transformed a ruin into her home, inspired "I will make up a song and sing it in a theatre with the night sky above my head," a multimedia exploration of Egyptian Modernist architecture and climate adaptation.

Collins' recent collaboration with musician Duncan Bellamy highlights her innovative cross-disciplinary approach. Their work at the Barbican, featuring large-scale projections with original music, demonstrates her ability to push artistic boundaries while maintaining emotional resonance.

Social consciousness threads through Collins' work, most notably in her curation of "We Will Walk - Art and Resistance in the American South." This exhibition showcased African American self-taught artists, presenting their works within a broader cultural context rather than limiting them to the outsider art category.

Memory serves as a cornerstone of Collins' artistic practice. Her installations create mental spaces where viewers can explore connections between time, place, and human experience. Works like "The Course of Time(6) – Factory Krakow" and the "True Stories" series demonstrate her talent for weaving together different eras and locations into cohesive visual narratives.

Collins' artistic journey reflects a consistent commitment to expanding visual language while maintaining clear artistic boundaries. Her work, housed in prestigious institutions like MoMA NY and the Reina Sofia Museum, continues to challenge and inspire viewers to see the world through a more nuanced lens.

The artist's unique vision transforms ordinary spaces into profound meditations on human existence. Through her lens, interiors and exteriors become metaphors for life's complexities, while her attention to historical depth and social relevance creates work that resonates across cultural boundaries.

Collins' contribution to contemporary art extends beyond traditional photography into a realm where medium, message, and meaning converge to create something truly extraordinary. Her ongoing exploration of human experience and cultural memory continues to evolve, marking her as one of the most significant artists of our time.

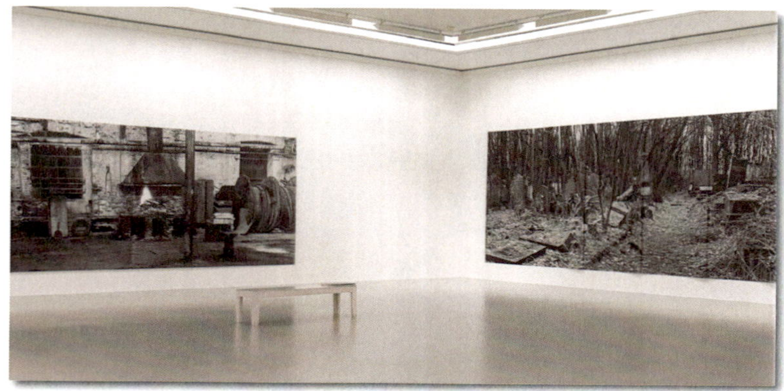

I try to give the viewer a large mental space to wander within so the mind can find a way to relate elements of place or time."

Hannah Colins

A Master of Color and Form

Louise P. Sloane Collins, an abstract painter, masterfully combines minimalist ideologies with vibrant color and texture, creating dynamic compositions that engage viewers through geometric forms and personal narratives.

Louise P. Sloane Collins, a distinguished abstract painter, has been a vibrant force in the art world since 1974. Her work, celebrated in an interview conducted for Mosaic Digest, is a testament to her mastery of color, texture, and form, seamlessly blending minimalist ideologies with expressive color and human mark-making. Sloane's paintings are a visual symphony, where the elements of mark-making, color, and geometry compete for the viewer's focus, keeping the eyes and mind in constant motion.

Sloane's artistic journey is deeply rooted in the minimalist movement of the late 1960s, a period that significantly influenced her style. Her early exposure to American Minimalists, some of whom were her studio instructors, inspired her to contribute to the genre while developing her unique "signature style." This style is characterized by dense, raised markings that initially mimicked writing, evolving into a complex interplay of color and texture. Her use of color is particularly striking: she employs it straight-up, without mixing, allowing the hues to blend optically and enhance the texture and luminosity of her work.

The square, a recurring motif in Sloane's work, serves as a central structure in her paintings. This geometric form, often set within a grid, anchors the surface and draws the viewer's gaze, creating a focal point that is both simple and profound. Over the years, the square has evolved in meaning, becoming a symbol of stability and focus in her compositions.

Sloane's paintings are renowned for their complex color contrasts and layered textures. She skillfully layers colors, whether through beeswax fused with heat or applied paint, creating a dynamic interplay of movement and depth. This layering technique ensures that no color obliterates what lies beneath, adding to the emotional and visual experience of the viewer.

A distinctive feature of Sloane's work is her incorporation of written words, religious symbols, and number codes. These elements create a richly textured surface that interacts with the geometric forms and color contrasts. The "writing" in her paintings is not meant to be read but serves as a vehicle for the paint's color and depth, engaging the viewer with its recognizable nuance.

The physicality of paint and texture is paramount in Sloane's process. Her works, whether on canvas, linen, metal, or paper, are imbued with a tactile quality that invites touch. This emphasis on texture has been a significant thread throughout her 50-year career, offering viewers a tactile experience that is both engaging and immersive.

Sloane's work bridges the gap between abstraction and representation, fitting into the dialogue between modernism and postmodernism. Inspired by geometric abstraction and the Suprematist movement, her art reflects the influence of pioneers like Kazimir Malevich and Joseph Albers. The narratives within her abstract compositions are deeply personal, drawn from journals, poems, and song lyrics that hold meaning only to her. These narratives, however, are not meant to be deciphered; instead, they serve to emphasize the surface texture and color, forming a connection that transcends labels and movements.

Louise P. Sloane Collins's work is a celebration of color, texture, and form, a testament to her enduring influence in the art world. Her paintings, housed in prestigious collections such as the Heckscher Museum of Art and the Virginia Museum of Fine Arts, continue to captivate and inspire, offering a unique blend of minimalist ideology and expressive artistry.

Louise P. Sloane Collins blends minimalist ideologies with expressive color, creating a unique visual language that captivates and inspires

Her paintings are a mesmerizing blend of color and texture, offering a tactile experience that captivates and inspires viewers.

My goal then and now was/is to add to the conversation of the genre of minimalism while creating my own 'signature style.'

Louise P. Sloane

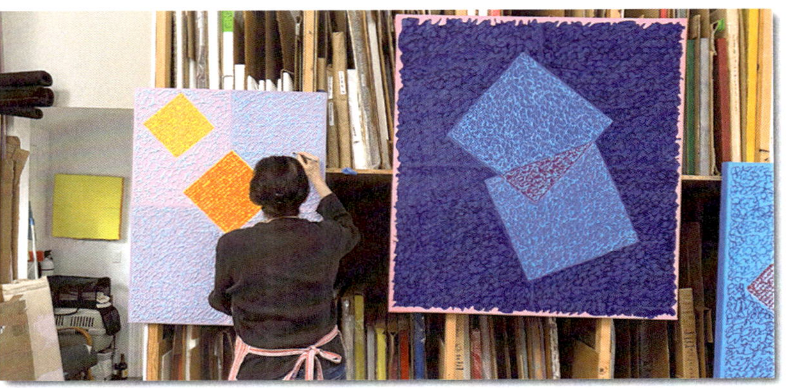

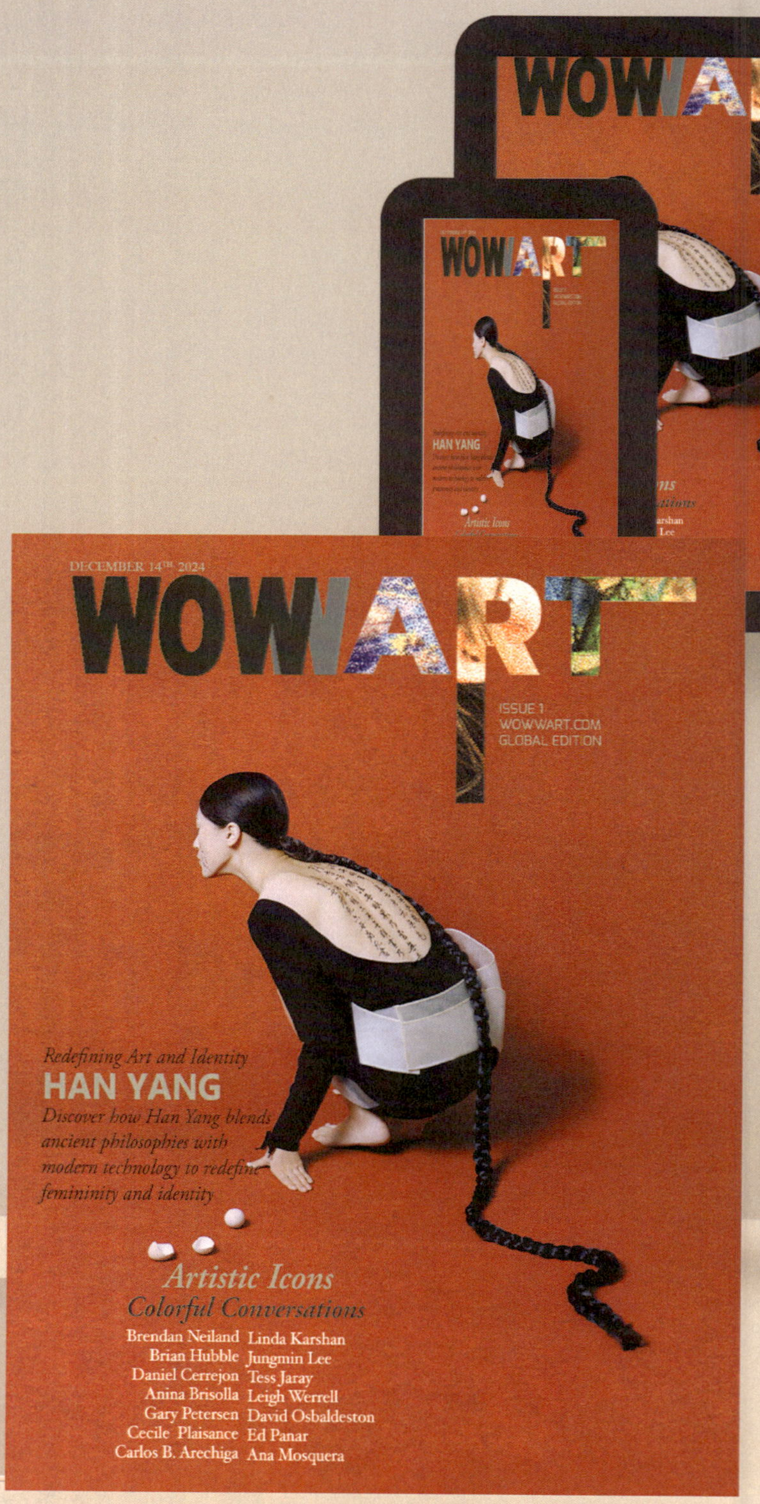

Available in
PRINT

It can be found in over 190 countries, from the Americas to Australia and Europe to Africa. It is accessible through thousands of retailers and platforms, including Amazon, Barnes & Noble, Walmart, and Waterstones.

ELECTRONIC

It is available in an electronic flip book format and is interactive. You can access it from various electronic devices, including PCs, smartphones, and tablets.

ONLINE

All the interviews we conduct are accessible online at www.wowwart.com

SOCIAL MEDIA

You can find us on Facebook, Instagram, and X. Please follow us on social media @wowwartmag

contact us today for an interview opportunity at editor@wowwart.com

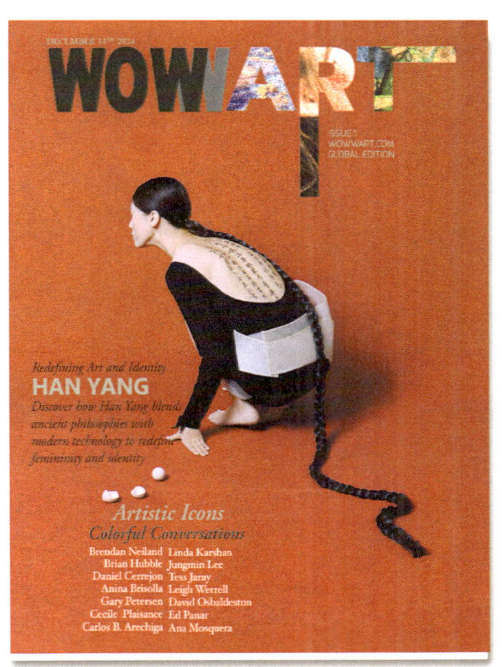

Save up to 50% when you order 10 or more from the same issue

YES! I would like a subscription to

☐ Current Issue for £24.99

☐ One-Year Subscription (__12__ Issues) for £270.00

☐ Two-Year Subscription (__24__ Issues) for £490.00

☐ I am a renewing a current subscription   ☐ I am a new subscriber

Name: _________________________________   Phone: _______________________

Shipping Address: ____

Billing Address: ____

Email: ____

☐ Yes, I would like to receive updates, newsletters and special offers
☐ No, I would NOT like to receive updates, newsletters and special offers

Payment Type: ☐ Check   ☐ Bank transfer   ☐ Wise   ☐ PayPal

____

____

Please mail this form to:
Magazine Name: WOWwART by Newyox 200 Suite, 134-146 Curtain Road EC2A 3AR London   https://wowwart.com

Subscribe Now!

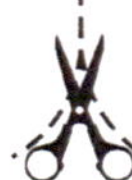

9 781642 264173

il-uh-streyt

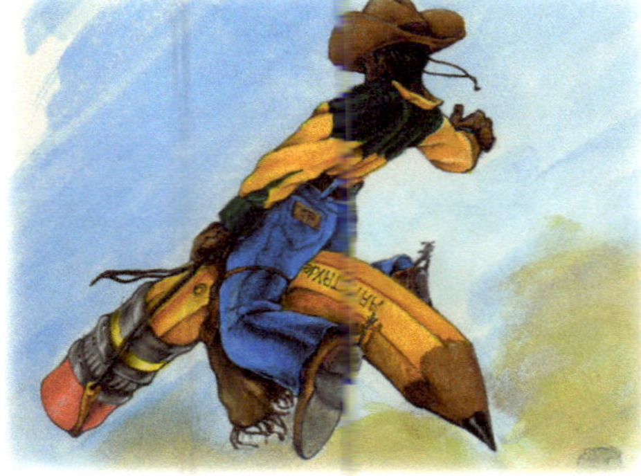

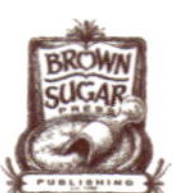
Brown Sugar Press Books LLC
Raleigh, NC
www.brownsugarpress.com

My Vantage Point: Through the Eyes of an Illustrator

T. BROWN

Introduction By Matt Hart, Ph.D.
Foreword By Flávia Bastos Ph.D.
Edited By Katherine Pickett, POP Editorial Services, LLC

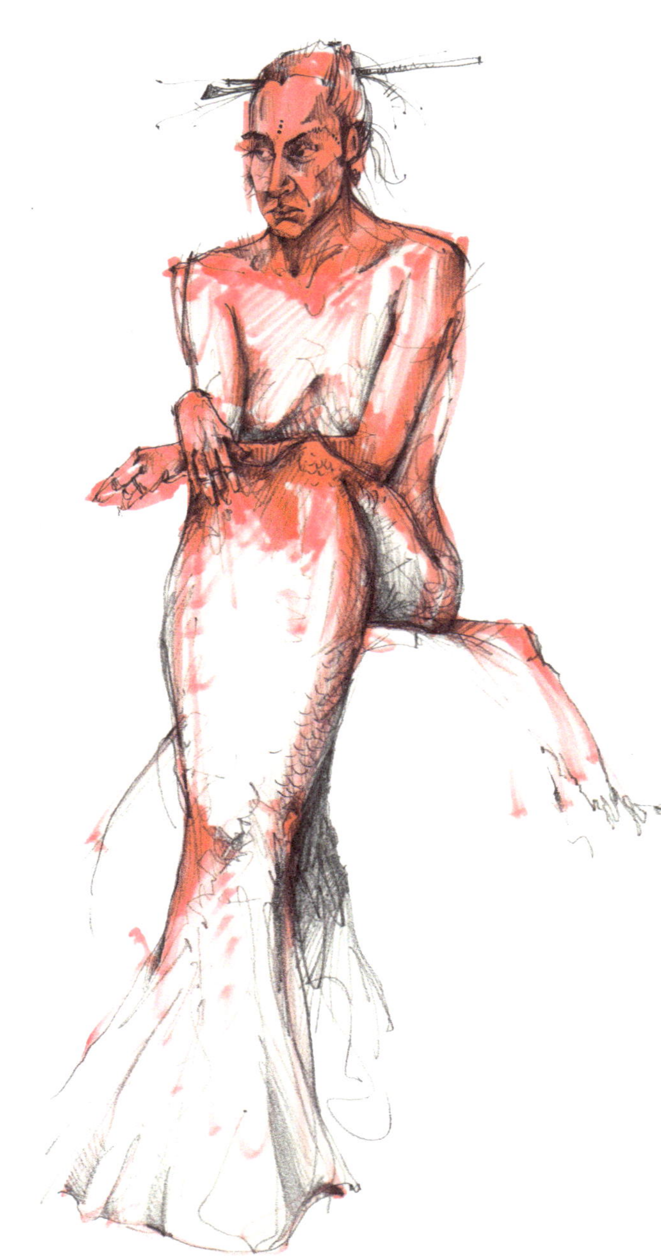

Table of Contents

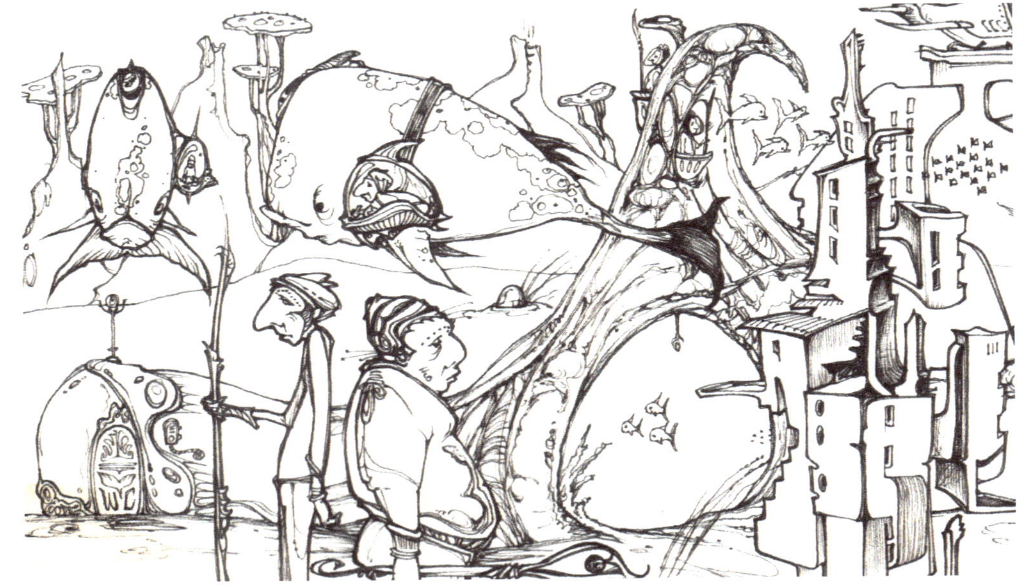

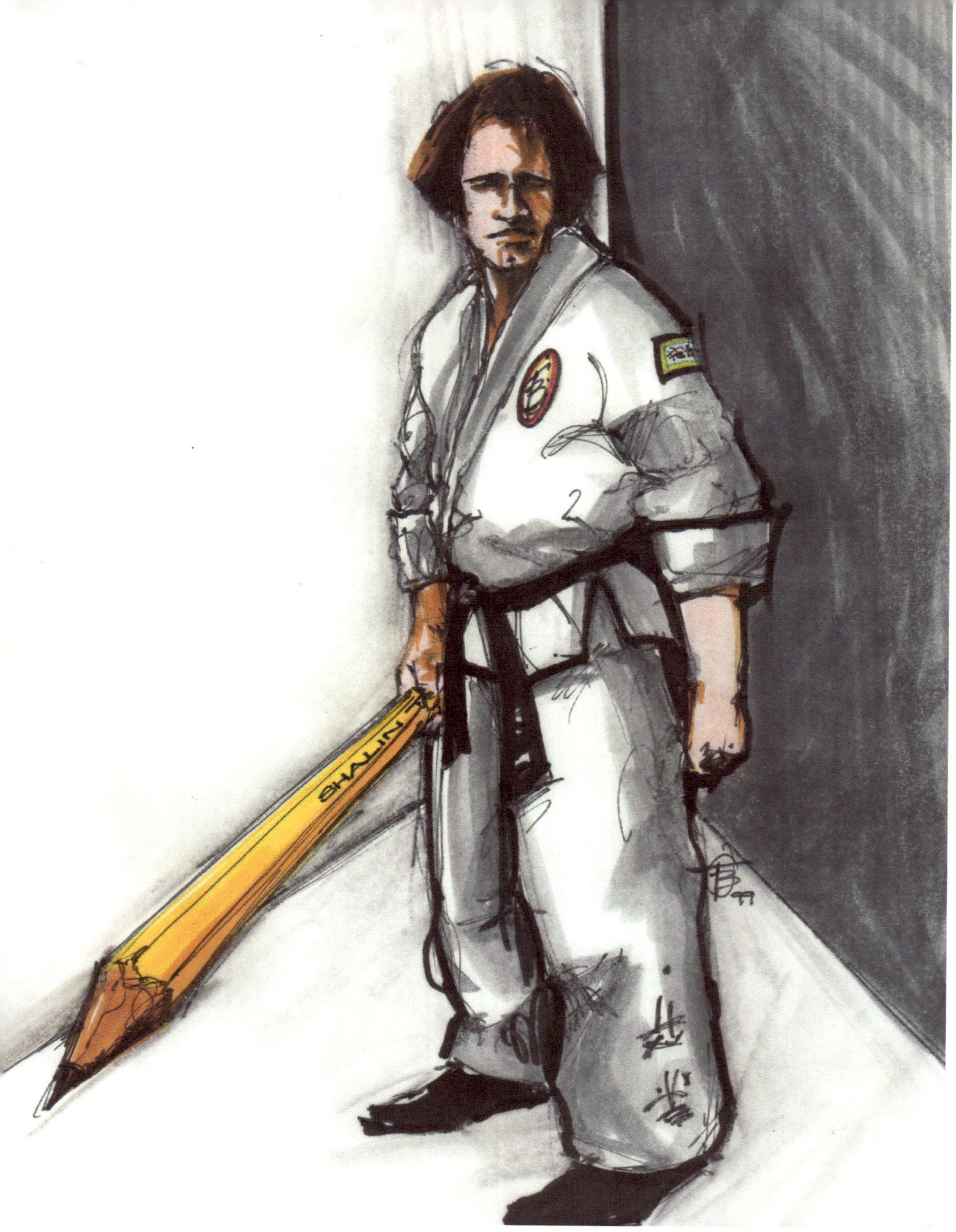

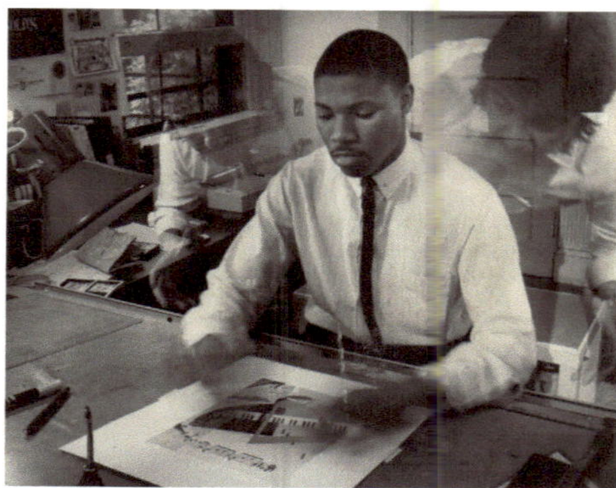

Top: Troy at The Pipkins Group Design Firm in Cincinnati, Ohio being photographed for a promotional piece with his first Art Director, Dan Britt.

Left: 'Kung Fu Ideas'
Marker color study, 10" x 12"

A Note from the Illustrator

The Background of this book.

This Art Book stems from a workshop and lecture titled Illustration and Beyond: The Hybridized Tool of Com-munication, which I gave at Maryville College at the seat of the mountains of Tennessee. A fellow artist and friend of mine, Carl Gombert, had for two years been asking me to visit the college when I would see him during our summer excursions to Utah to facilitate the AP Studio Art Reading via Education Testing Service (ETS). After we completed reading for the summer of 2018, I thought I should give Carl a call. To my surprise, he was slightly unsettled. He told me Maryville's proposed artist-in-residence had dropped out and the col-lege was entertaining the prospect of someone else being offered the spot. It seemed I had called at just the right time.

The exhibit that would accompany my lecture featured about forty works that spanned a good part of my career to date. Since I was going to be giving the workshop for primarily illustration students, we decided to make the exhibit a type of retrospective of my illustration practice. So, about forty works in two galleries became the task, with a limited edition print to commemorate the school's bicentennial celebration. While planning this exhibition, I thought of how illustration has transitioned over the decades from an artform known as a distant cousin of fine art to a highly skilled tool of communication. We see its impact from early notables like N.C. Wyeth and Maxfield Parrish to the more contemporary figures of Seymour Chwast and Brad Holland. This exhibit demonstrates the many genres that illustration spans while giving the viewer a hint as to the thinking of a visual communicator. The works move from familiar genres like children's books to more conceptual topics that are research based. The exhibit demonstrates the flexible nature of illustration and its ability to communicate, from the simplistic to the complex. Today's illustrator has morphed to remain relevant in a world inundated with imagery. The discipline itself has become a hybrid of sorts, giving practi-tioners the opportunity to forge new genres in the industry and to adjust to suit its demands.

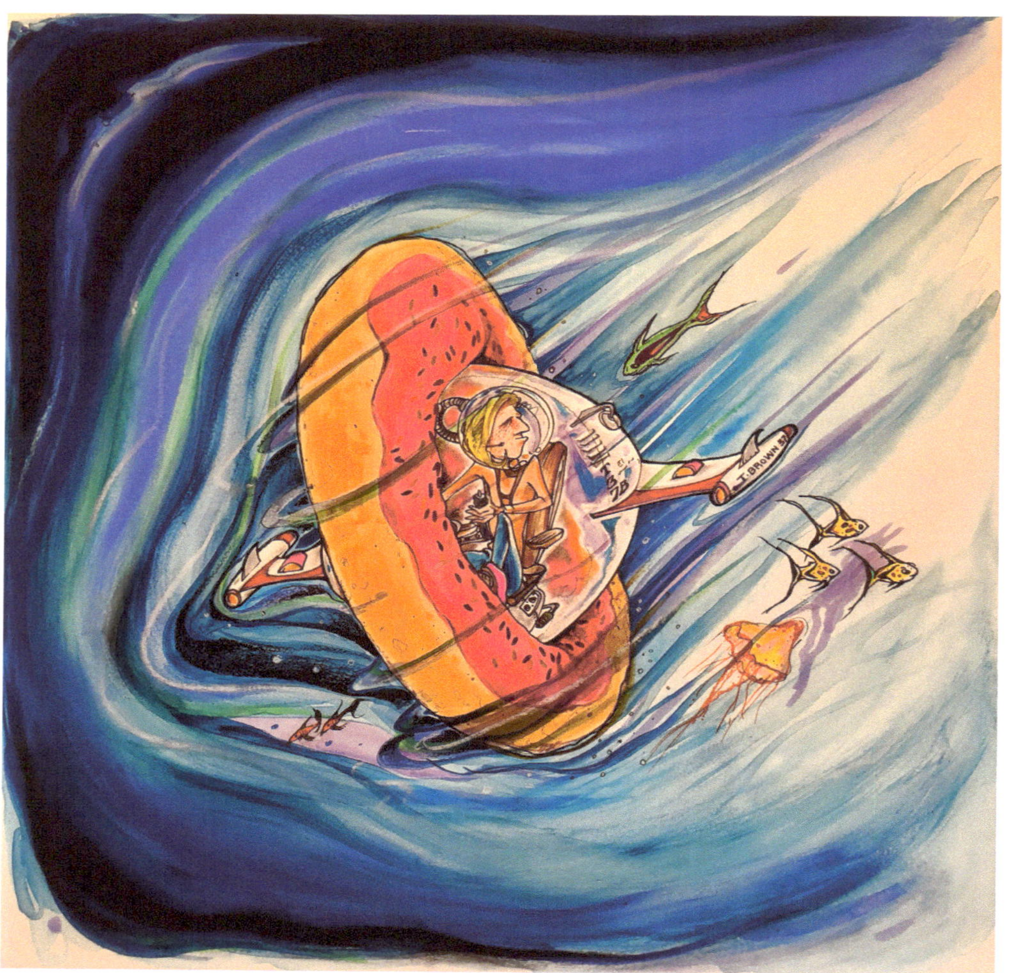

Top: Illustration from upcoming concept book.

Artist Introduction: My Concept of Illustration

By T. Brown

My earliest concept of illustration grew out of two distinct genres: the Bible and comic books. I know these two might not seem related at all, but to me they were one and the same. Both were about the power of good versus evil and the world that defined them. They both were about story, narrative, and imagination. Last, they were about mythical characters that infused their worlds with mystery and power.

The Bible called it faith; comics called it imagination. The Bible had giants, angels, demons, heroes, and villains; so did comics. Much of my early life was shaped by the fantasy and spectacle of these two genres. My interest in the Bible was laced within the illustrated pages more so than the text. The older Bibles were filled with illustrations, unlike the present-day versions. I longed to see how the paintings would illuminate the text. Jesus has been painted more times and by more civilizations than any other individual—each culture endeavoring to demonstrate another aspect of man's humanity or God's deity. Only an illustrator would have the audacity to think they could illustrate God.

Similarly, it was the images that moved me through those comics, with the text bubbles being the backdrop. Later, my seventh-grade art teacher, Mr. Smiddle, would introduce me to illustrators like Frank Frazetta and Howard Pyle, whose work provoked me to examine deeper the purpose of the illustrated text. Frazetta developed a language of his own with his monstrous paintings, which most cast off, and his ambiguous fantasy works. I understood the subtle power he longed to give his characters. His sensuous female characters were more feminine to me than those in the Hollywood movies. He illustrated the feminist archetypes before feminism discovered its worth. His version of Rosie the Riveter brandished a sword from Middle Earth. His curvy female characters made men swoon, but their swords filled their hearts with caution, understanding that one wrong word could cause them to have an out-of-body experience with their head lying next to it. Howard Pyle gave his images for such classic texts as Treasure Island a cinematic backdrop for us to dream. He paved the way for the young directors and writers who would take us into the glorious age of movies. It was the illustrator who put context to films like Star Wars, King Kong, and the James Bond series through those epic movie posters that gave our heroes and villains a face. Without Bob Peak's illuminous posters, how could we have imagined sitting in the seats to watch a Star Trek film?

My illustrations, like others, have very much been a product of my visual environment. A type of visual up-bringing, so to speak. A culmination of many genres, experiences, and, yes, faith. I've tried to not only let my illustration be an exercise of technical ability or prowess—not limited to just a facility of the text . —but also allow it to be a tool of the soul. To infuse it with a sense of discovery that goes beyond my own interpretations or understanding. This journey has been for me a determination to experience growth, and that pursuit will allow me to know more about myself: The self that was known before I was given a name or arrived on this earth. The self that we see that looks and appears very different from the one we see each day. The self that most frightens us while simultaneously amazes us. This propels my work beyond a client proposal or a children's book manuscript to a place fraught with endless mystery and intrigue.

Most illustrators talk about their work in the confines of a career, but my true goal moves in a realm void of career goals and temporal accomplishments. Like musicians or composers, we illustrators exist beyond the accolades, or we should. We endeavor to complete something that is never finished, explore a place that has no map, write that song that has a sound not heard before. Then share it. The courage is not in the creating, but in the sharing .

I understand that just like many before me I am here to share the sum of my gift. I can't determine what measure of consumption the gift takes, only the measure in which I share it. And I hope it will yield that unseen immeasurable purpose that knew me before I had a name.

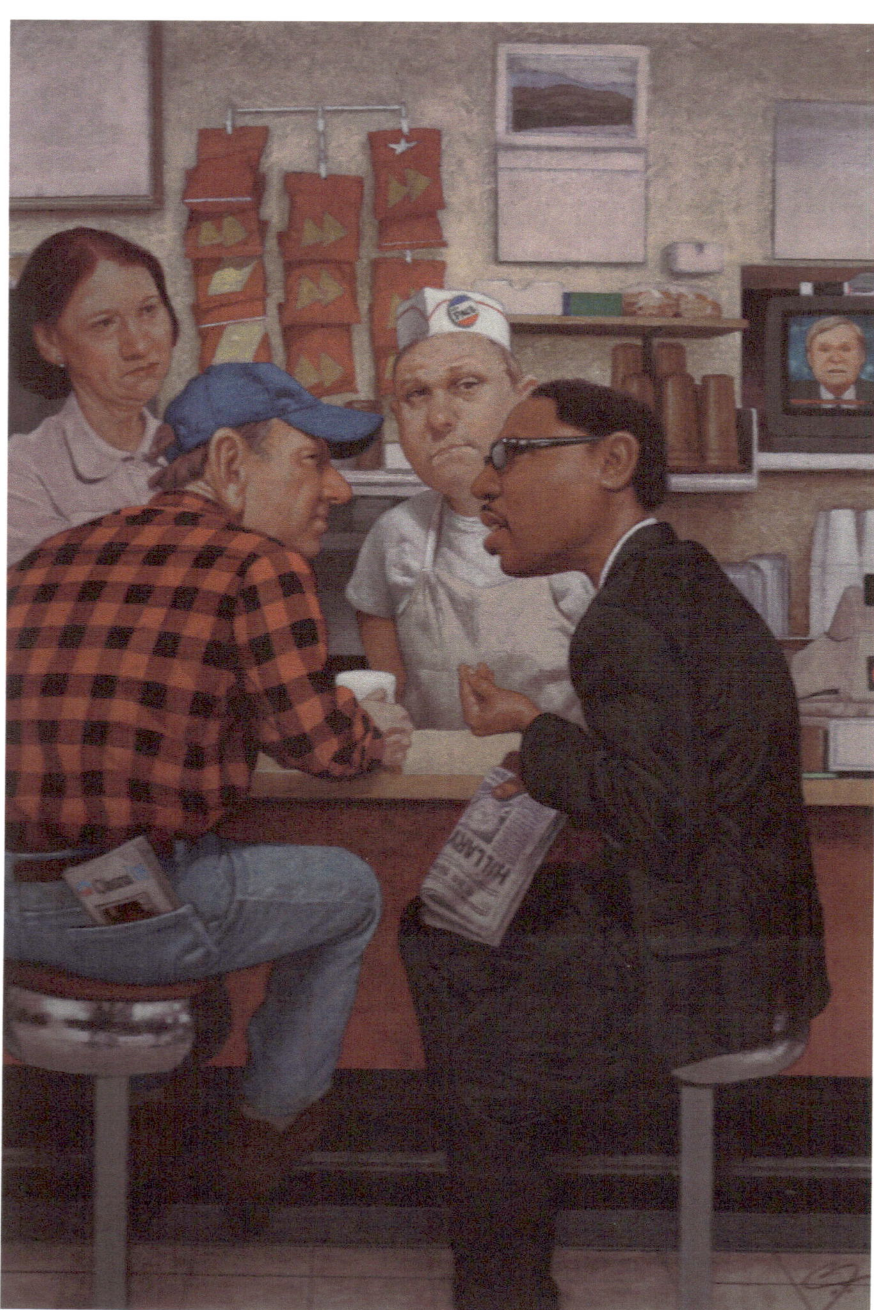

Left: Troy posing in this illustration by C.F. Payne for an article that appeared in the New Republic Magazine during the Democratic primary race between Barack Obama and Hillary Clinton.

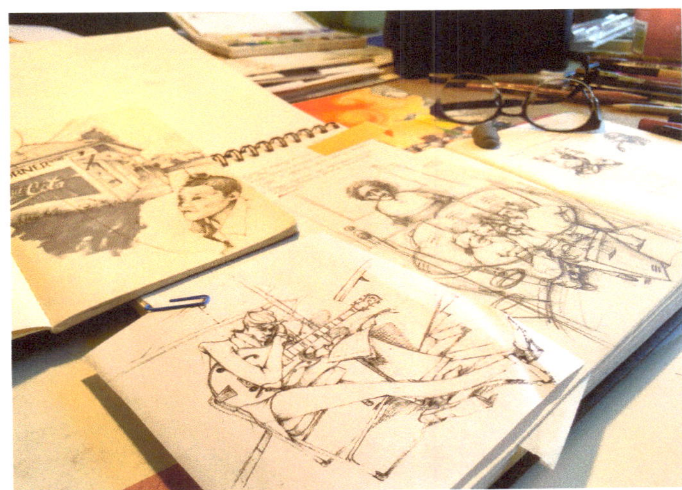

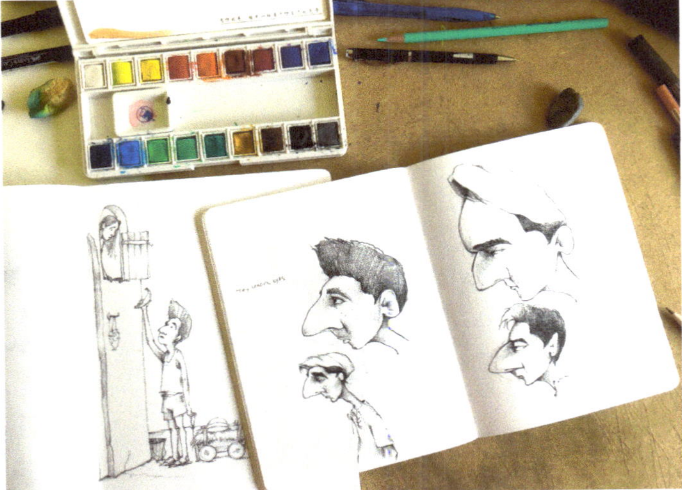

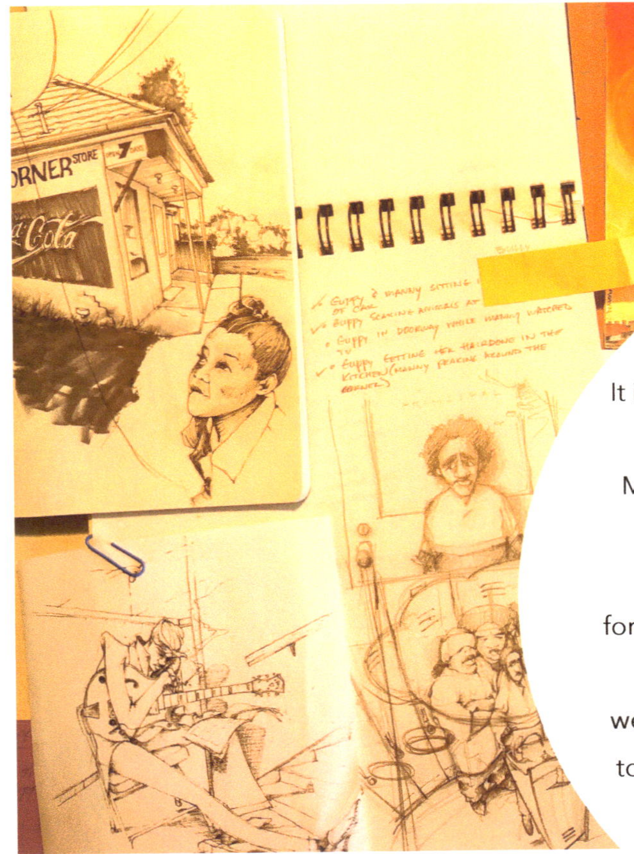

The most sacred place for me as
artist is within the walls of my studio.
It is filled with my silent swears, my catalogue
of dreams, and deepest thoughts.
Most of all it's filled with my vulnerable parts
as an artist.
No matter how fragile, how broken, how
fortified or fleeting my confidence may be, it's
the studio that still
welcomes a new opportunity for my creativity
to once again emerge and santify that space.

- T. Brown

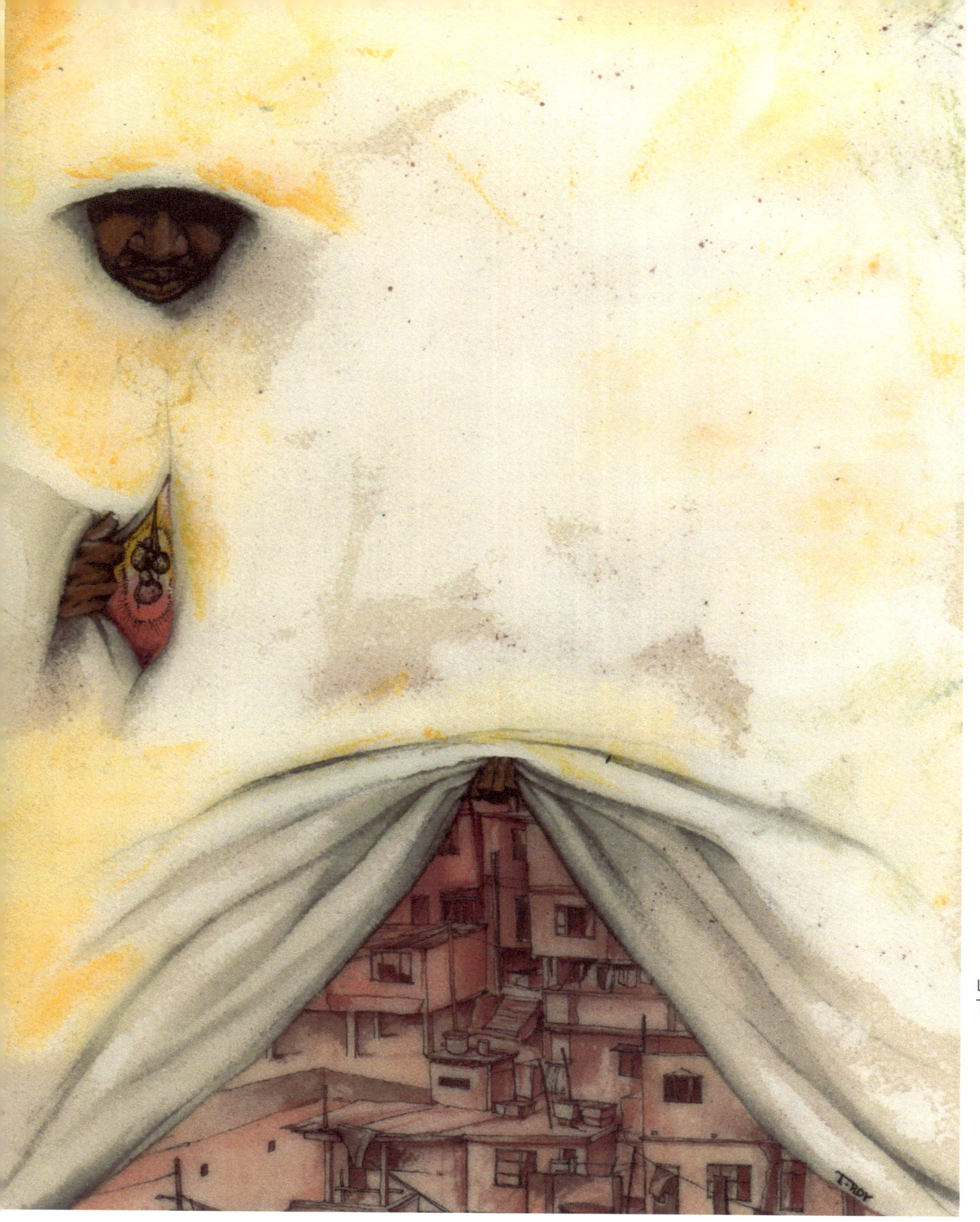

Left: 'Favela Sanctum' mixed media, on board in resin.
This piece was part of the Brasil Series.

WRITING IS DRAWING AND THE OTHER WAY AROUND

By MATT HART Ph.D. - Liberal Arts Chair, Creative Writing

I'm drawing a picture of the rain coming down
Wet concrete and crying mailboxes
Or dogs outside going back inside, shaking
themselves violently, briefly, letting fly
in performative displays of doggedness
that sometimes catch the light just right,
so you see the whole rainbow, or the reflection
of the sun's wild corona, like a halo in a fresco
commissioned by a pope   Additionally
there are meanings that are hidden when I draw
Weirdly/contortedly they're grinning
among the trees—the trees which I also drew
They're not thinking about Dutch Elm disease
or ruining the forest for the resources they need
Meanwhile, I'm thinking about this paper,
and how the rain beating down on it
would create a blur of inky pulp, and also how
that blur might resemble coagulated milk,
the inside of cactus, a million ways
to destroy myself—pass out in the rain
and inhale a shallow puddle   Is it obvious,
or not obvious what this drawing's all about
I just want to dream, which is writing

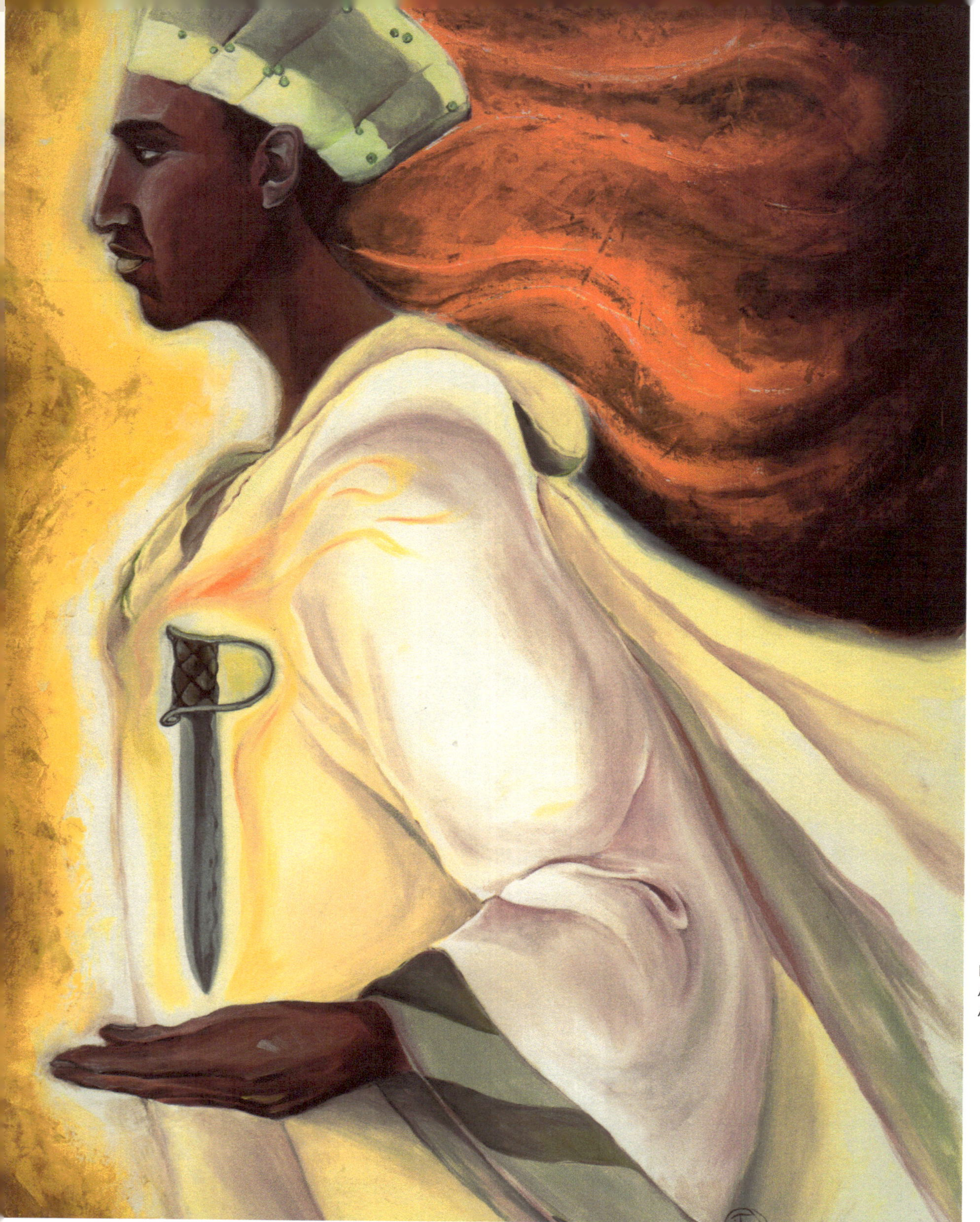

Left: 'The Favela Protector' from the Brasil Series of paintings.
Acrylic on canvas, 16" x 20'
Also limited edition prints were made.

FLÁVIA BASTOS Ph.D.

Professor in the School of Art, in the College of Design, Architecture, Art and Planning at the University of Cincinnati

Discovery is a journey, not a destination. My professional journey as an art educator intersected with that of Troy Brown's nearly twenty years ago. We met when he came to graduate school, already a wide-eyed and differentiated student—more mature, an experienced artist/illustrator, a father, a husband, a self-determined person. It was the early 2000s and I was learning how to be a professor.
Troy and I shared a common ancestry, the Black Atlantic culture that connects Brazil and the United States through the spirit of Africa. In the fields of art and education, people of color are quite underrepresented. It was lucky that we found each other, and we were able to develop a rewarding and mutually supportive relationship. You see, Troy allowed me to share my culture with him, and in the process, I saw it with different eyes. We traveled to Brazil together in (2007) and he made the most amazing illustrations of what he saw, a culture whose roots he recognized, and I understood in a novel way how our heritage was shared. The student educated me.

In his book, Troy walks us through his process of making meaning through art. As an artist and as an educator, he embraces the complexities of the visual world, inviting us to understand and to connect through it. That happens because the visual world is integral to culture; it's part of our experience; it reflects and at the same transcends us.

In the years I have known Troy Brown, I have witnessed his growth as an artist and teacher. I feel part of his development, which is richly documented in this book. He shares his way of seeing, which will unleash your own. It's about discovery. It's about culture. It's about the unmeasurable transformation that takes place when we recognize each other, and allow ourselves to see otherwise.

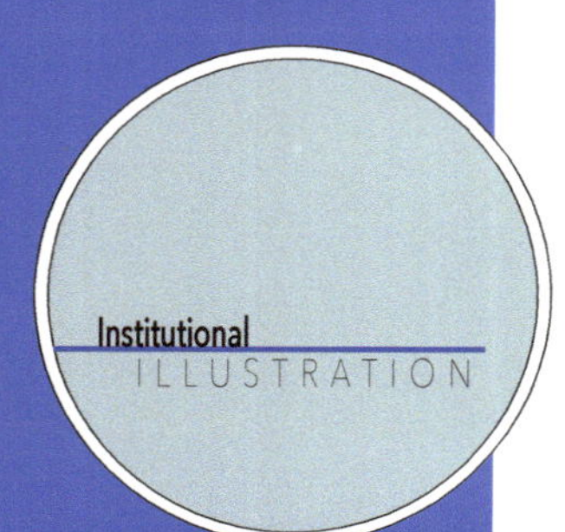

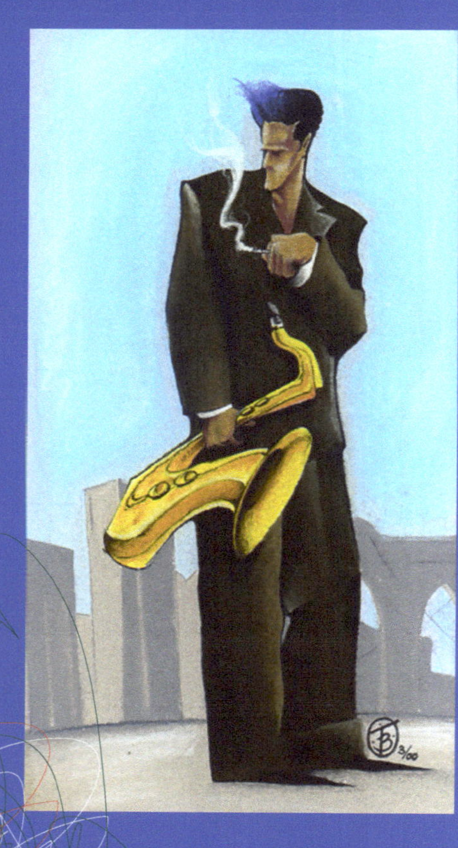

The works compiled in this section reflect my very first client after leaving the Pipkins design studio that had given me my start. The Fifth Third Bank Jazz Series still exists today and is one of the longest-running free jazz events in the nation. The project gave me a chance to experience the solitude of creating from concept to finished product. This was significant in the sense that most of the creative work prior to this point in my career was the product of a collaborative experience with other designers, photographers, and creative staff. The Fifth Third Bank Jazz Series was indeed liberating on many levels and served as a catalyst that allowed me to carve out my own niche both creatively and visually for years to come.

Left: From the Fifth Third Bank Jazz Series
Title: Leavem Smoking
Pastel on 140 lb. Lana, 16" x 20"

Right: Let it Rest

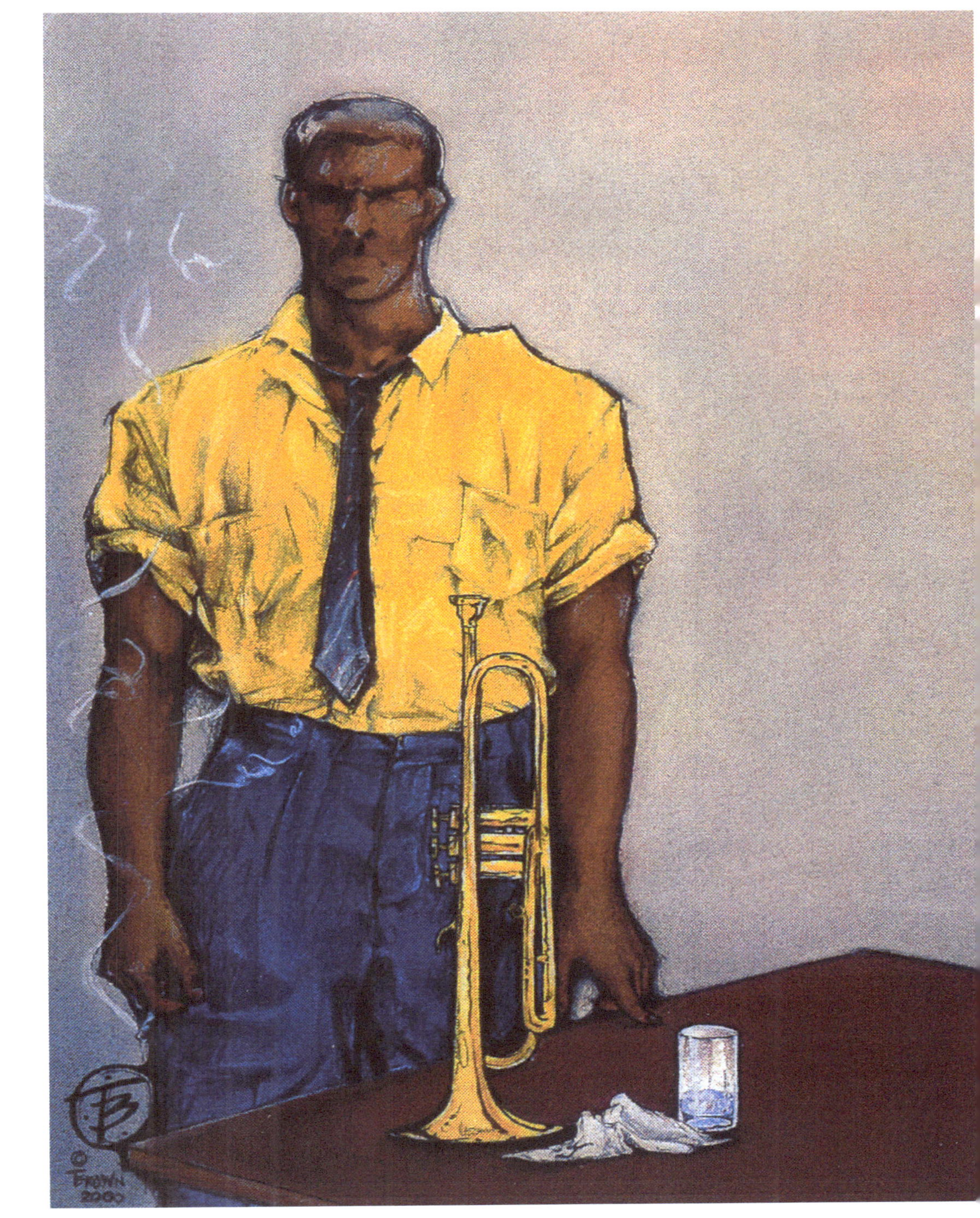

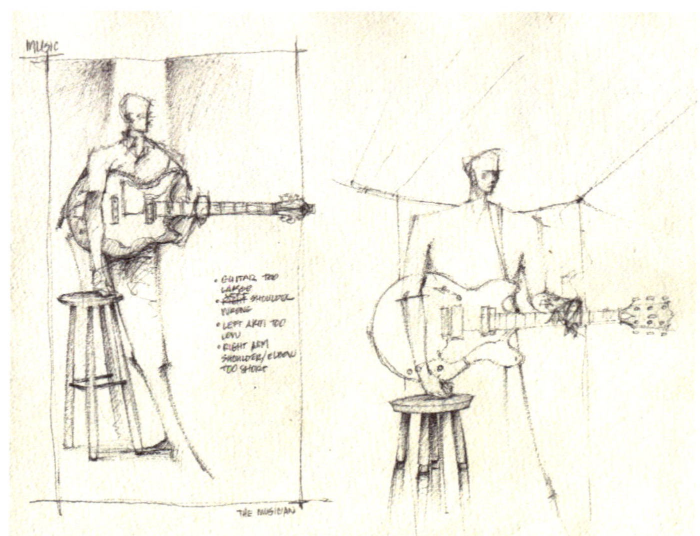

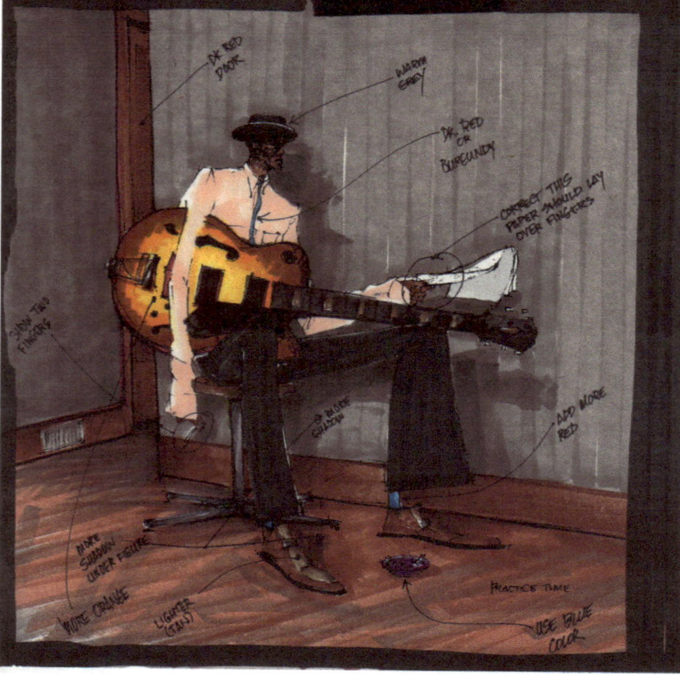

This image was presented to the director of the Fifth Third Bank Jazz Series, but was unfortunately not accepted in 1996 Instead, they chose the illustration on the next page (Leavem Smokin). The main artist performing that year was a saxophone player.

Left: Early sketch featuring Les Paul styled guitars
graphite on tissue paper.
Below left: Marker color study

Right: Hallway Practice
Pastel on 140 lb. Lana, 16" x 20"

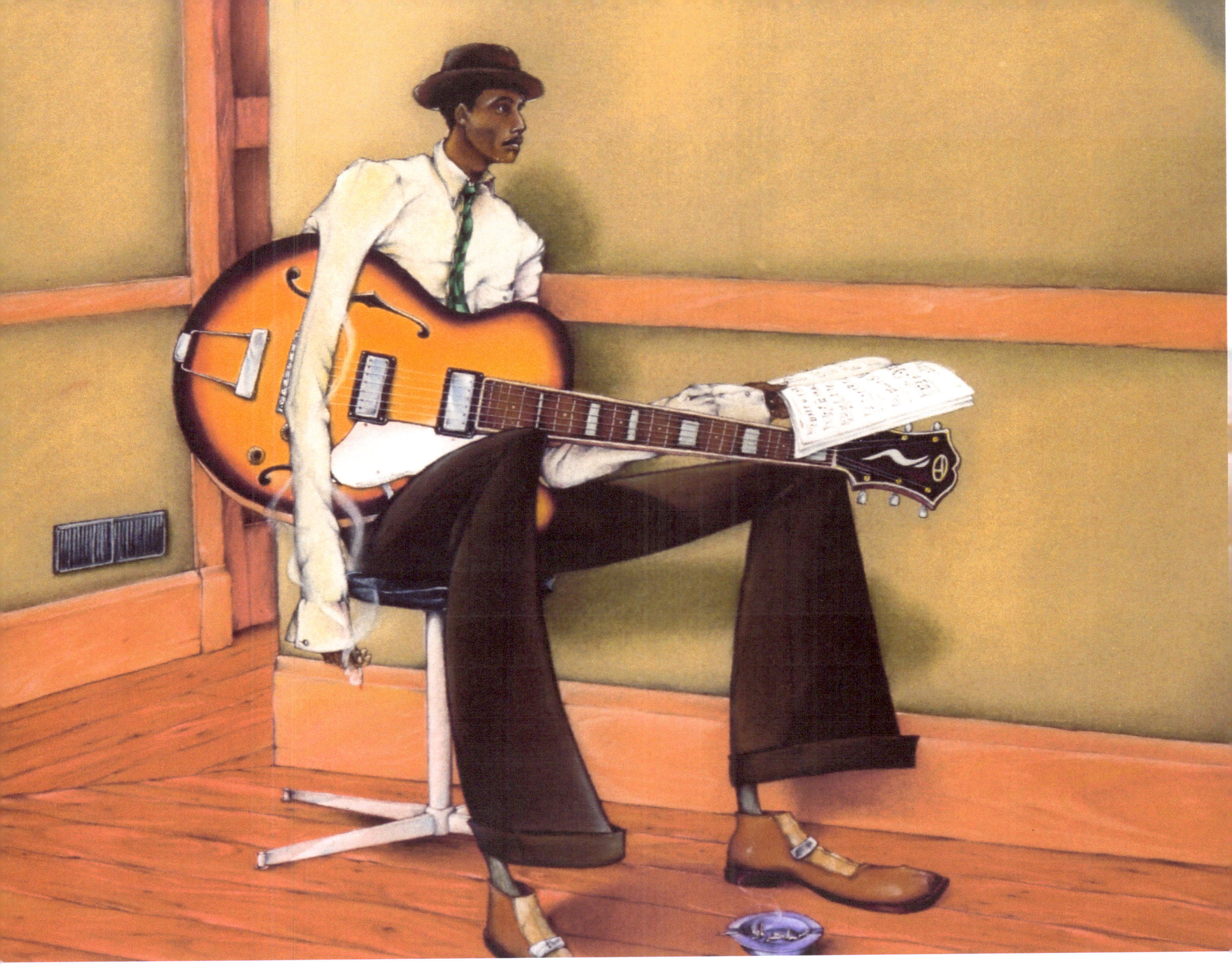

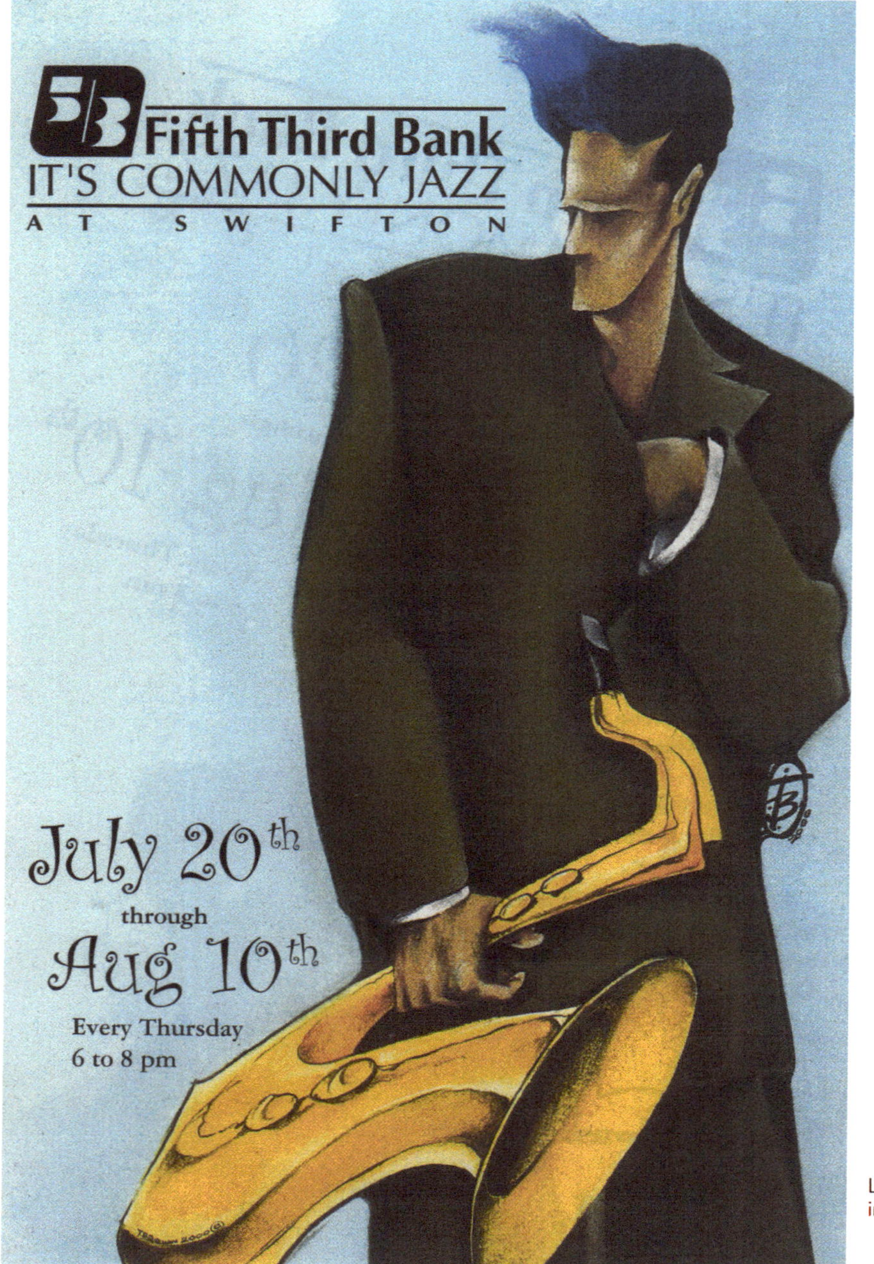

This image was chosen for the Fifth Third Bank Jazz Series, but I was later told I needed to remove the cigarette from his hand (why his hand is tucked in his jacket). This was in the late nineties, when attitudes were changing about what was socially accepted. The request was made the night before the illustration was due to go to the printer for the additional printings for various collateral items.

Left: Table tent, one of the many collateral items that would use this image that year.

This piece, titled Jazz Migration, was a popular addition to the series. It was the second year I had worked on the series and the first figurative piece presented to the director. I was nervous because this was my first big client. I presented several other pieces as well, but this was the winning choice. The director called me after many of the collateral items had been printed and told me several bus shelters featuring the image were having an issue. She then told me that the image was being stolen out of the shelters and they needed to replace them. I was elated people enjoyed the image, but equally uncomfortable about the collateral items being stolen. Looking back, we should have created some type of commemorative poster that people could collect.

Right: 'Jazz Migration' was one of the first figurative pieces used for the series.
Pastel on 140 lb. Lana, 30" x 40

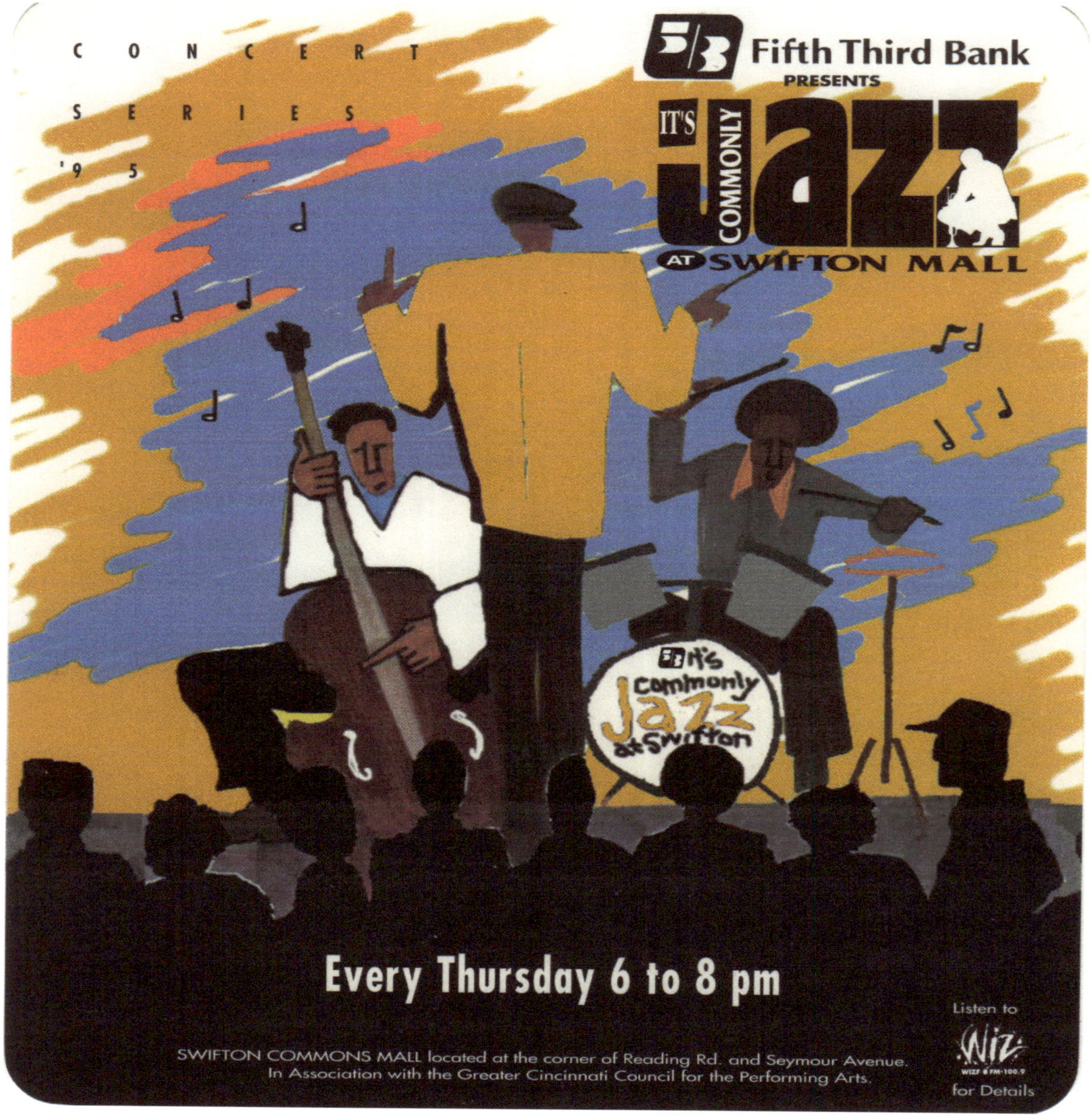

Left: 'The Trio' Digital
A two-sided Fan one of the many collateral items that would use this image that year. It was the first and only digital illustration used for the series.

Right: Year 1993, Front of the fan. This was the only graphic presentation for the series. All the other years illustration was used.

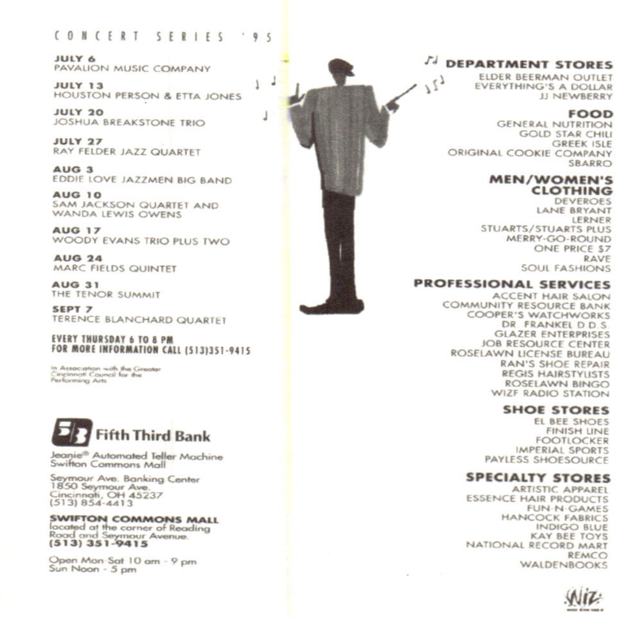

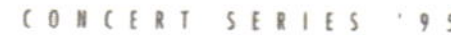

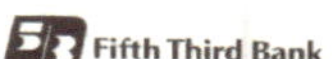

Below: This was an early image that we used to establish the Brand. The figure was a trumpet player and native of Cincinnati that agreed to be photographer for the initial logo for the event.

Right: Year 1992, Front of the fan. This was the very first image I created for the series. The headliner that year was a trumpet player, so that was the only direction given. The original piece is owned by the promotor and organizer for the event. Carolyn Wallace still organizes the event every year for the faithfull jazz lovers of Cincinnati.

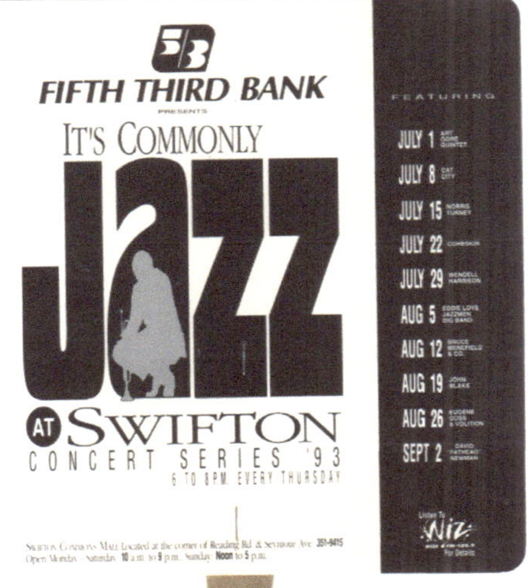

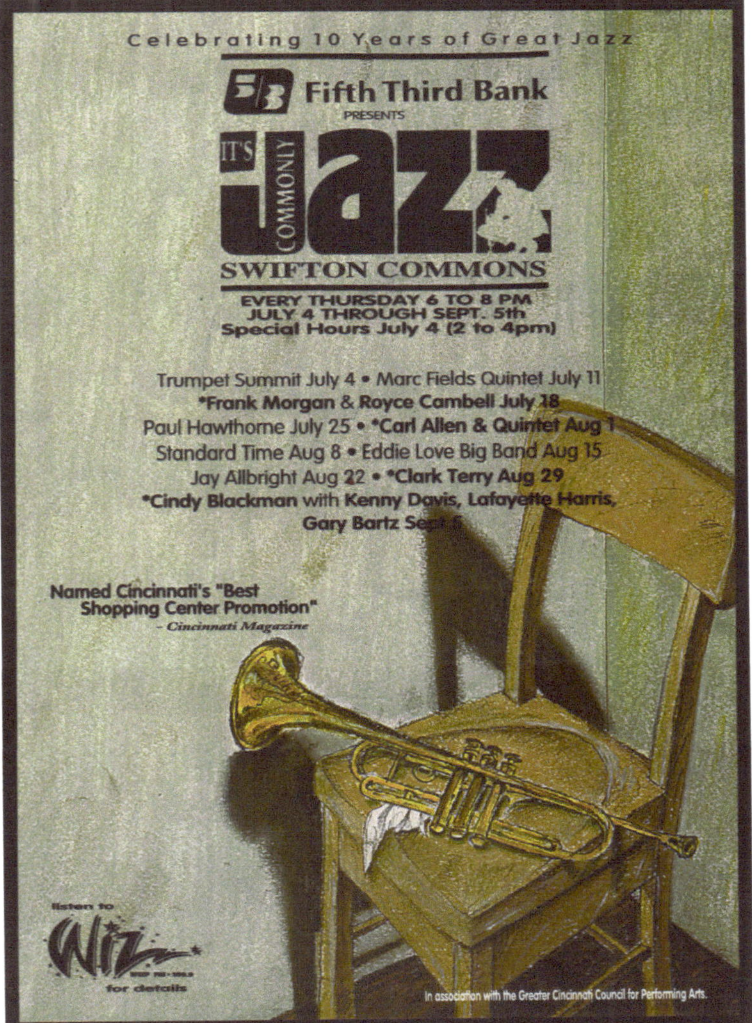

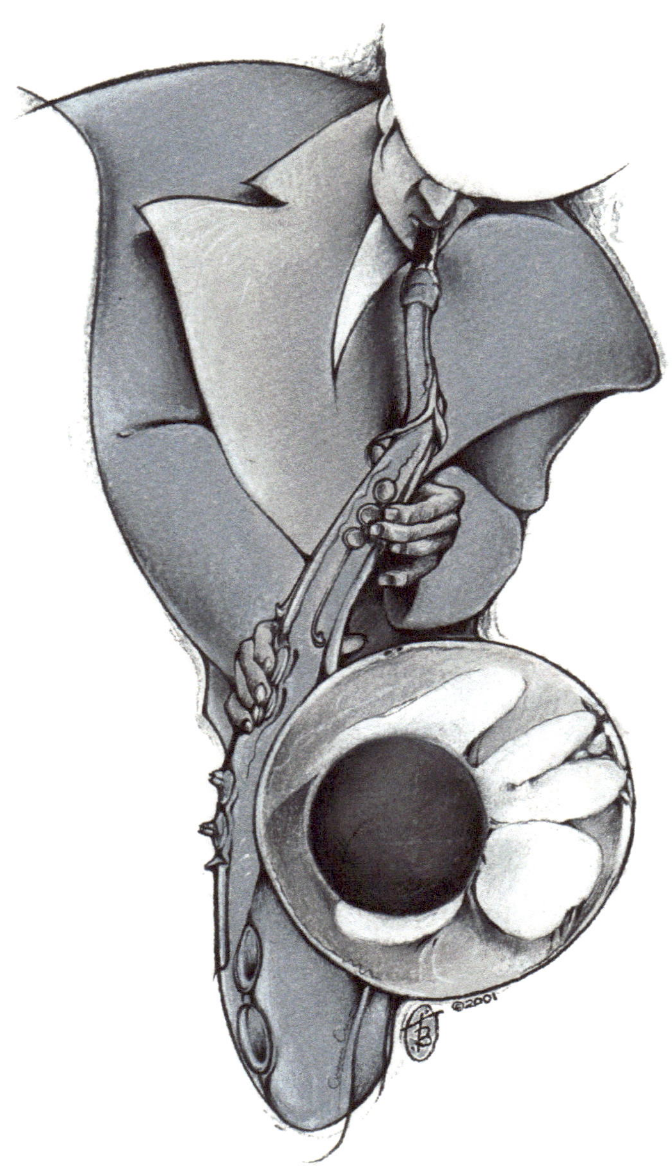
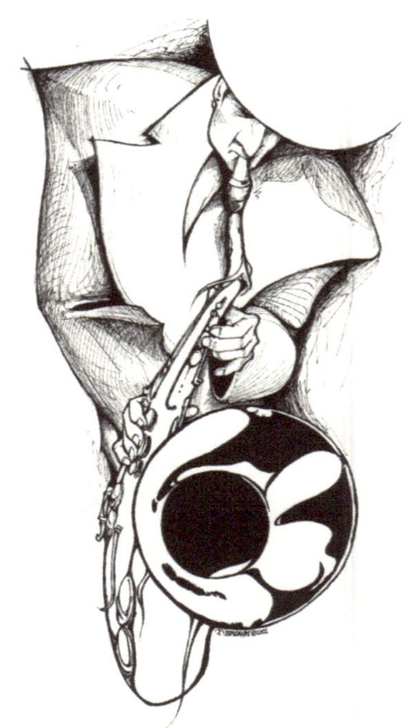

The two images on the left represent an abstract approach to my concepts that particular year. Until then,
most of my images had been traditional in approach and
I was looking for a way to somehow reflect the varied
expressions I felt jazz represented.

The image on this page was presented with a few others
that year and was frowned upon because of the cigarette. This was back in the mid-nineties, when smoking
was newly beginning to fall out of vogue. Some restaurants had begun to ban smoking at the time. All of my
reference materials, unfortunately, had cigarettes in their
hands.

Left: 'Abstract Sax'
Pastel on 100 lb. Lana paper.
14" x 20"

Left: Pen & Ink study for Abstract Sax

Right: 'Between Sets' Pastel on 100 lb. Lana paper.
24" x 30"

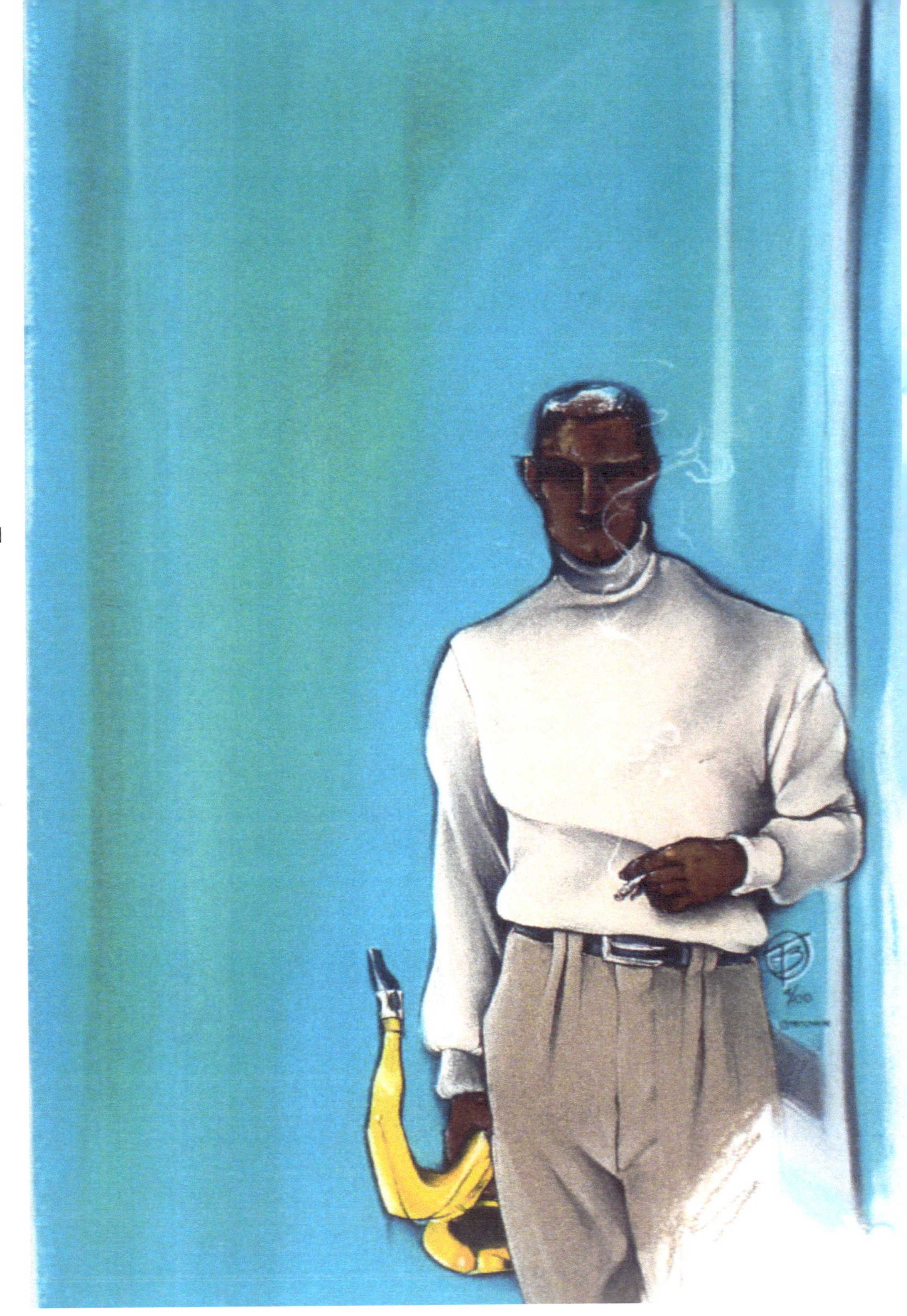

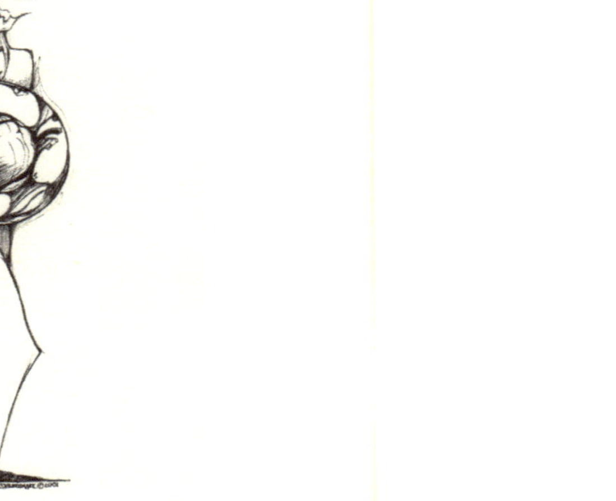

Left: 'Bass Moods'
Pastel on 100 lb. Lana, 11" x 20"

Top: 'Just Smokin' Pen & ink study, 8" x 10"

Right: Early sketches for the 5/3 Bank Jazz Series.

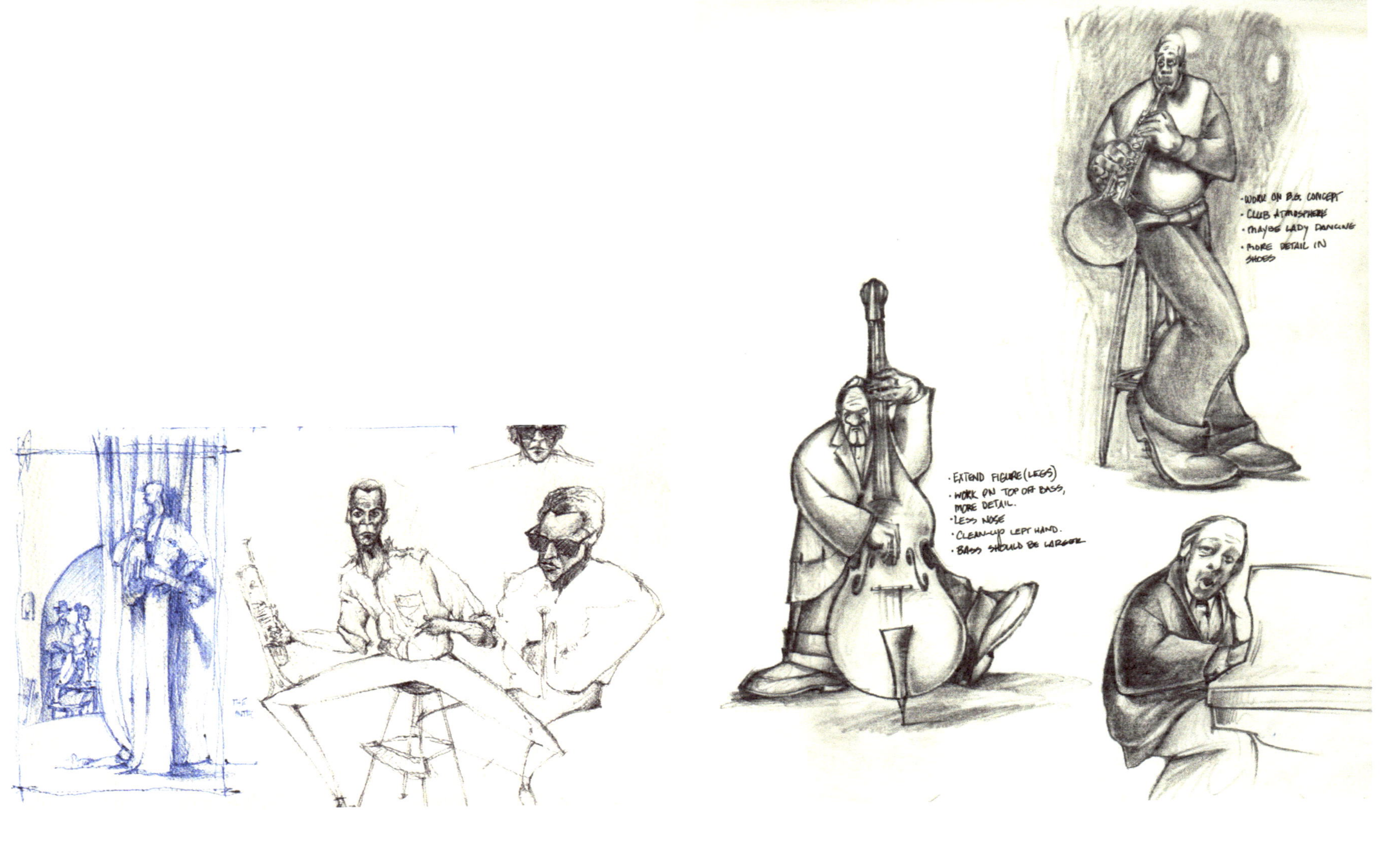
· WORK ON B.G. CONCEPT
· CLUB ATMOSPHERE
· MAYBE LADY DANCING
· MORE DETAIL IN SHOES
· EXTEND FIGURE (LEGS)
· WORK ON TOP OFF BASS, MORE DETAIL.
· LESS NOSE
· CLEAN-UP LEFT HAND.
· BASS SHOULD BE LARGER

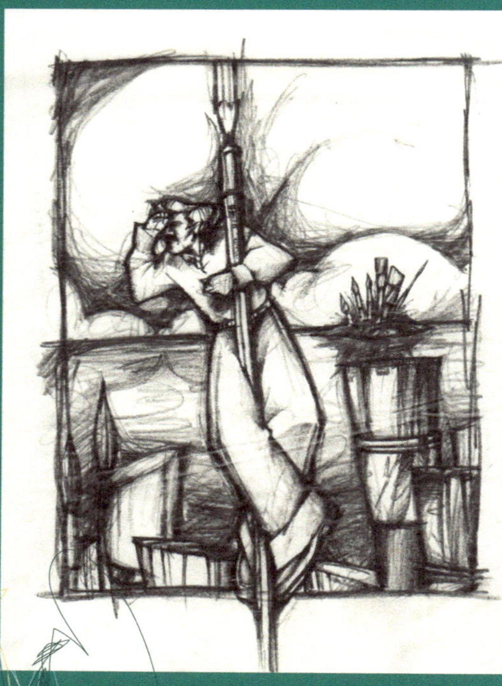

My approach to this collection was to create a series of works that focus on the importance of the "concept" within the genre of illustration. So, I set out to see how many renditions I could come up with that demonstrated this concept in as many interesting approaches as possible. The early pieces were large in scale (30" x 40"), but as I continue to work on the pieces, they have decreased in size considerably. There are many more that are not displayed in the book and still many others that are stuck on the pages of my sketchbook. I do plan to return to the subject at some point because I always consider the "concept" to be so important.

Left: Sketch for the pencil concepts, graphite on tissue paper.

Right: 'The Taming of Ideas'
Pastel on 140 lb. Lana, 30" x 30"

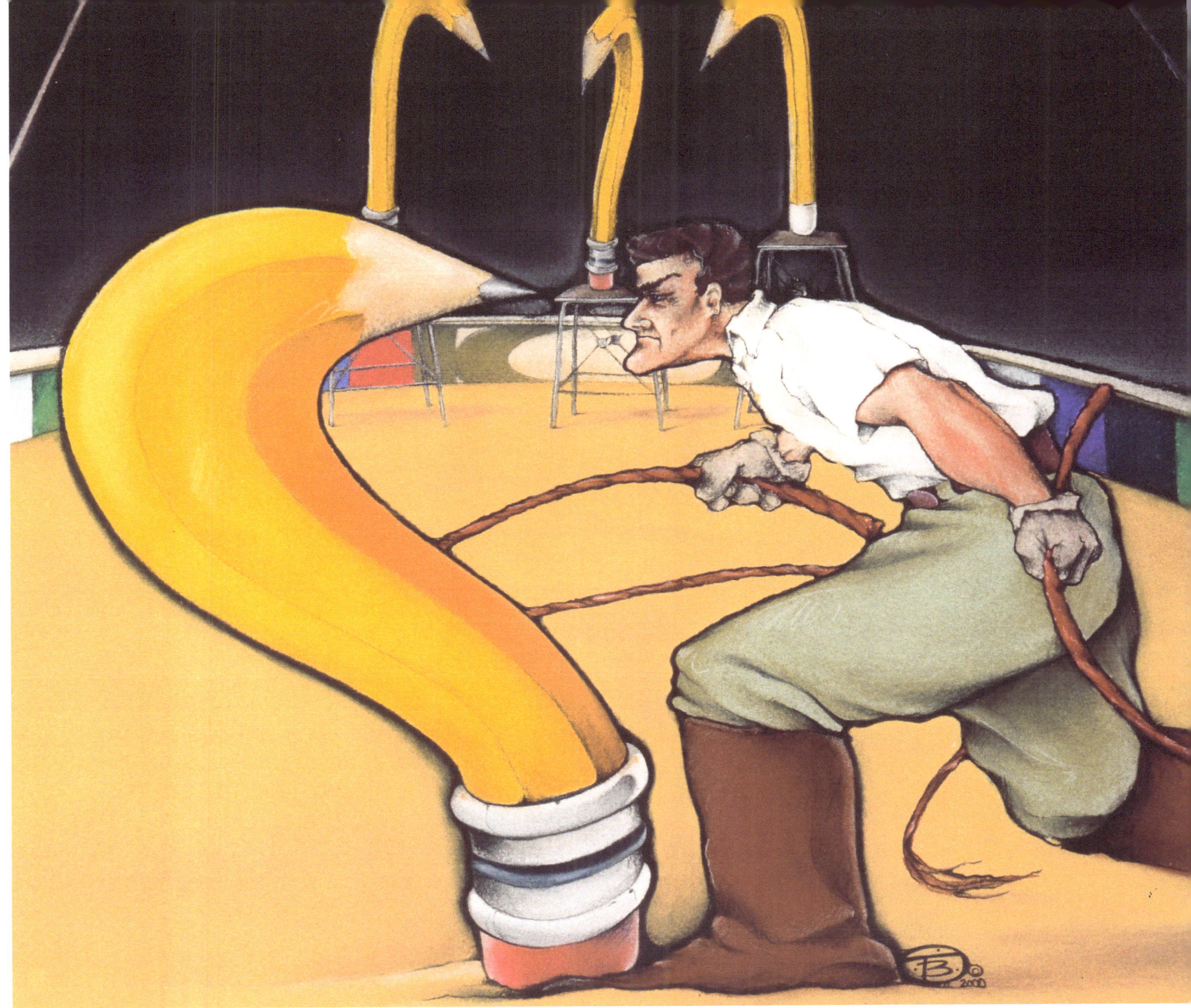

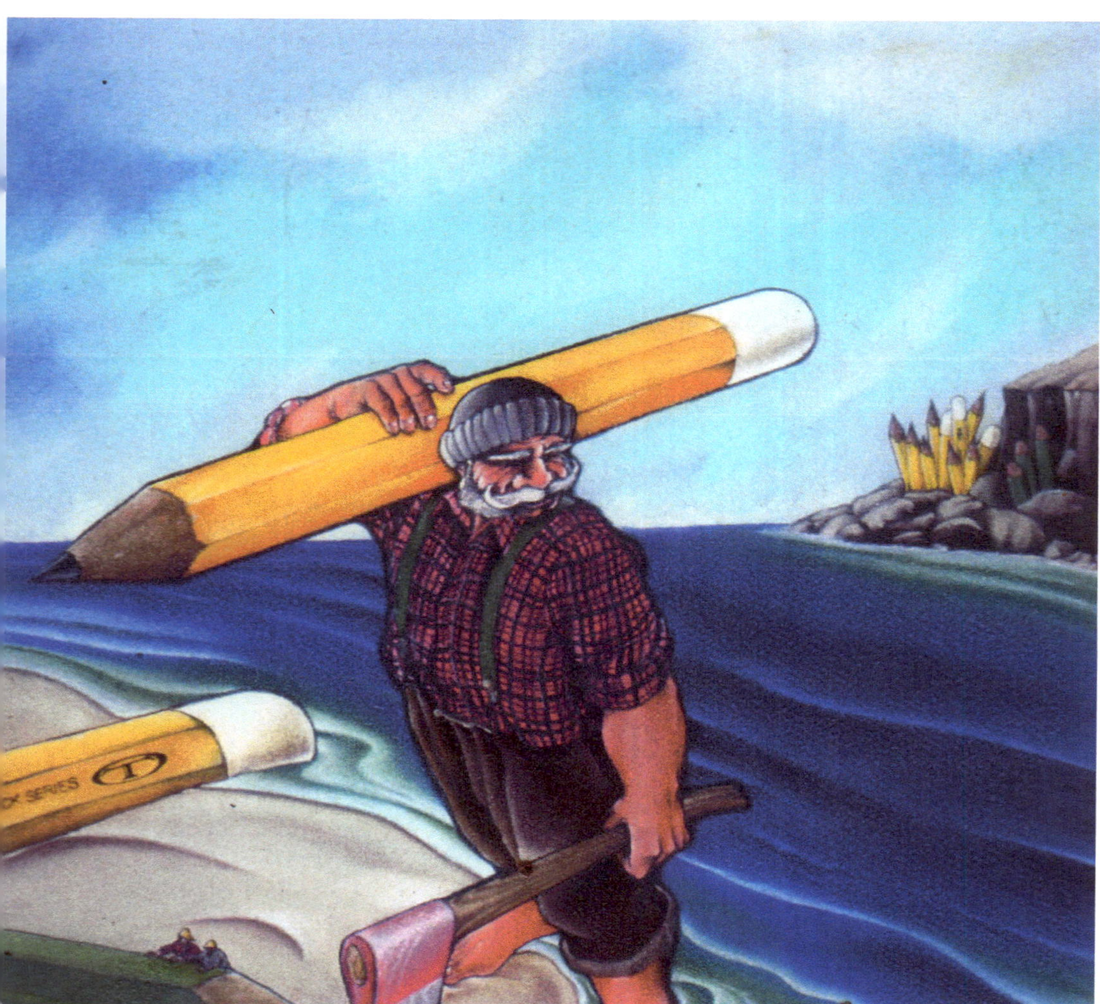

Left: 'Bunyan Concepts'
Pastel on 140 lb. Lana, 30" x 30"

Right Top: A page from CMYK National Magazine. Troy won selection for Harvesting Ideas illustration in 2003 and for the illustration 'Hallway Practive the following year while at the Art Academy completing his BFA in Illustration.

Right: The Illustrators Harvest
Pastel on 140 lb. Lana, 24" x 30" along with an early sketch.

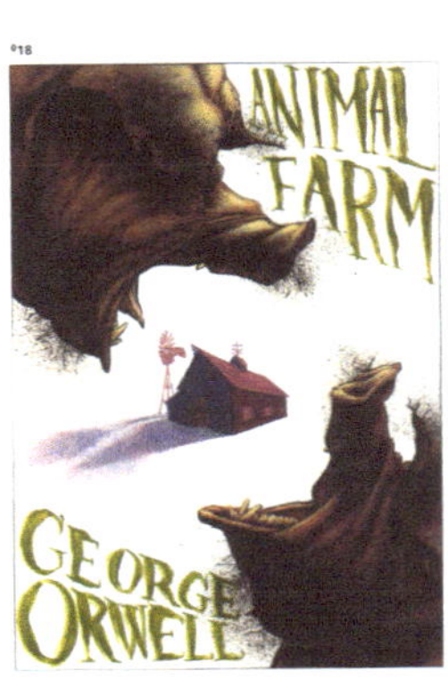

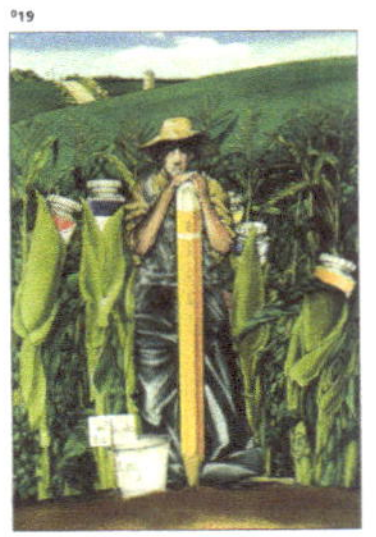

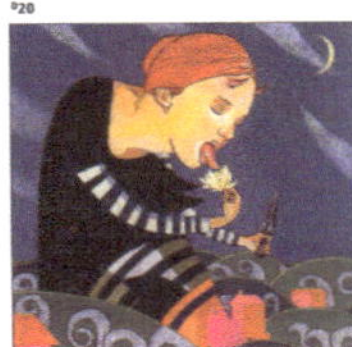

#18

"The Seven Commandments"
Eric Seat, illustrator
Robert Meganck/Sterling Hundley, instructors
Virginia Commonwealth University
(Richmond, Va.)

"The assignment was to create cover and interior illustrations for George Orwell's famous novella Animal Farm." — www.ericseat.com

#19

"Harvesting Ideas"
Troy Brown, illustrator
Mark Thomas, instructor
Art Academy of Cincinnati (Cincinnati, Ohio)

"I was trying to demonstrate the close organic relationship artists have with their materials."

#20

"The Lotus Queen"
Mario C. Sam, illustrator
Jeanne Turner, instructor
Maryland Institute College of Art
(Baltimore, Md.)

"Illustration done for children's book on dreams and nightmares."

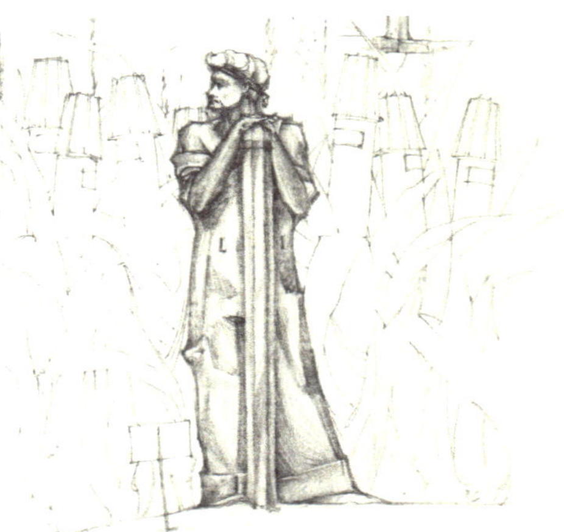

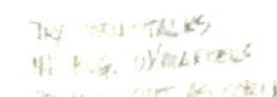

EMPHASIS OF
BOOK ILLUS.

• GOOD ILLUSTRATION
TAKES CULTIVATION OF
THE IMAGINATION.

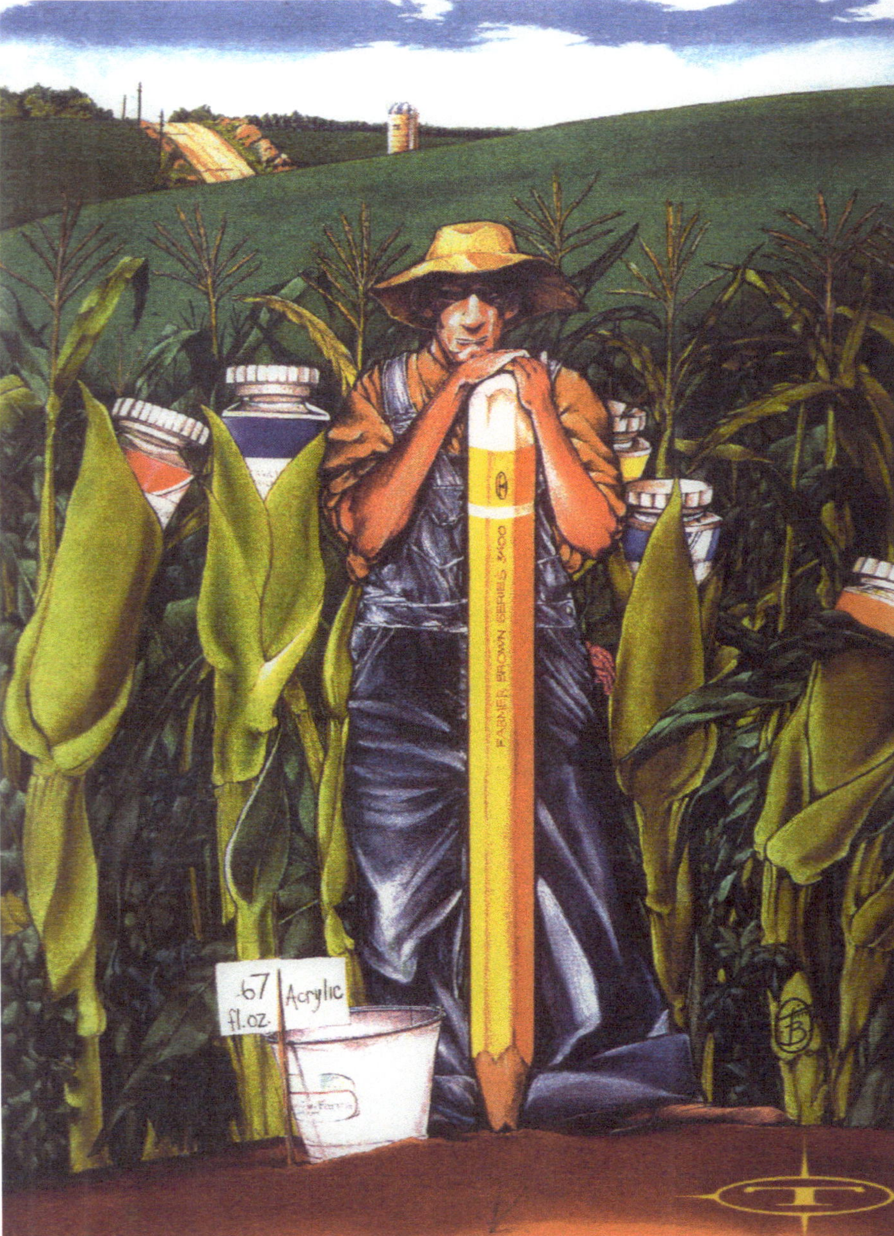

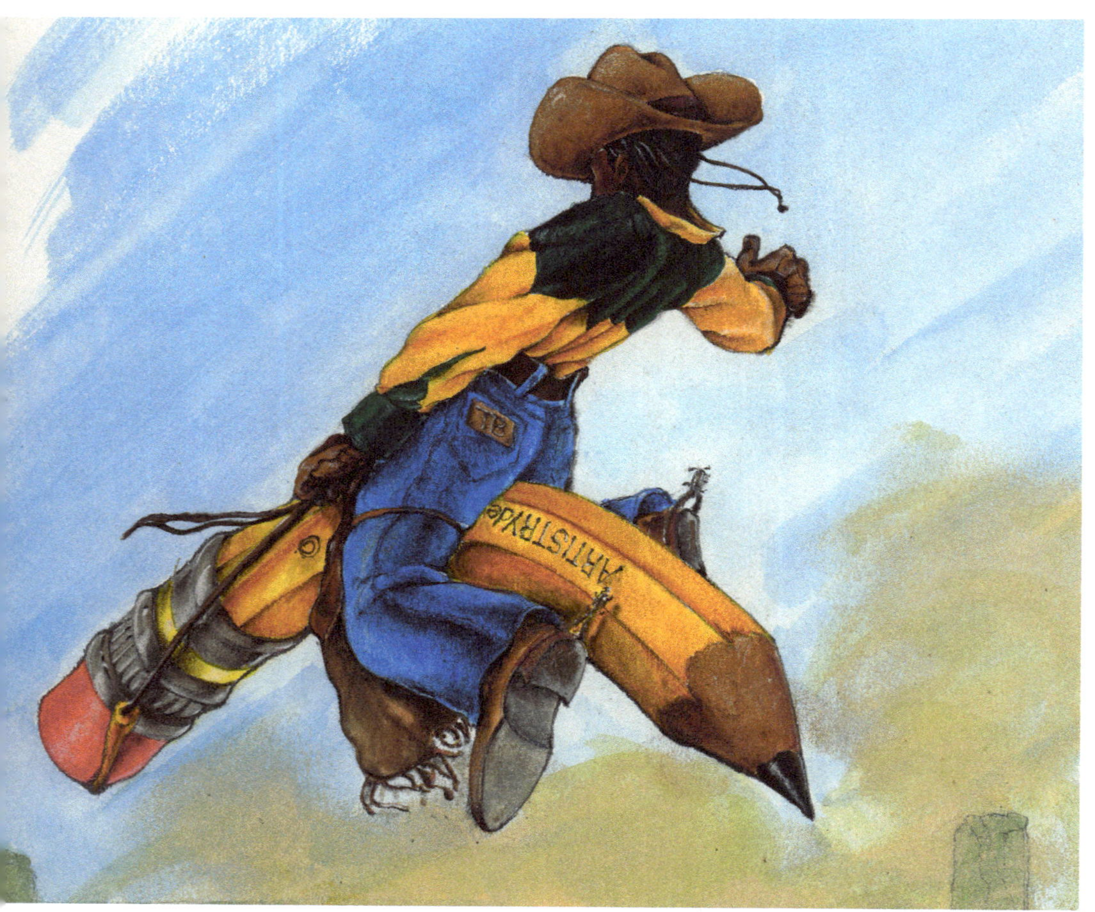

This image became very popular and was used on much of my promotional items during the late nineties. It embodied my creative approach to challenging client concepts. Seven seconds to tame that idea and get it under control to the point its presentable to the client and ready for use.

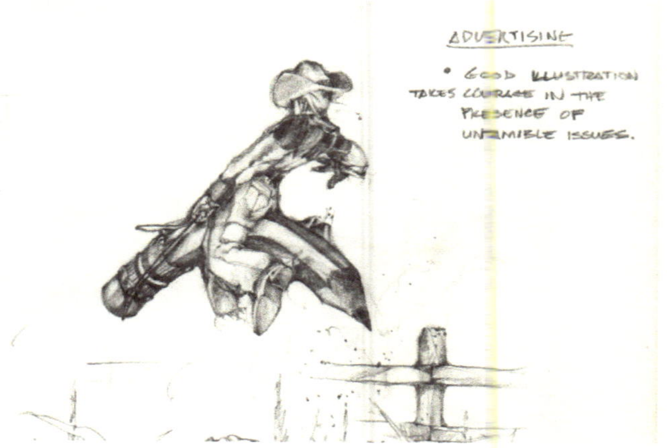

Left: 'Rodeo Concepts'
Pastel on 140 lb. Lana, 30" x 30"

Right: 'Bullseye Concepts'
Pastel on illustration board, 24" x 30" along with some early sketches.

The Bull's-eye piece is similar to the Rodeo illustration in theory. Sometimes you are able to present a variety of concepts to the client that will work, but this illustration was about the difficult task of choosing which concept would hit the exact needs of the client. It was never seen in my promotional materials.

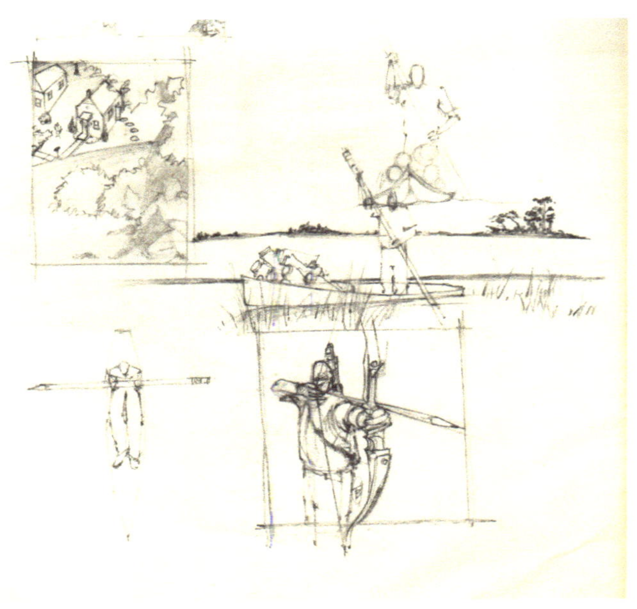

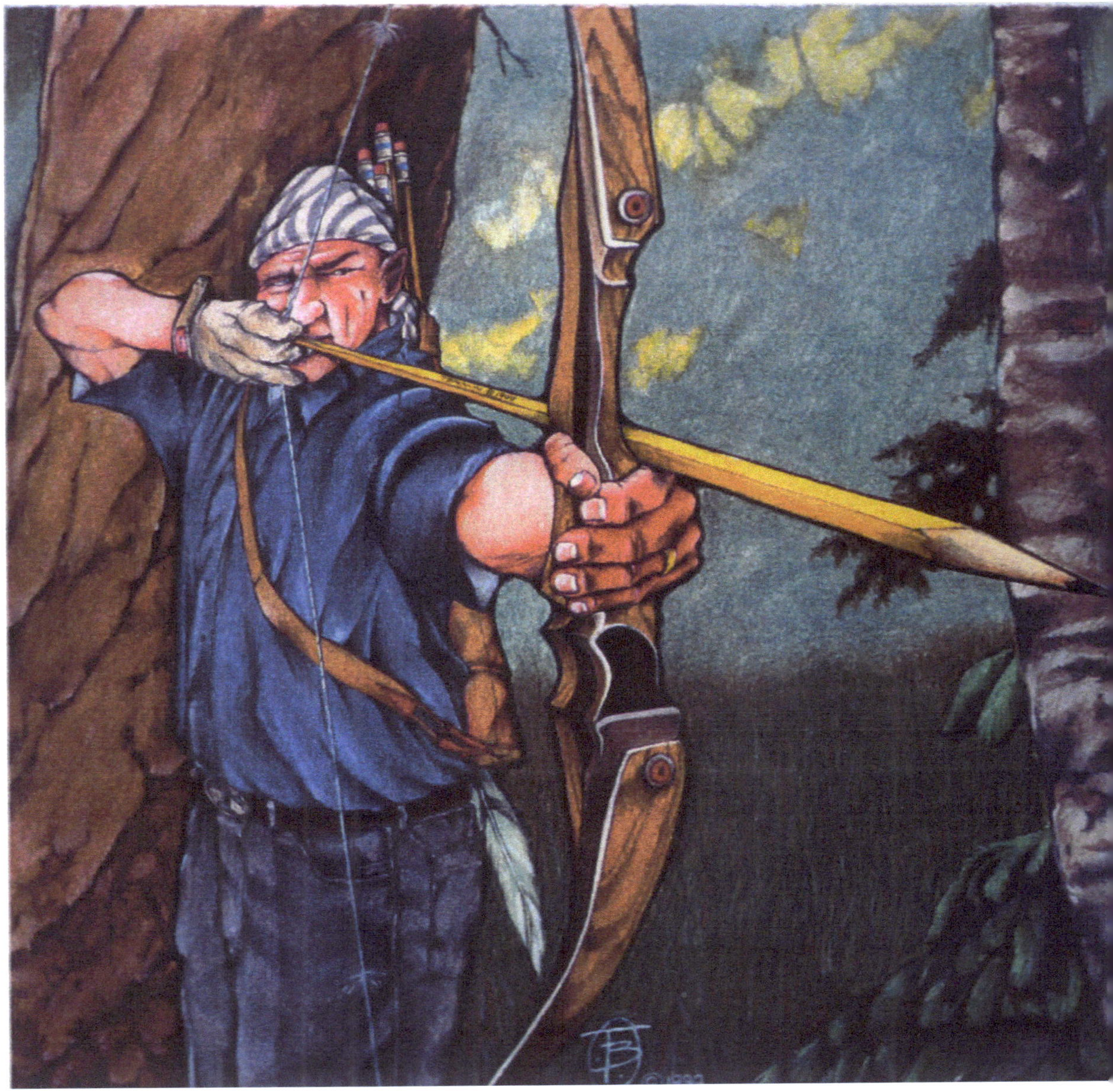

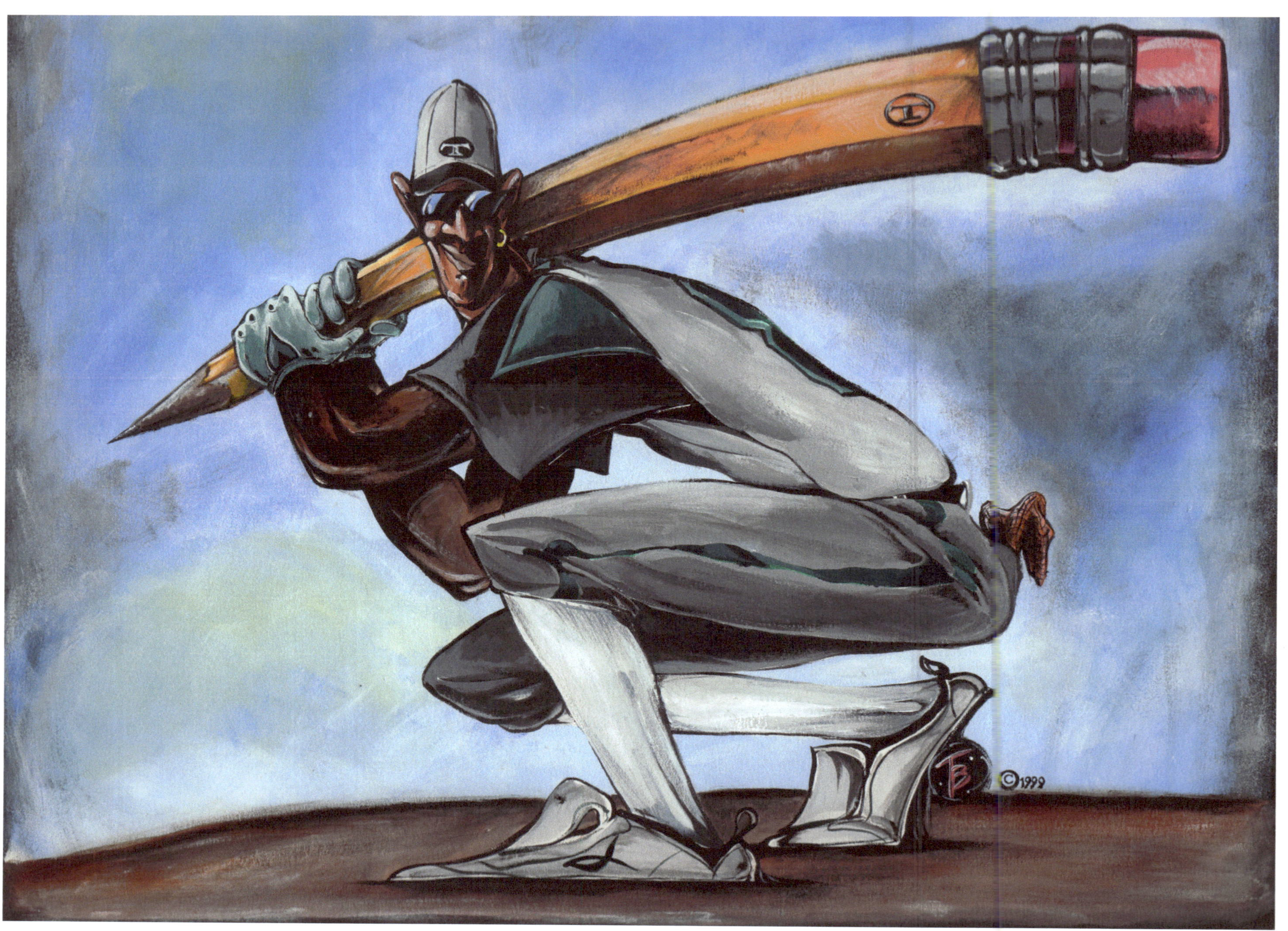

©1999

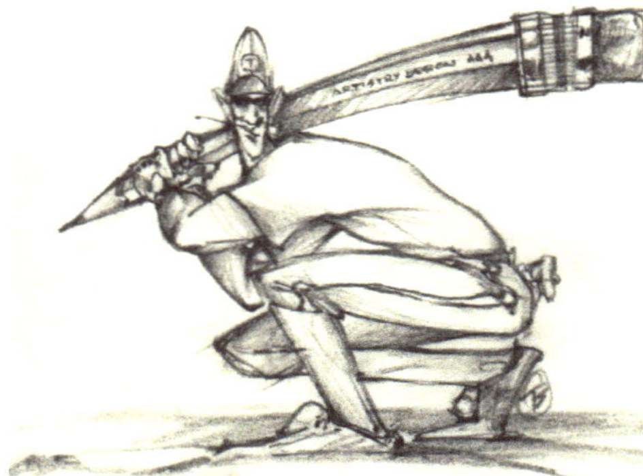

This piece is titled Hector. ESPN did a story on how Major League Baseball was enjoying an influx of Cuban players. I wanted to celebrate the story and the new era it marked for the league, even though I am not a huge baseball fan. The original piece, in the bottom right, is owned by C. F. Payne. Chris worked on a piece for the cover of a magazine called The Republic. The piece featured a scene in a small-town diner during the primary election between the Democratic candidates Hilary Clinton and Barack Obama. I was one of the models for the piece and I later asked him if he would consider trading that piece for Hector, since I knew Chris was such a big baseball fan.

Left: 'Hector' acrylic on illustration board. This was a study to determine if the final would be executed in paint or pastel.

Right Top: Early sketch for Hector on tissue paper.
Bottom: 'Hector' Pastel version, 20" x 16"

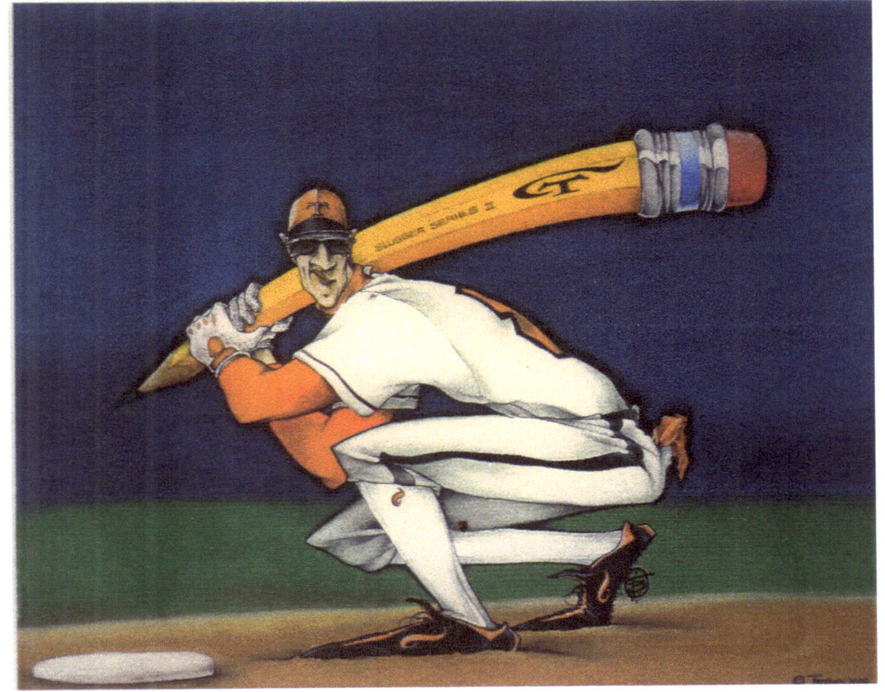

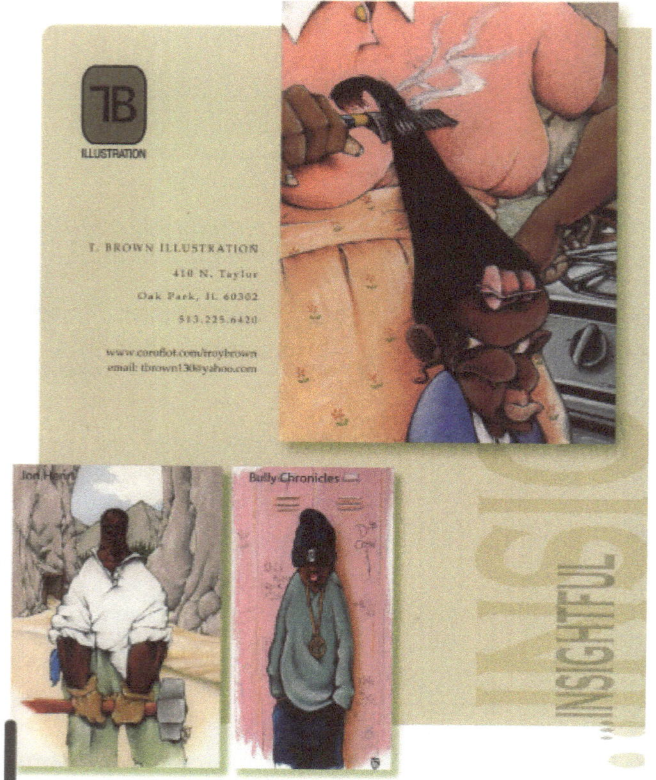

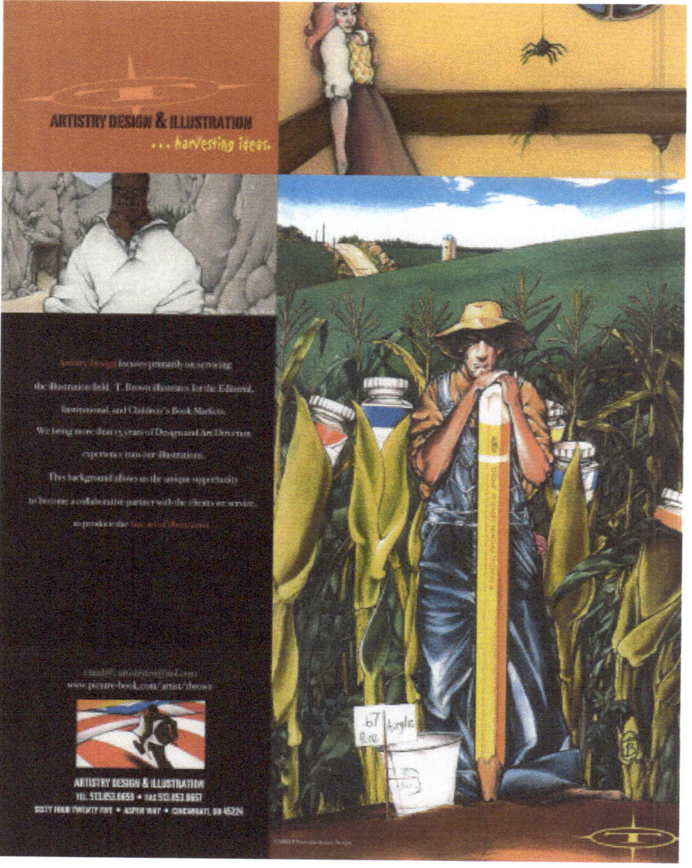

Left: An early advertisement page that appeared in Black Book Directory of Illustration.
This book was distributed to Art Directors and Editors that purchased illustration around the country.
The one-page directory ad appeared around 2003 through 2006.

Right, postcard front: Promotional postcard direct mailer for Artistry Design. Troy's freelance design company was at the time named Artistry Design & Illustration.

Bottom: Back of postcard mailer

TROY BROWN

ILLUSTRATOR
PO BOX 9555
CINCINNATI, OH 45209
513.321.5632
FAX 513.321.5602

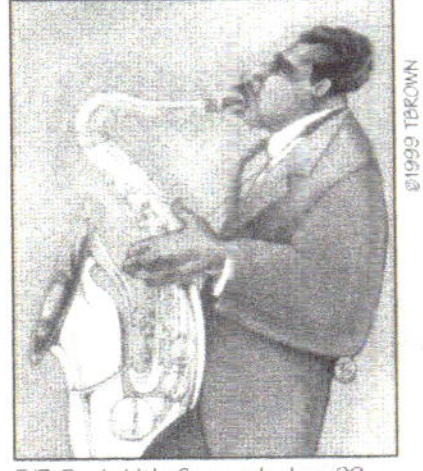

5/3 Bank / It's Commonly Jazz 99
postcard illustration

On cover The Illustrator's Open
©1999 TBROWN for ARTISTRY design

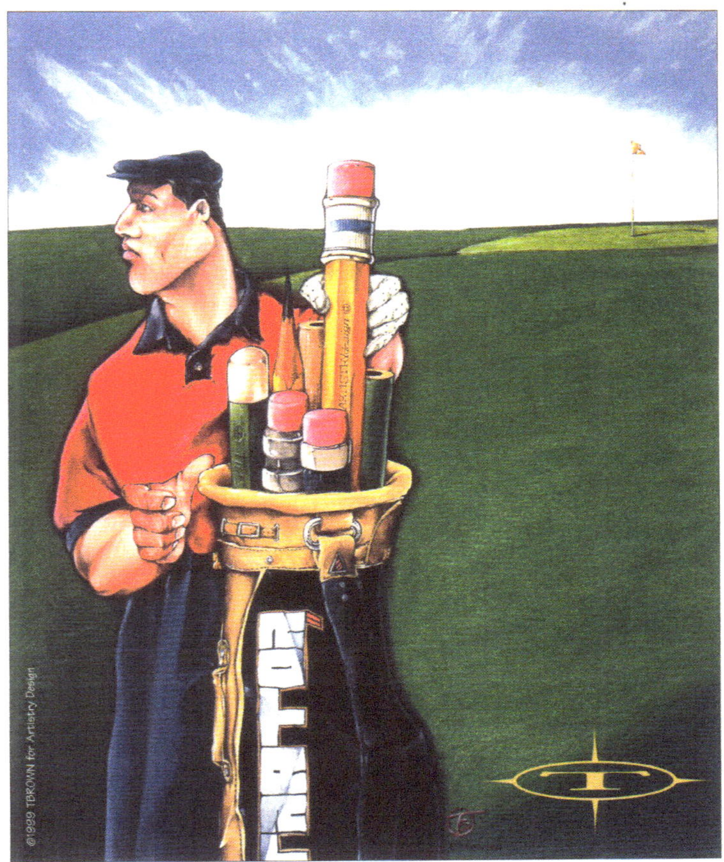

T·BROWN · ILLUSTRATOR
513.321.5632

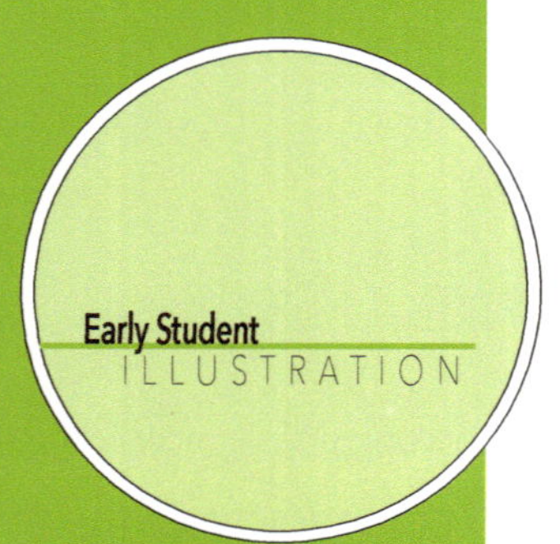

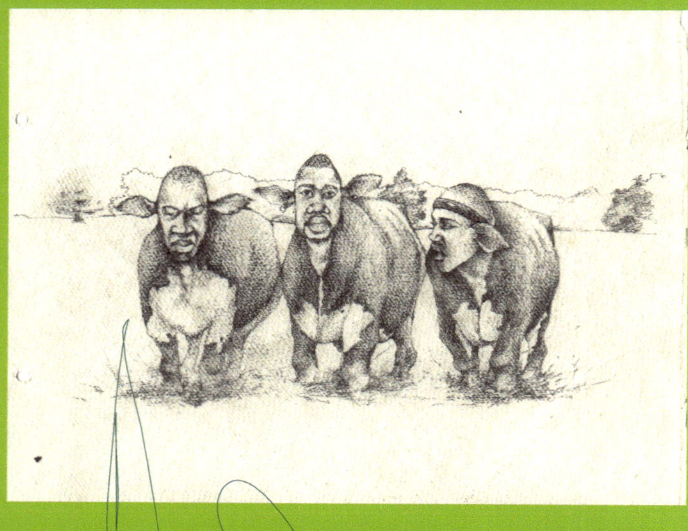

This section presents work I produced while a student at the Art Academy of Cincinnati. This was my second academic degree, the pursuit of which involved me leaving my full-time gig. The Art Academy of Cincinnati exists in a space that constantly serves as a source of creative reflection and nourishment. The memories and experiences were the spark to my awakening as a creative, the organic structure that still functions as my hidden scaffolding to which all my creative ventures connect. It is like many things in our lives that, through profound subtlety, manage to remain a sort of creative conduit that in the end leaves us at a loss when trying to describe its impact in our lives.

Title: Bovine Records
Acrylic on canvas
16" x 20"

Left: Out to Pasture, based on a Source Magazine Article
Graphite on watercolor paper

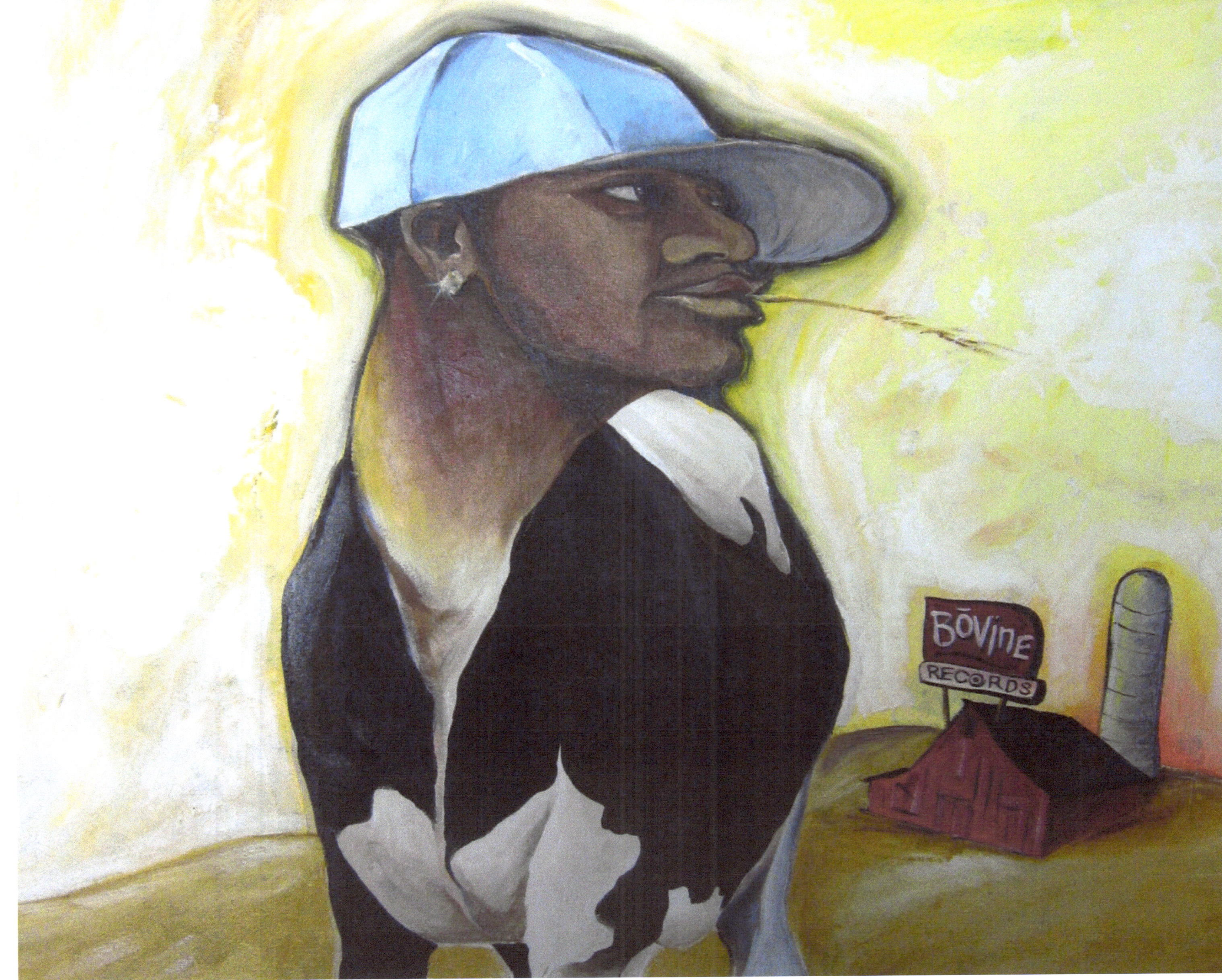
BōVINE
RECORDS

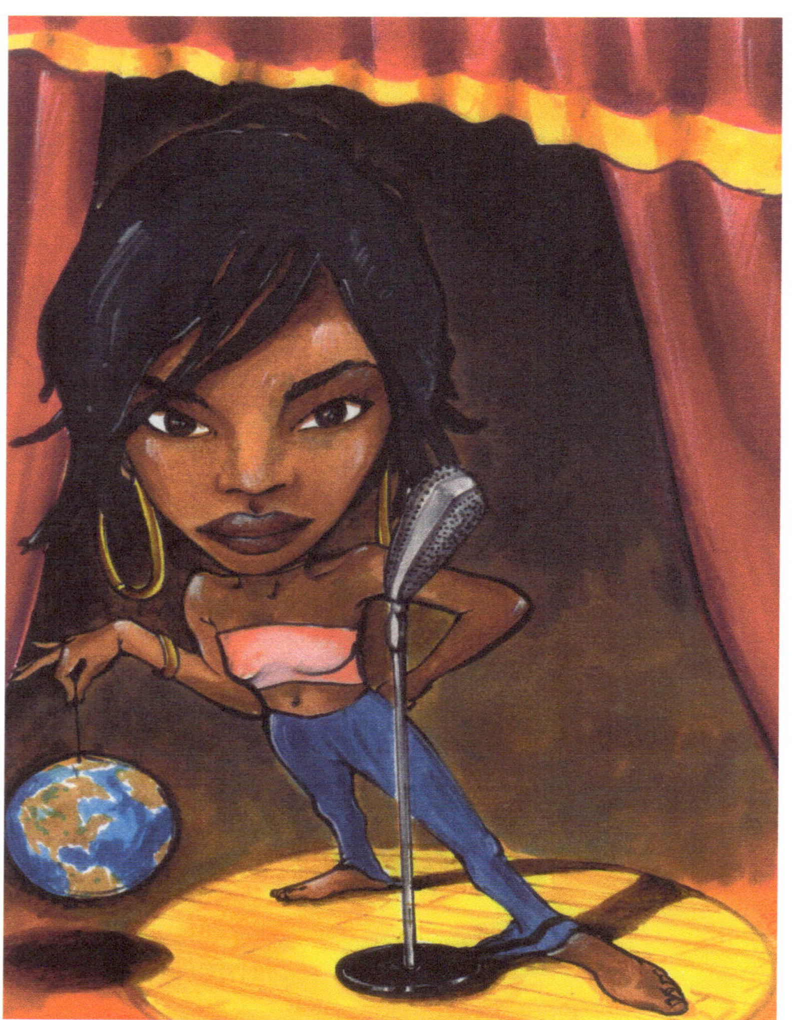

Left: 'Lauryn Rules'
This was a marker rough in preparation for the final, which was never completed. The illustration was based on an article out of Source Magazine at the time.

Below: This piece was an ink study that was inspired by a Source Magazine article chronicalling the members of Tupac's crew that were their friend after he had been shot. The article talked about how they would navigate their careers post Tupac.

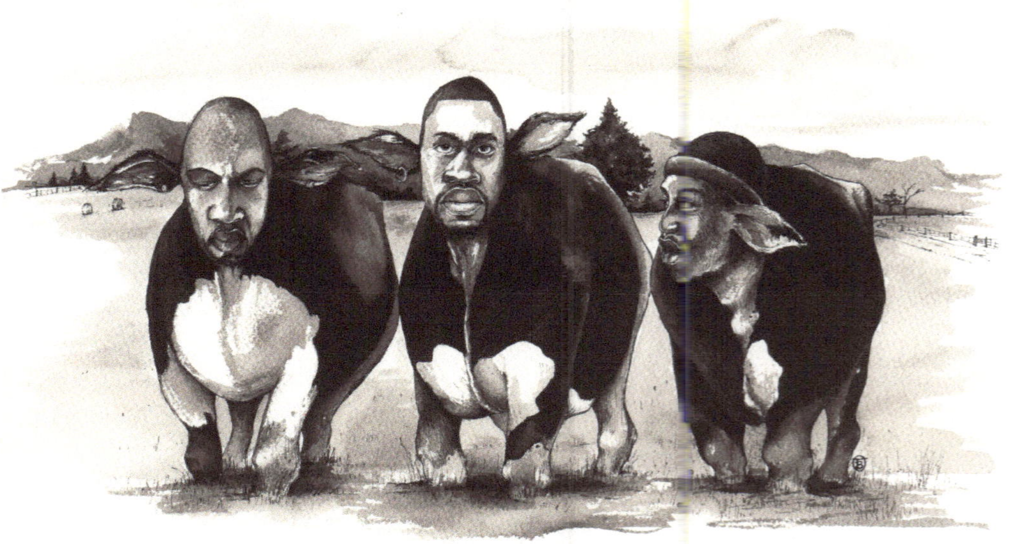

Bottom: Every year the AAC illustration students would submit illustrations for the annual Reindeer Parade, held in Mt. Adams in Cincinnati, Ohio. An odd parade that featured dogs dressed in christmas costumes. The winning illustration would be featured as a poster for the event.

Right: 'Hip Hop Heartless'
Acrylic on canvas, 18" x 20"

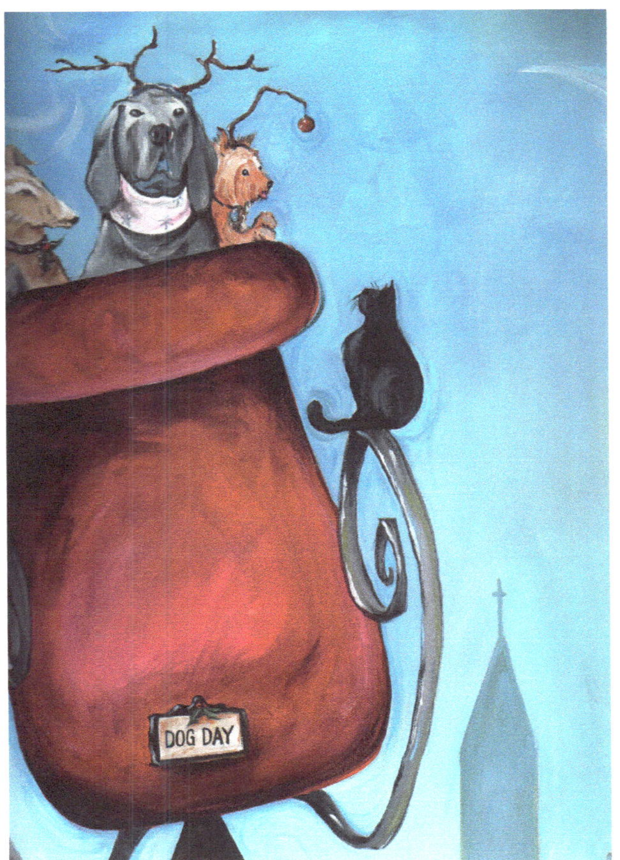

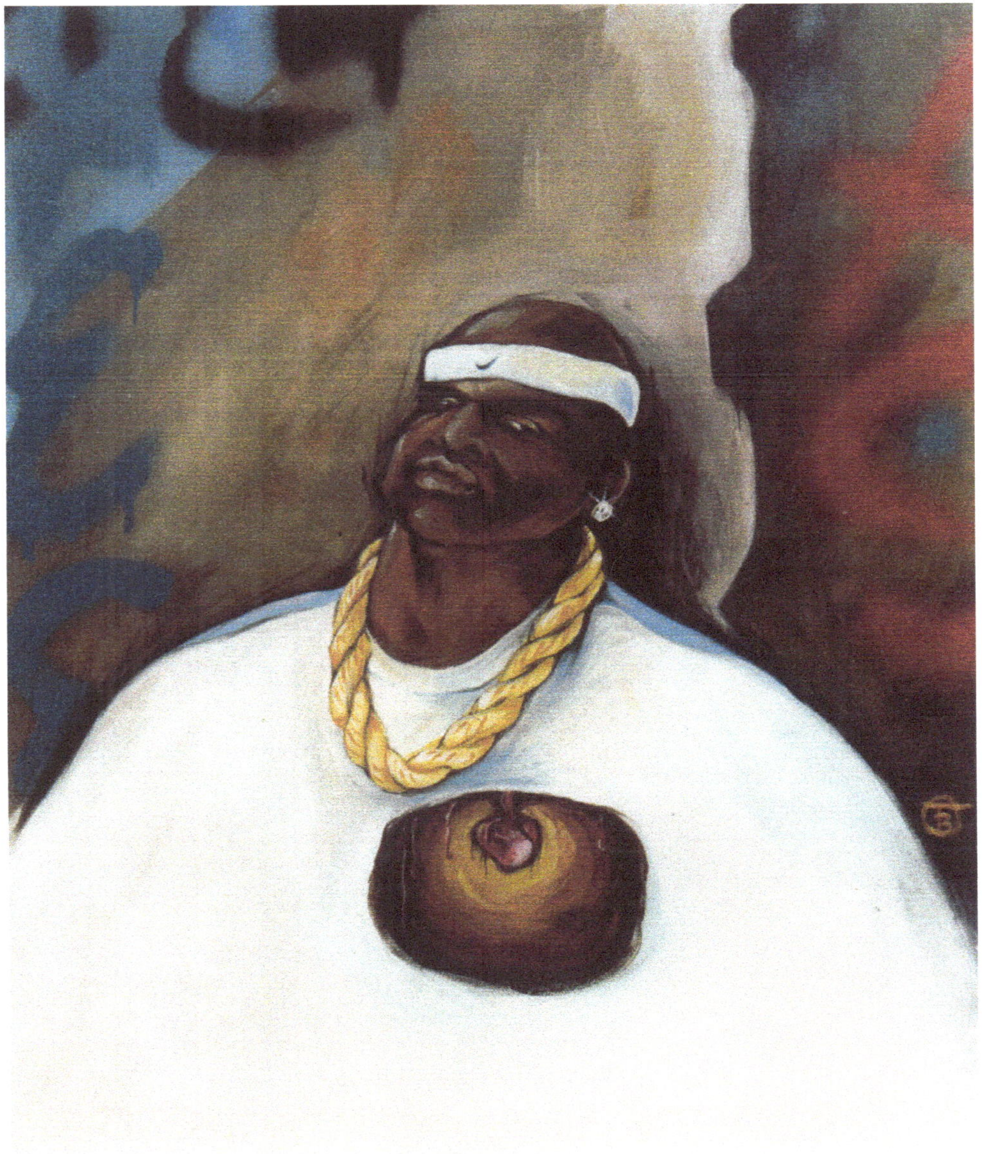

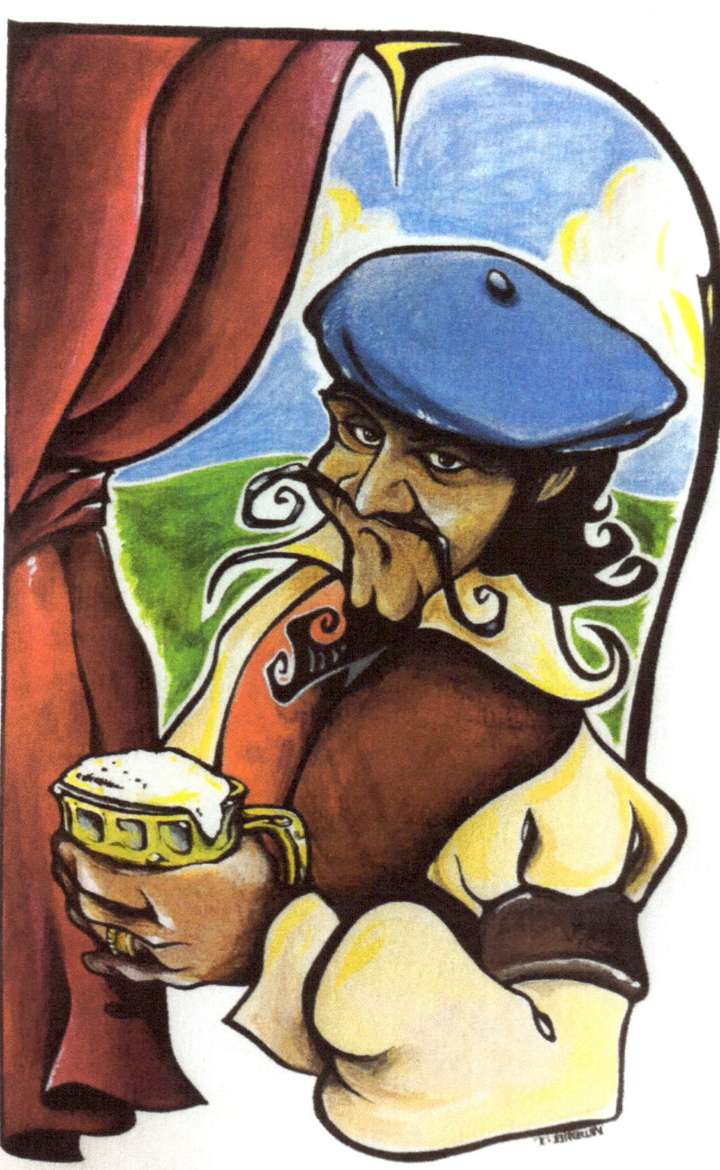

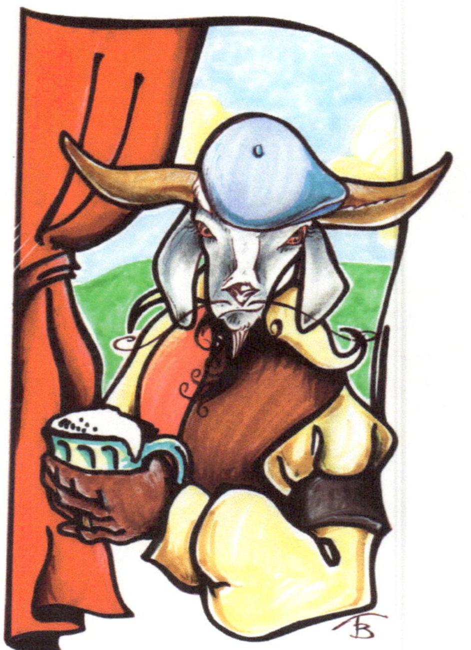

Left: These pieces were done for a local Shakespear Theater in Cincinnati. The illustration lll students at the Art Academy all submitted concepts for the annual poster.
The final piece was done in acrylic on canvas, 16" x 20"

Right: A promotional piece actually never ended up using called 'The Other Santa.' One piece was done in pastel on lana, the other was done in ink on water color paper.

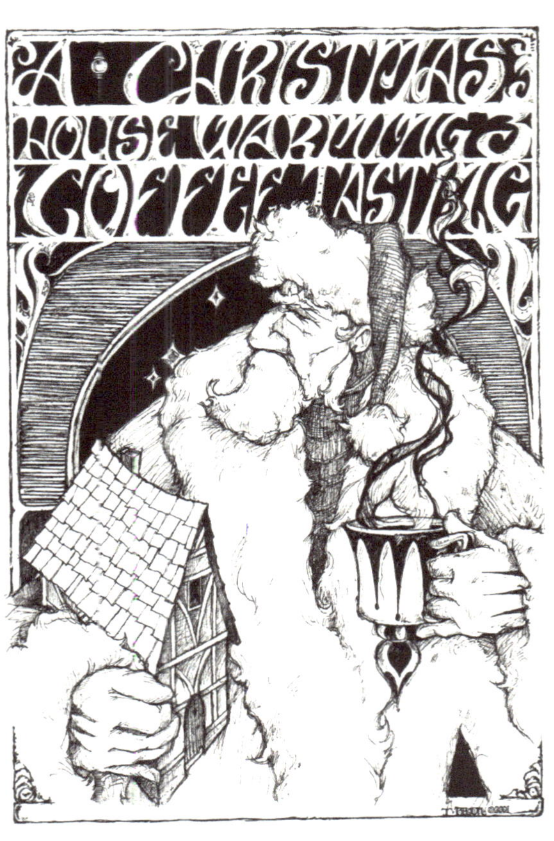

A CHRISTMAS
HOUSEWARMING
COFFEE TASTING

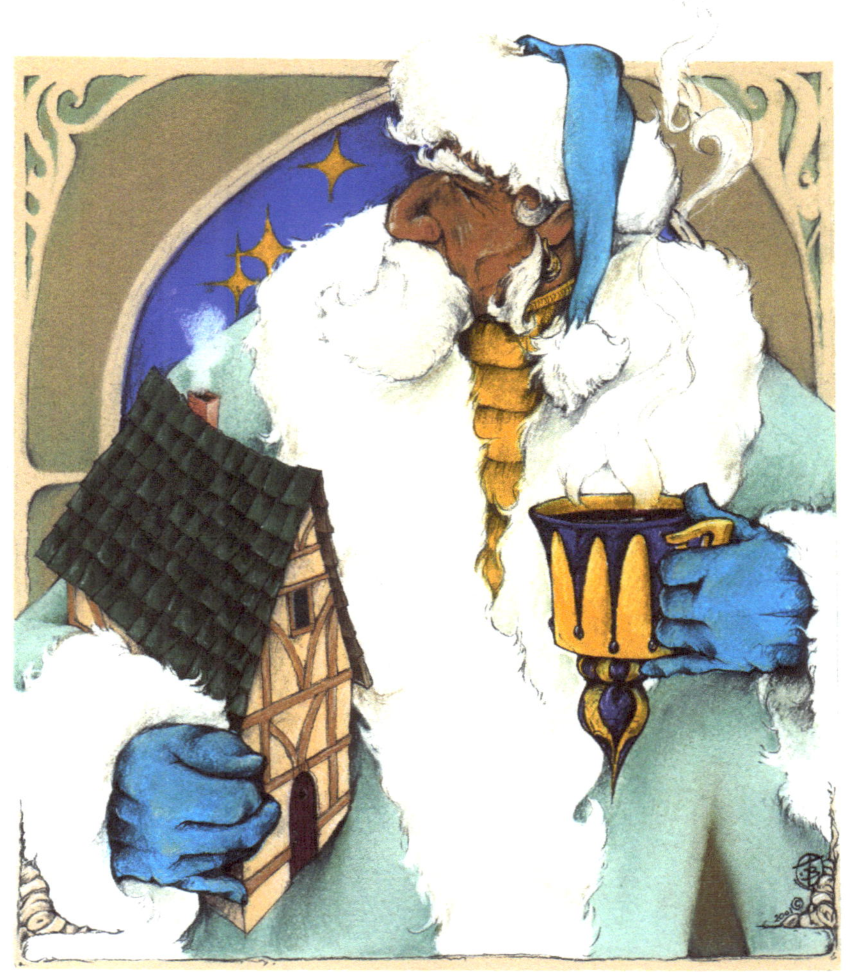

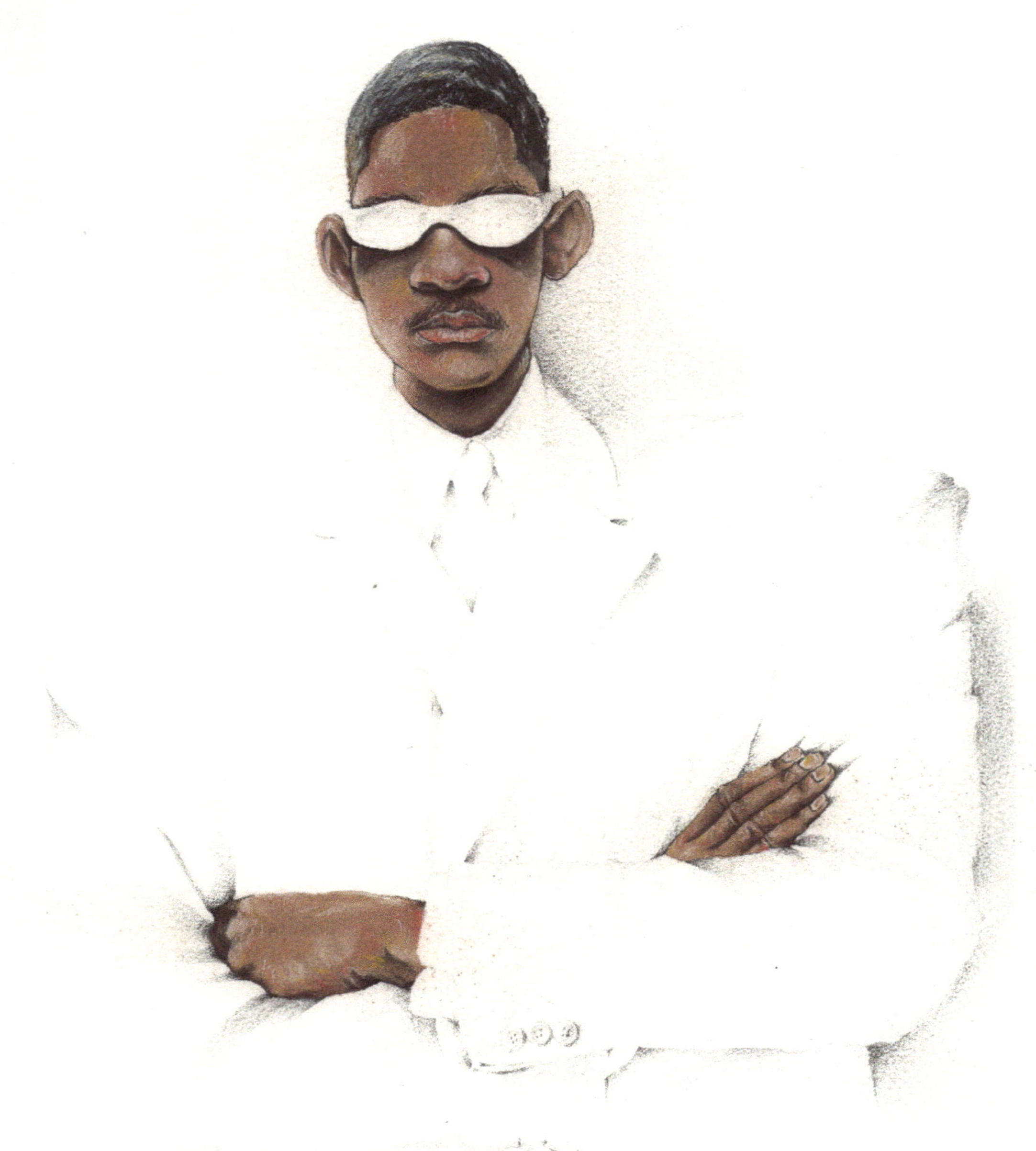

This illustration was done in 2001 while I was studying at Virginia Commonwealth University (VCU) during a summer intensive called the Illustration Academy. The program was run by John English, the son of renowned illustrator Mark English. The assignment was to produce an illustration based on an existing article from a national publication.

The article I chose came from one of the movie magazines of the day, which featured a story on Will Smith and how he maintained such a squeaky-clean image in Hollywood. The article was released just a month before Men in Black hit theaters. That year, students worked with John English, Anita Kunz, and Sterling Hunley during the three-week session. All of them were heavy in portrait work, and although I didn't do many portraits, my work was influenced by the program for a short while. That was also the year I met my longtime mentor, Alex Bostic, who was a professor at VCU at the time. Alex would encourage me to pursue teaching in higher education.

Left: 'Clean Willie' Pastel on lana, 16" x 20"
Complete while Troy attended the Illustration Academy at Virginia Commonwealth University 2003, where he met mentor Alexander Bostic.

Right: 'Old Memories' This was an assignment while at the Art Academy of Cincinnati. We had to choose an article from a major magazine and illustrate the text. The article I chose focused on racism and the long history of discrimmination in this country. The article equated discrimination to the memories of African Elephants.

Right: A few early draft sketches and a color study for the Old Memories piece.

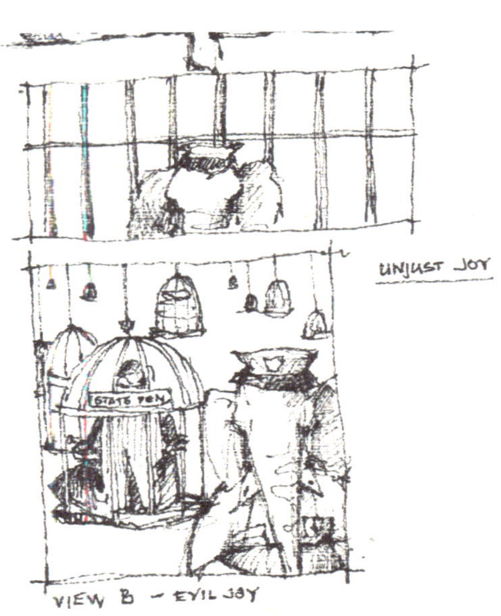

STATE PEN
UNJUST JOY
VIEW B - EVIL JOY

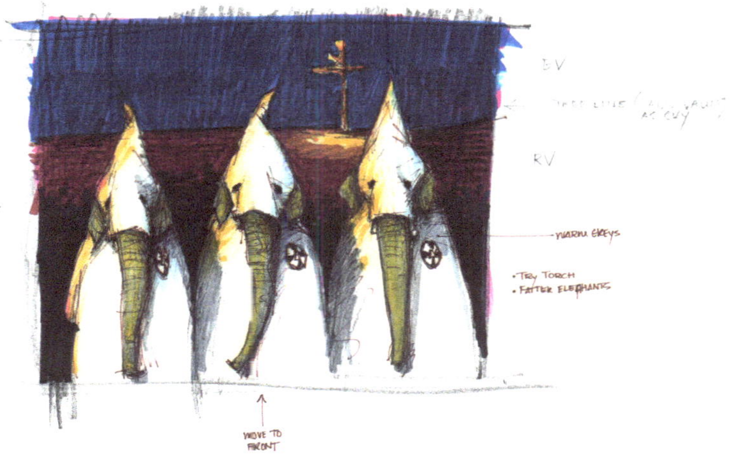

WARM GREYS
TRY TORCH
FETTER ELEPHANTS
MOVE TO FRONT

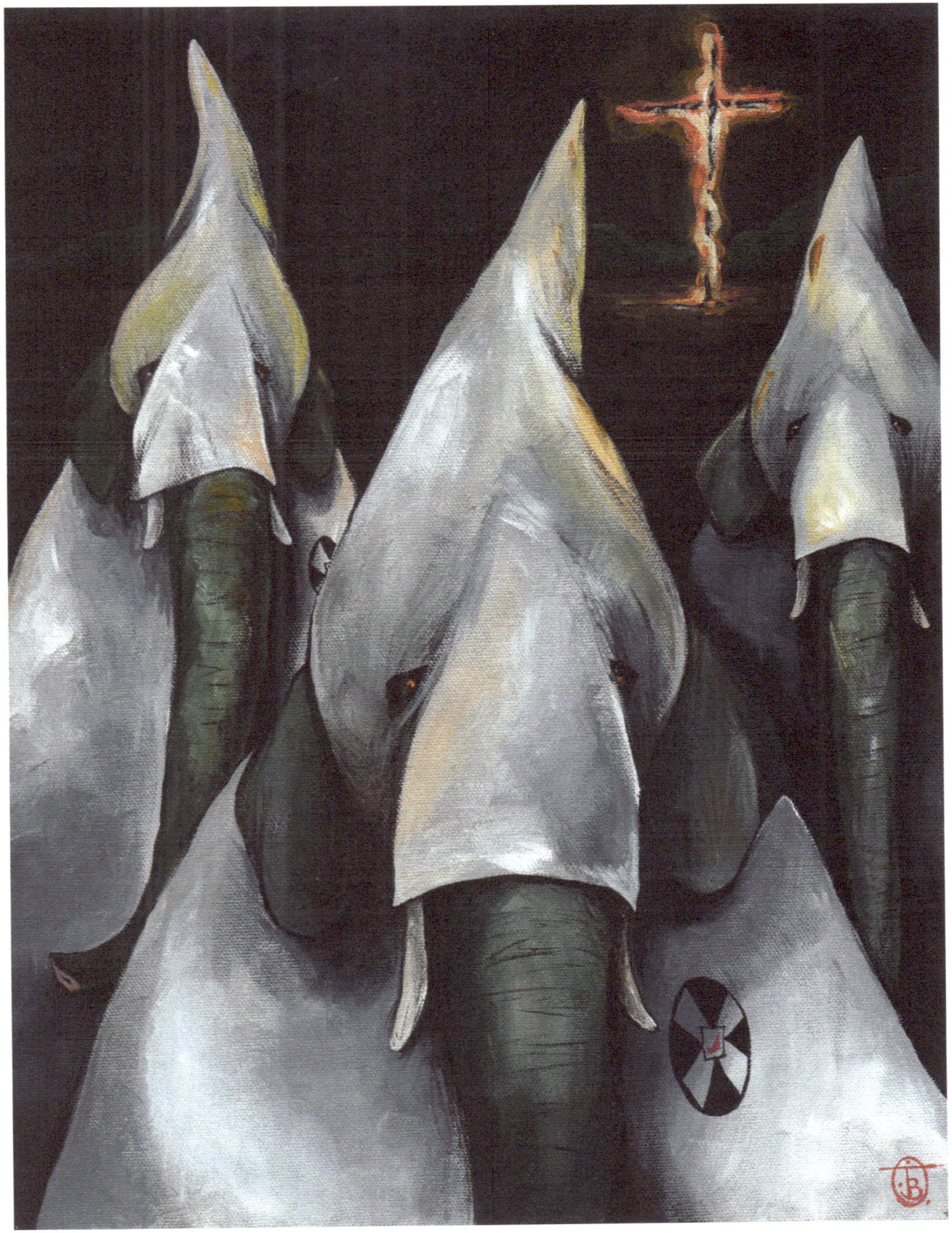

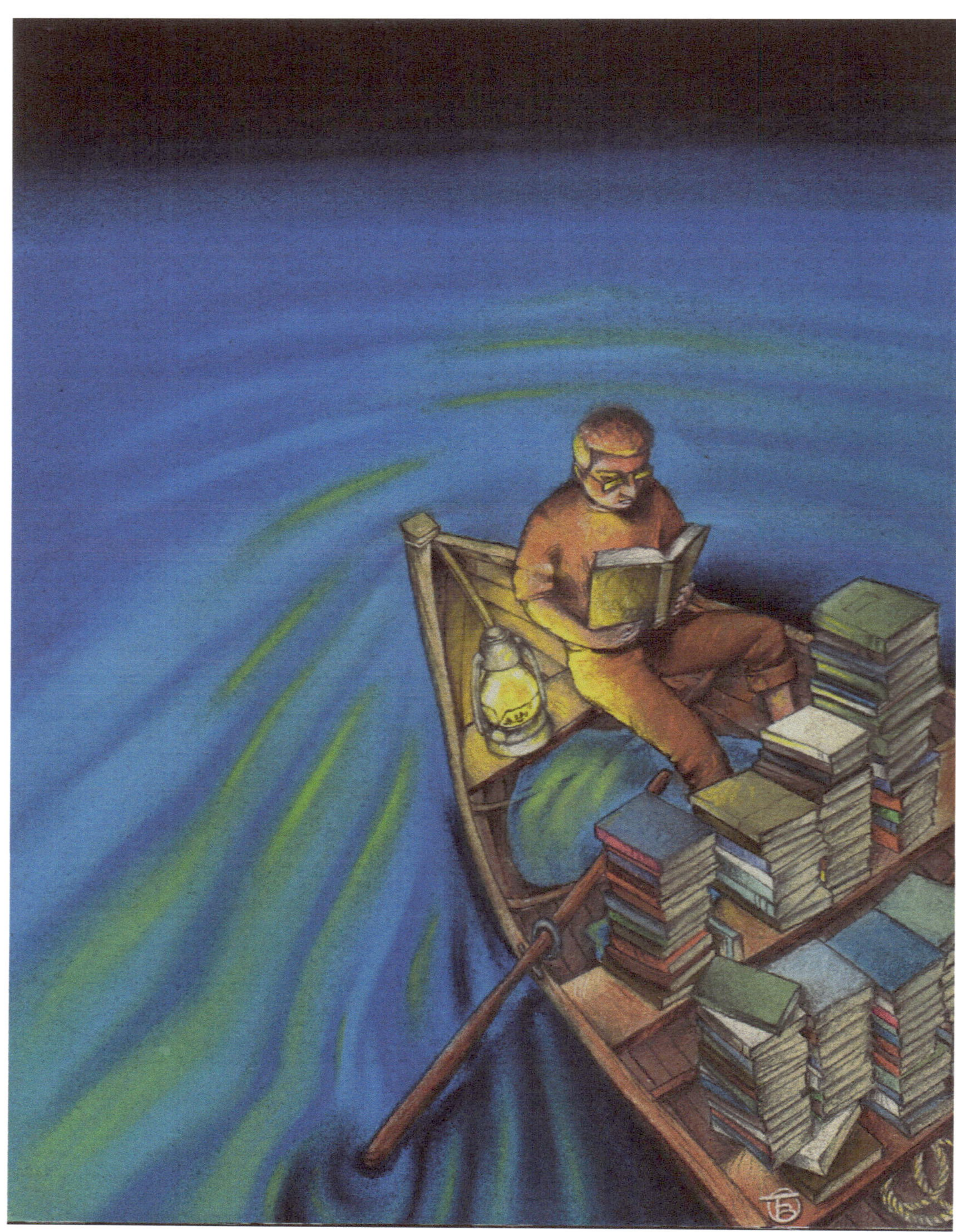

Left: 'Books Adrift' Pastel on lana, 10" x 12"
The assignment was to illustrate a cover for a national magazine.
Troy chose The New American Review.

Right: The first thumbnail sketch for the final piece.

Right: A color layout with tissue overlay magazine header as a draft.

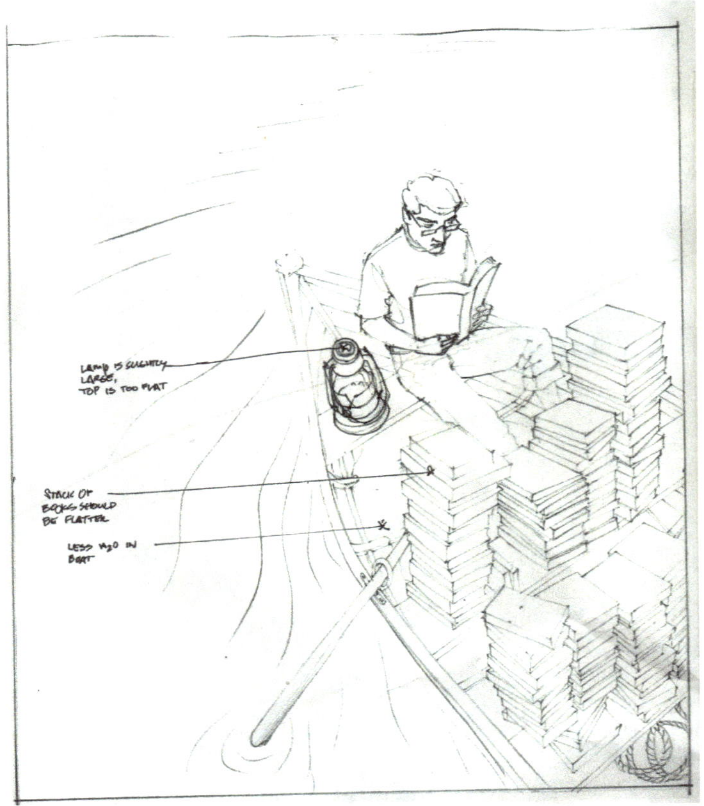

LAMP IS SLIGHTLY LARGE, TOP IS TOO FLAT
STACK OF BOOKS SHOULD BE FLATTER
LESS H₂0 IN BOAT

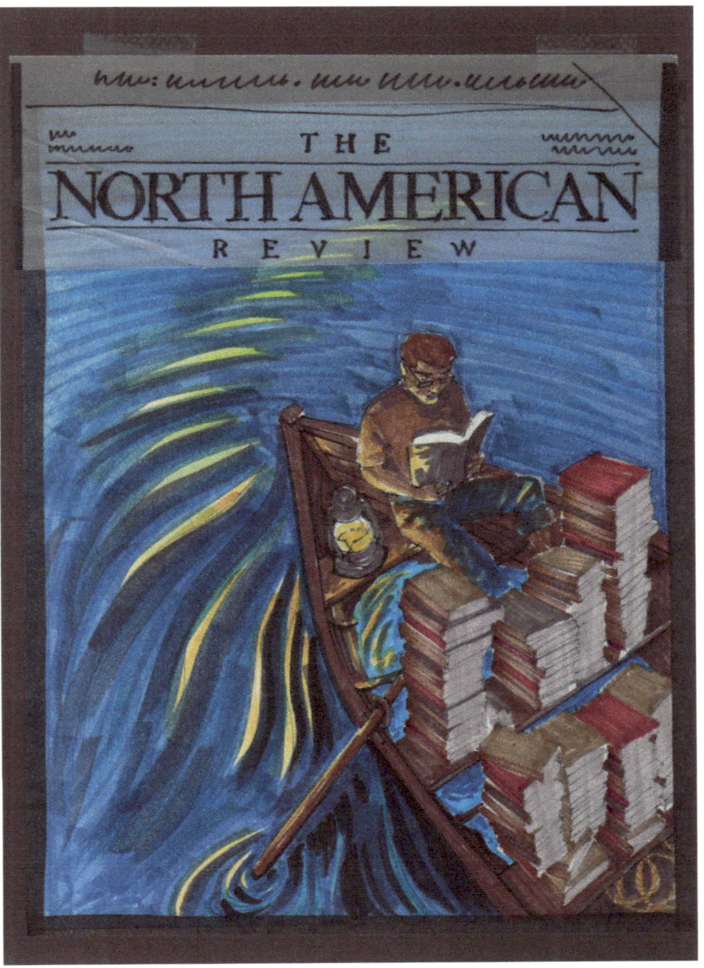

THE
NORTH AMERICAN
REVIEW

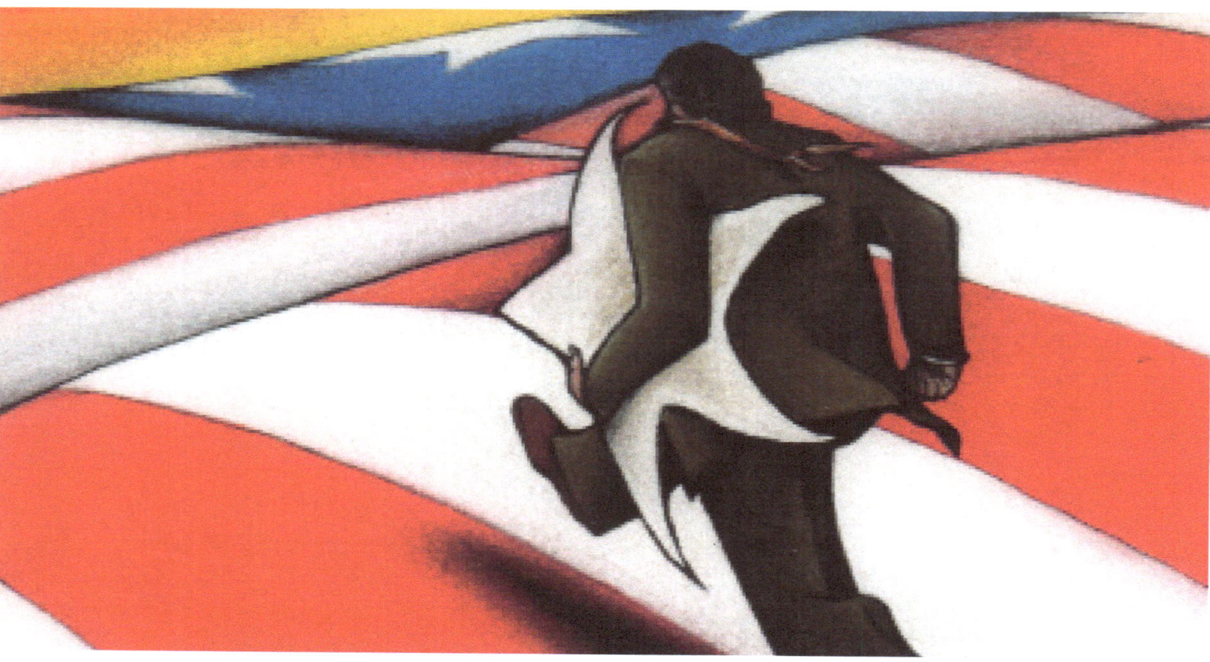

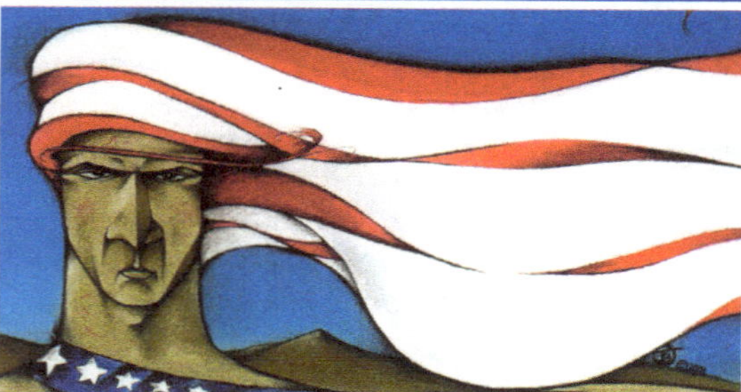

Left: 'Lady Liberty Rises' Pastel on lana.
Client: Bramkamp Printing Company in Memory of 911.

Top: Study for Bramkamp Printing Company 911 Project, '*Repairing Our Nation*' Pastel on lana

Right: 'Unload Presents Here'
Pastel on lana, digitally edited.
Client: The Powers Agency in Cincinnati, Ohio

While at the Art Academy of Cincinnati I was asked to contribute an illustration, along with other illustrators and photographers, in memory of 9/11.
The client, the Bramkamp Printing Company, wanted us to somehow show America's resilience in the face of mass brokenness.
I presented two concepts to be used as a promotional tabletop calendar for the company. They chose the more abstract concept, Lady Liberty Rising. My approach was to embody America figuratively rising up to defeat her foes. The second concept, Repairing the Nation, fostered a hope that we could repair the damage the nation had suffered and slowly heal in time.

The piece on this page was done for a design firm in Cincinnati, Ohio for their Christmas Card that year. The theme was 'Unload Presents Here'

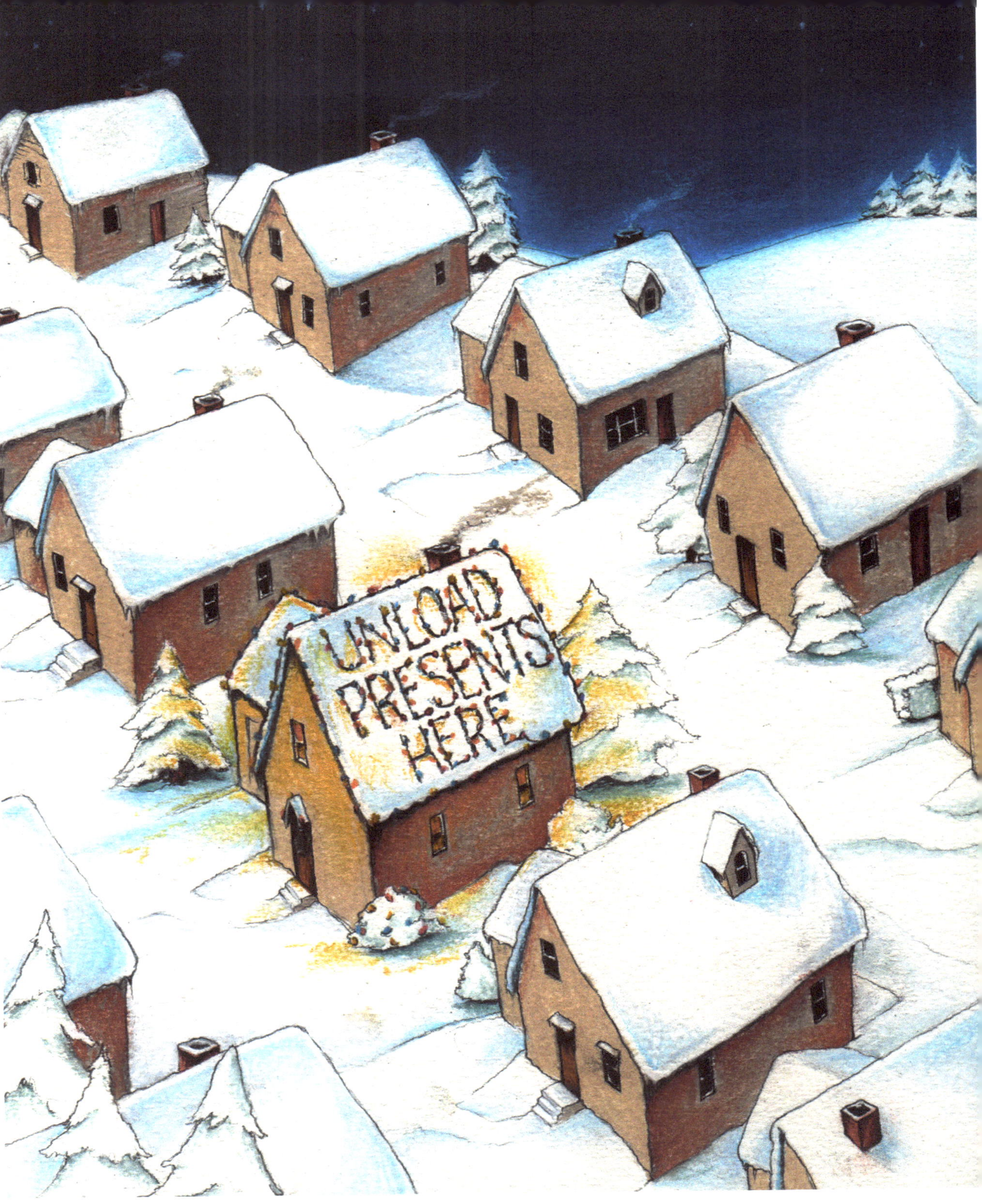

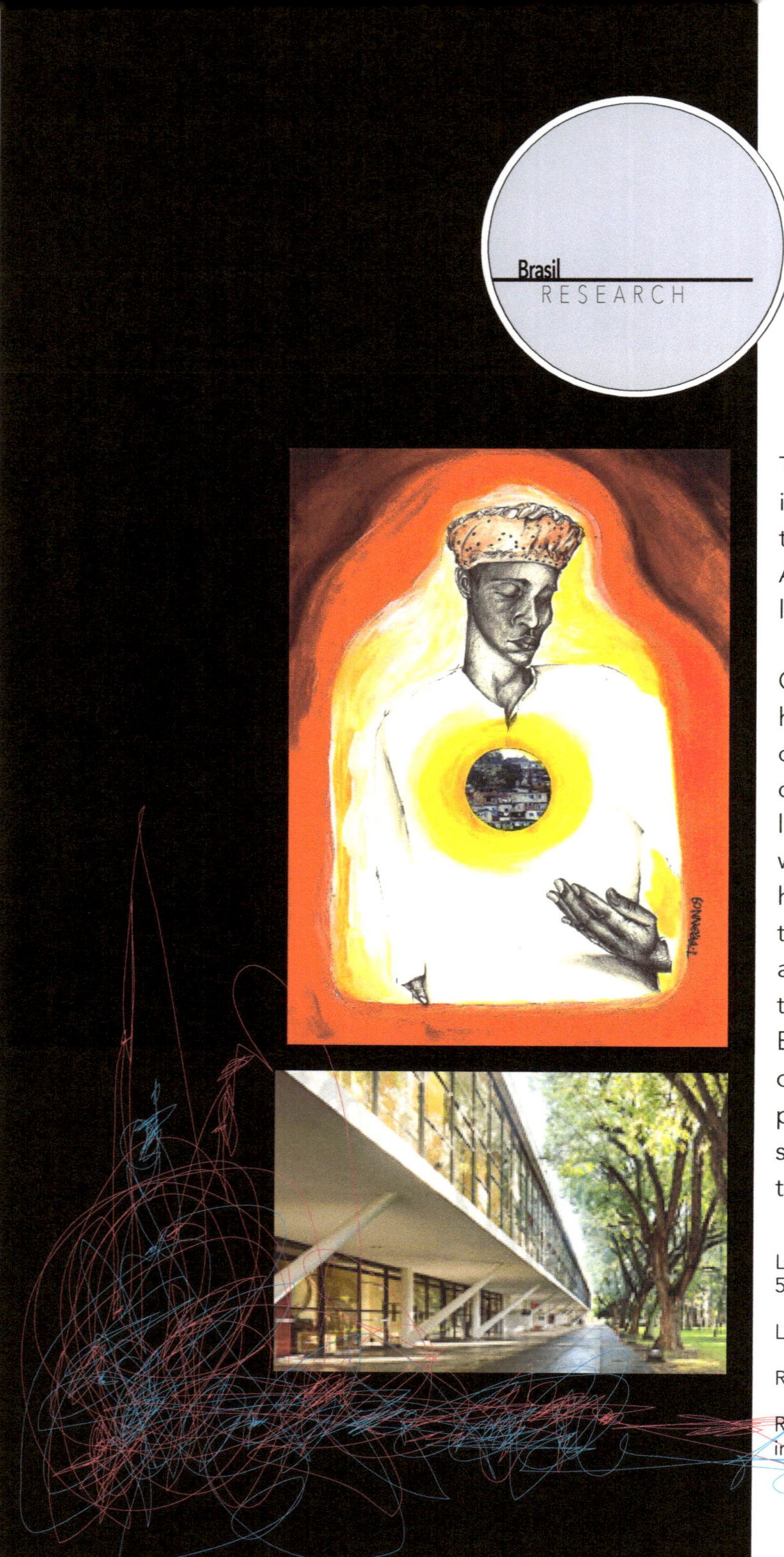

This section begins with the artwork that extended from my research while completing my thesis work in São Paulo, Brasil. In X year2007, I was employed as an educator in the Museu Afro Brasil along with a team of educators and my translator, Renato Ajaujó, who is my dear friend to this day. The experience was profound on many levels and helped shape my approach to research as it relates to visual content.

One day in particular served as a paradigm-shifting experience. After several long hours of presenting to the various school groups that would visit the museum, as our day was coming to a close, Renato took some time to acquaint me with some of the more unfamiliar galleries in the museum. One gallery contained some excellently painted traditional European salon-trained pieces that I assumed were lesser works executed by artists of the nineteenth century. As I looked closely at the pieces, however, I noticed a few obvious alarming images that would have been contrary to the time period. Several Black artists were depicted painting a white female nude in an open figure session. My first response was, how could this take place, considering the colonial-based society that still at the time viewed slavery as a necessity? These Black students we sitting as equals to their white counterparts, committing what was considered a lynchable offense of the day. Renato went on to tell me that all of the paintings I was seeing in this particular gallery were in fact done by Afro-Brasilian slaves who had been sent by their slaveowners to Europe to develop their found talents in the salons. This was a path to freedom for some of them who would even-

Left: Favela Prince, based on images from Condomble.
5" x 7" mixed media on clay board, in Resin.

Left Bottom: Front entry of de Museu Afro Brasil, Sao Paulo, Brasil.

Right: Study for Young Elder, 5" x 5" graphite and oil on clay board

Right(Detail): Early study for Young Elder, 5" x 5" mixed media, on clay board, in Resin.

tually return to Brasil and—through extreme difficulty—managed to carve out a living from their paintings.

For the first time in my life I was face to face with astonishing works created by slaves, people who looked like me and had similar ancestral origins. The life I had lived to that point mirrored theirs in many ways. They understood how it felt to be the only person of color in the classroom. They understood the weight of having to silently justify your presence, that you are just as talented and equipped to be in the room as your white counterparts. That your work deserved space on the same gallery walls as the next artist. It is one thing to believe you belong, but it is another thing altogether to see you belong. It changes your entire sense of reasoning.

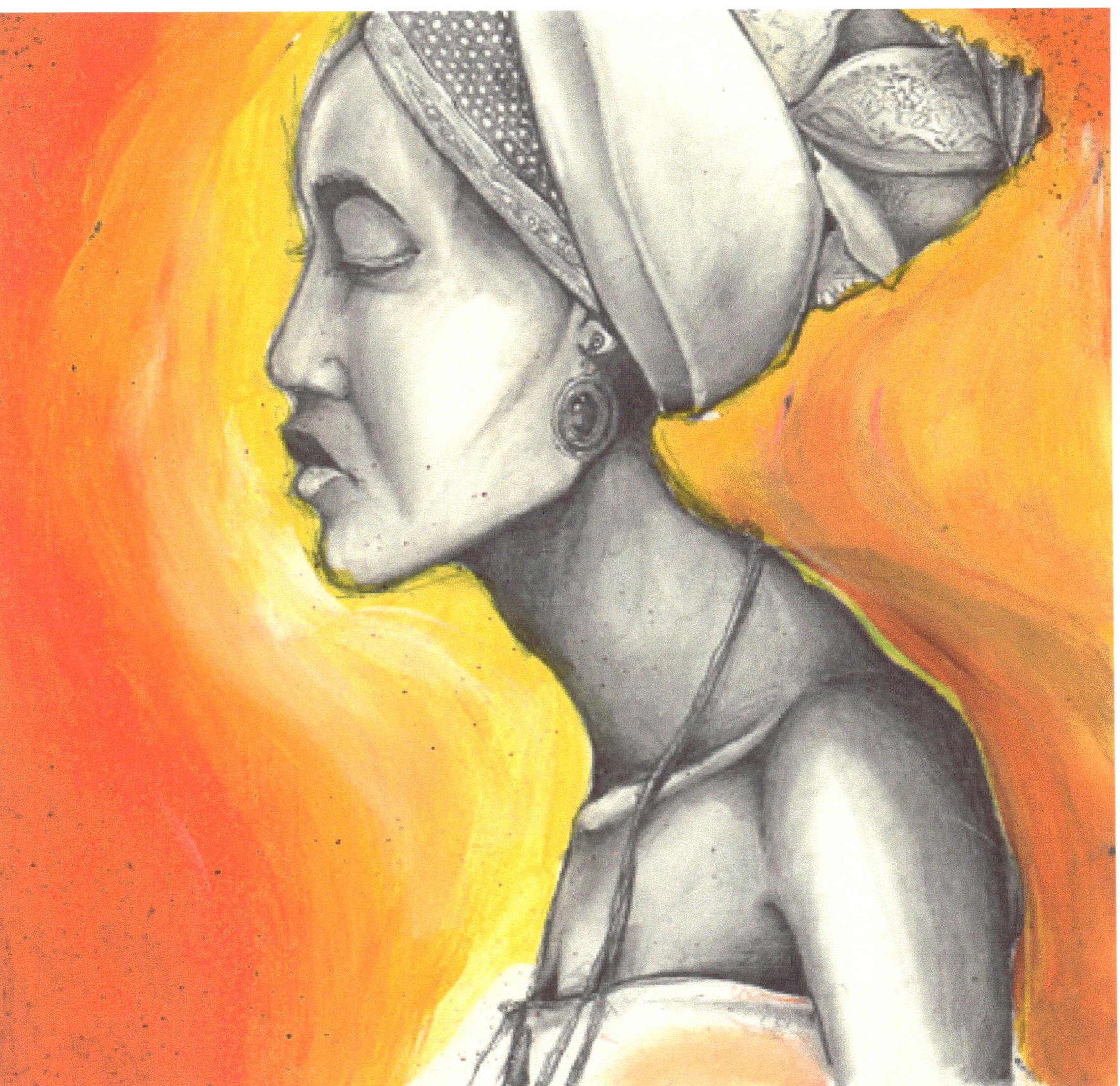

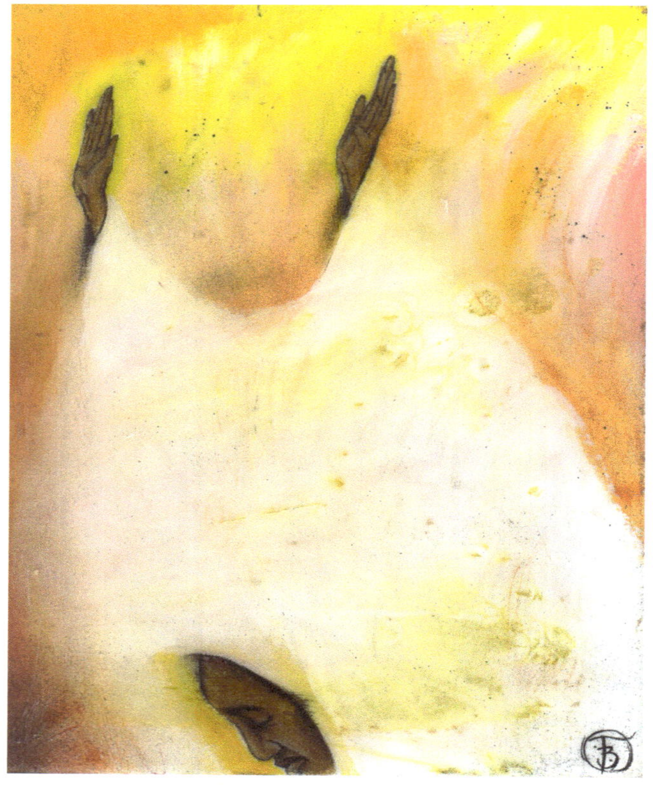

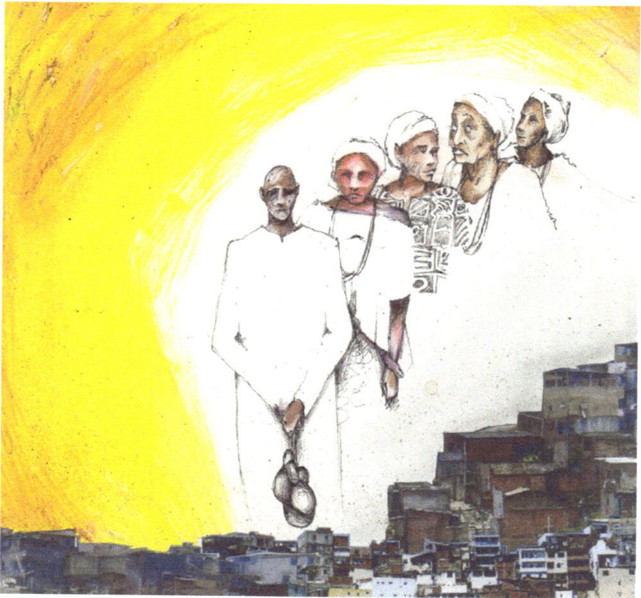

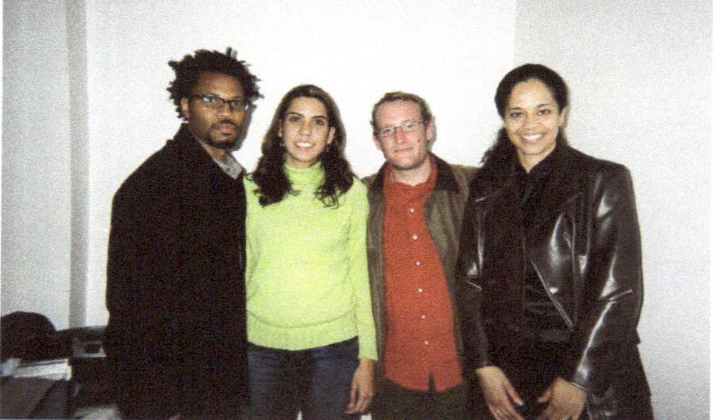

Above photo: Troy with educator Juliana, her husband and Ranato's wife Alessandra

Left Top: Favela Sanctum, 5" x 7" mixed media on clay board, in Resin.

Left Bottom: Elders Watching, 5" x 5" mixed media, collage, oil on clay board

Right (Detail): Sherie in Downtown Goiania, acrylic on canvas, 16" x 20"

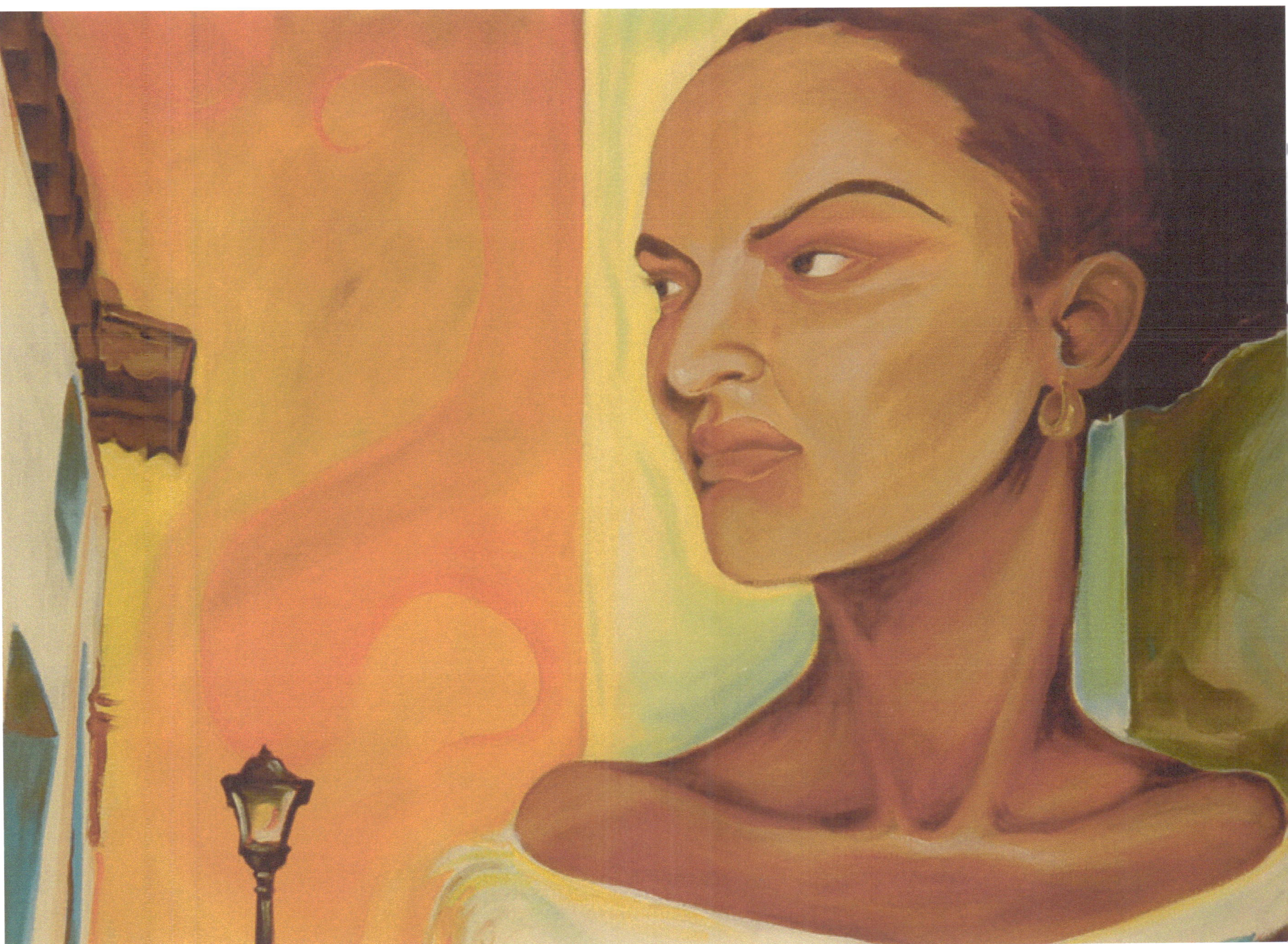

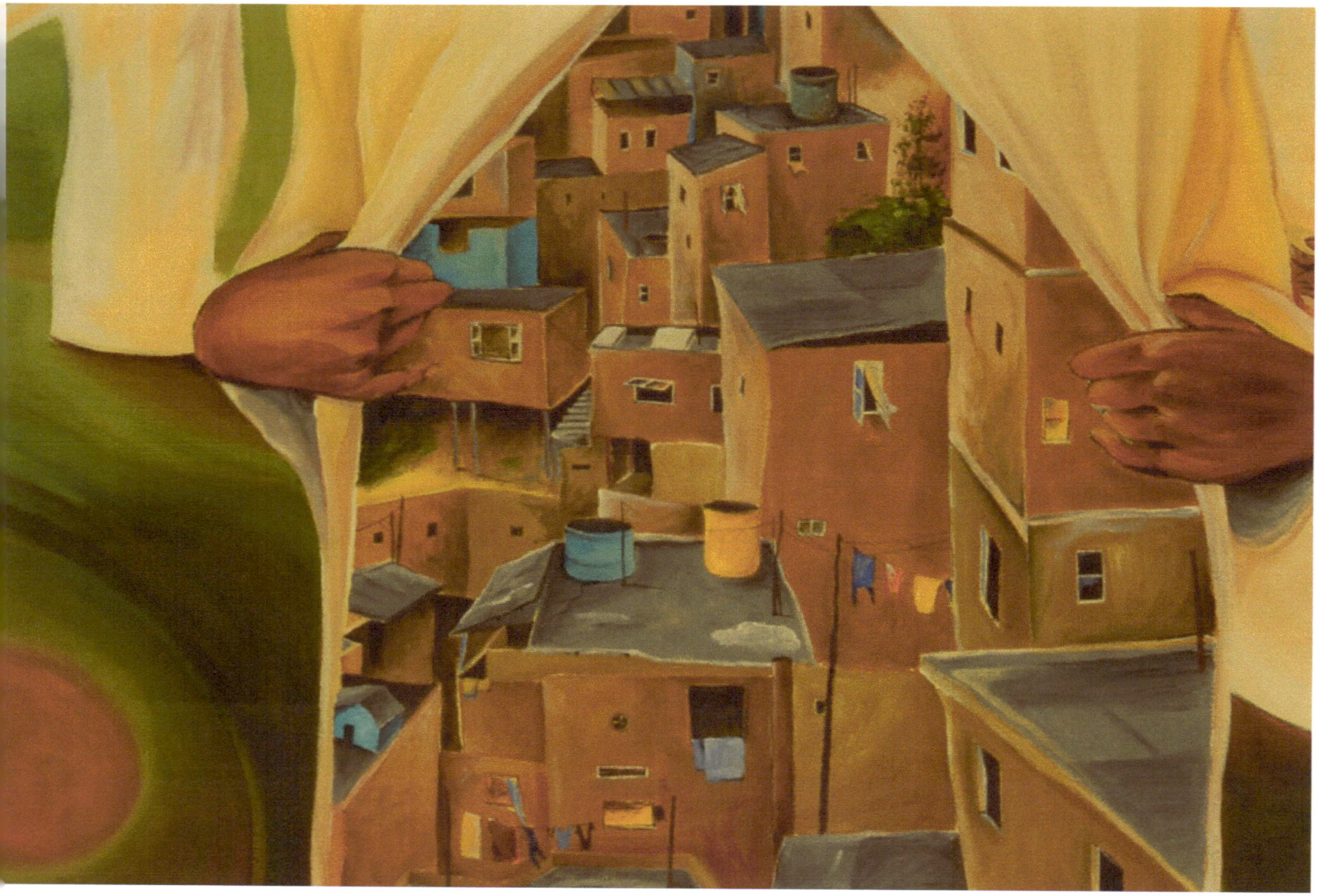

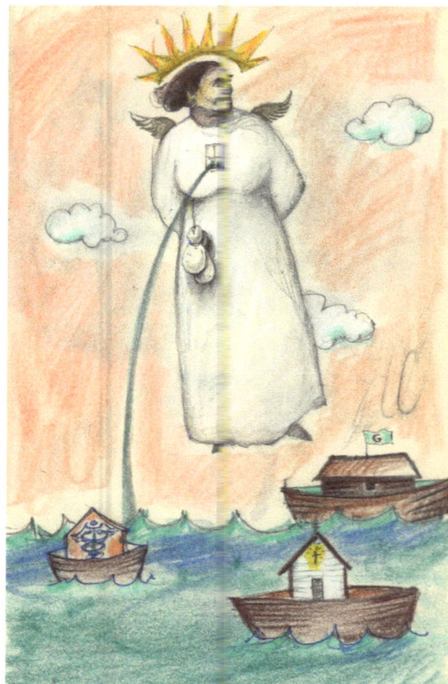

Above: Concept sketch for a commissioned portrait of the client Anthony Gooding's mother.

Left Top: Renato (Detail), acrylic on canvas, 24" x 30"

Right Top: African exhibition on view while Troy worked as The Museum Afro Brasil education staff.

Right: Renato (Detail), acrylic on canvas, 24" x 30"

Right Bottom: Troy's translator and Troy standing in the Museum with his translator Renato before a presentation.

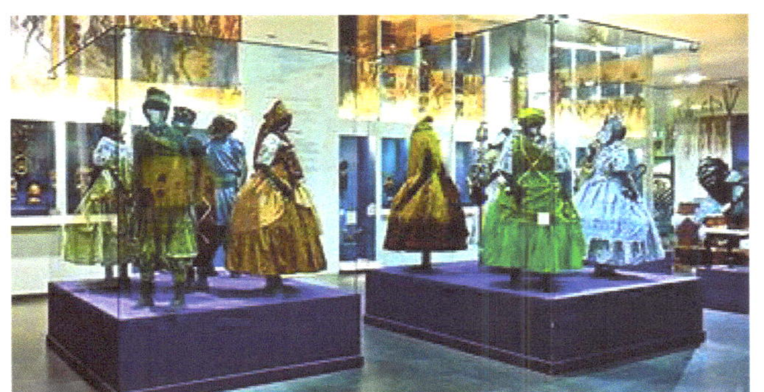

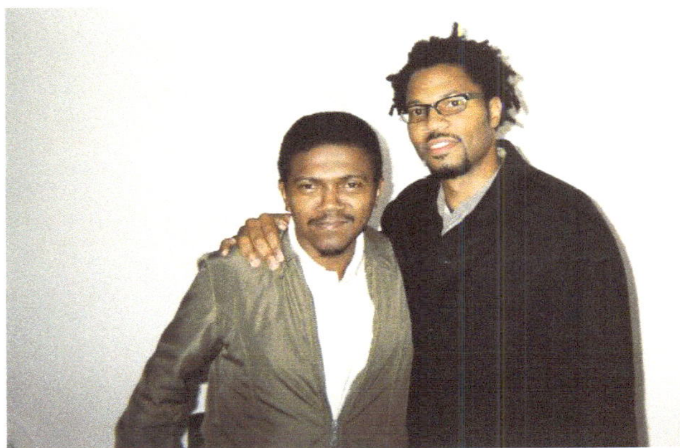

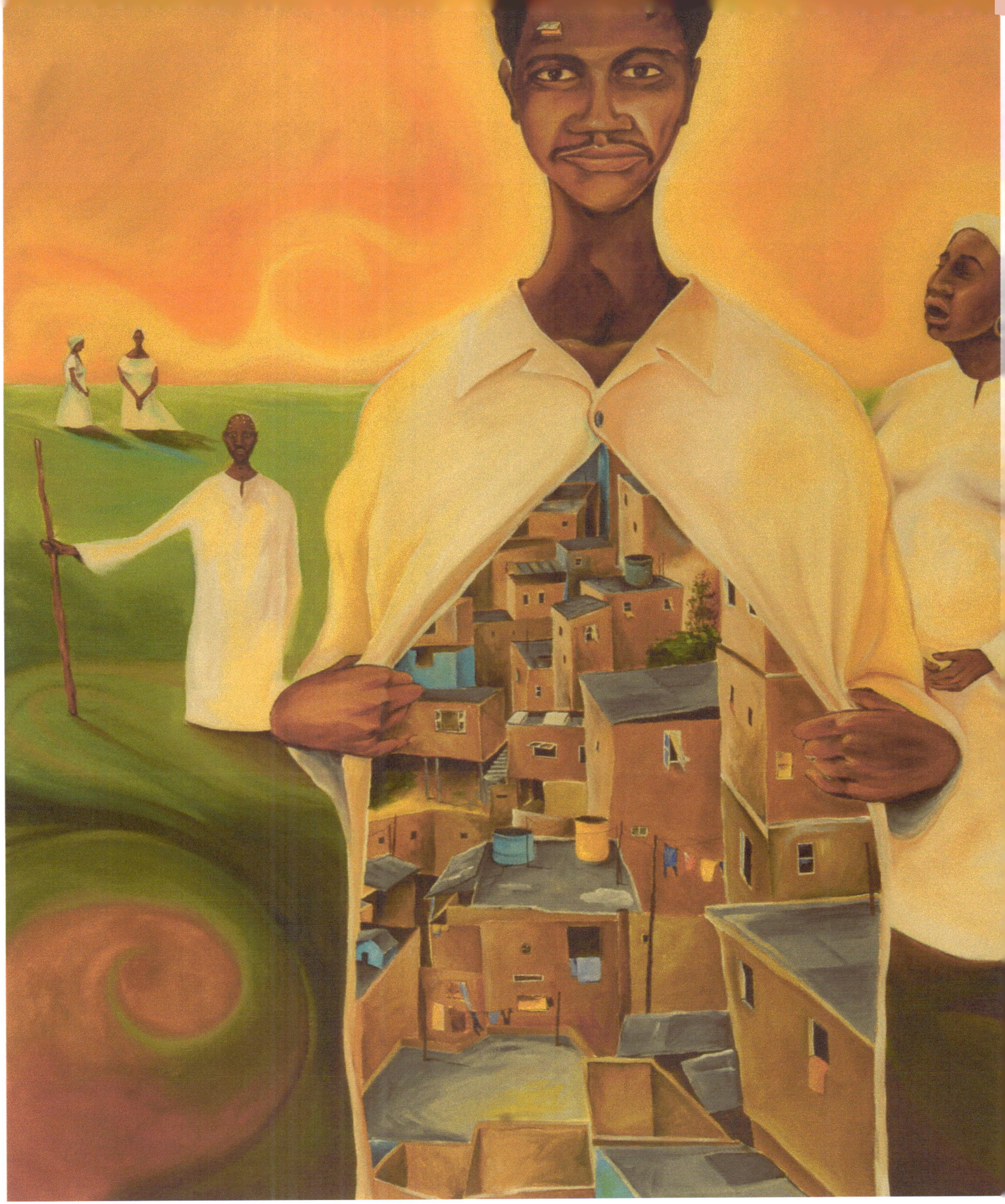

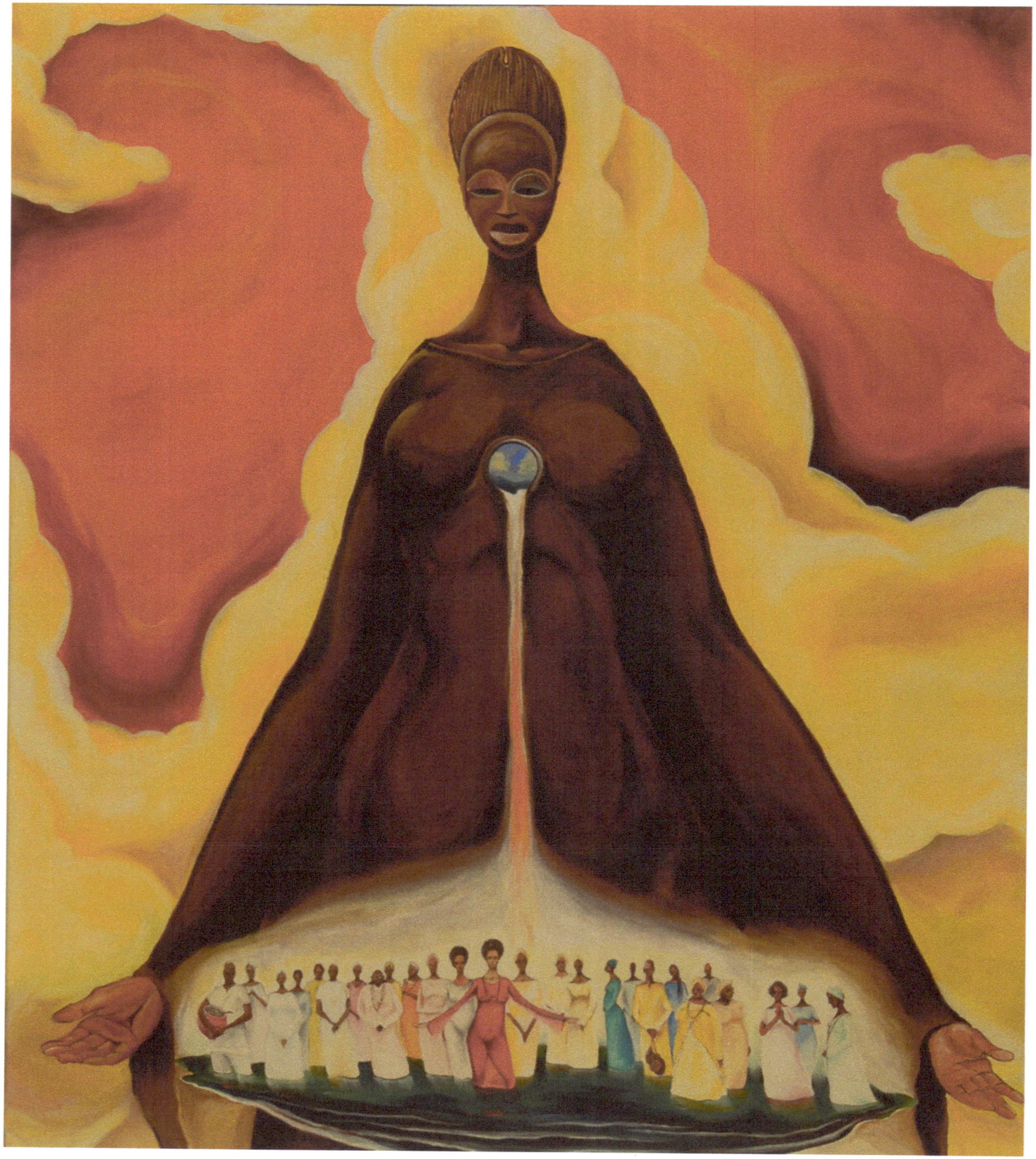

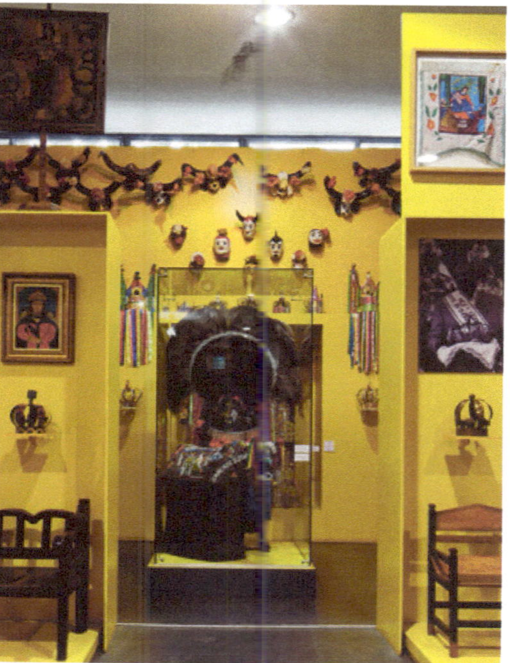

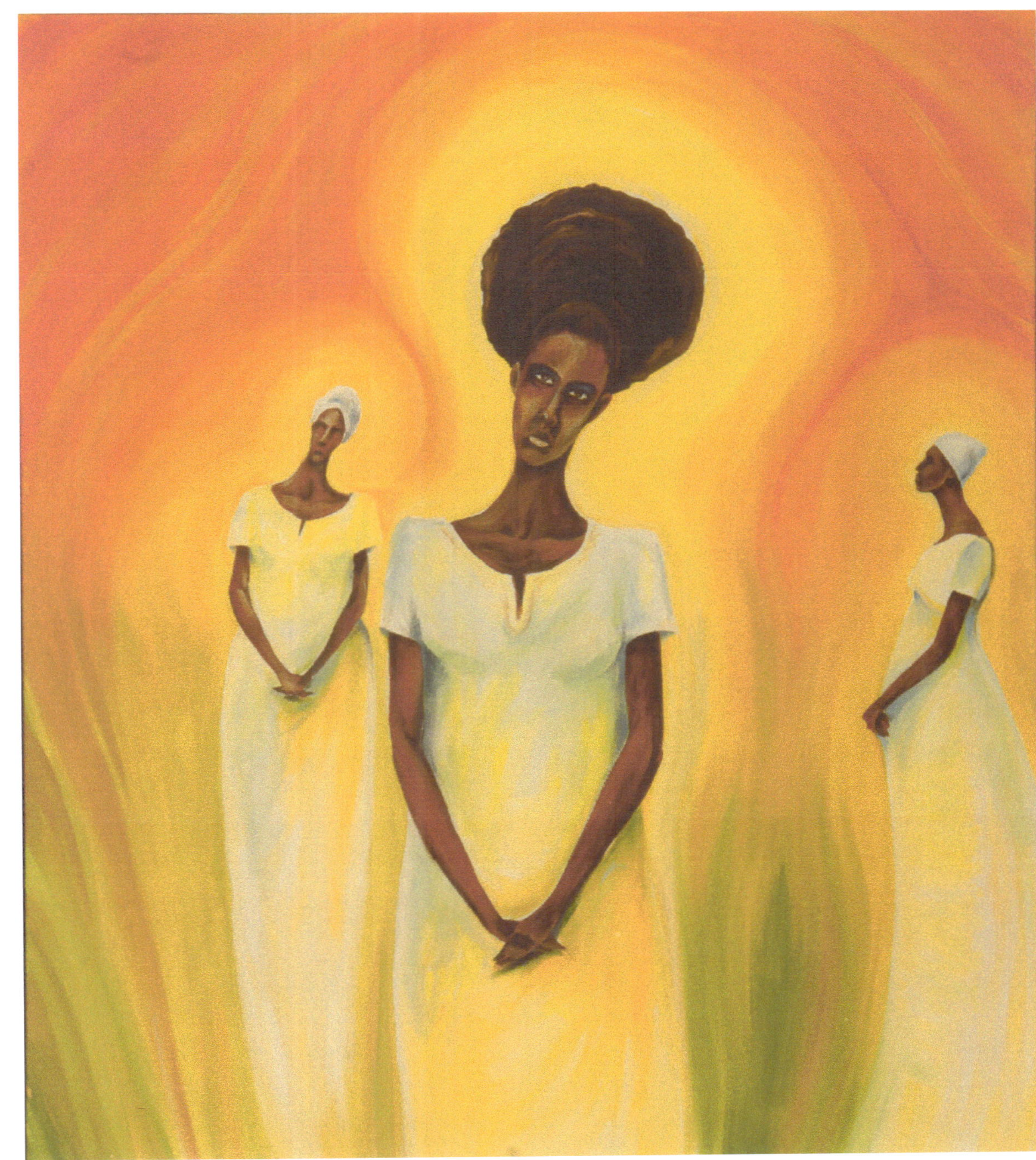

Left: 3 Elders, acrylic on canvas, 16" x 20"

Left: This is a photo from one of the exhibits at the Museum Afro Brasil while Troy was staff.

Right: 3 Elders
Acrylic on canvas, 16" x 20"

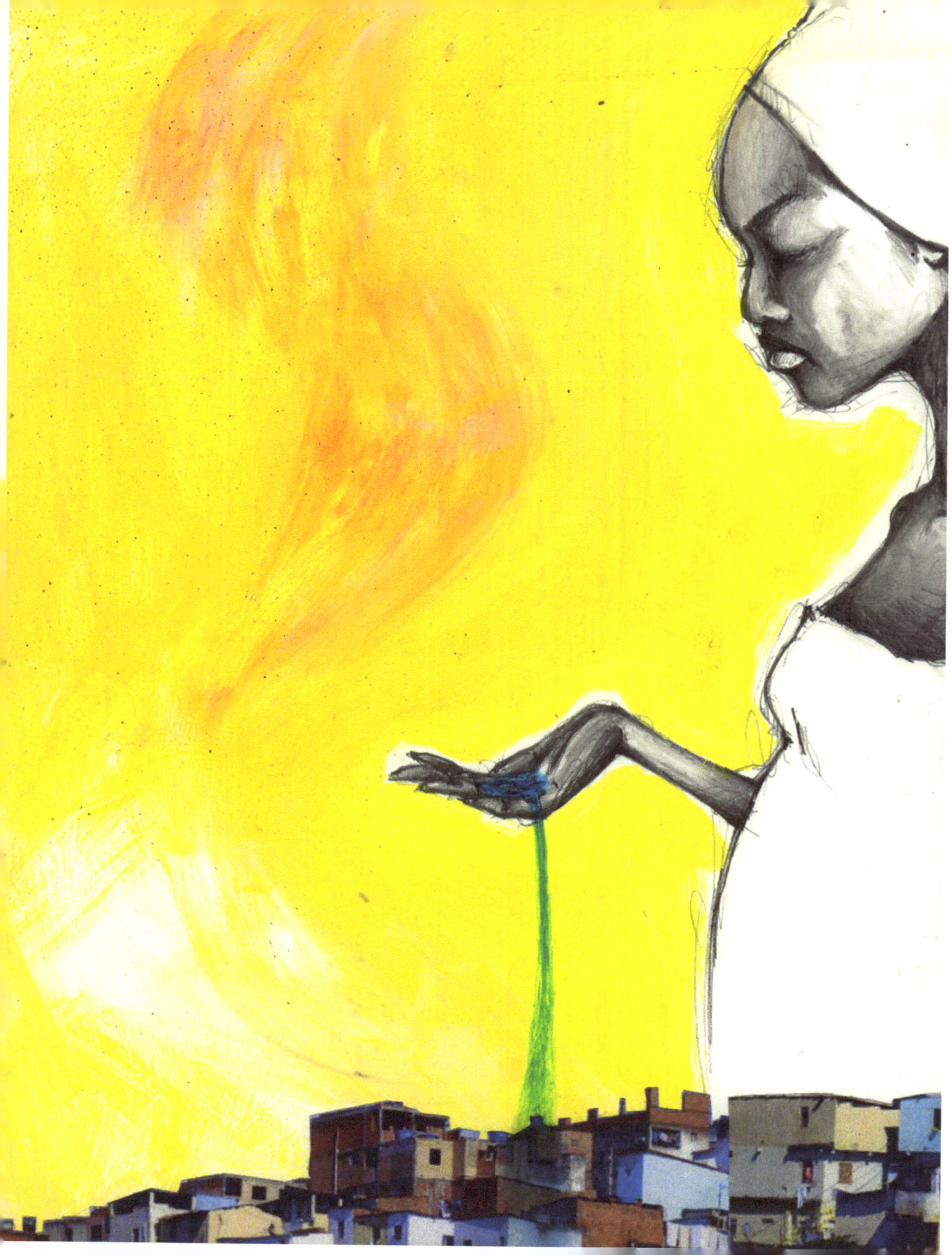

Left: 'Nourishing the Favela'
mixed media, acrylic on board, 16" x 20"

Bottom: Troy, a fellow student Jamie and a prominent
sculptor they met while in Brasil. In total there were about
four University of Cincinnati students and eight Ohio
State students on the trip.

Right: A photo of the University of Cincinnati Group visiting a local artists studio in Sao Paulo.
Troy, one of the groups translators, Ross, Caroline, the
gallery director, a professor from Ohio State, Jamie and
professor Bastos.

Right Below: Ross and Troy during our presentation as
Guest Lecturers at the Universidade Federal De Goias,
Brasil Lab School.

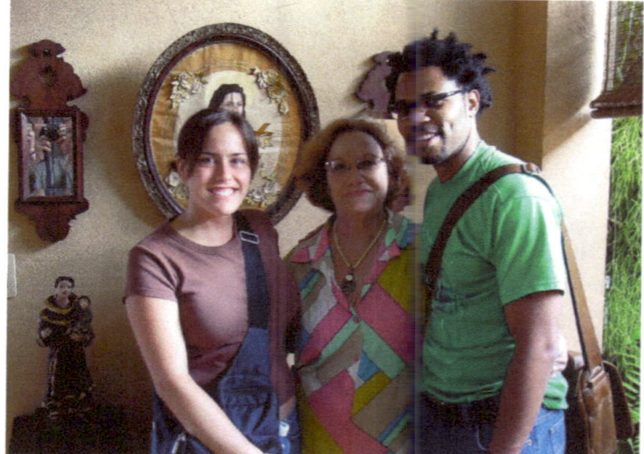

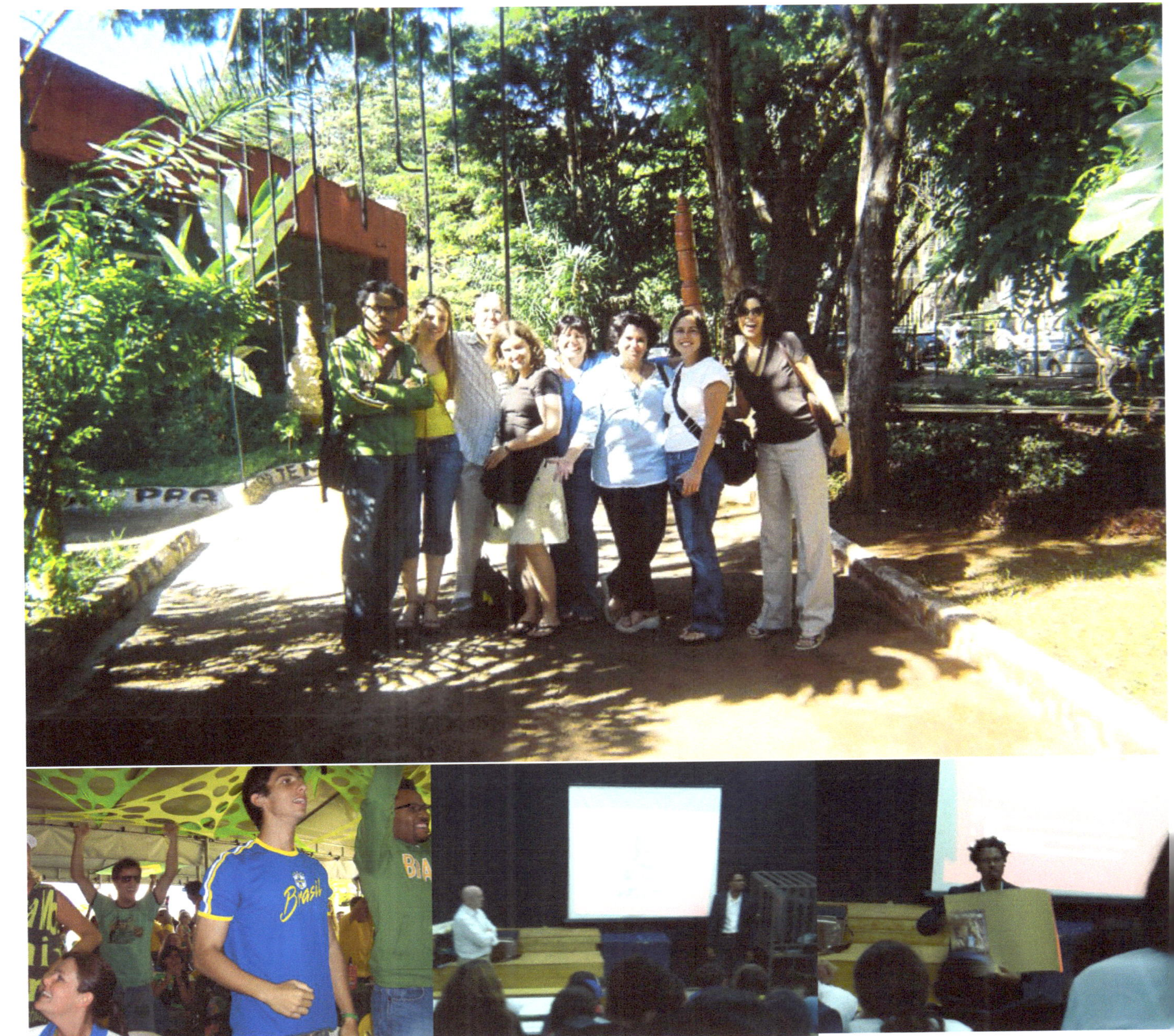

Left: Photo of the UC group while visiting a Museum in Goias, Brasil.

Left middle: The Receptionist at the Museum Afro Brasil.

Bottom: Myself with my fellow educators at the Museum.

Right: A rural town outside of Goiania, Brasil. The UC group traveled further to a farm outside the city to enjoy a traditional meal.

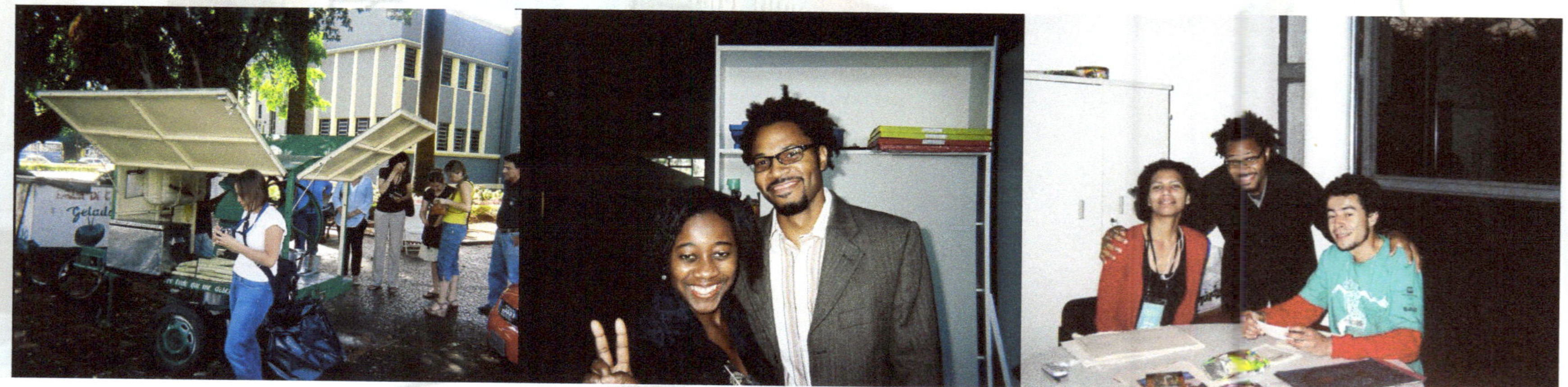

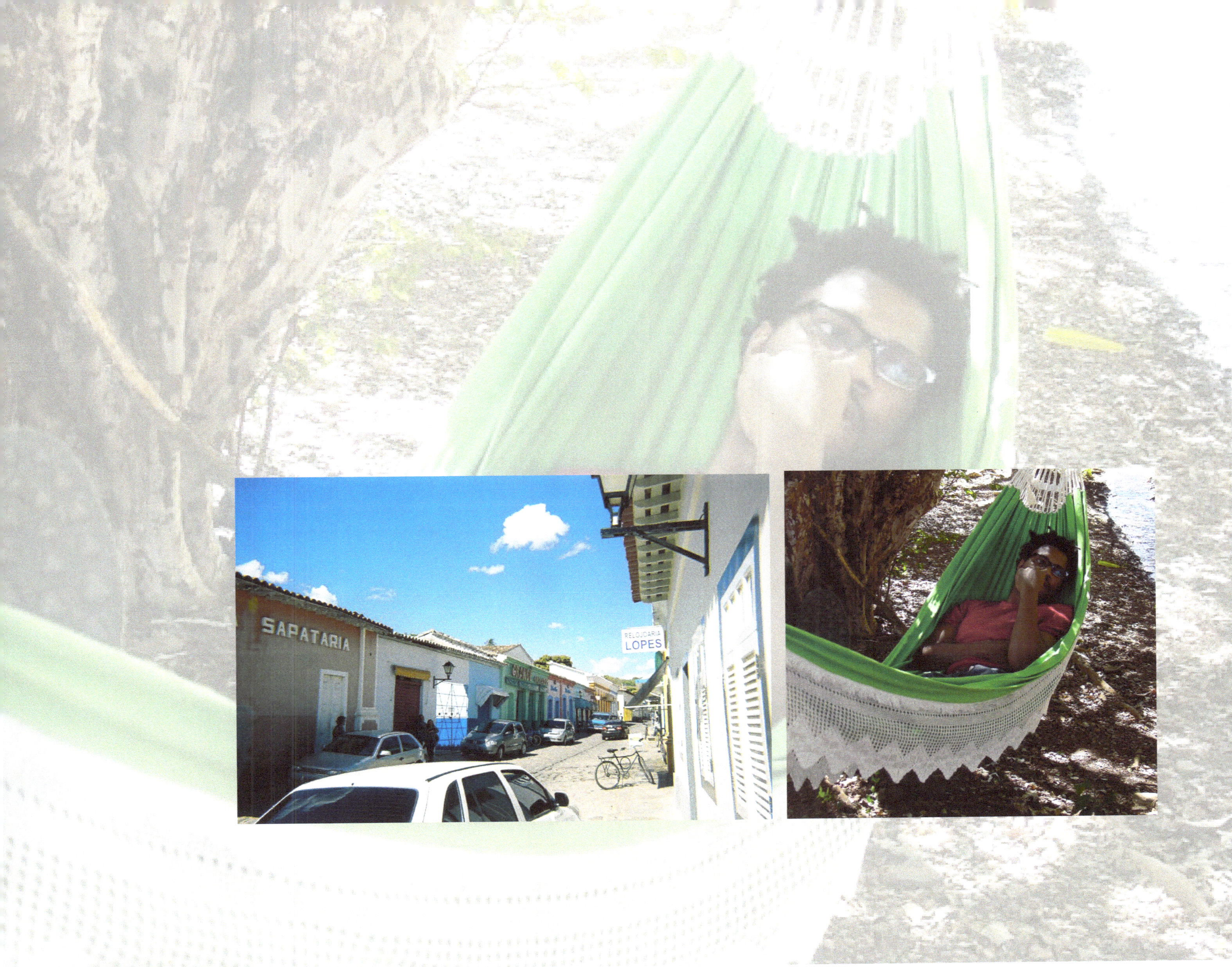
SAPATARIA
RELOJOARIA
LOPES

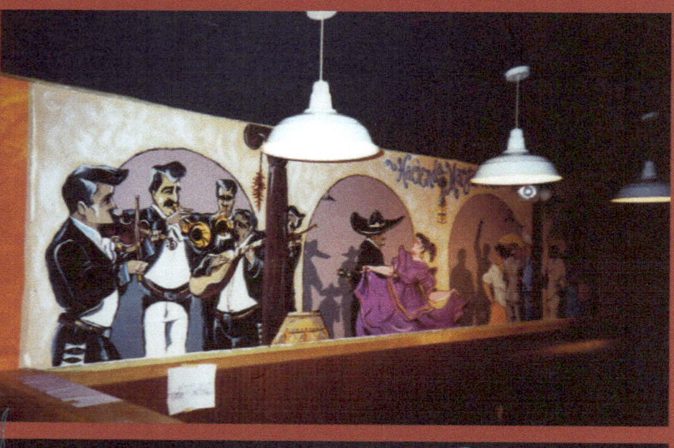

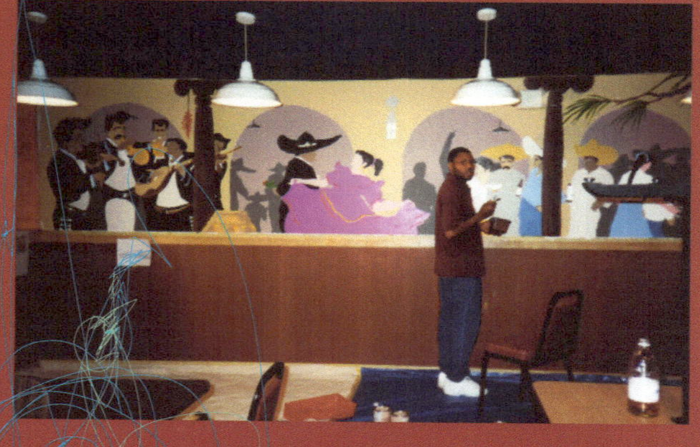

The works presented here represent a series of client-based projects from a time when I ventured out as a freelance illustrator after leaving Pipkins Design. These photos originate from murals done for a restaurant named Margaritas in Cincinnati, Ohio, and northern Kentucky. Margaritas was owned by Tony VanJohnson, who was married to Tiffany, our account executive when I worked at Pipkins Design. By this time Tony was opening his second location and he needed someone to complete the decor. It took about four to six months to complete all the components for each location, and each had a little different end product. The first two restaurants were largely mural based and influenced by traditional Mexican themes. The owner and I finally settled on a series of framed images that would go into each store. The images were inspired by photos he had taken while he spent time outside Mexico City observing the Tarahumara Indians. The framed ink-and-watercolor-wash paintings represented a much cleaner aesthetic for the restaurants, which I think he wanted. Two of the five restaurants are still in service today.

Left: Photo of Troy painting the east wall at the Florence, Kentucky location of Margaritas Restaurant.

A Pastel Mock-up (1/8 Scale) of the Margaritas Mural was done as a guide to completing the finished mural. The study was also done in the event the owner wanted to print it as wallpaper and use in other locations.

Top right: Photo of the finished mural.

Both these images are part of the prints created for Margaritas Restaurant located in Tower Place Mall in Downtown Cincinnati.

Right: Lone Mariachi
Pen & ink on watercolor paper, 12" x 14"

Bottom: Pen & ink 8" x 10"

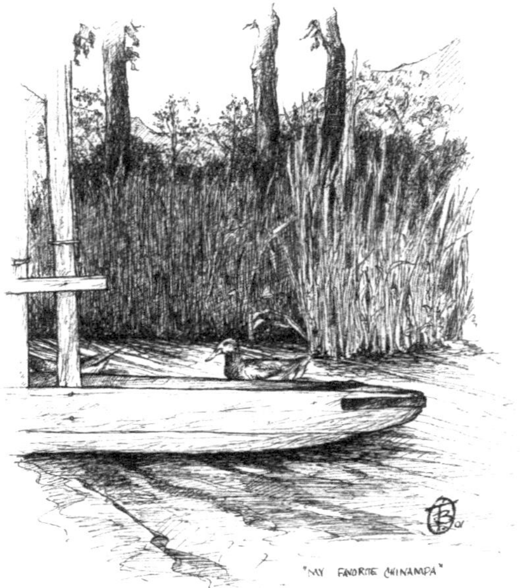

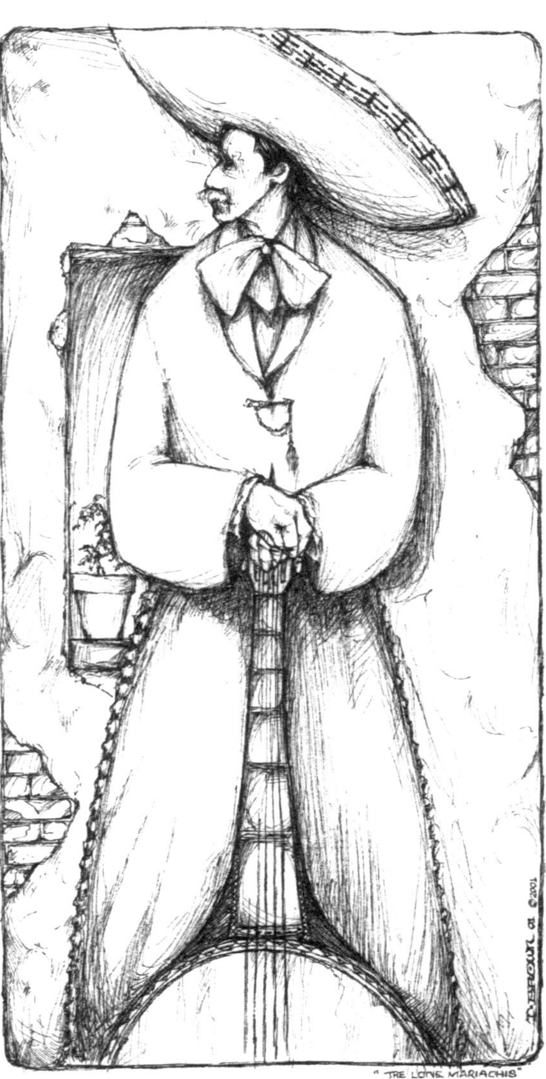

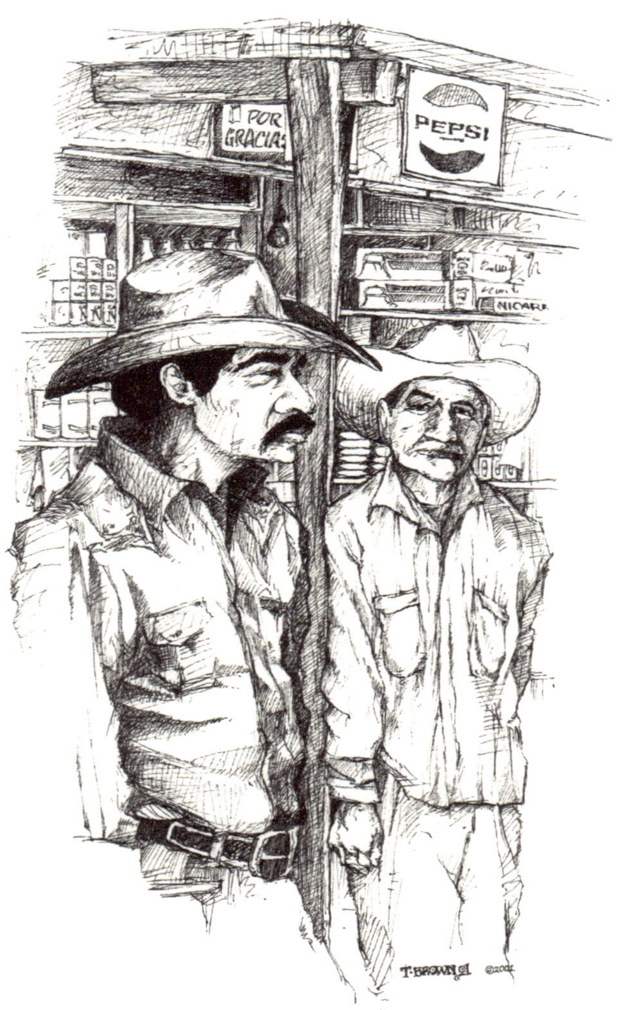

POR
GRACIAS
PEPSI
T·BROWN·01 ©2002

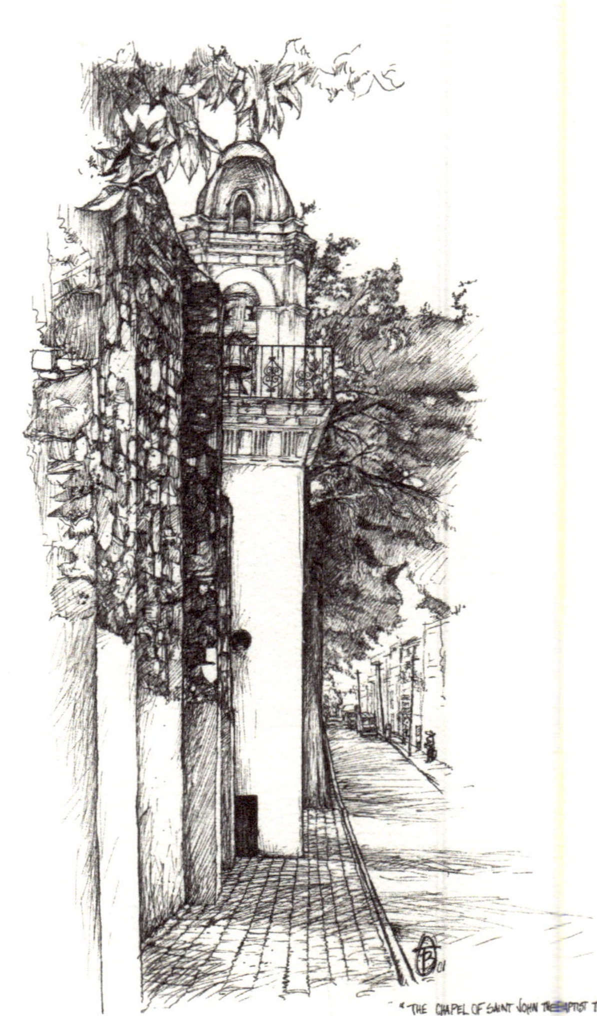

"THE CHAPEL OF SAINT JOHN THE BAPTIST TBATENCHI"
IN XOCHIMIL, MEXICO

Left: The Gringos
Pen & Ink on watercolor paper

Left: The Chapel in Mexico
Pen & Ink on watercolor paper

Right Bottom: Photos of the Tower Place Mall in Downtown
Cincinnati while I was working on the murals for Margaritas
Restraurants.

Right: 'My Drum'
Pen & Ink, watercolor wash.
This was one of the framed prints that also hung in the Tower
Place Mall in Downtown Cincinnati restraurant.

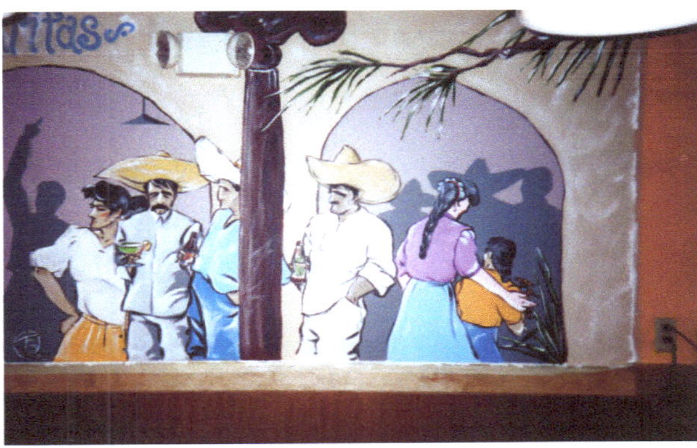

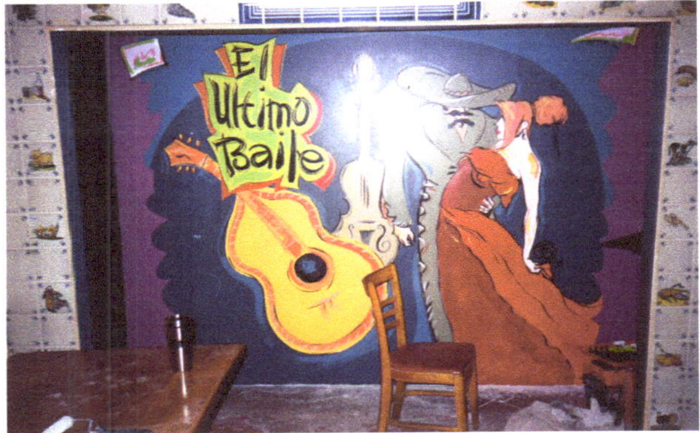

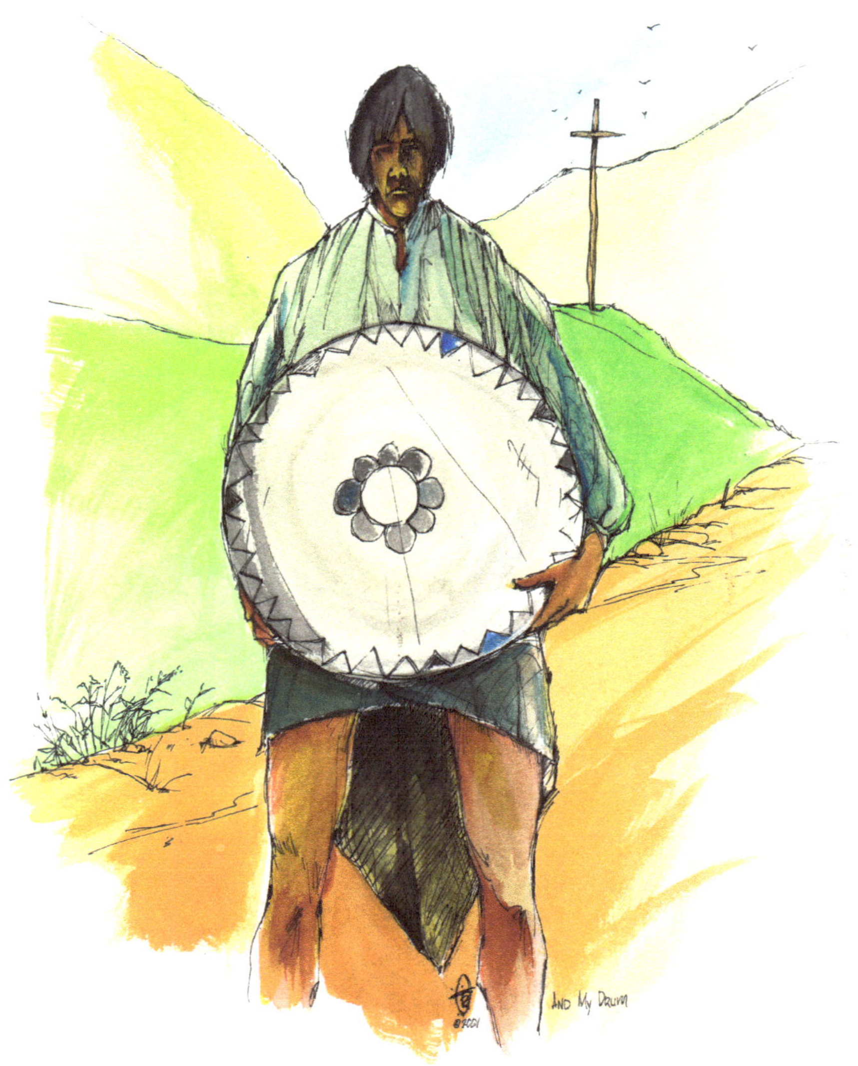

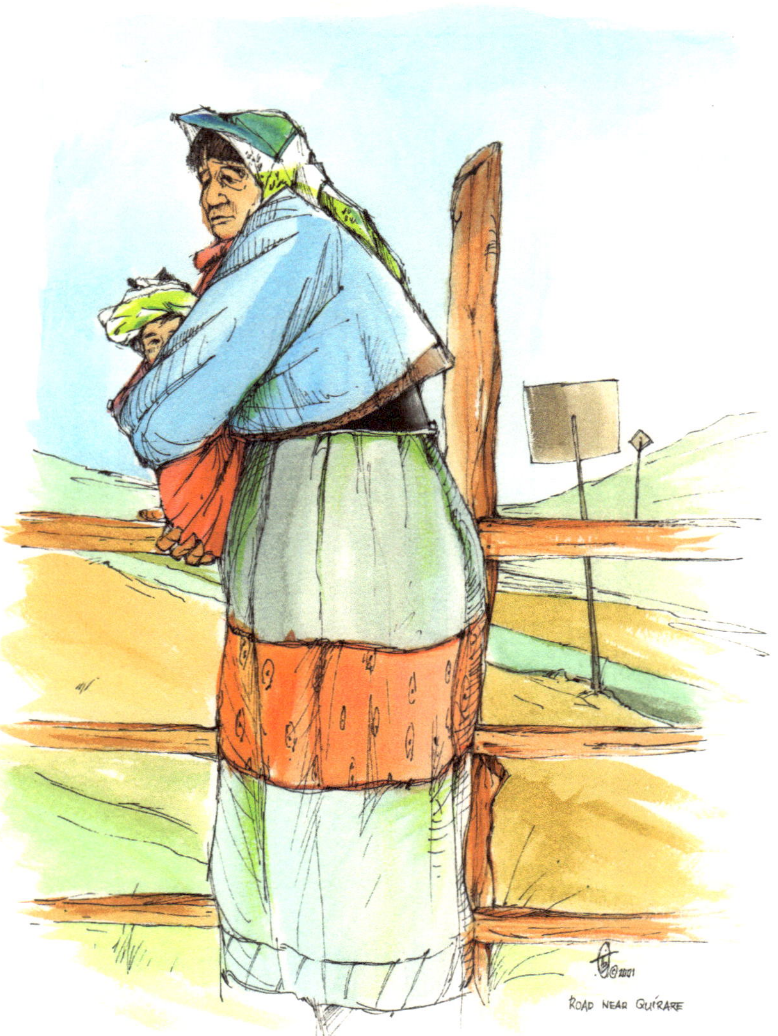

Left: Another framed print that was created for Maragaritas Restraurant, Eigth St. location, downtown, Cincinnati.
Pen & ink, water color wash.

Bottom: A photo of the framed prints after they were installec in the restraurant.

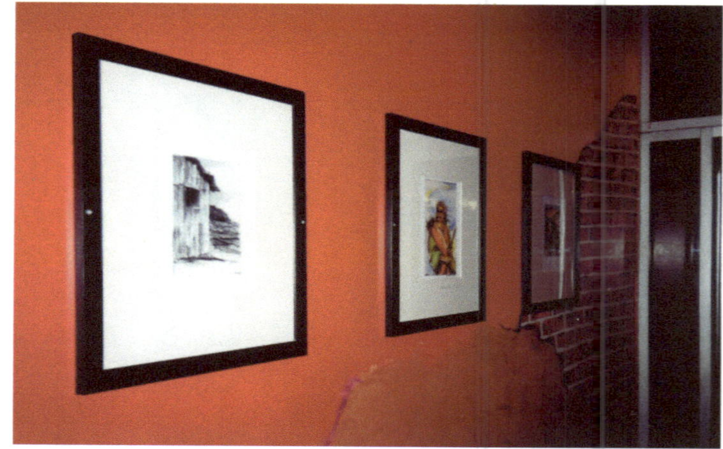

Left: 'The O d Mexican' Another framed print that was created for Maragaritas Restraurant, Tower Place Mall in Downtown Cincinnati. Pen & ink, wate- color wash.

Bottom: A photo of the framed prints after they were installed in the restraurant.

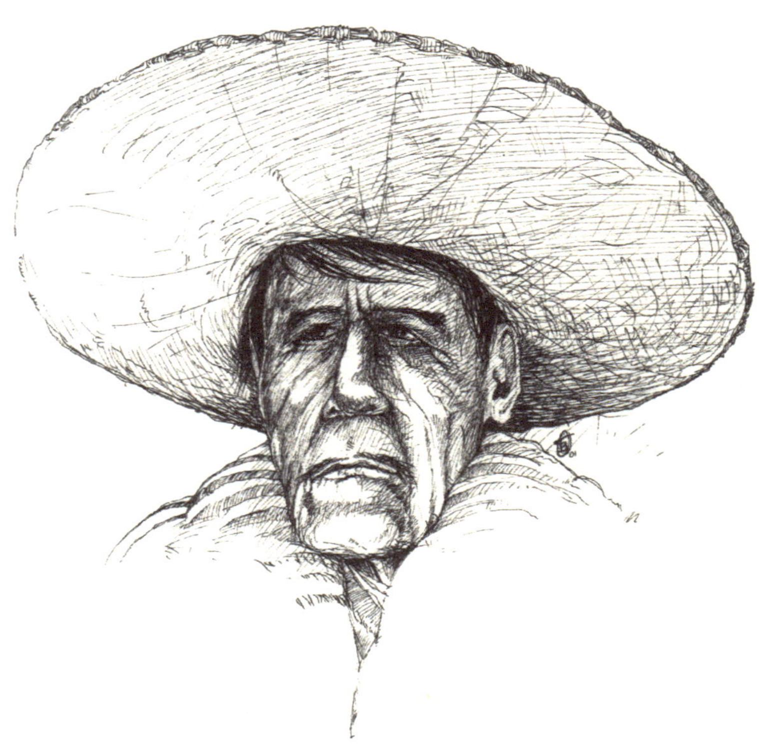

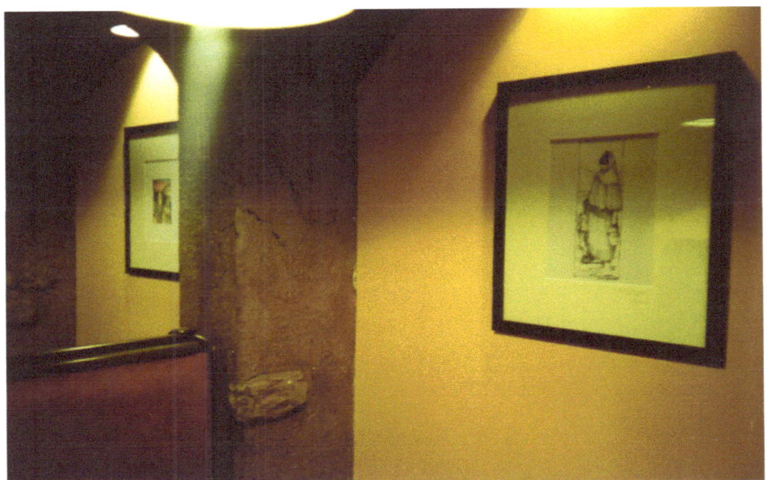

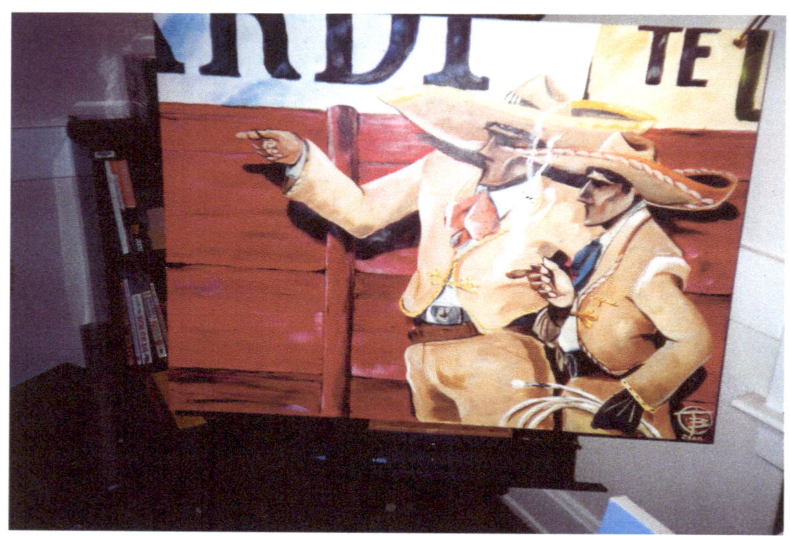

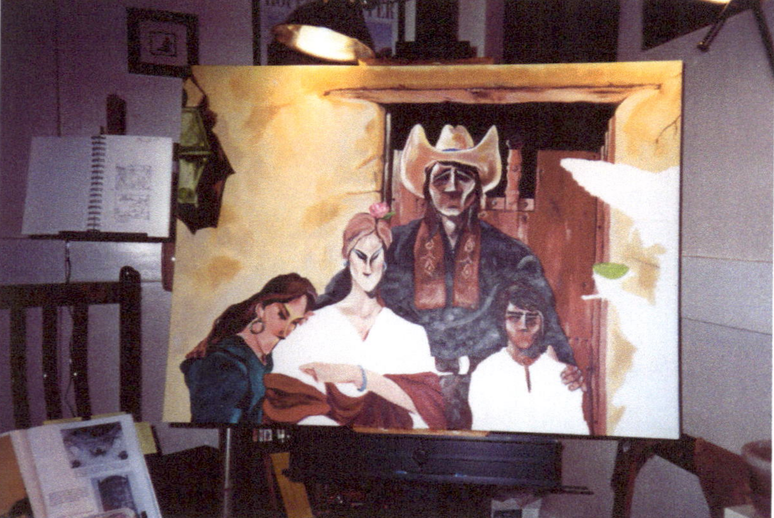

Left: Two paintings were also created for Maragaritas Restraurant, Florence, Kentucky location.
Acrylic on canvas. Both painting were 40" x 30."

Right: Another framed print that was created for Maragaritas Restrau*r*t,
Tower Place Mall in Downtown Cincinnati.
Pen & ink, water color wash.
The owner wanted Troy to capture the railroad history and tradition in Mexico.

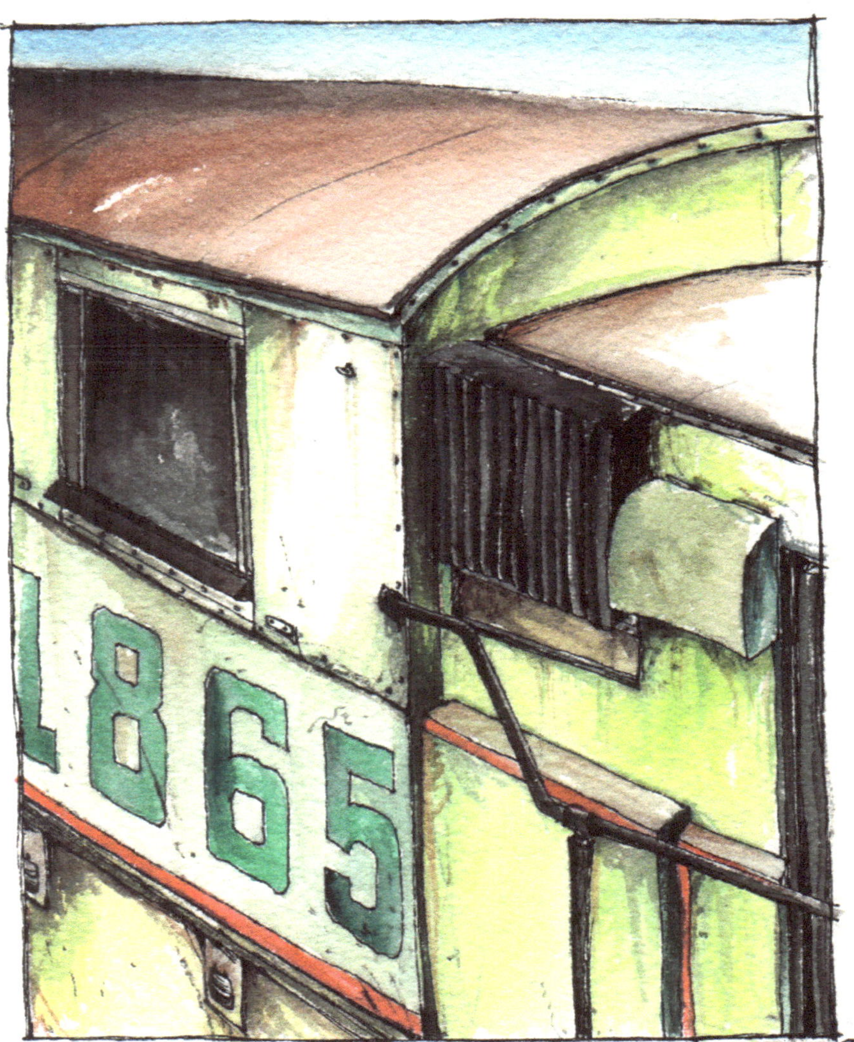

Engine 1865, from Los Mochis.

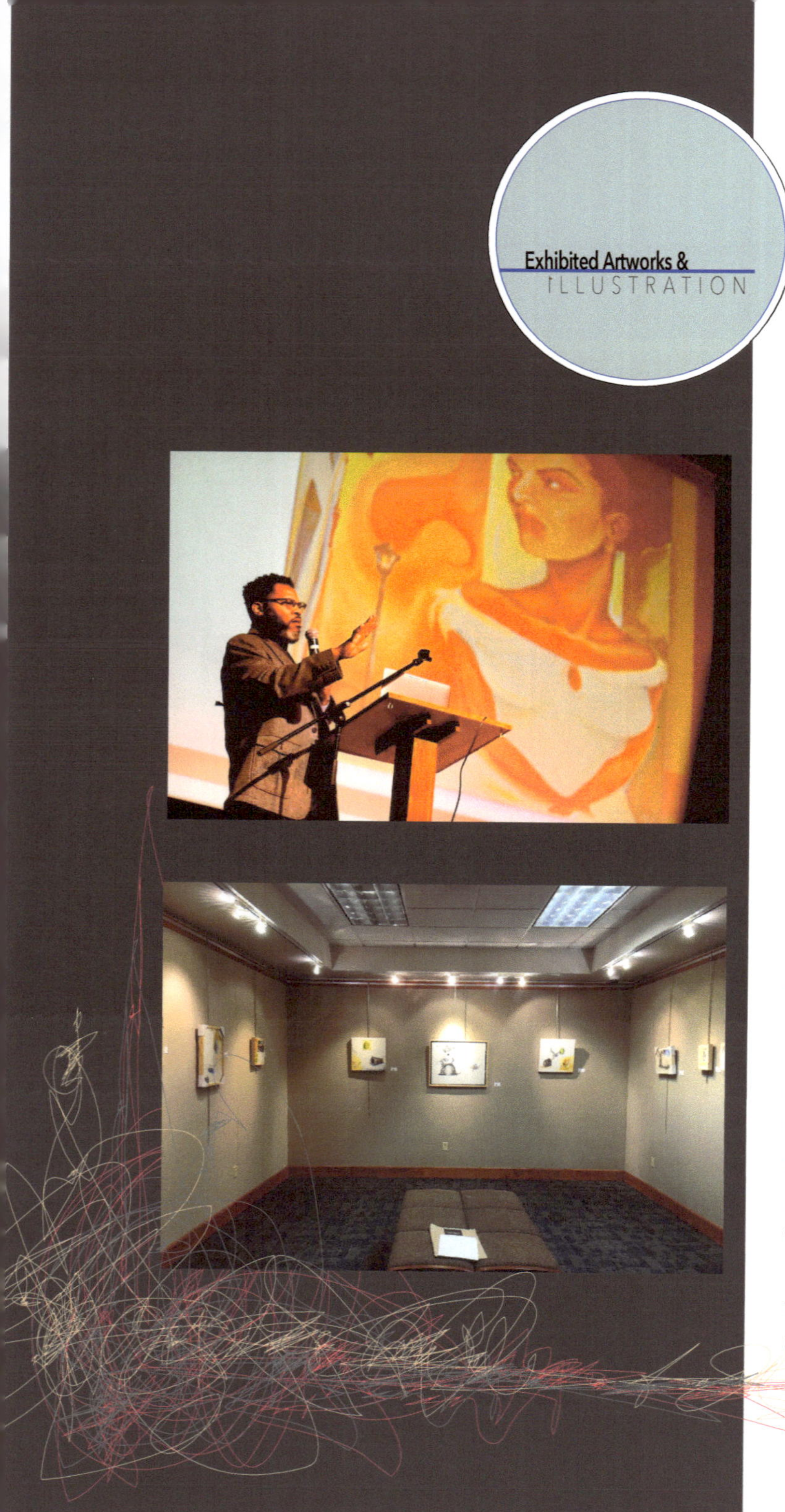

Troy Brown brings art and advice to Maryville College

Maryville College Publication - The Highland Echo, Founded in 1915
Sarah Cardell March 2019

On Monday, Feb. 25, Troy Brown inspired students and faculty members alike through sharing his story of personal growth as an artist with charisma and enthusiasm.

This was only the first event of Brown's stay at Maryville College as the week-long artist-in-residence, and it surely left all wishing he could stay a week longer.

Brown currently works as an art professor at the North Carolina Central University and illustrates his own children's books. He and his wife own their own publishing company, Brown Sugar Press Books, and have experienced much success.

"It's so nice to be your own publisher!" Brown said. "You can print your books exactly how you want and when you want." Brown has published four books thus far, which have sold in Indie book festivals all around the world. He wrote his first book, Lois and the Red Balloon, about his mother.

"My mom made a lot of sacrifices for me to be where I am today. I felt like she deserved to be the subject of my first book project," Brown said. Personal, sentimental connections like these can be found in all of Brown's art.

"Everybody is walking around with their own little worlds of memories and experiences and emotions," Brown said. "I want to look for stories of people everywhere I go and put them in my work."

His earliest freelance professional works were promotional posters for the Fifth Third Bank Jazz Series Collection, which all depicted jazz musicians with distinct character and energy. These posters used vivid colors and exaggerated the musicians' hands and lips and feet, giving the work a dynamic, unexpected impression—much like the impression that jazz music leaves.

"I really liked the response I got from these posters," Brown said. "People were even stealing them right out of bus shelter advertisement bulletin boards all over the city! I knew I must've made those people feel something."

Left Top: Photos taken during exhibition at Maryville College, TN and the Saul Alexander Gallery, Charleston, SC.

Left: Photo from *The Memoirs and Memory Exhibition* at Saul Alexander Gallery inside The Charleston Public Library.

Right: 'Old Merc 2,' Mixed media on board, 16' x 20"

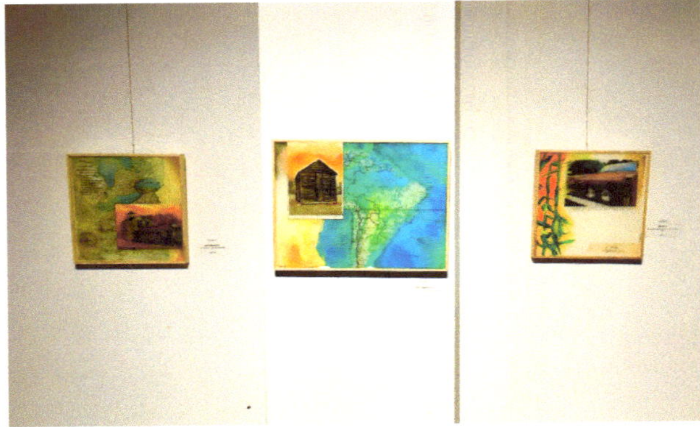

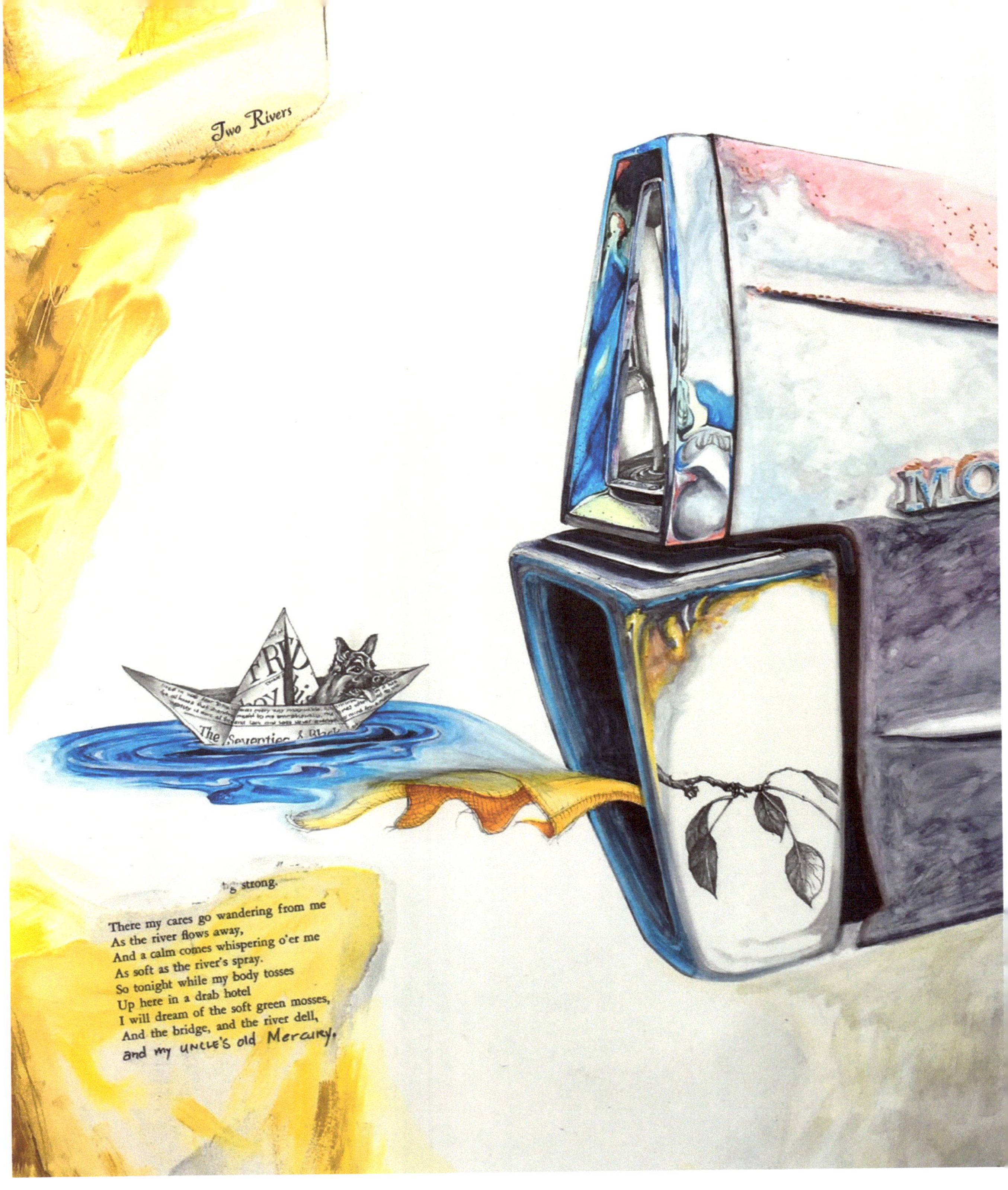

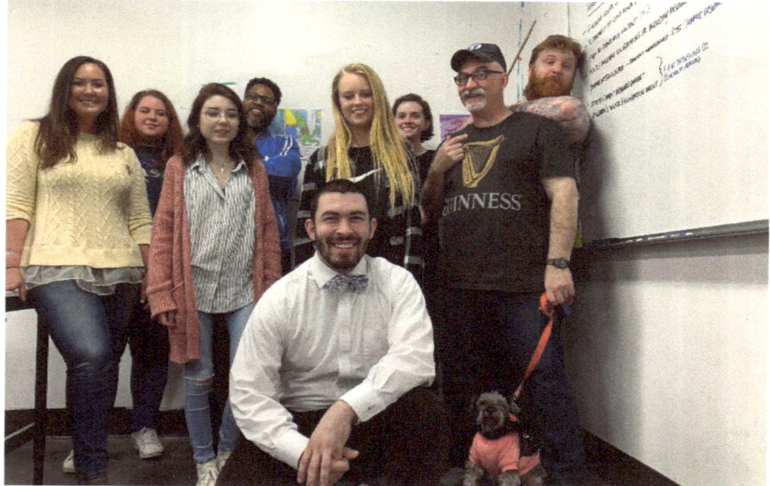

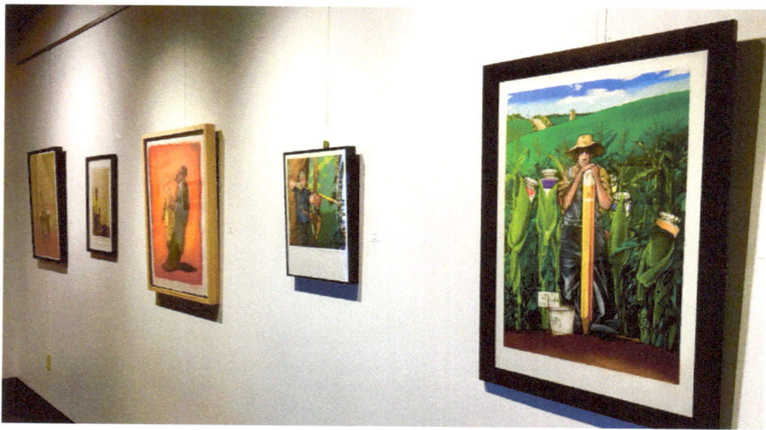

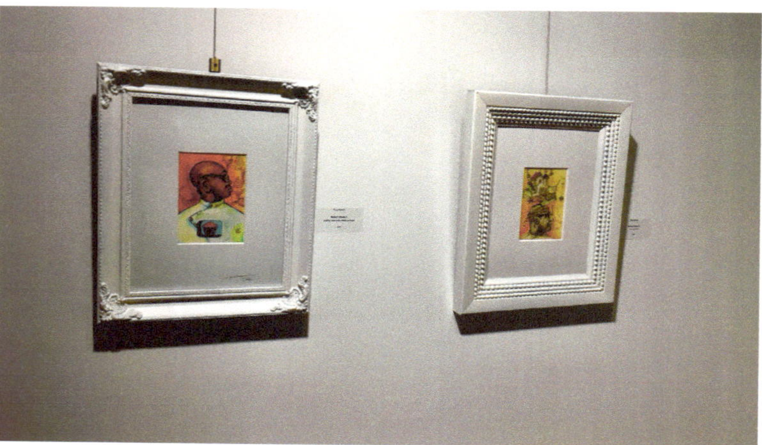

A later series of paintings were reflective of Brown's experiences while on a trip to Brazil, and, again, his goal was to reveal some level of the subject's character and evoke a personal emotional response from the viewer.

For example, in the painting Renato, a Brazilian man opens his shirt to reveal a scene from a favela, or a ghetto, which indicates that the experiences he's had in this certain area has shaped who he is on the inside.

Brown continued to play with this kind of pictorial storytelling when he moved to North Carolina. He was intrigued by old wooden Appalachian barns and homes and often drove around town just to take pictures of the rural structures.

He later photo-transferred these images onto materials such as aquaboards, and then combined them with snippets of old poems salvaged from an antique book store selling the works of regional writers.

Harley White, a junior psychology major, enjoyed this series of Brown's work the most because they themselves write poetry and felt that they were able to connect better with the art that had words accompanying the images.

"It was an amazing experience to actually meet the artist. I felt like I appreciated the art even more after hearing the thoughts of the guy who created it," said White.

Brown dedicated his time on campus to meeting with students for individual art critiques and hosting workshops. He did, additionally, have some wise words he wanted to share with the general audience of Maryville College.

"Accept your personal story. Be open to it, let it shape you. And then share it with others. Because when people share themselves through their art or even just through a conversation, they contribute to this sea of rich stories that gives people the chance to connect with each other."

Photos taken at Maryville College, TN during Troy's residency. Maryville students that participated in Troy's the children's book workshop during the residency.

Left: The artist in Saul Alexander Gallery, standing in front of Branches of Memory
Ink, color pencil on 140 Lana paper

Right: Old Merc 1
Mixed media, photo transfer, hand colored in resin.

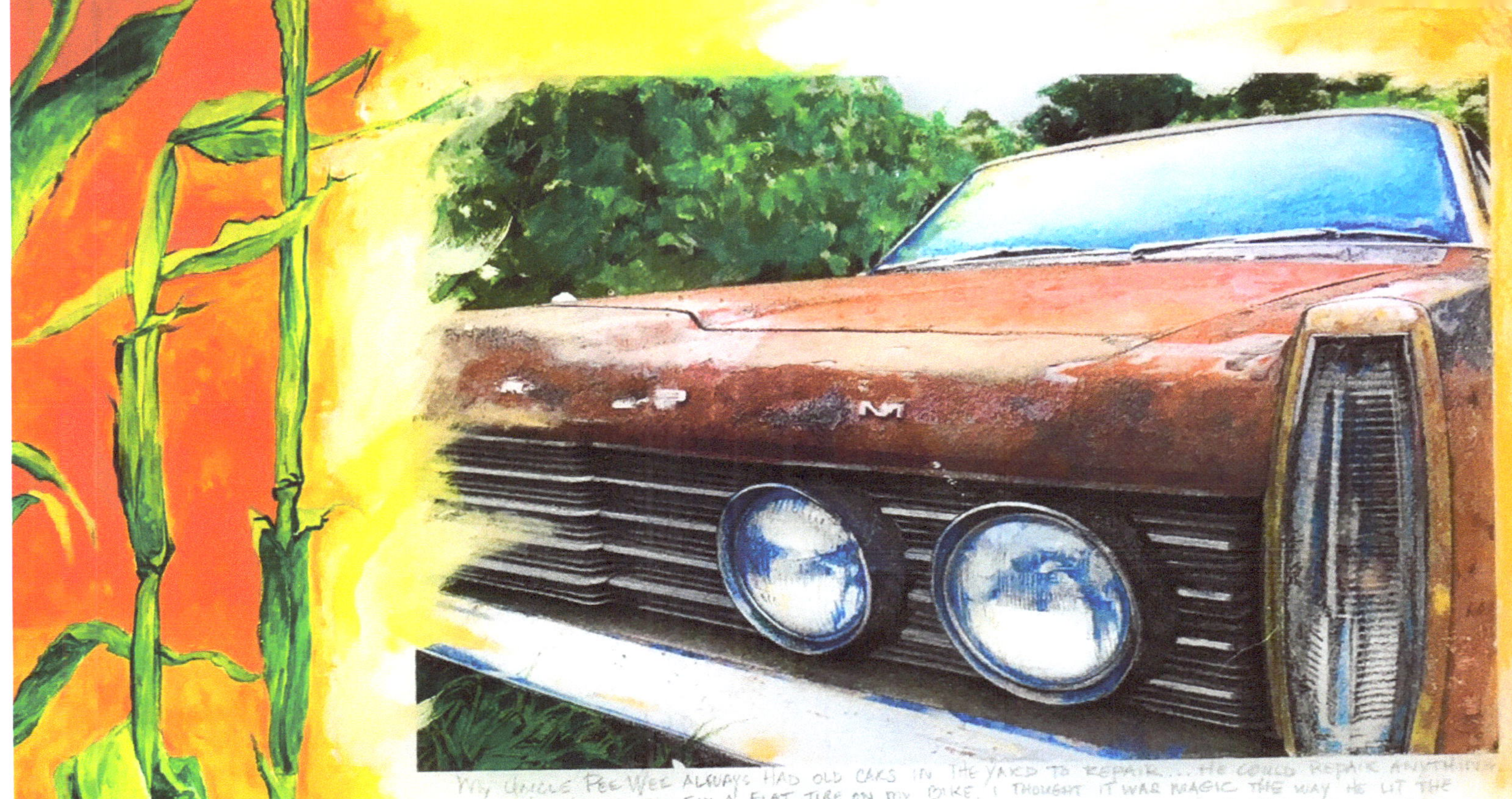

MY UNCLE PEE WEE ALWAYS HAD OLD CARS IN THE YARD TO REPAIR....HE COULD REPAIR ANYTHING. HE HELPED ME FIX A FLAT TIRE ON MY BIKE, I THOUGHT IT WAS MAGIC THE WAY HE LIT THE FLAME ON THE GLUE. THANKS UNCLE FOR THOSE LITTLE SLICES OF MEMORY MAGIC.

Boy
v
MEMORIES

They bring forth nostalgic memories
Of my ~~girl~~hood days at my Grandmother's:

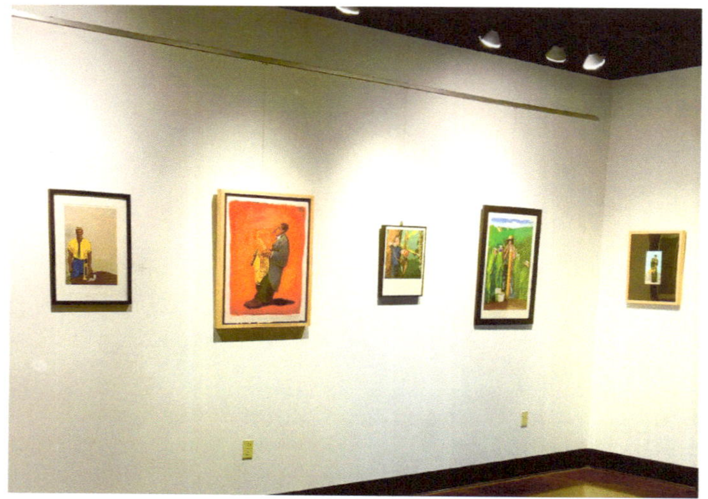

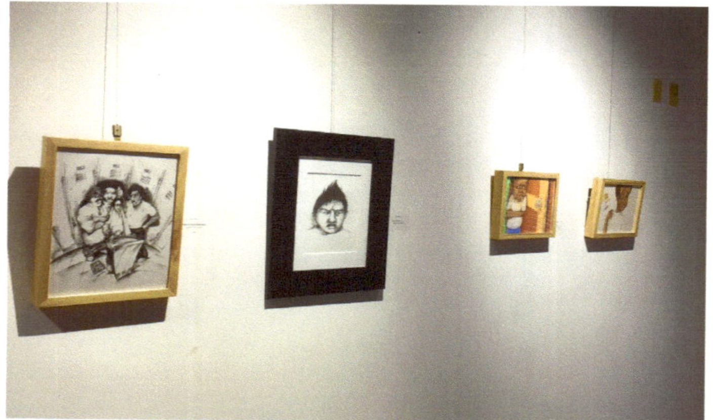

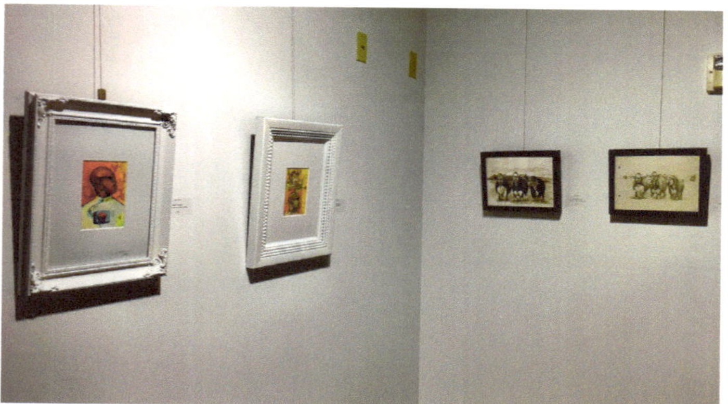

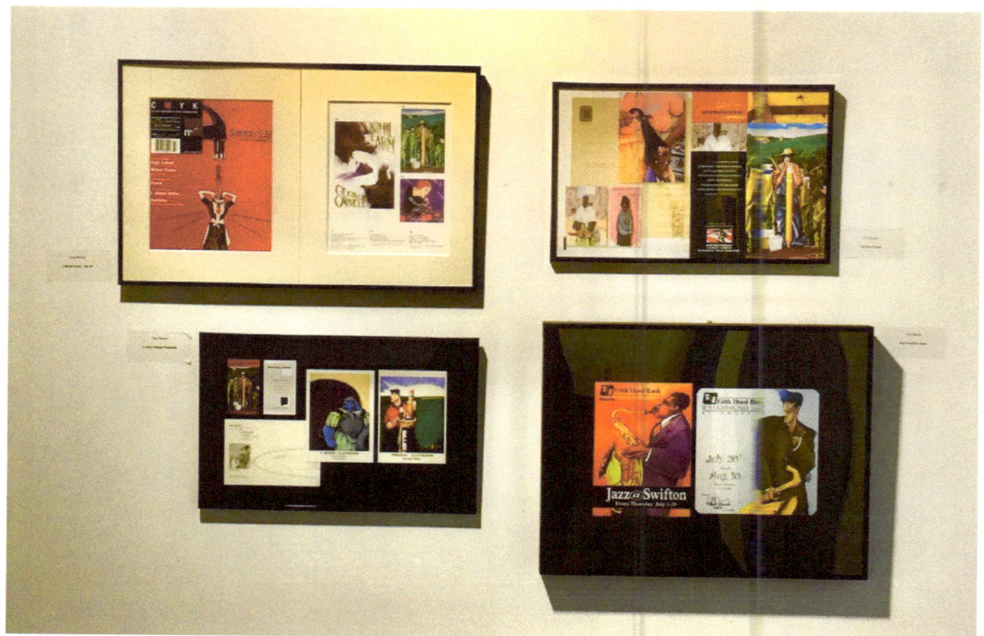

Photos taken during exhibits at Maryville College, TN.

Right: Barn Thoughts 2
Mixed media, water soluble oils, photo transfer hand colored, clock
components, 12" x 12" on Board

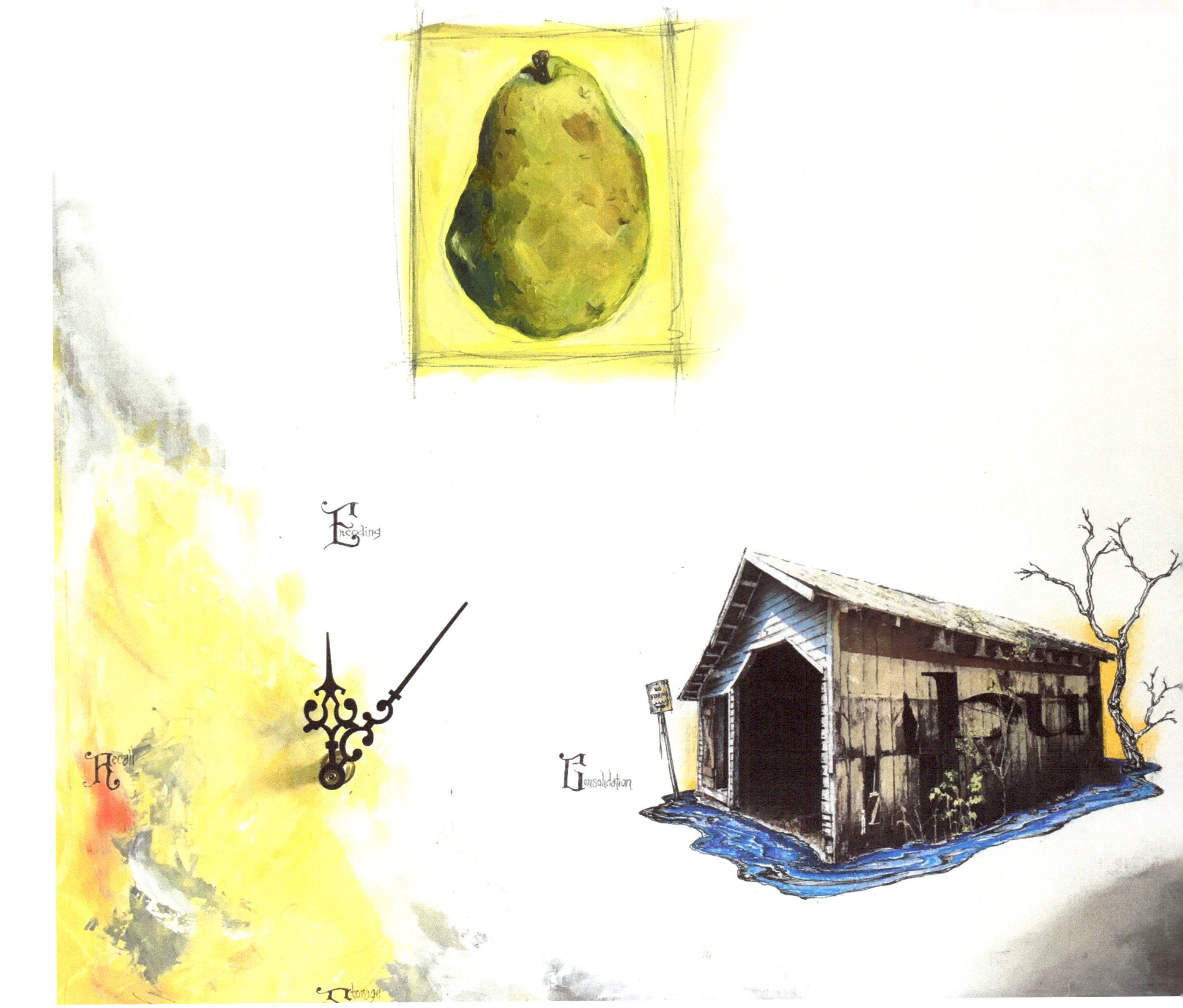

Encoding
Recall
Storage
Consolidation

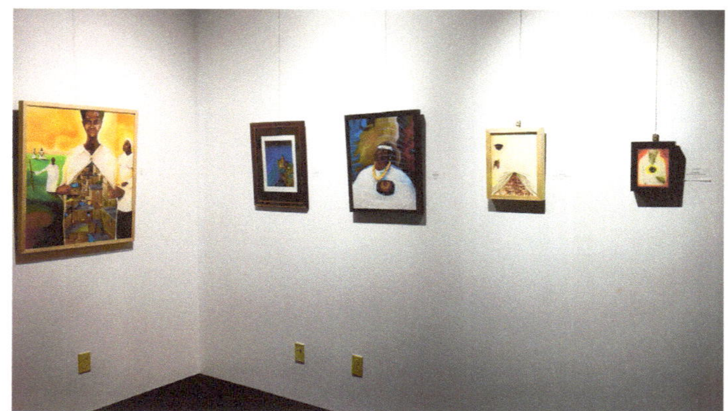

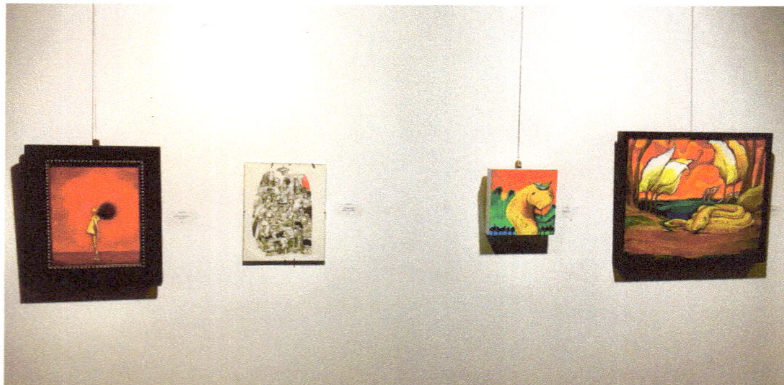

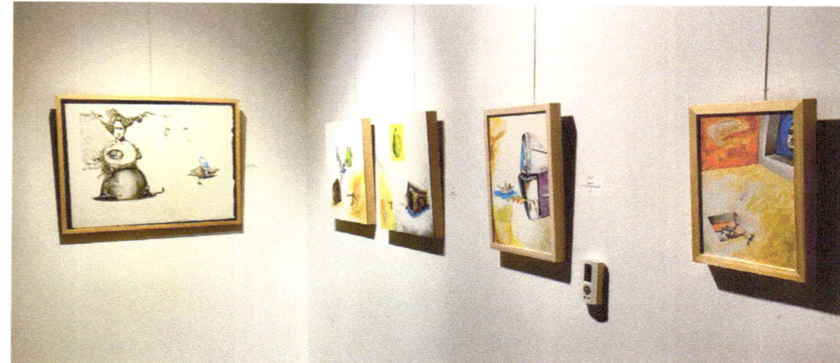

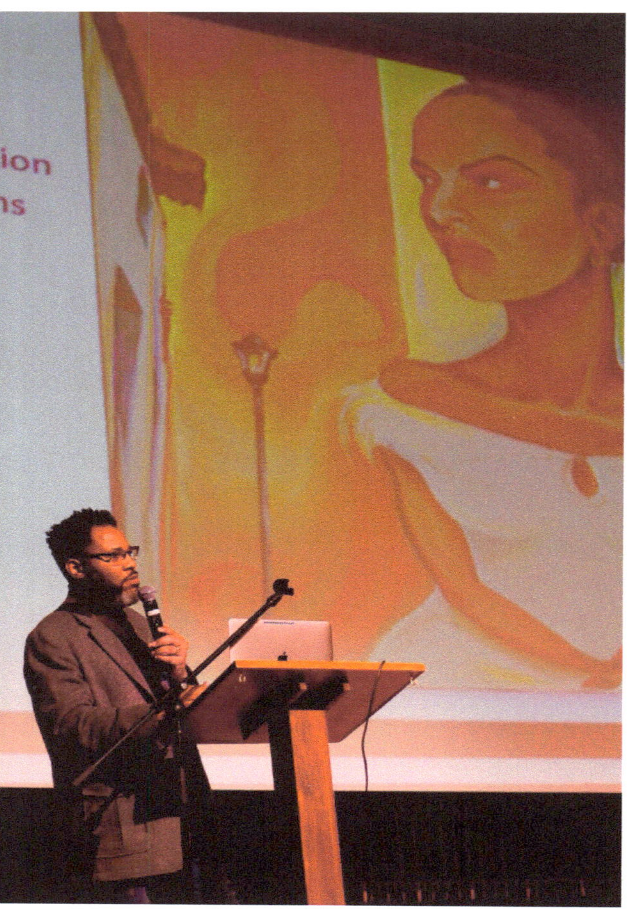

Above: Troy lecturing during the Maryville College Residency.
Photos taken during exhibit and residency at Maryville College, TN.

Barn Thoughts 1
Mixed media, water soluble oils, photo transfer hand colored, clock components
12" x 12" on Board

Previous page: Barn Thoughts 2
Mixed media, water soluble oils, photo transfer hand colored, clock components
12" x 12" on Board

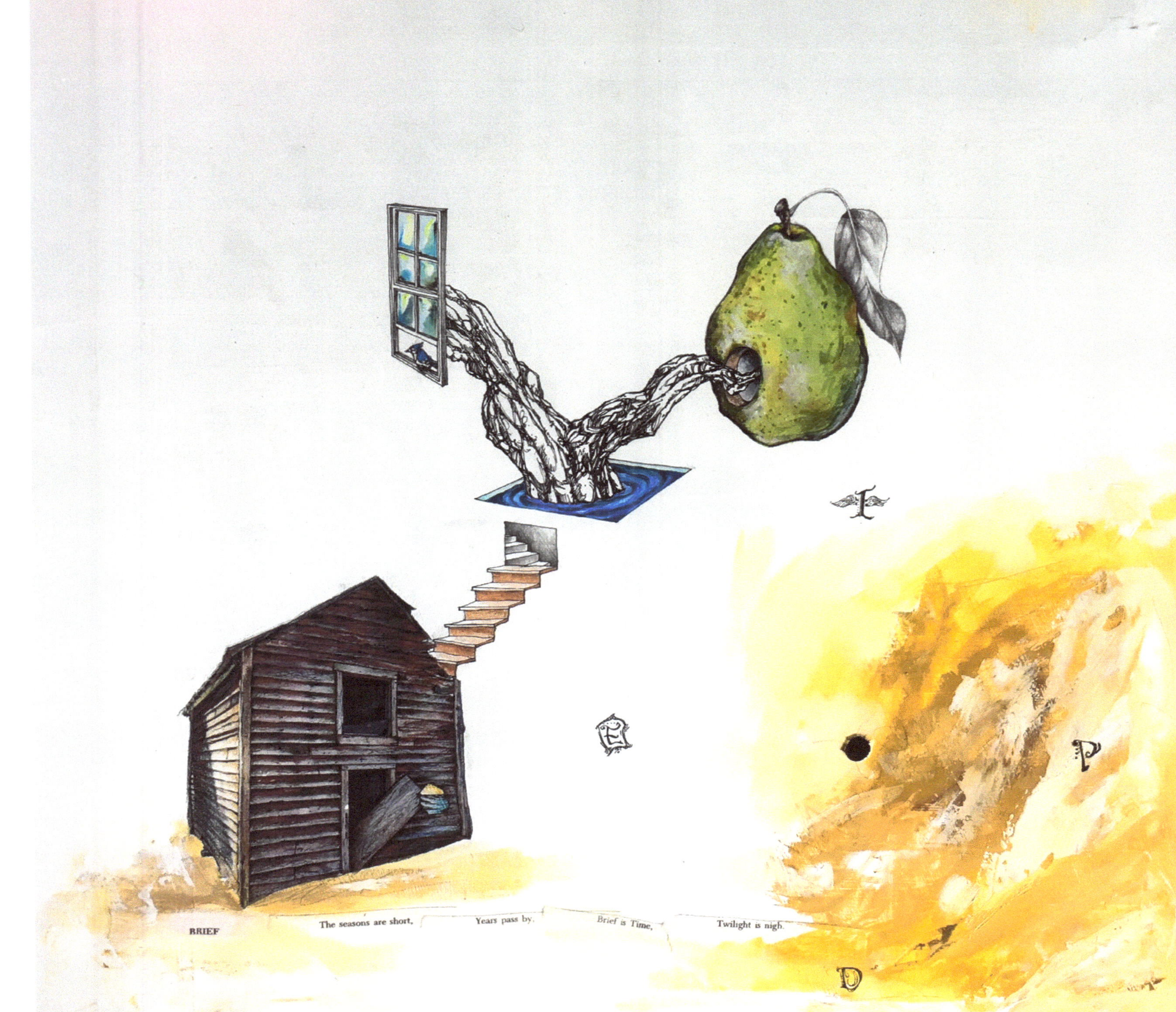

BRIEF
The seasons are short,
Years pass by.
Brief is Time,
Twilight is nigh.

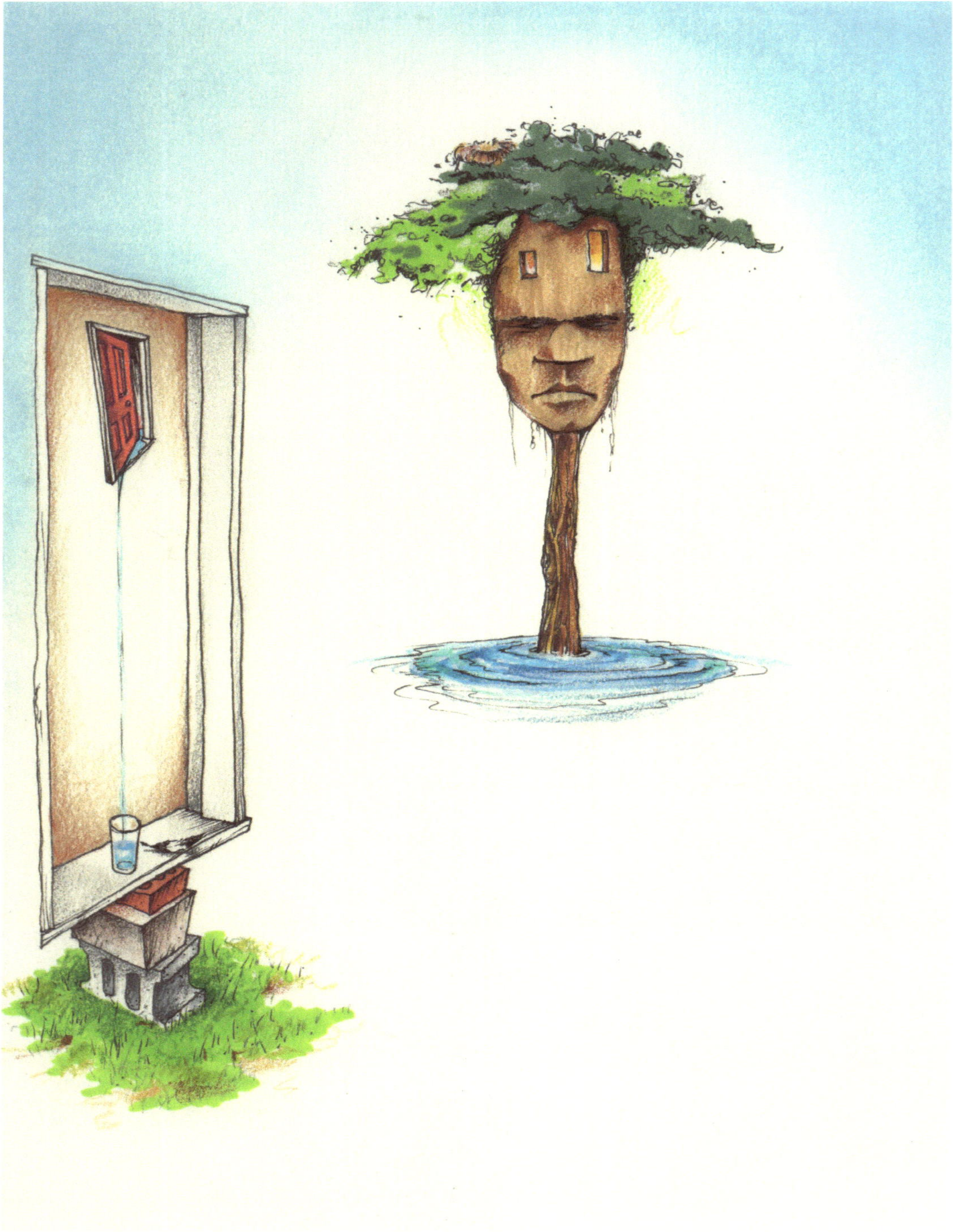

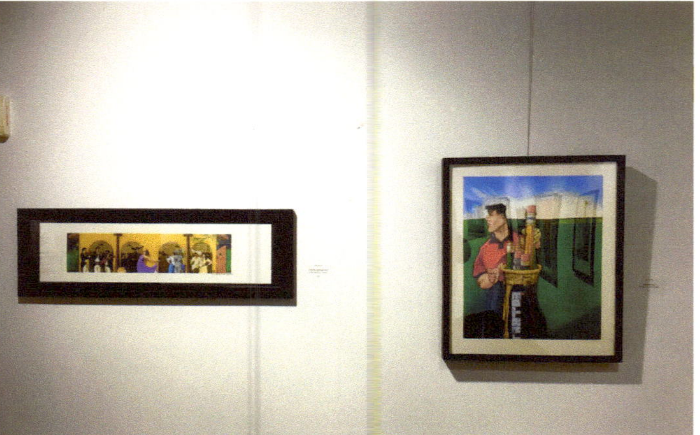

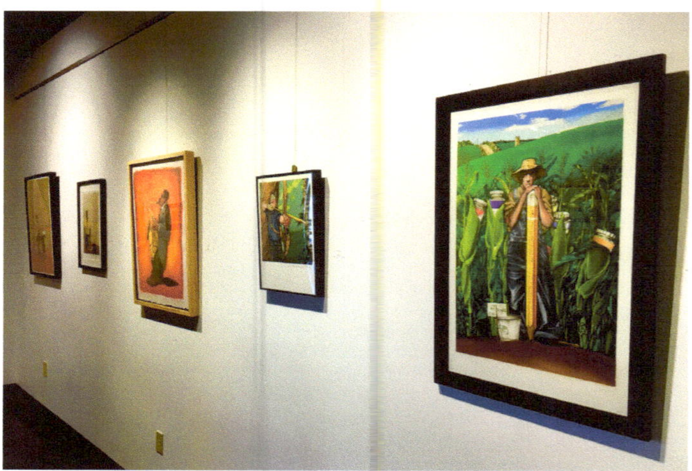

Above: Photos taken during exhibit at Maryville College, TN.

Right: Professor Carl Gombert and Troy after presenting the Commemorative Poster for the 150th of Maryville College.

Left: Subliminal Trees
8" x 10"
Color pencil, micro pens

Right: Subliminal Outtakes
8" x 10"
Color pencil, micro pens

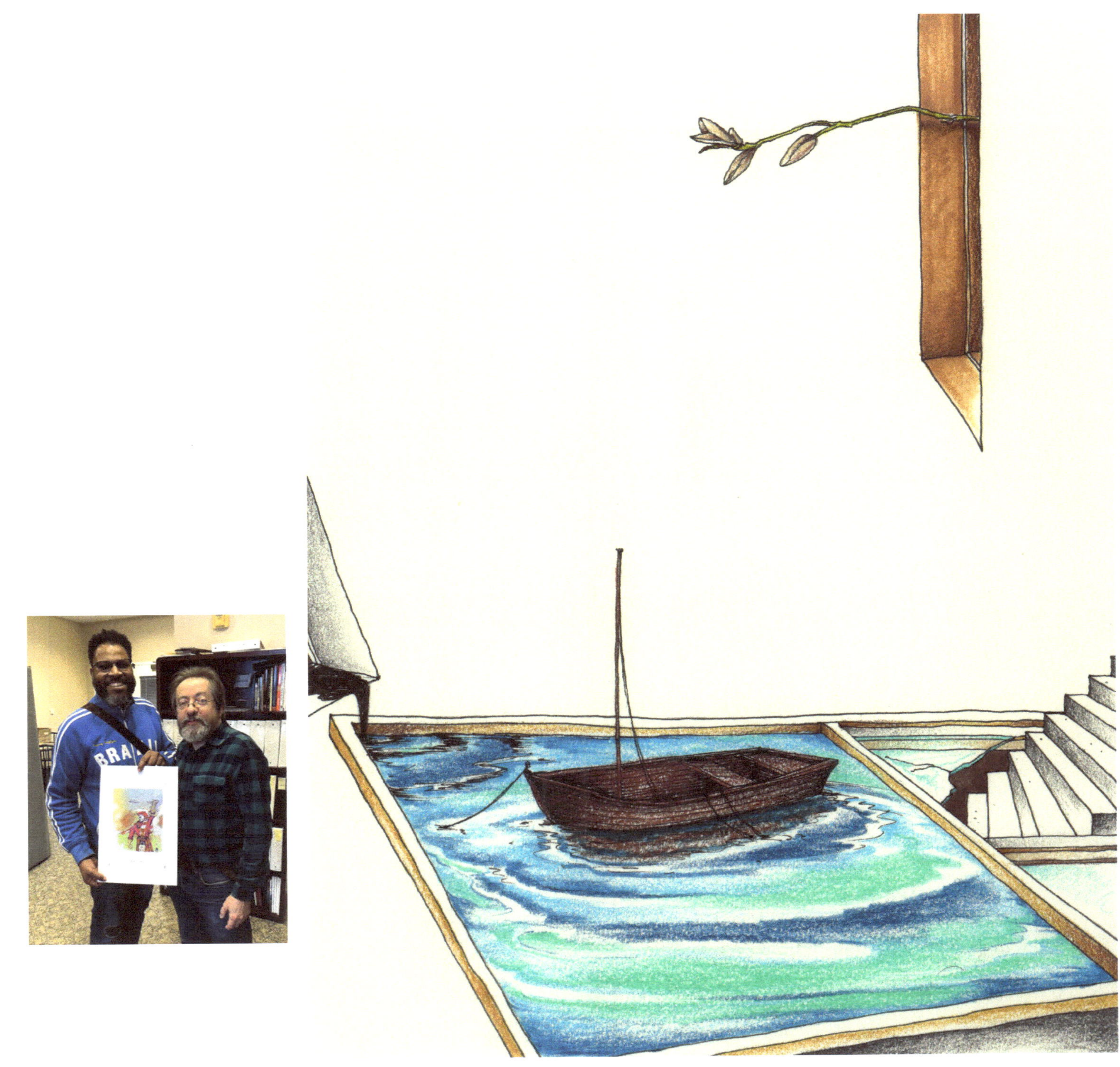

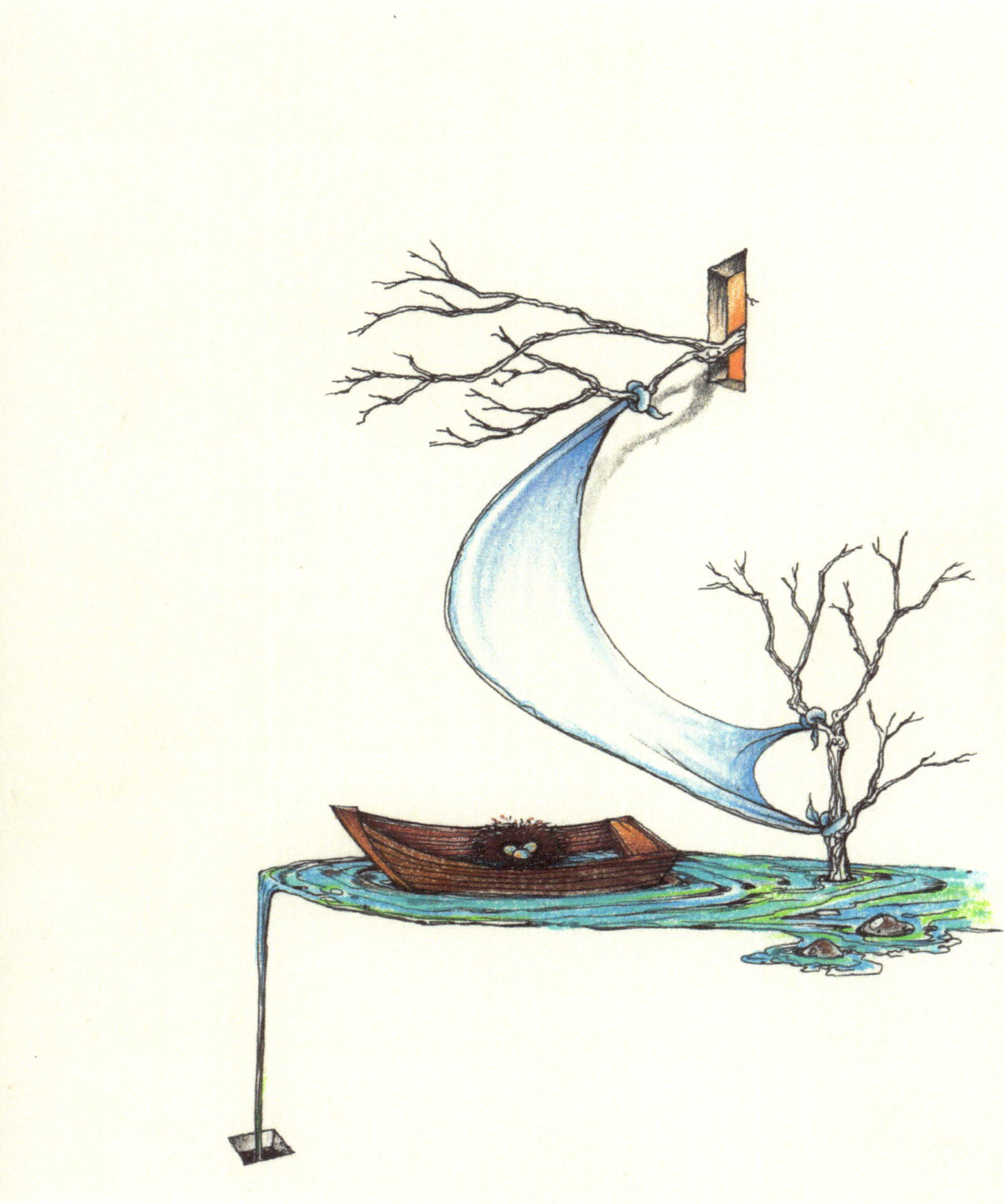

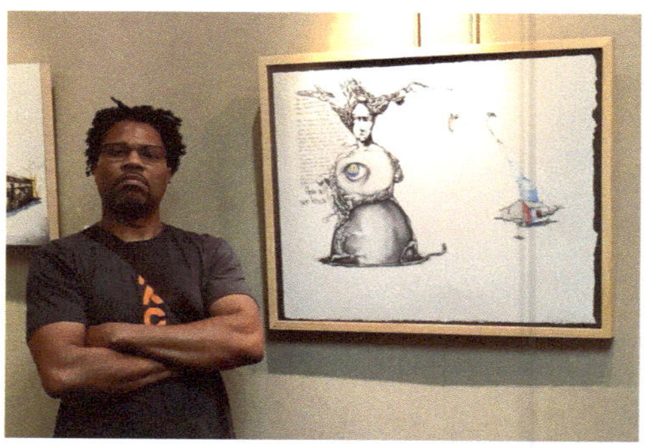

Above: These pieces were created to exhibit at The Saul Alexander Gallery in Charleston, SC. The artists after installing pieces in the gallery.

Left: Subliminal Streams
8” x 10”
Color pencil, micro pens

Right: Subliminal Streams 2
8” x 10”
Color pencil, micro pens

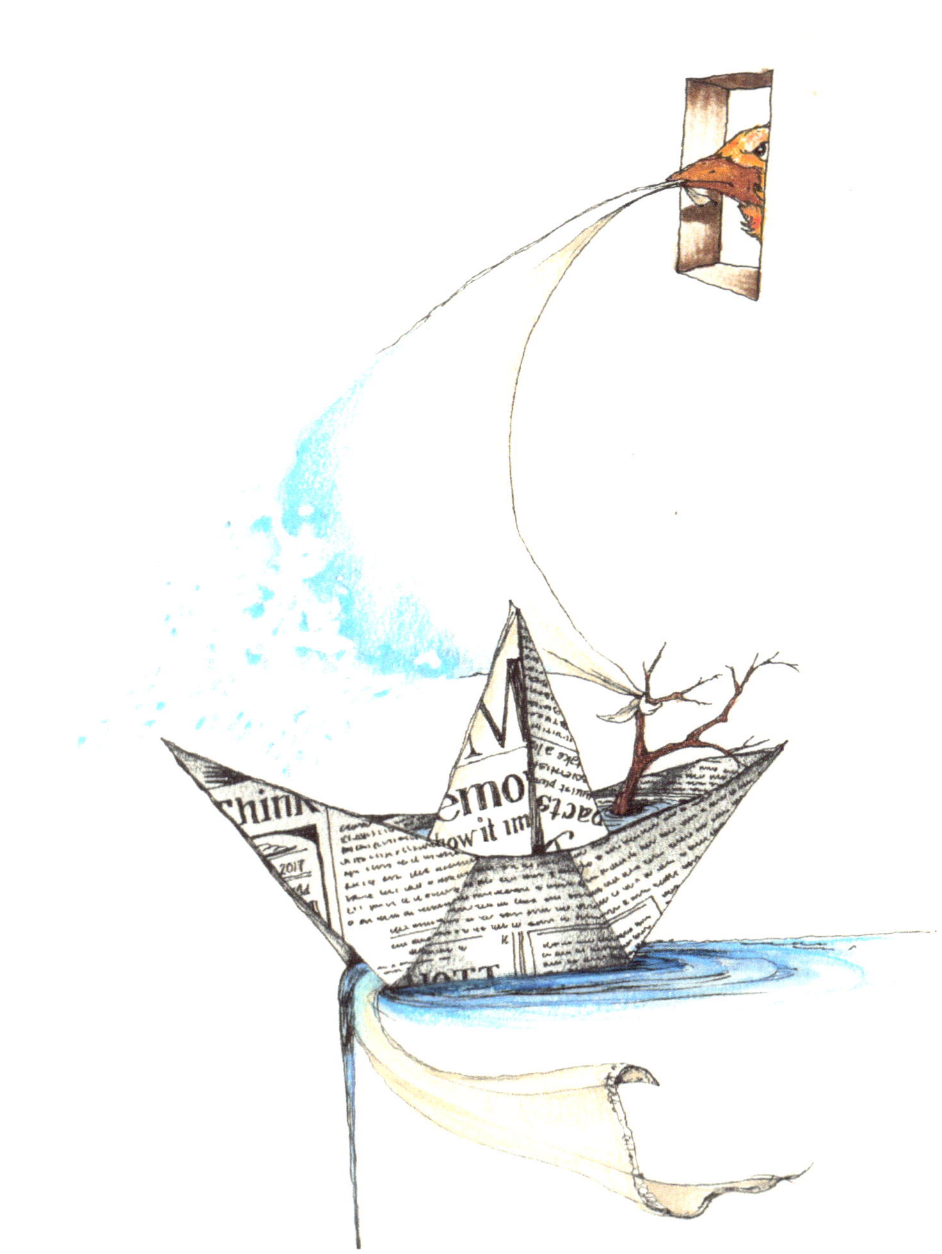

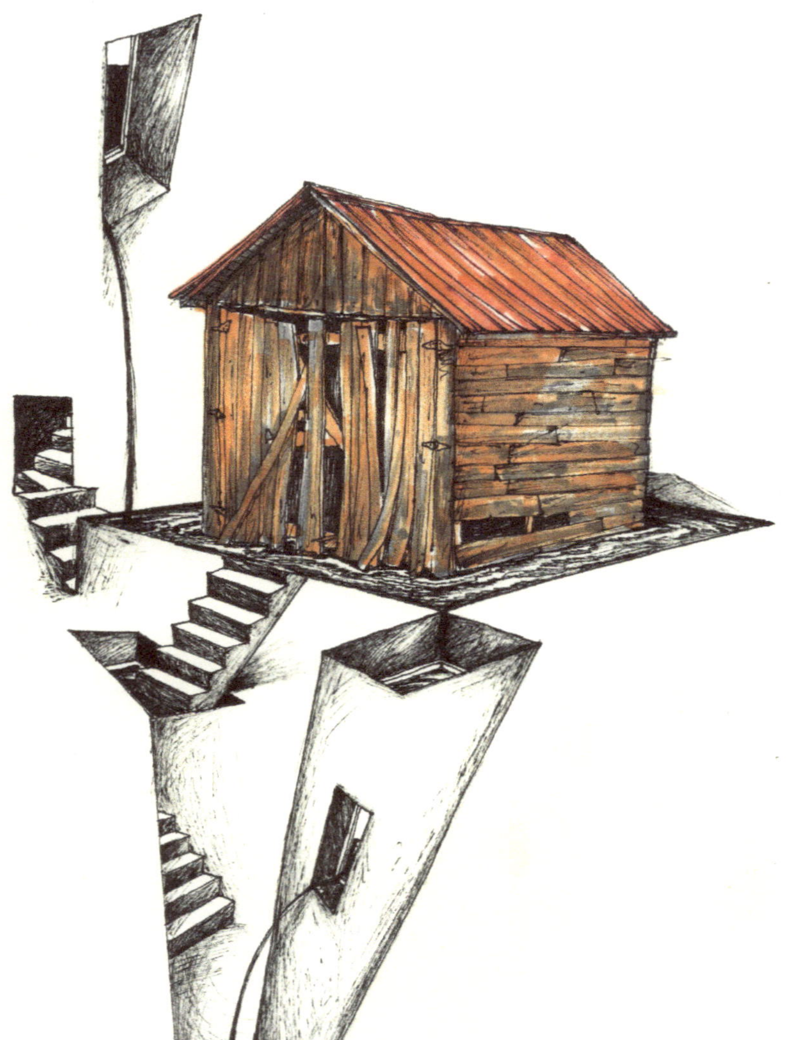

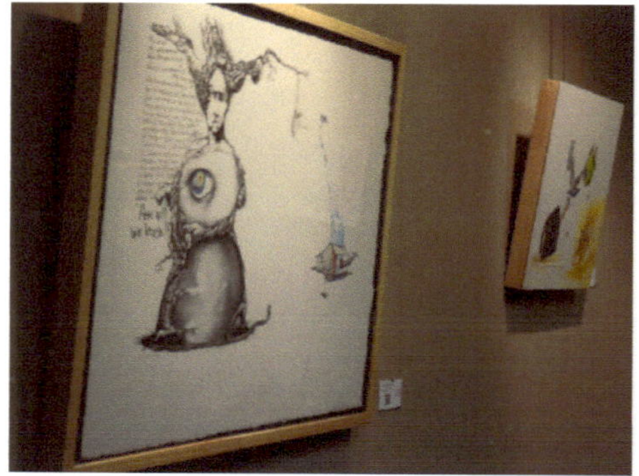

These pieces were created to exhibit at The Saul Alexander Gallery in Charleston, SC.

Left: Barn Transitions
8" x 10"
Color pencil, micro pens

Right: Subliminal Journeys
8" x 10"
Color pencil, micro pens

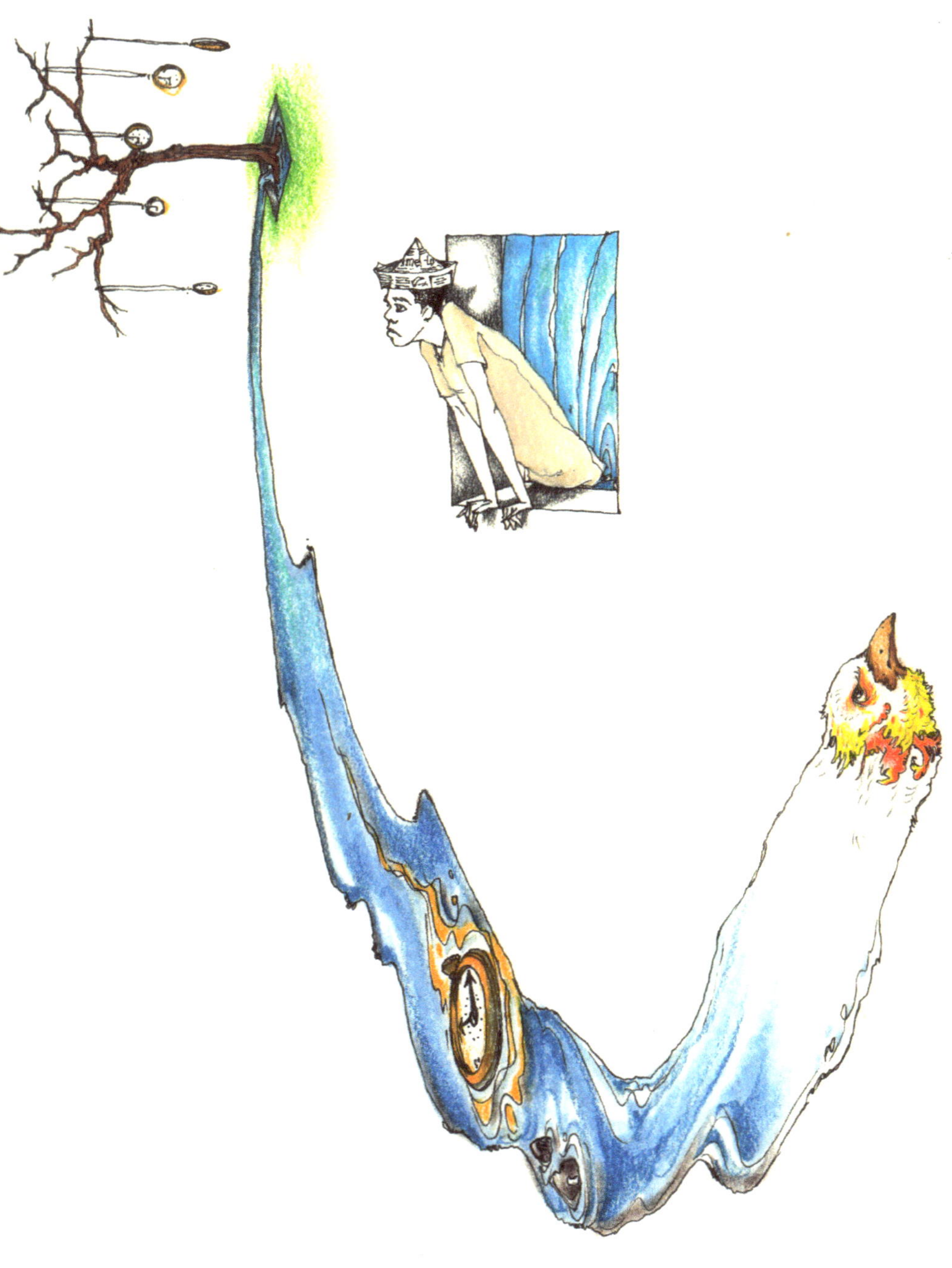

"Accept your personal story. Be open to it, let it shape you. And then share it with others. Because when people share themselves through their art or even just through a conversation, they contribute to this sea of rich stories that gives people the chance to connect with each other."

- T. Brown

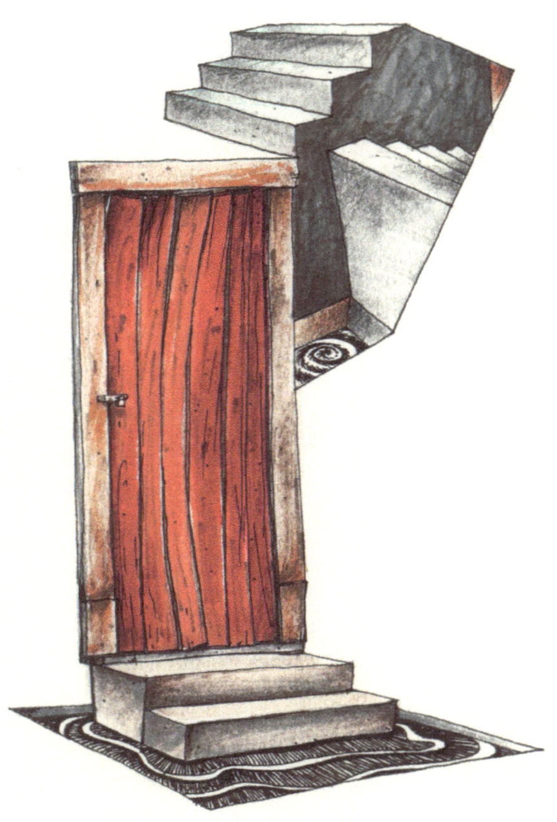

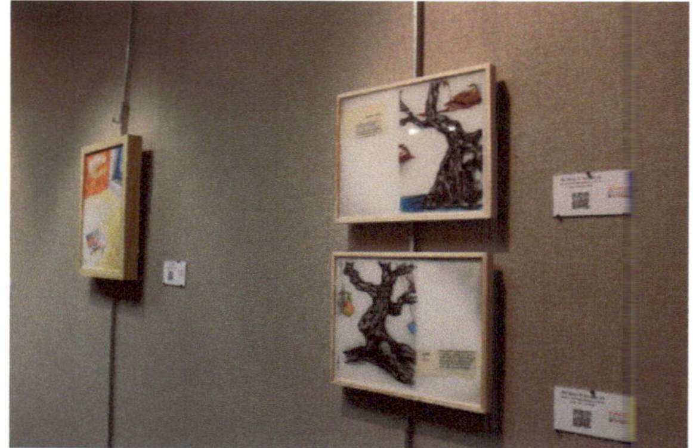

These pieces were created to exhibit at The Saul Alexander Gallery in Charleston, SC.

Left: Fluid Levels
8" x 10"
Color pencil, micro pens

Right: Subliminal Memories 1
8" x 10"
Color pencil, micro pens

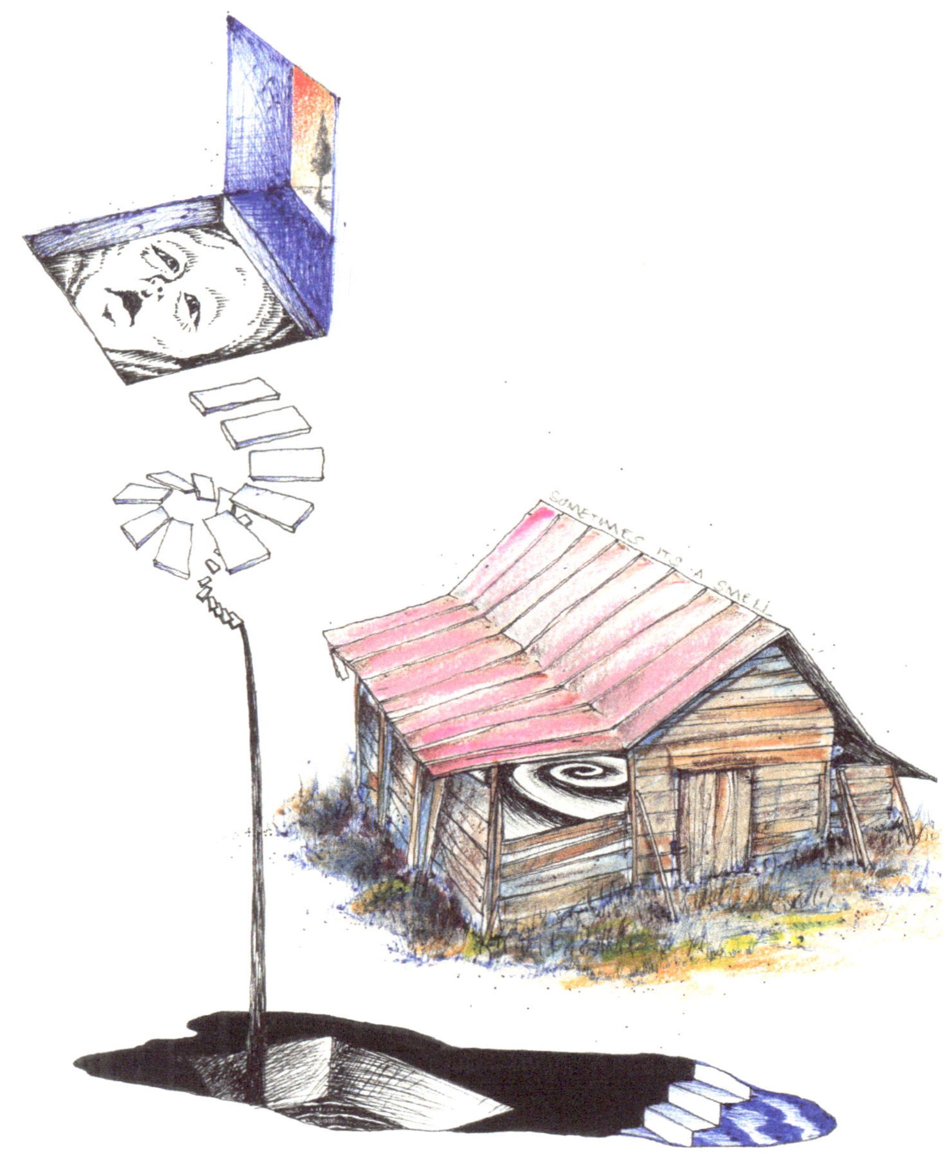
SOMETIMES IT'S A SMELL

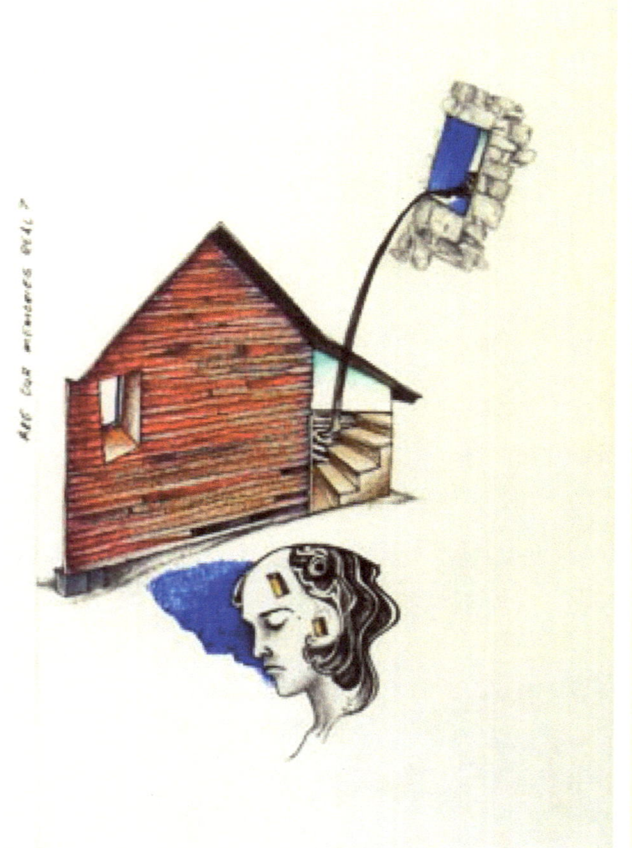

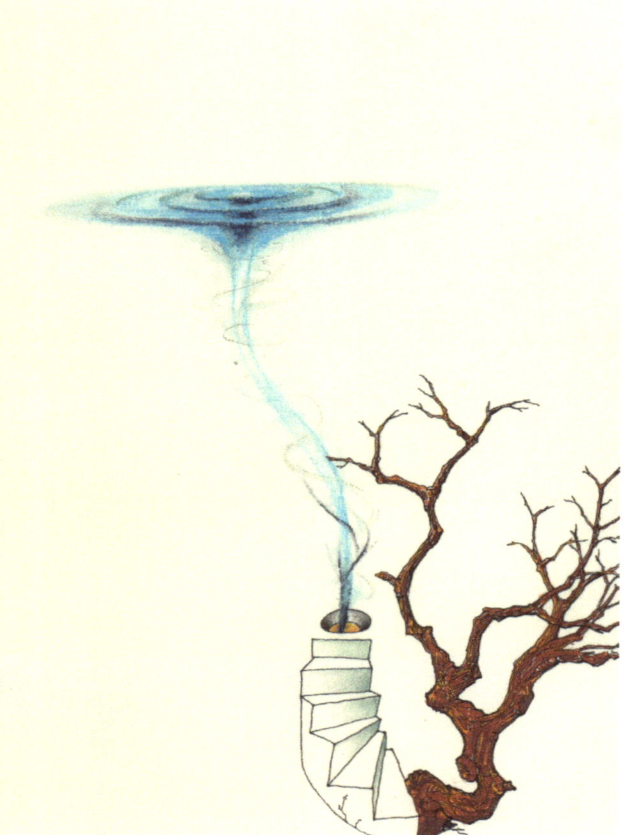

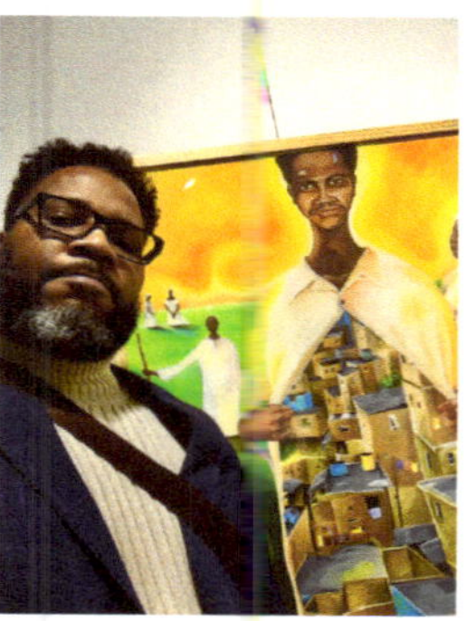

Above: Photo taken while at the Saul Alexander Gallery, Charleston, SC. Opening.

Left: Subliminal Memories 2, 8" x 10"
Color pencil, micro pens

Upward Streams, color pencil, micro pens, 8" x 10"

Right: Branches of Memory, 20" x 16"
Color pencil, micro pens on Lana

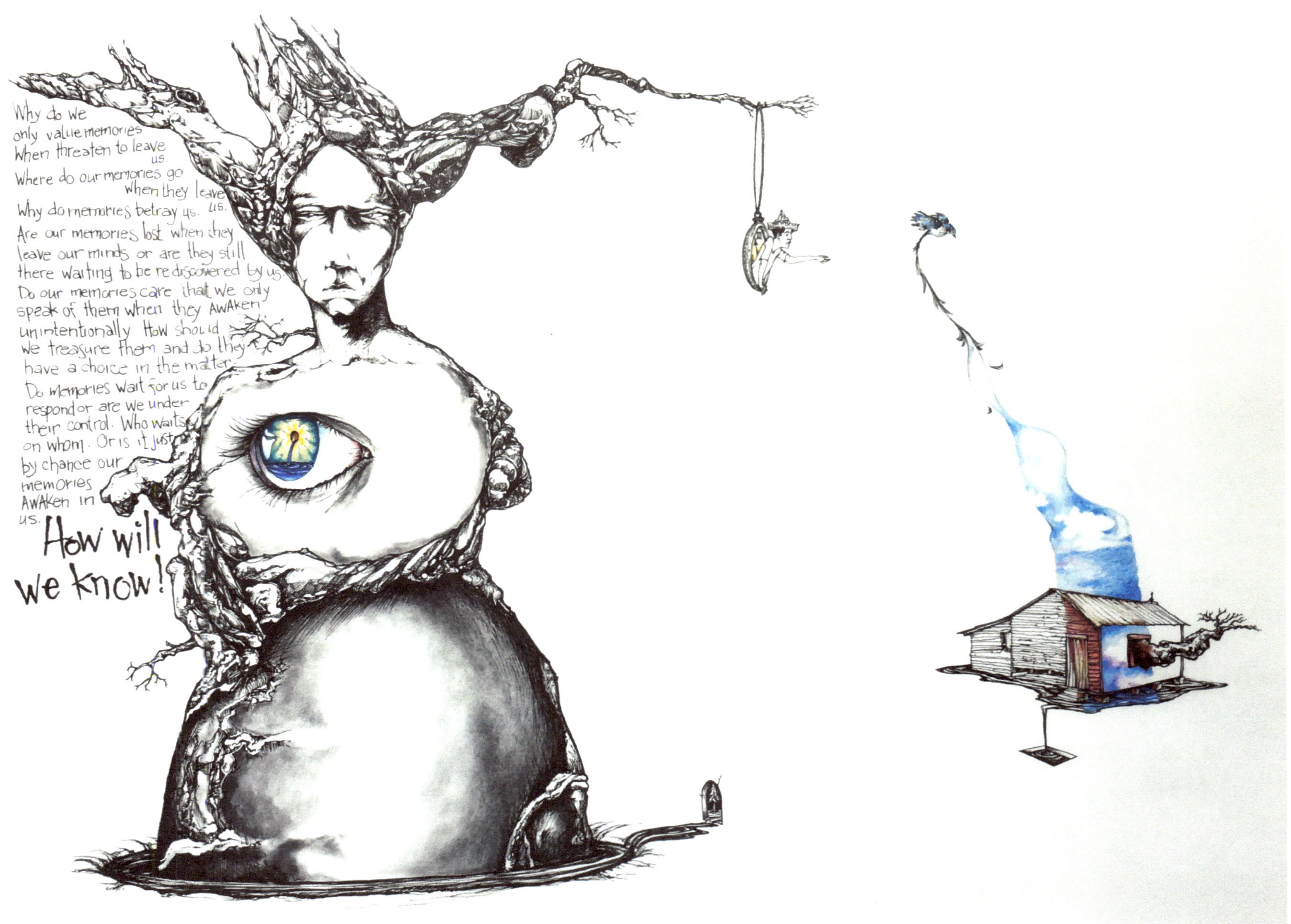

Why do we
only value memories
When threaten to leave
us.
Where do our memories go
when they leave
Why do memories betray us. us.
Are our memories lost when they
leave our minds or are they still
there waiting to be re discovered by us.
Do our memories care that we only
speak of them when they AwAken
unintentionally. How should
we treasure them and do they
have a choice in the matter.
Do memories wait for us to
respond or are we under
their control. Who waits
on whom. Or is it just
by chance our
memories
AwAken in
us.
How will
we know!

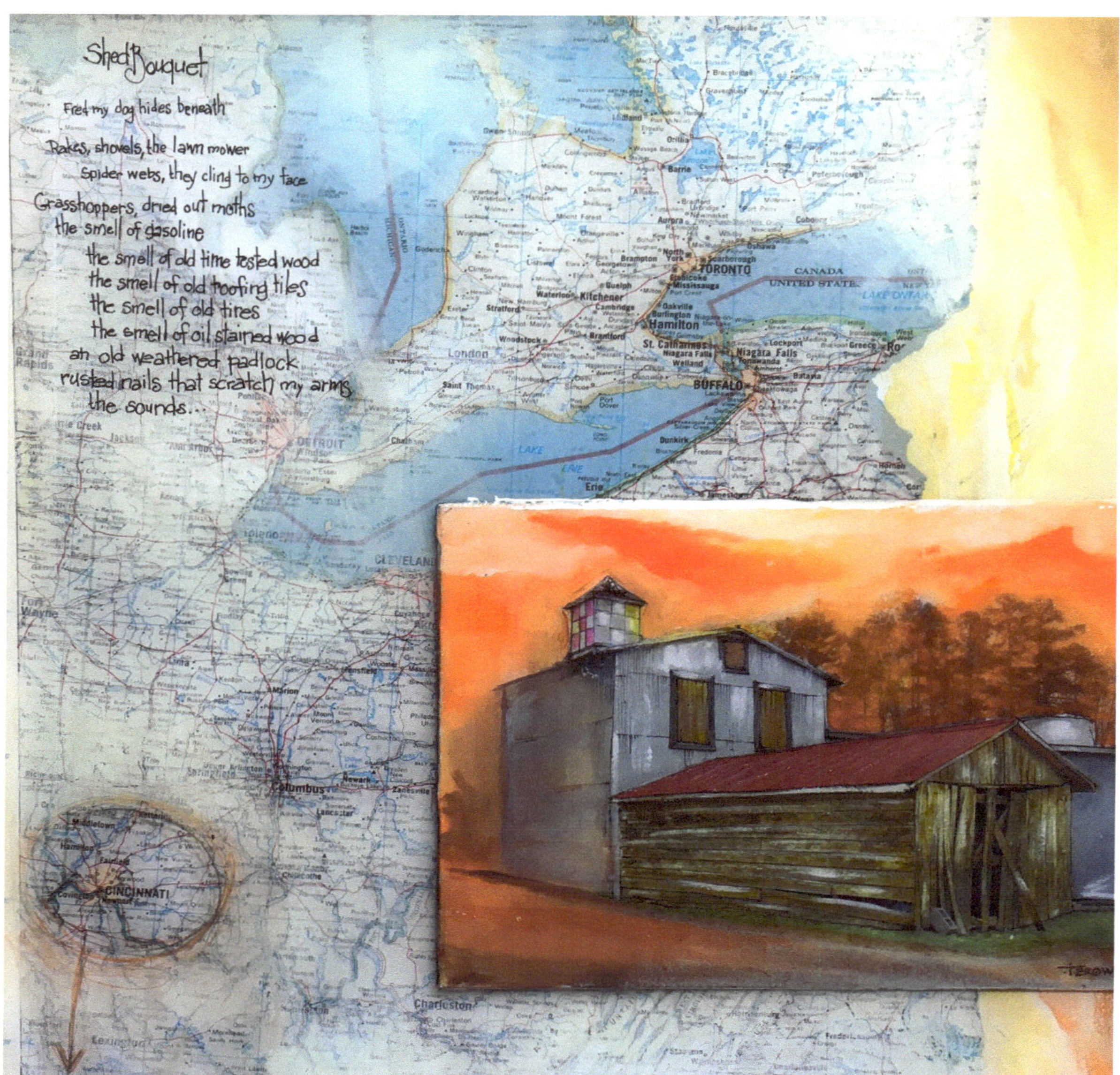

These pieces were created primarily in two parts. The smaller inset pieces were a combination of photo transfers that were hand painted and mounted on board. The maps were a combination of collage, hand written and printed poetry mounted on painted board. Both pieces were finalized in resin.

Left: Barn Origins Parts 1
Photo transfer, hand colored water-based oils on board in resin
18" x 18"

Right: Barn Origins Parts 2
Photo transfer, hand colored water-based oils on board in resin
18" x 18"

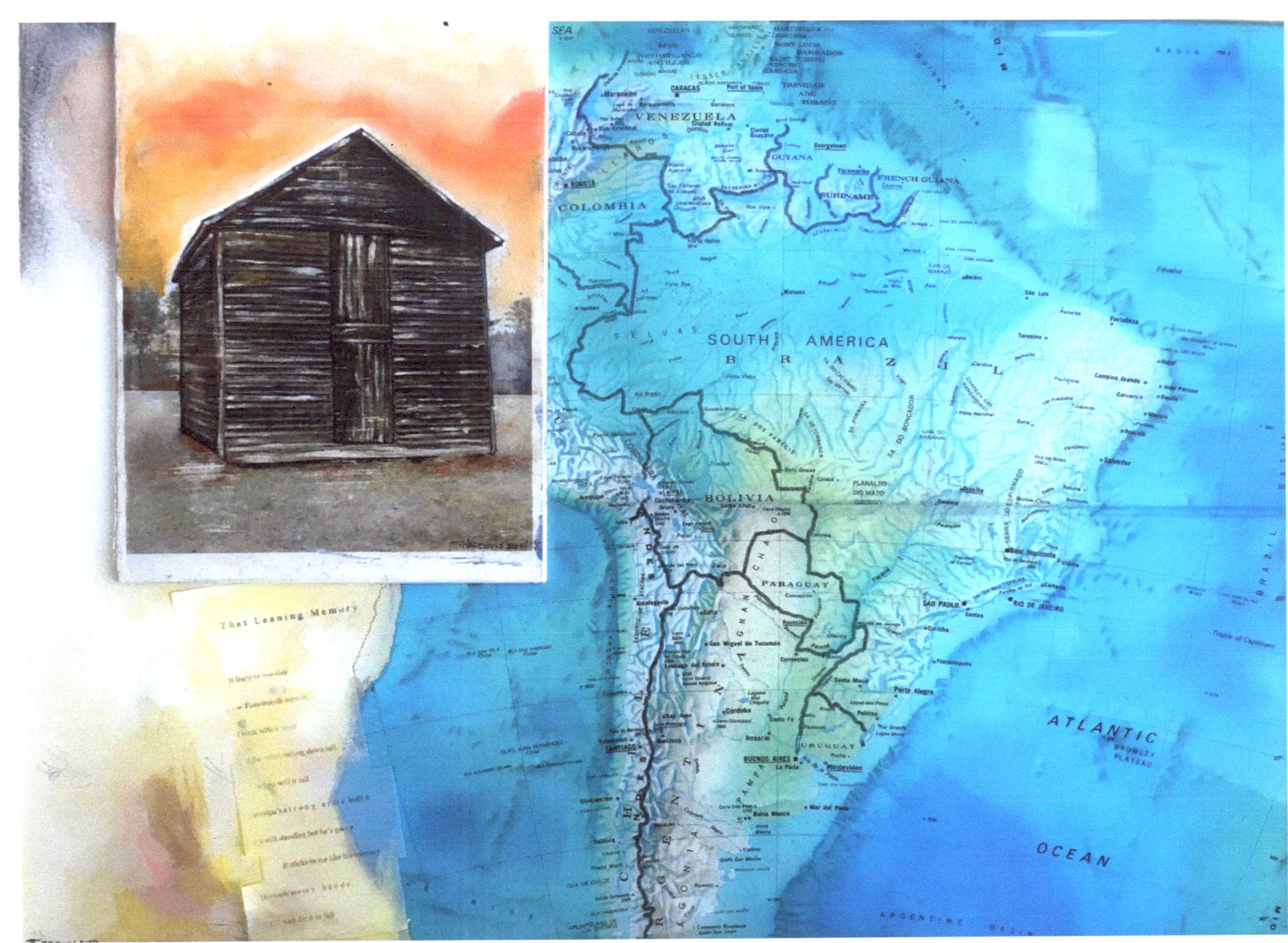
That Leaning Memory

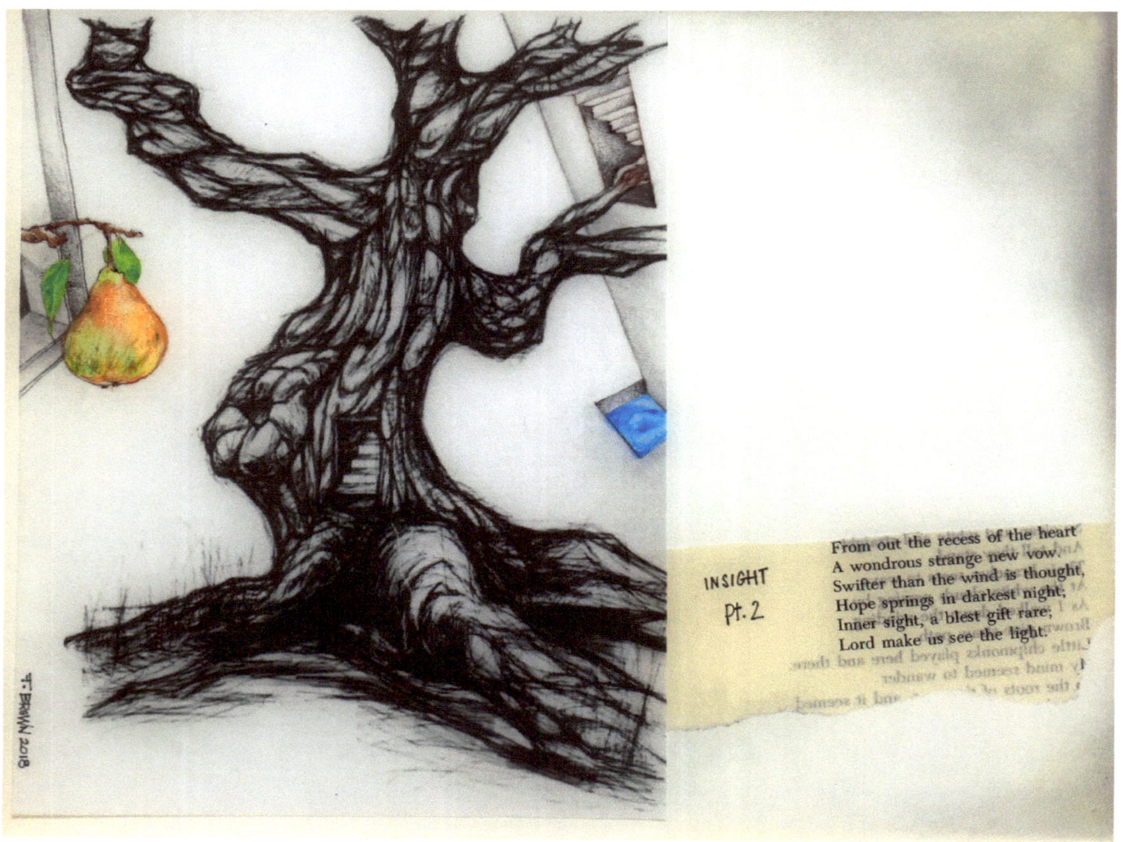

These pieces were created for the one man exhibit at The Saul Alexander Gallery in Charleston, SC. Both pieces were created by Troy while on his iPhone sitting in sunday worship service.

Left: My Roots 1
iPhone Drawing, printed 8" x 10" in resin.

Right: My Roots 2
iPhone Drawing, printed 8" x 10" in resin.

INSIGHT   Pt. 1

A treasure chest of memories
In the mind is hidden;
And in the very darkest hour
Some spring forth unbidden,
Unlocking secrets of the past,
Awareness of the now,

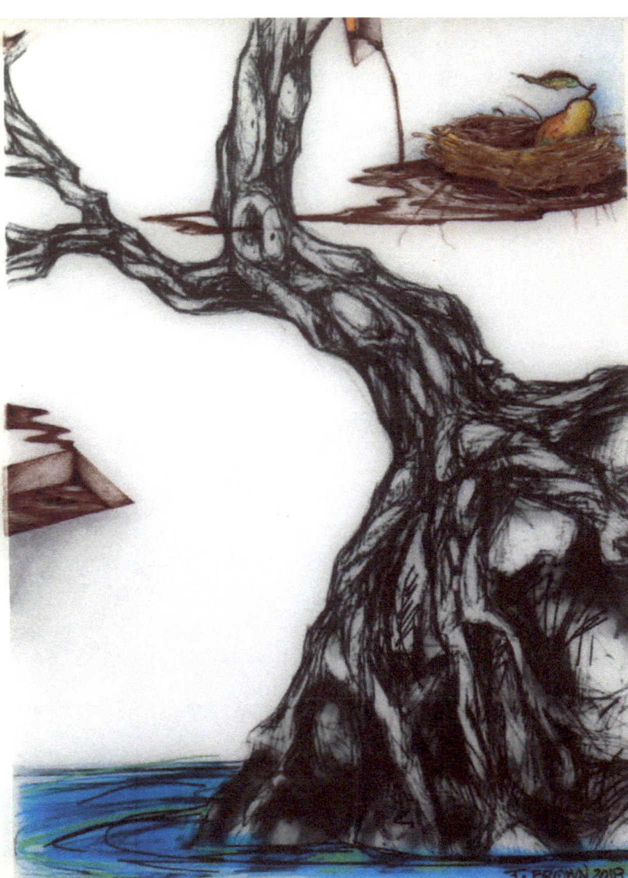

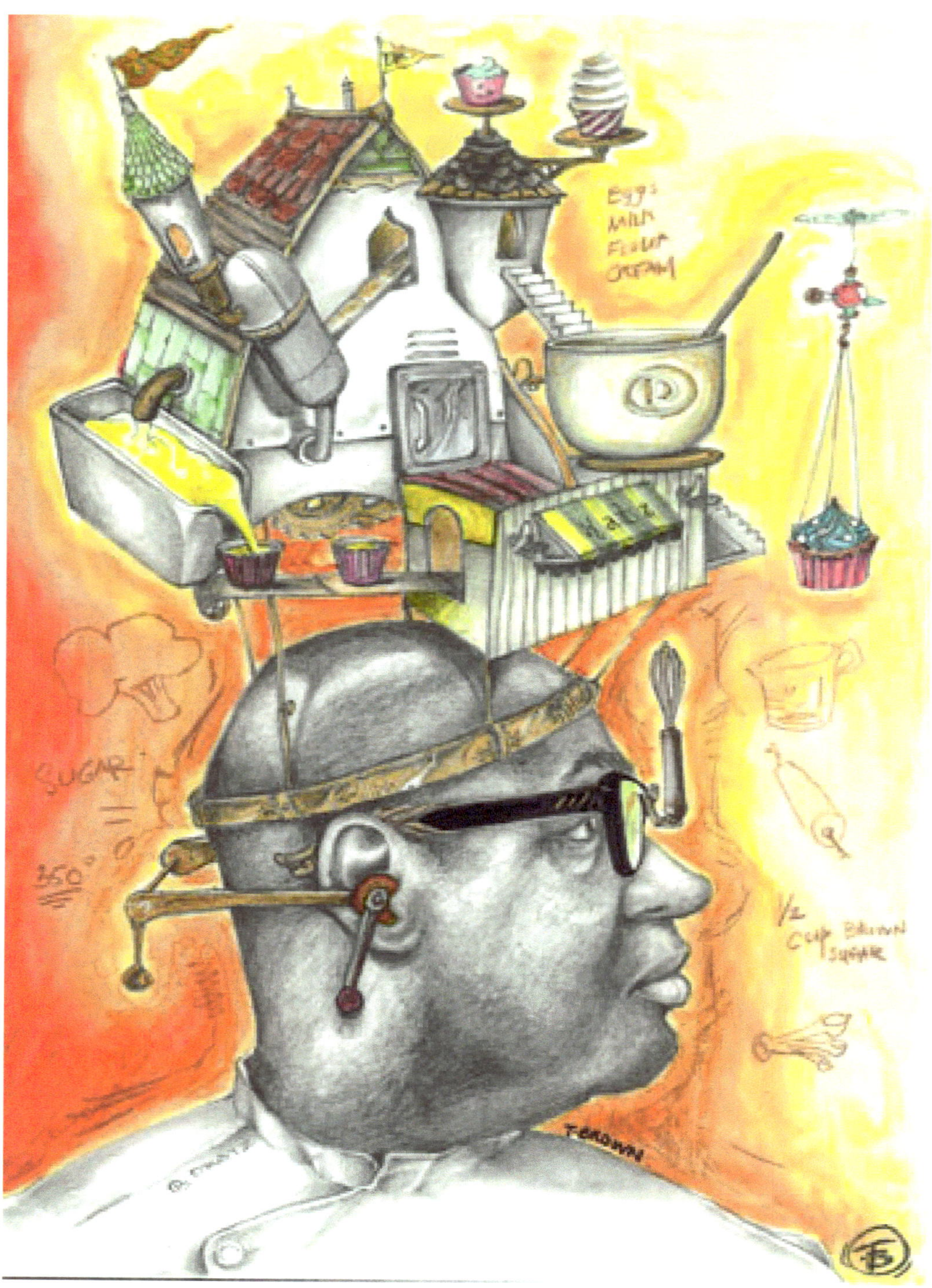

These pieces were created to exhibit at The Black Creativity Exhibition at the Museum of Science and Industry, Chicago. 'The Baker's Dream' appeared in the 2015 Exhibition.

Left: The Bakers Dream
Mixed media on 5 x 7 clay board

Right: The Baker's Heart
Water-based oils on clay board. The piece was inspired by a close friend and Pastry Chef, Daryl Watts.

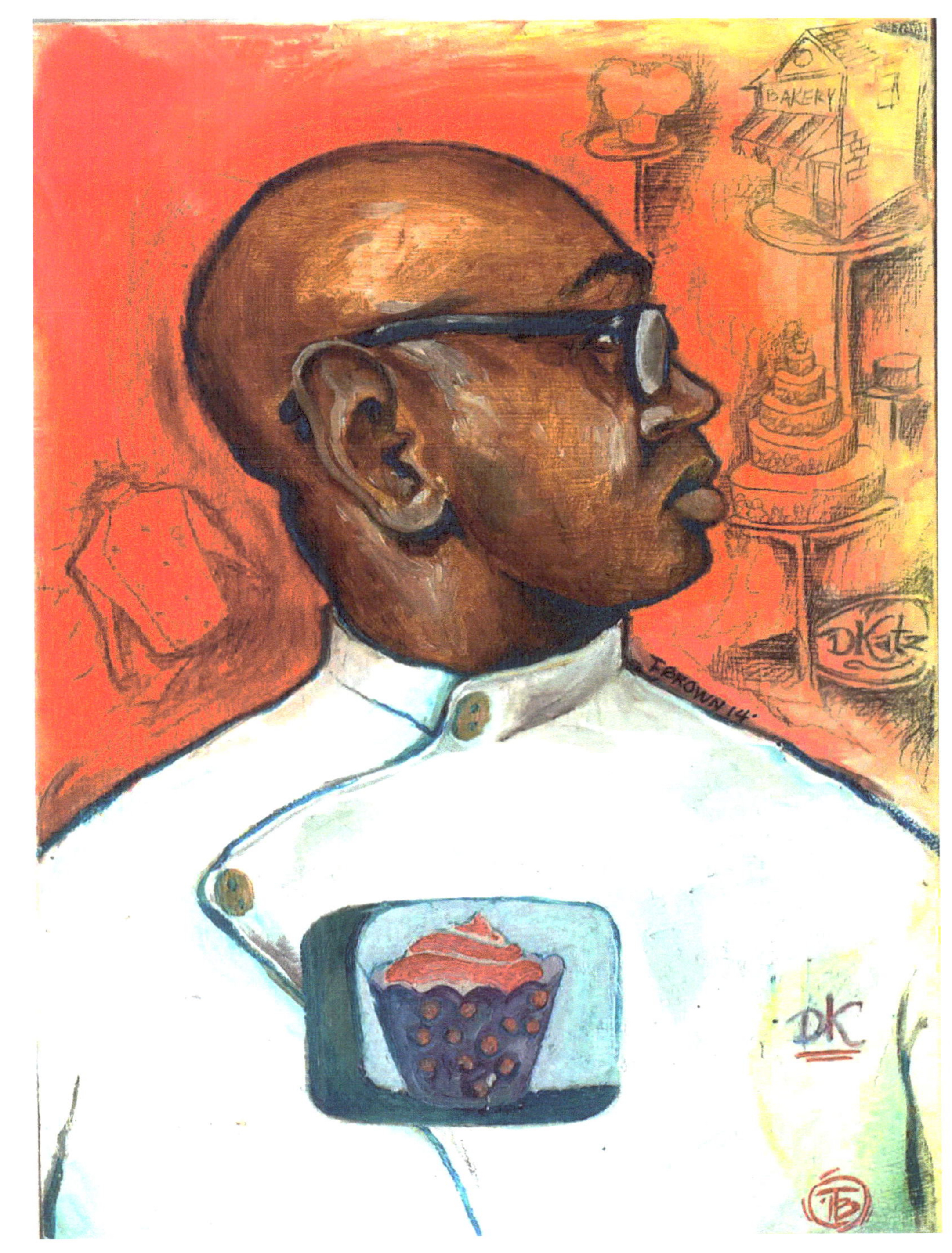

BAKERY
T BROWN 14.
DKatz
DK

Children's literature to me always was attached to my sense of destiny. My aesthetics ability even as a young graphic designer was innately attached to a sense of storytelling. To me, children's books function as a way to bring clarity to the text or subject in a way that only a children's book can. It is the supreme combination of text and images, words and pictures, living symbiotically in a state of perfect creative balance. Each enhances the other's qualities while still managing to somehow not alienate their own distinctive voice and attributes.

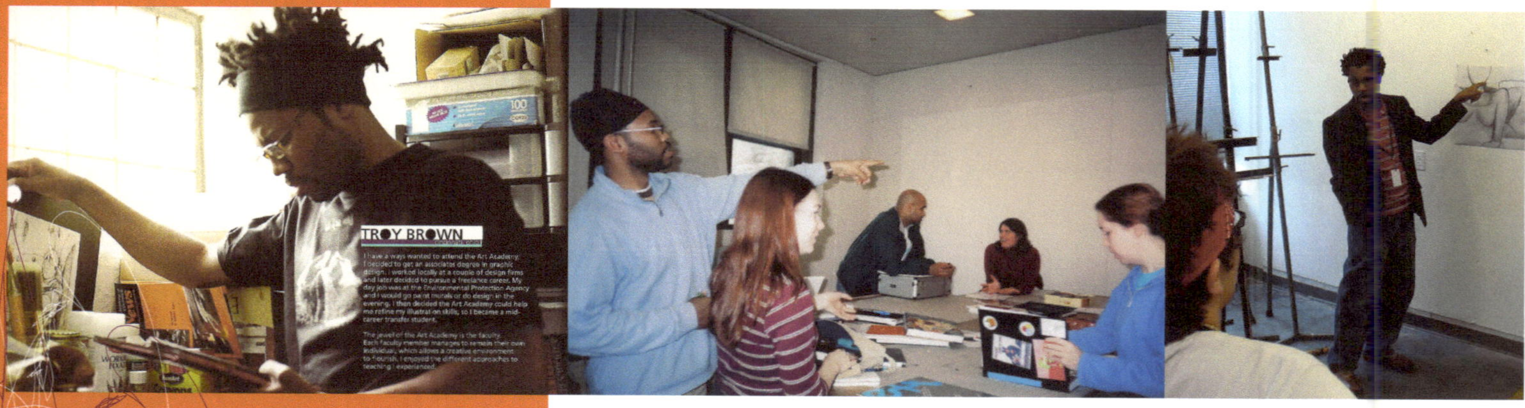

Left: Troy in his first studio on Aspen Way, Cincinnati, Ohio. The photo was taken for and article that appeared in the Art Academy of Cincinnati annual brochure section that follows accomplishments of alumnus.

Middle: Troy and fellow students during class at the former Art Academy Building that was adjacent to the Cincinnati Art Museum in Eden Park.

Above Right: Troy teaching a portfolio preparation class for high school students at the Art Academy Over-the-rhine location.

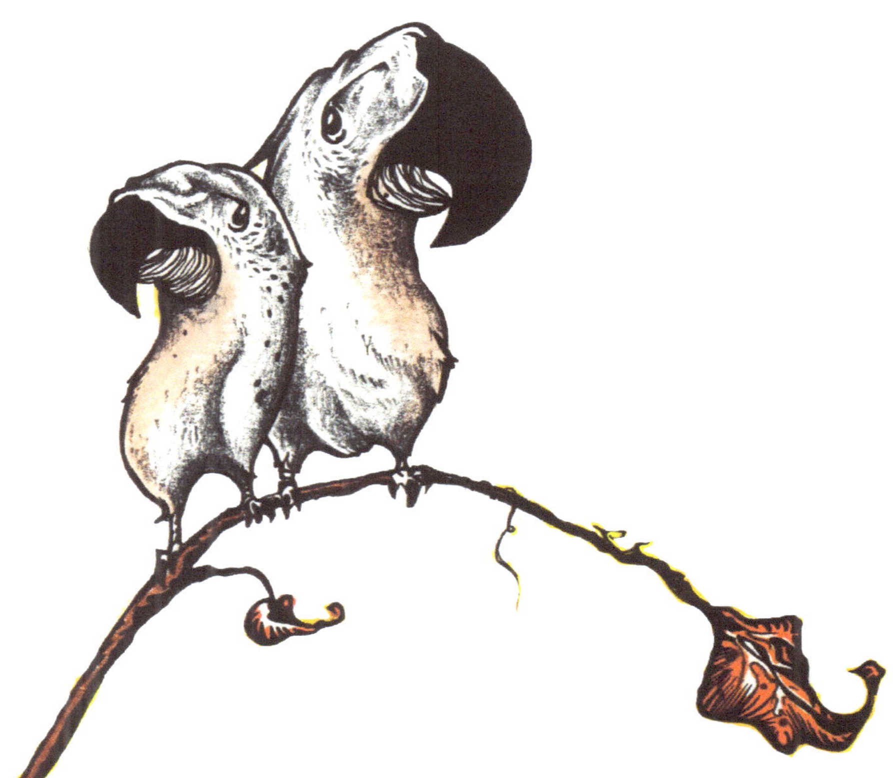

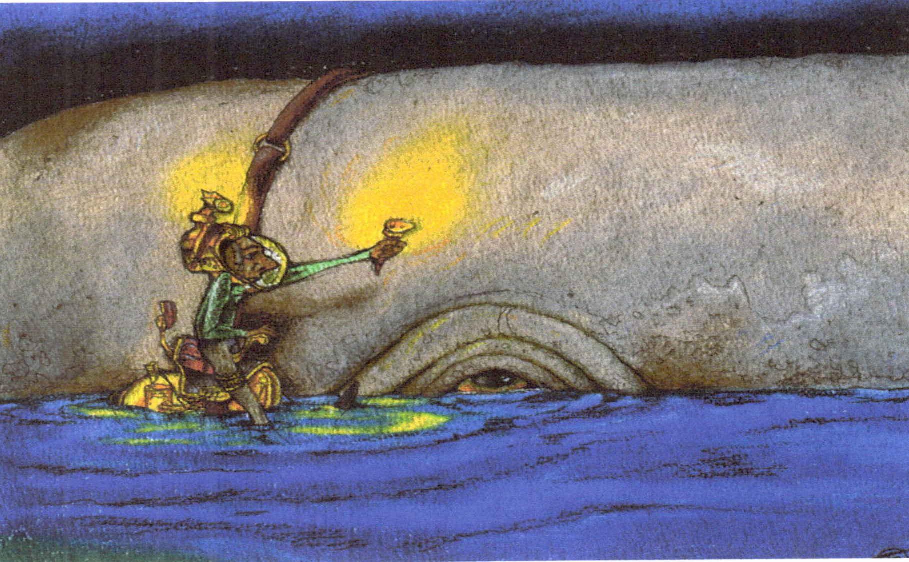

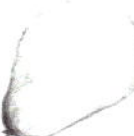

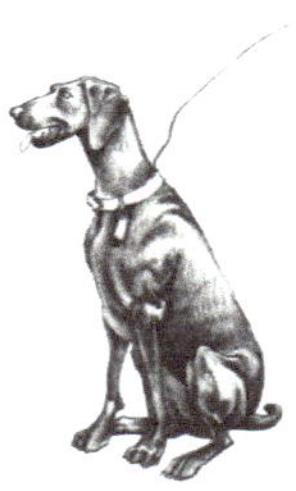

Above: The unofficial mascot at BSP Books.

Right top: Illustration from the children's book Feathers. The book had no words following the oral story telling tradition. The original publishers of the story wanted to the story to continue its rich heritage as an oral tale.

Right bottom: Illustration for upcoming book, 'Whale Riders'

My wife and I started our independent publishing label Brown Sugar Press in late 2015 after moving to North Carolina from Chicago. We began the company because we wanted to publish our own concepts apart from the constraints of traditional publishing and ultimately own our creative content. I wanted to produce books directly for the school system in which I taught at the time and other school systems where I had connections to teachers who taught in those school systems.

This book cover to the right represents the first picture book we published, called Lois and the Red Balloon. The book was dedicated to my mother and was inspired by her willingness to give up her dream of becoming a nurse to raise us kids.

Left: Cover illustration from the book, *Lois and the Red Balloon*
Published 2015
Brown Sugar Press Books LLC.

Right: Interior page illustration from the book, *Lois and the Red Balloon*
Graphite on watercolor paper, page 21.

Far Right: Interior page illustration, from the book, *Lois and the Red Balloon*
Graphite on watercolor paper, page 9.

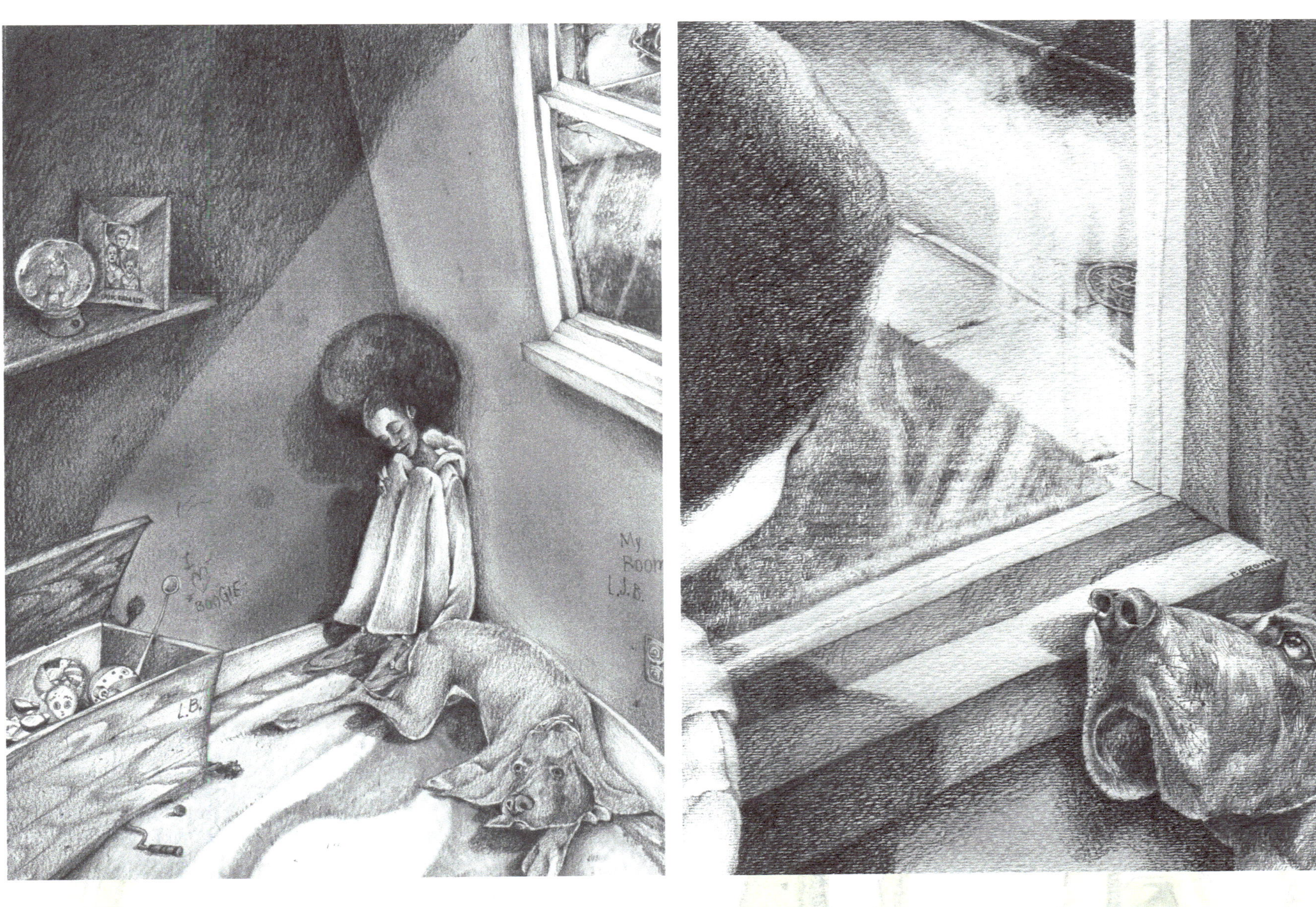

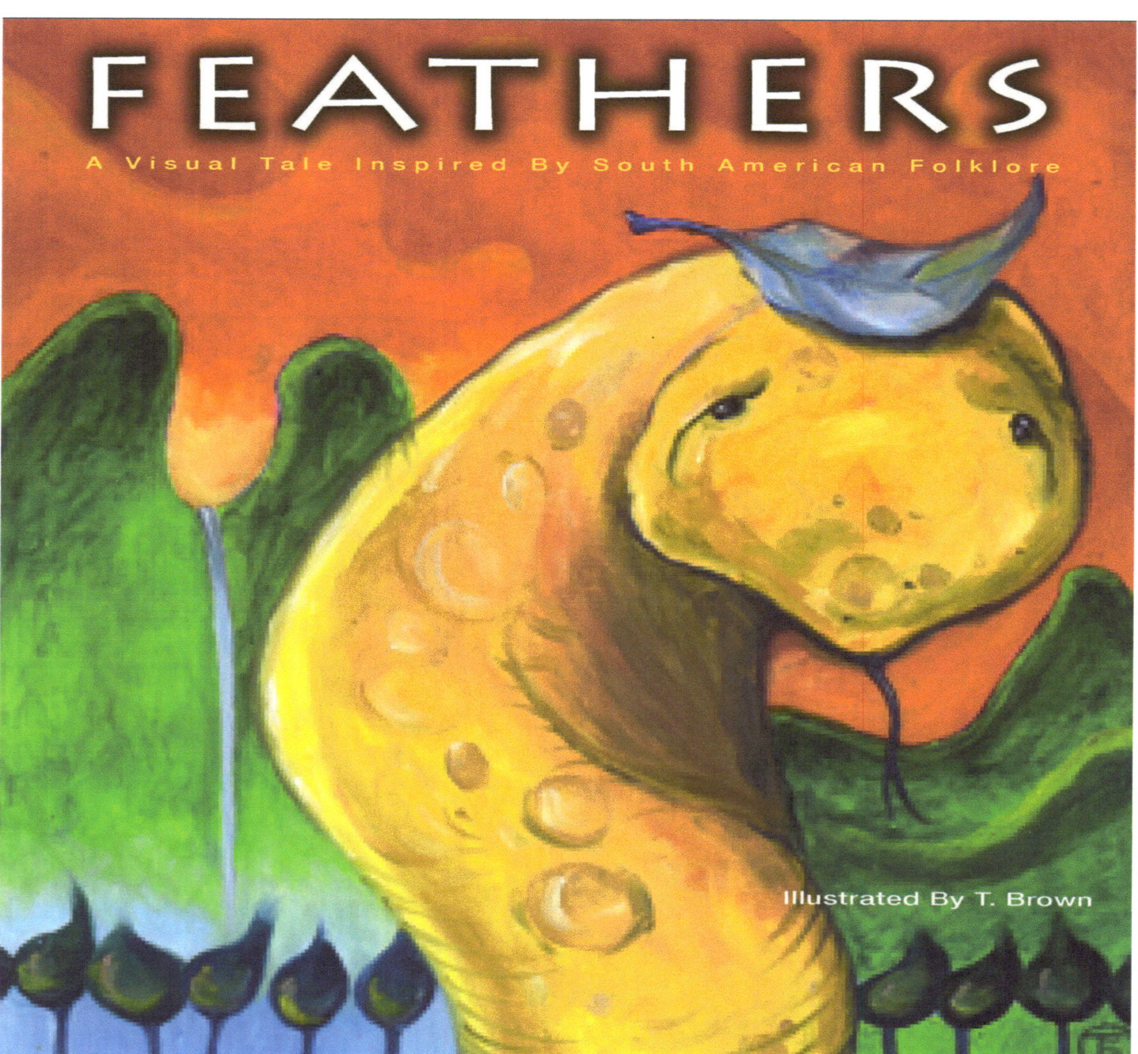

Left: Cover Illustration from the Book, *Feathers*
Published 2015
Brown Sugar Press Books LLC.

The picture book Feathers is inspired by an earlier text that was given to me as a gift by professor Flavia Bastos. Professor Bastos was instrumental in establishing my relationship with the Museu Afro Brasil in Sao Paulo, Brasil. The text was a collection of oral folklore from across the globe. The original tale is from South America and tells the story of how birds got the colored feathers. After contacting the publisher and one of the original oral storytellers they wanted to honor the lasting oral tradition and not allow the story to be re-told in text form again. So my version continues honoring that oral tradition and is only in pictures.

Right: Illustration from the Book, *Feathers*
interior illustrations
Prisma markers on 360 paper, inset cover.

Right Bottom: Illustration from the Book, *Feathers*
interior illustrations
Prisma markers on 360 paper, around page 14 (book has no page numbers).

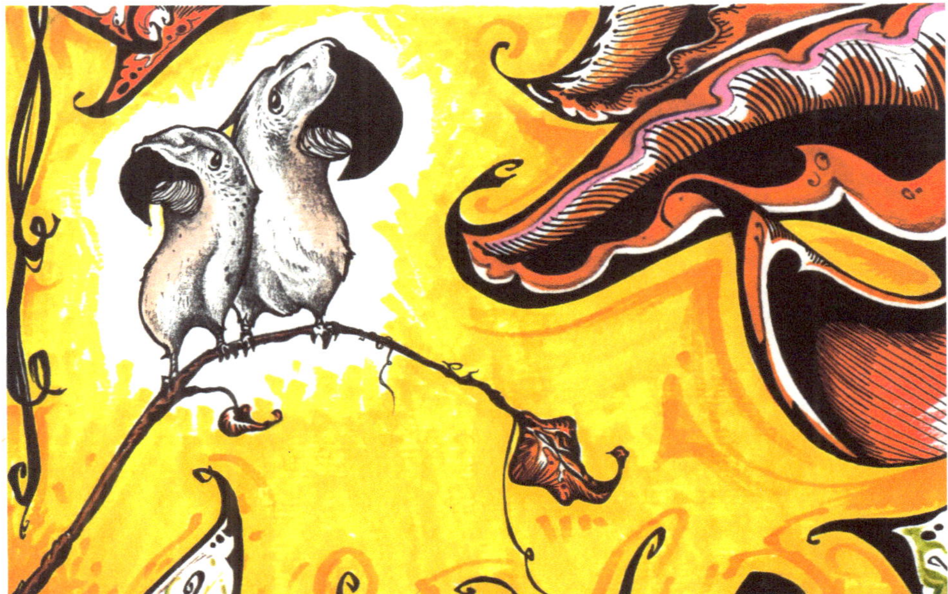

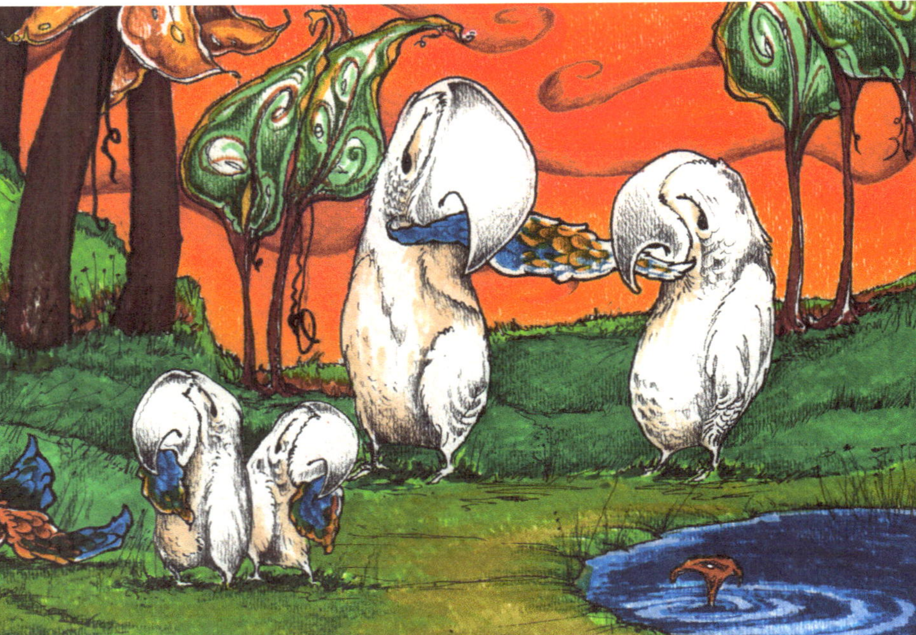

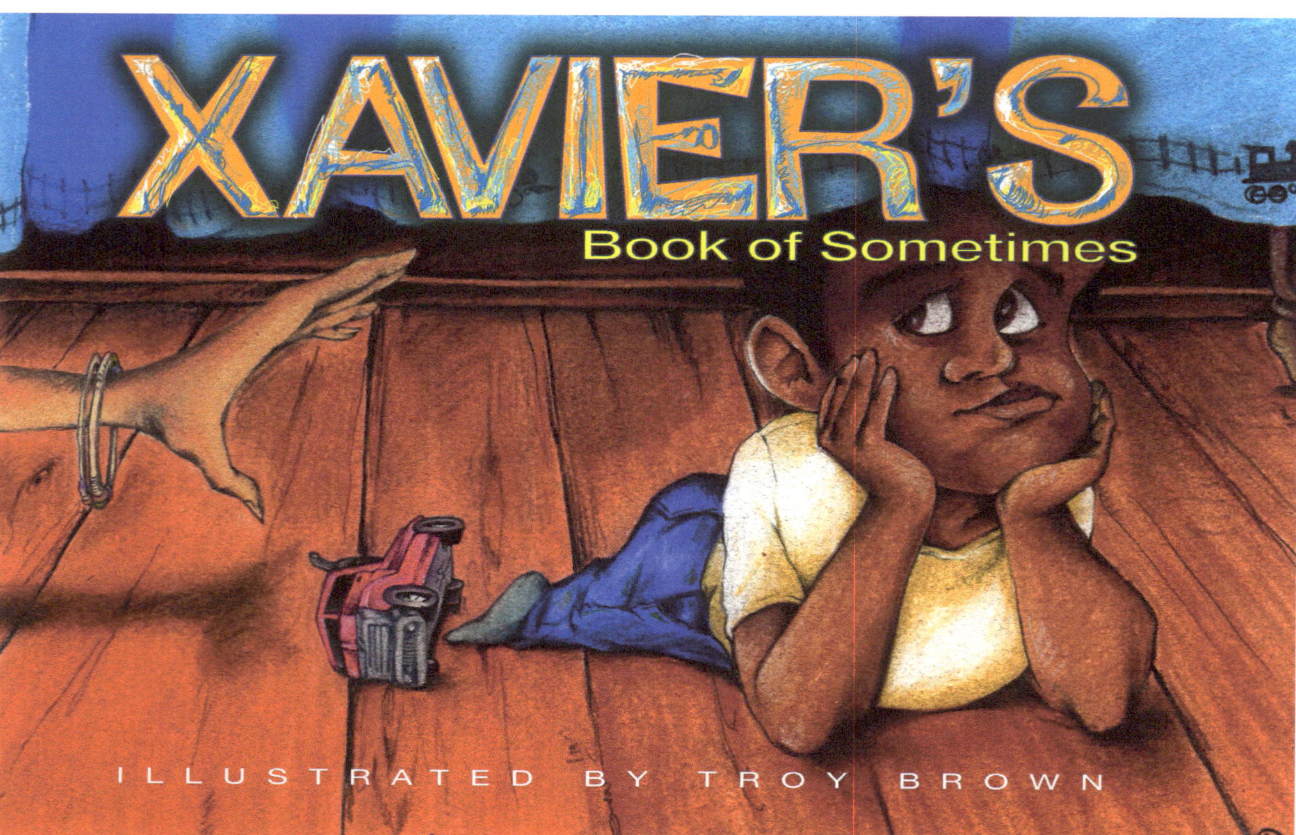

Left: Cover Illustration from the Book, *Xavier's Book of Sometimes*
Published 2015, Brown Sugar Press Books LLC.

Right: Illustration from the Book, *Xavier's Book of Sometimes*, Page 15 illustration
Pastel on Lana paper

Bottom Right: Xavier Book of Sometimes, Page 23 illustration, Pastel on Lana paper

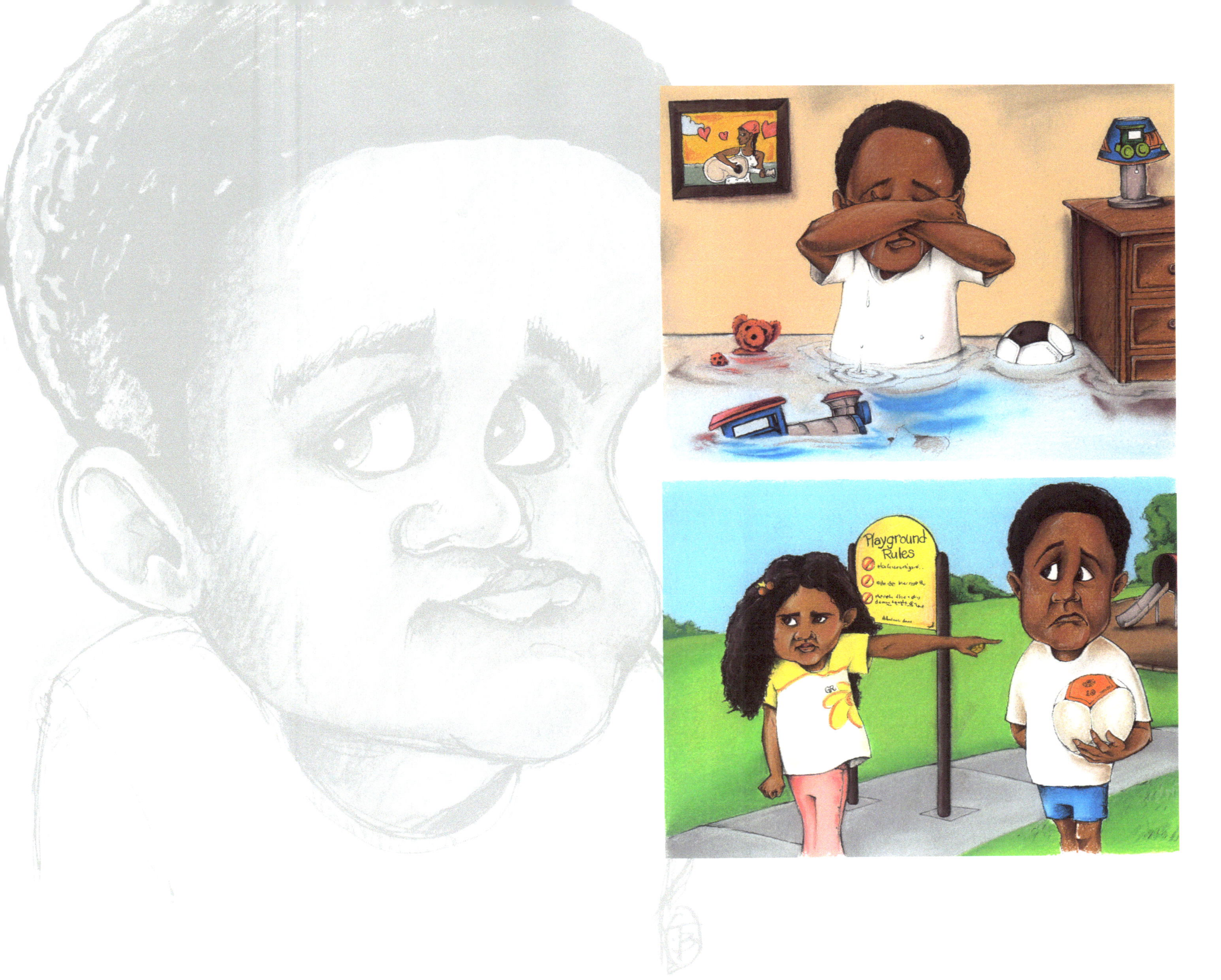
Playground
Rules

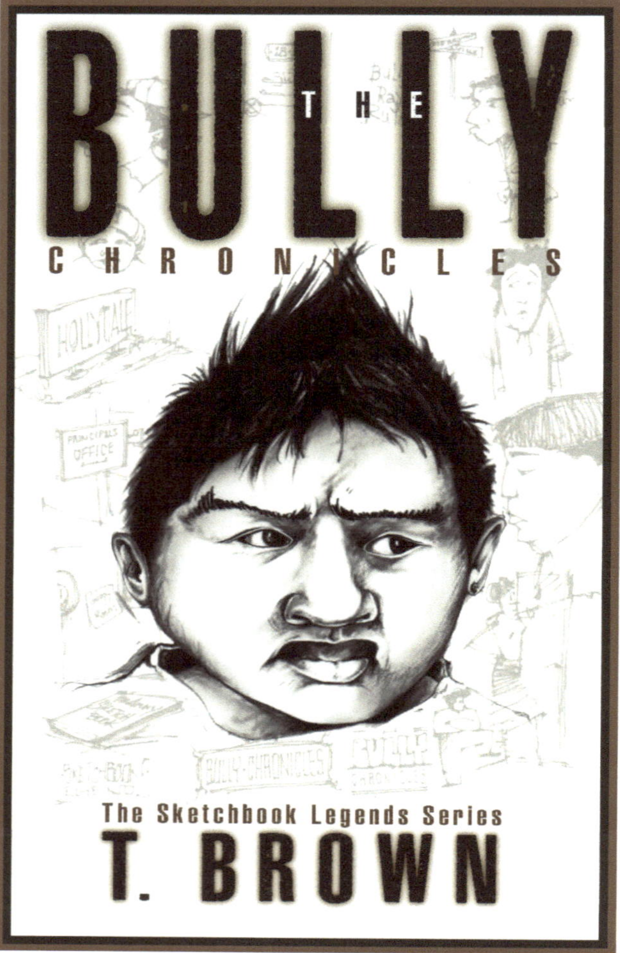

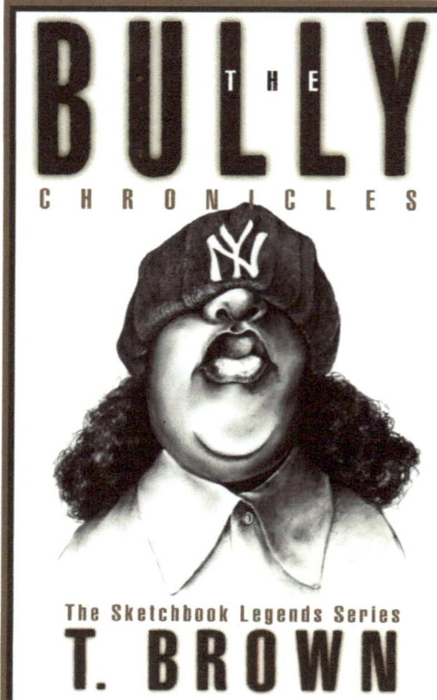

Bully Chronicles represented a new genre for our publishing company. We moved from picture books into the young reader genre or YA Market. This was important because my son Xavier was an avid reader and still is to this day. There never seemed to be enough titles for him to read and I noticed he was reading the same titles several times. This first book is a collection of short stories loosely based on my own experiences. Librarians I have spoken to were so welcoming of the title and agreed this segment is indeed starving for more quality content.

Left: The Bully Chronicles cover, Published 2019 Brown Sugar Press Books LLC. (Showing two versions of the cover)

Right: Illustration from the Book, *The Bully Chronicles*, 'Hallway Holdup'
Graphite on vellum

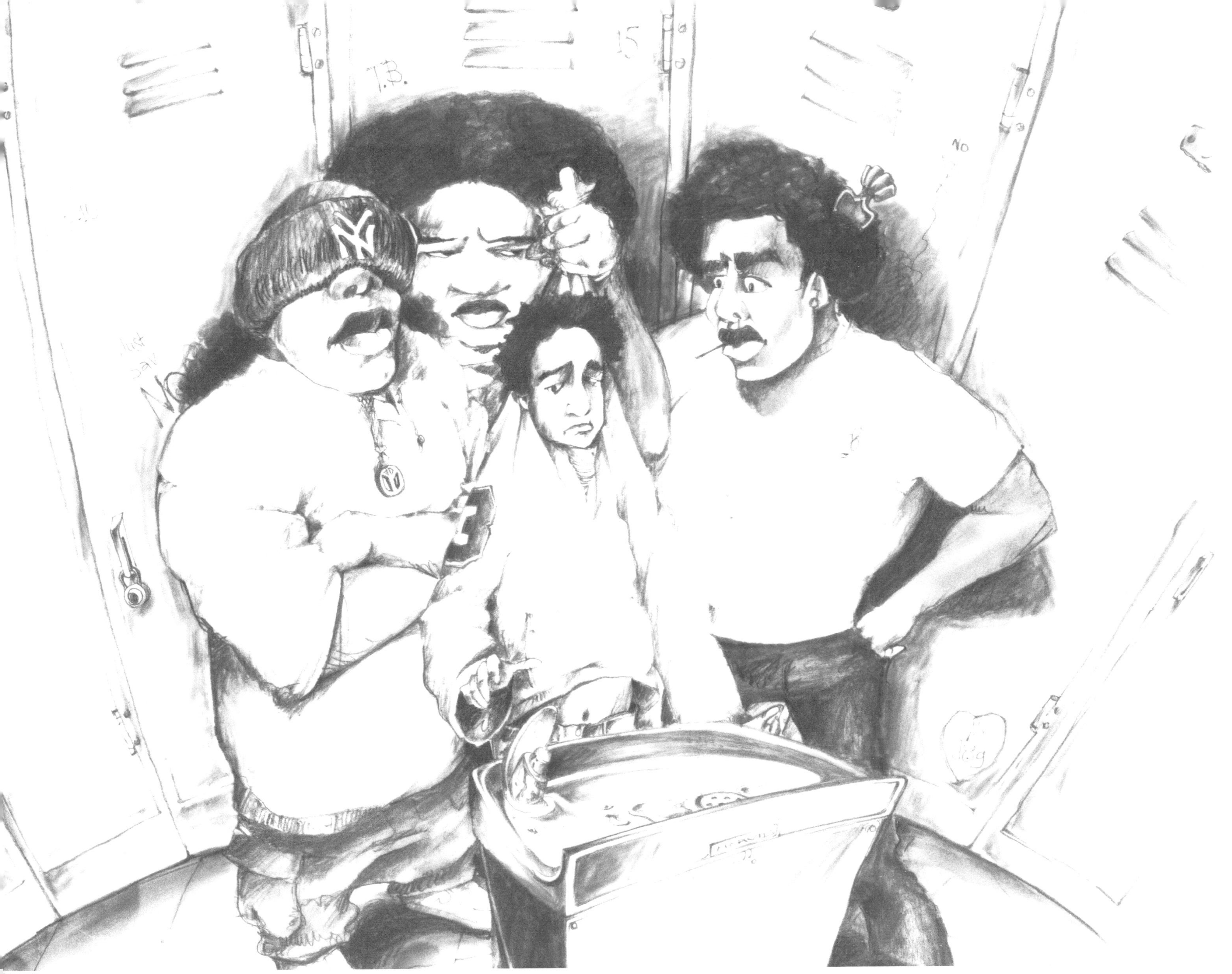

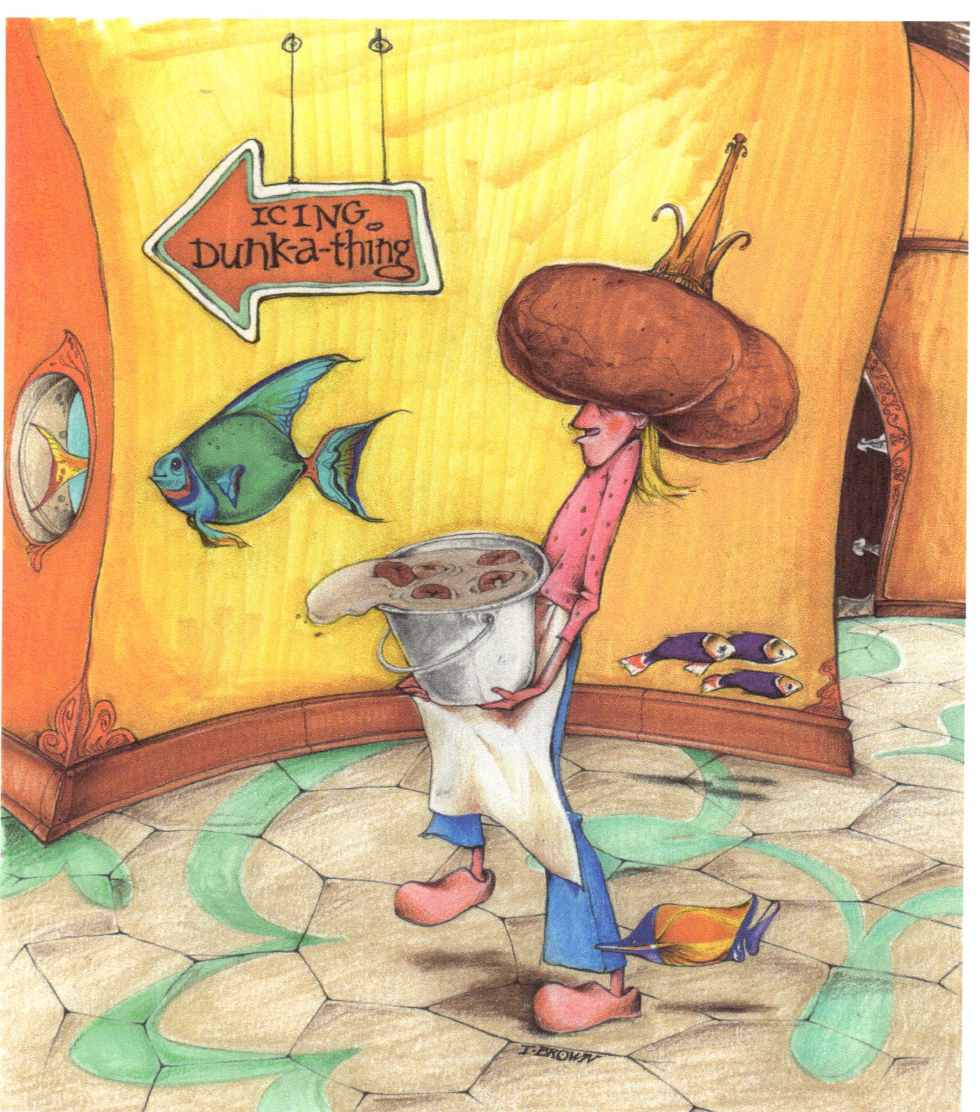

Left: Illustration from upcoming book about a baker
Color pencil, marker on 360 paper

Right (Background image):Illustration from the Book, *The Bully Chronicles*, 'Lunch takaway'
Pastel on Lana paper

Right: Illustration from the Book, *The Bully Chronicles*, 'Bully Bees'
Color pencil, marker on 360 paper

Right: Illustration from the Book, *The Bully Chronicles*, *Sunday Morning with Guppy*.

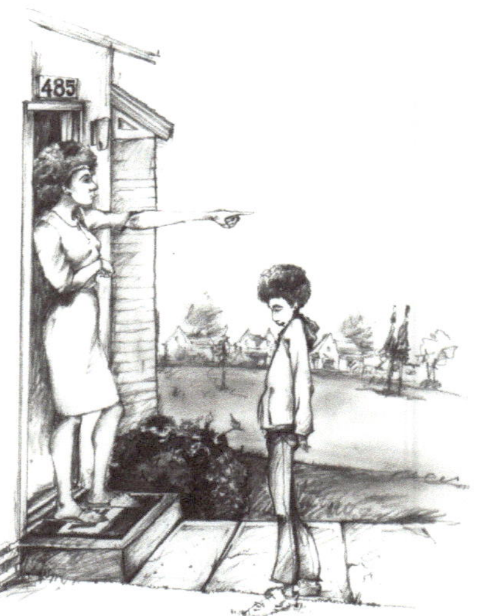

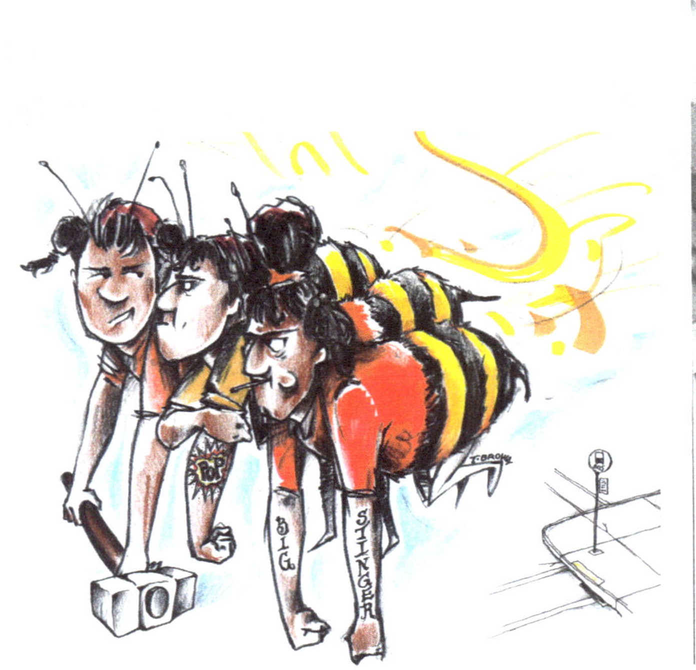

BIG
STINGER

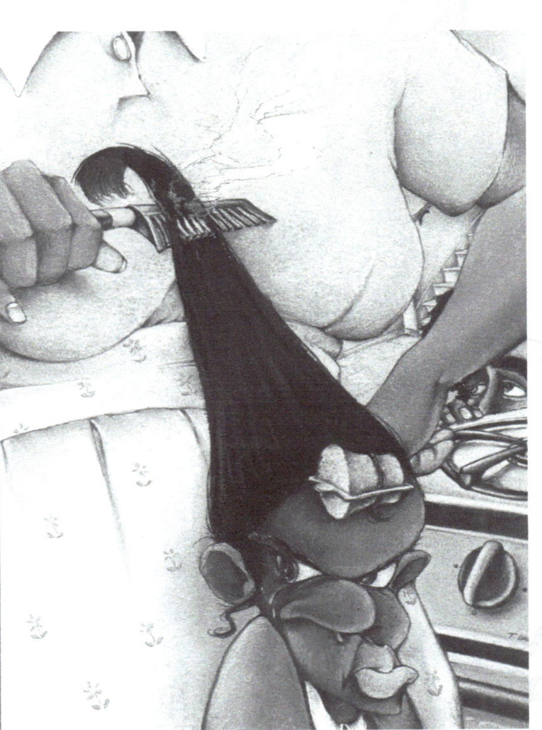

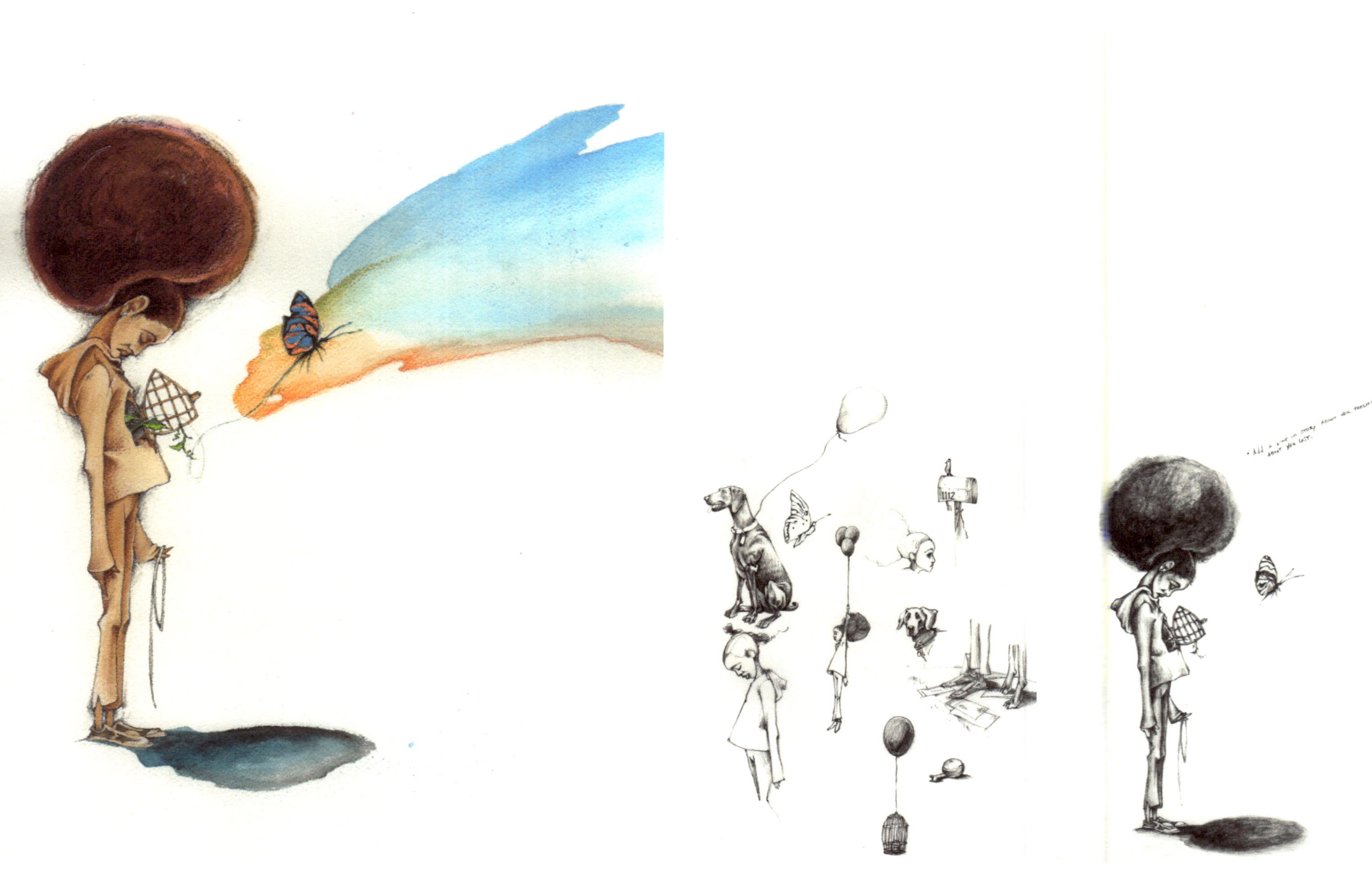

Add a line in story about her feeling about her lost.

Left: Illustration from the Children's Book, *Lois and the Red Balloon*.
Page 15. Early sketches for the Lois book. Graphite on tissue paper.

Right: Illustration from *Lois and the Red Balloon*. Page 11.
'The Family.'

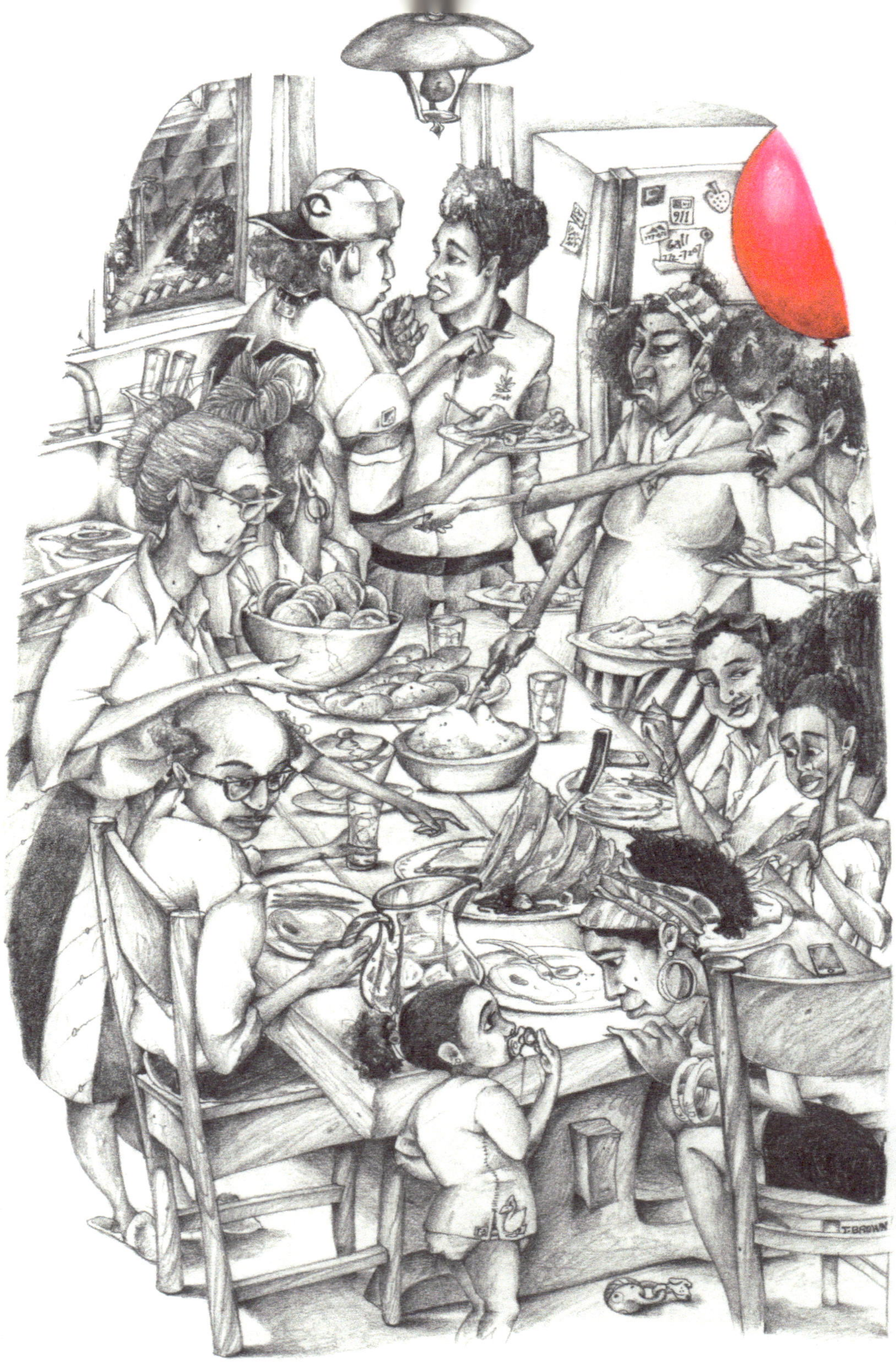

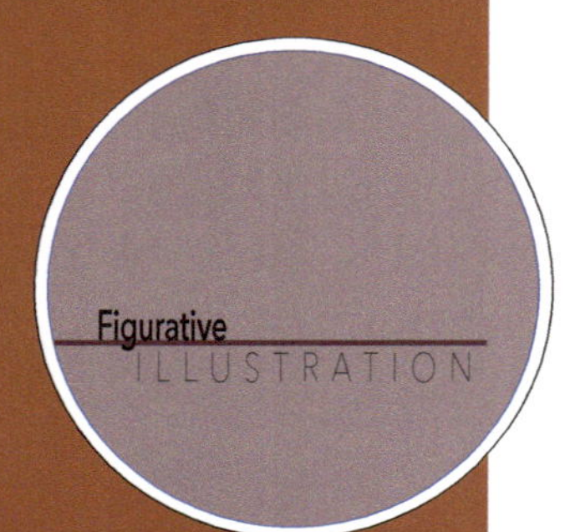

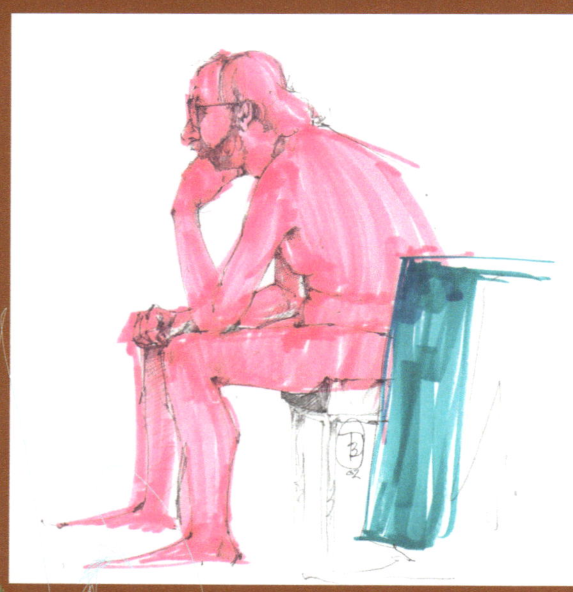

My very first professor at a school named Cincinnat Academy of De-sign, (Mike McGuire) was absolutely great at drawing the figure. He was the first person that actually inspired me to fall in love with the figure and commit myself to drawing all aspects of the better. Later it would prove to be an important aspect when I began working at a local design firm in Cincinnati. I was actually the only designer that could handle any figurative projects that involved the client look-ing at sketches of people. Thanks Mike. Most of these figure studies were completed during my participation in the Art Club Figure weekly drawing sessions. After design school I really had no place to practice developing my skills with the figure. With the advent of Macs, design-ers were drawing figuratively less and less. During the years of 1992 til around 1998, myself and an illustrator friend on mine from that great migration of illustrators out of Detroit named Dave Vermett attenced the weekly Art Club Figure drawing sessions to keep our skills sharp. The Art Club also had a annual exhibit if you wanted to enter your fa-vorit pieces from the sessions. Some entered drawings, some entered finished painting based on the subjects they sketched in the longer pose Wednseday sessions.

Left: Seated Nude
Marker and graphite on paper

Right: Seated Nude in Aqua (Detail)
Marker and graphite on paper

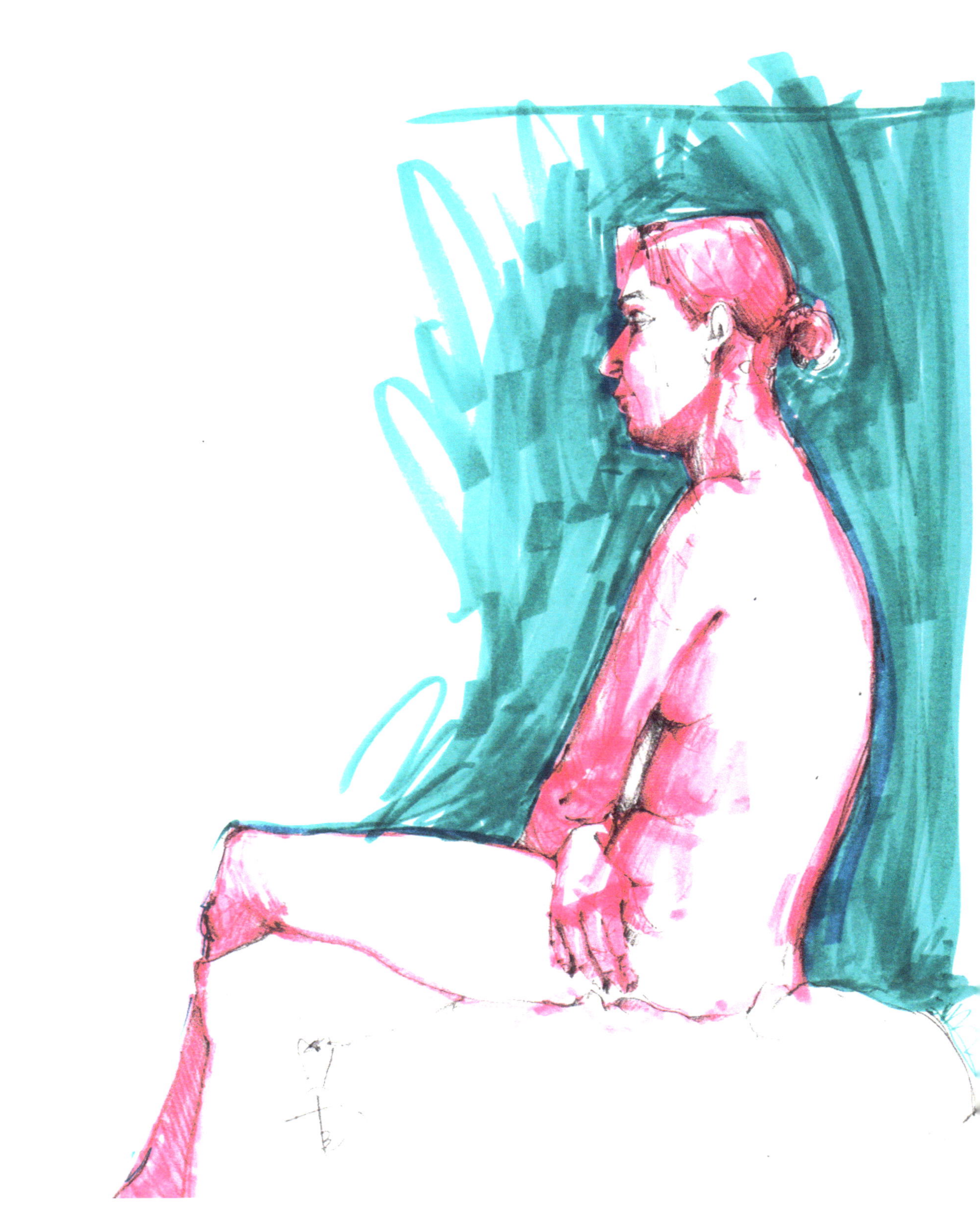

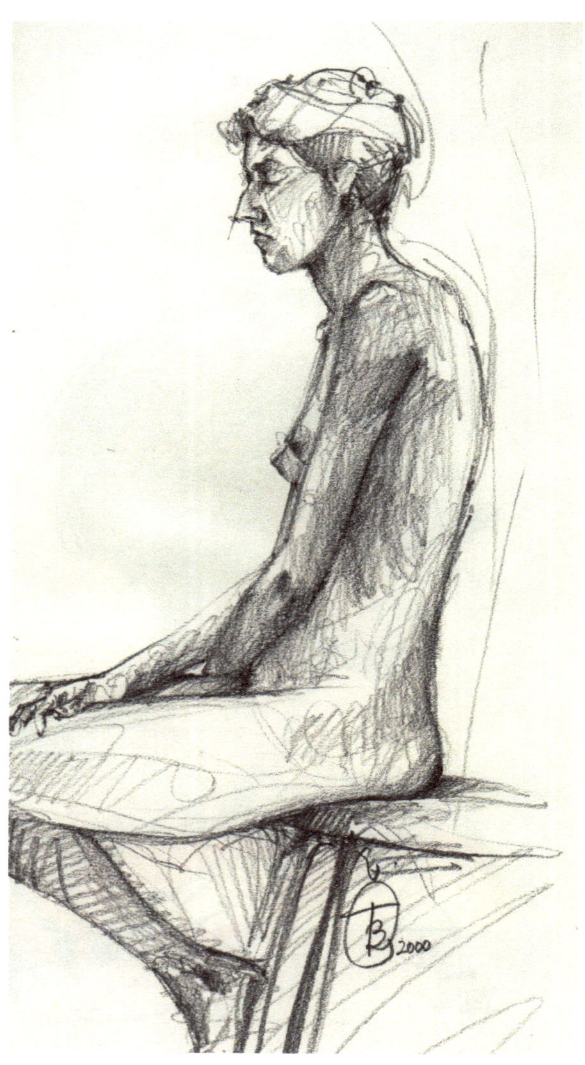

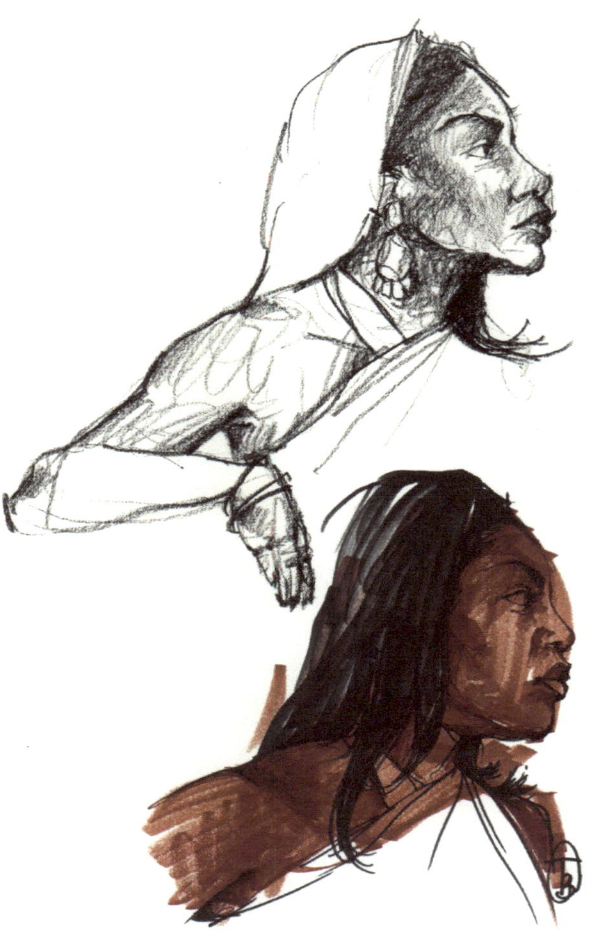

Left: Laura Seated
Graphite on paper

Left: The Sista (Head Study of Sandy)
Marker and charcole on paper

Right: Female Seated
Marker and graphite

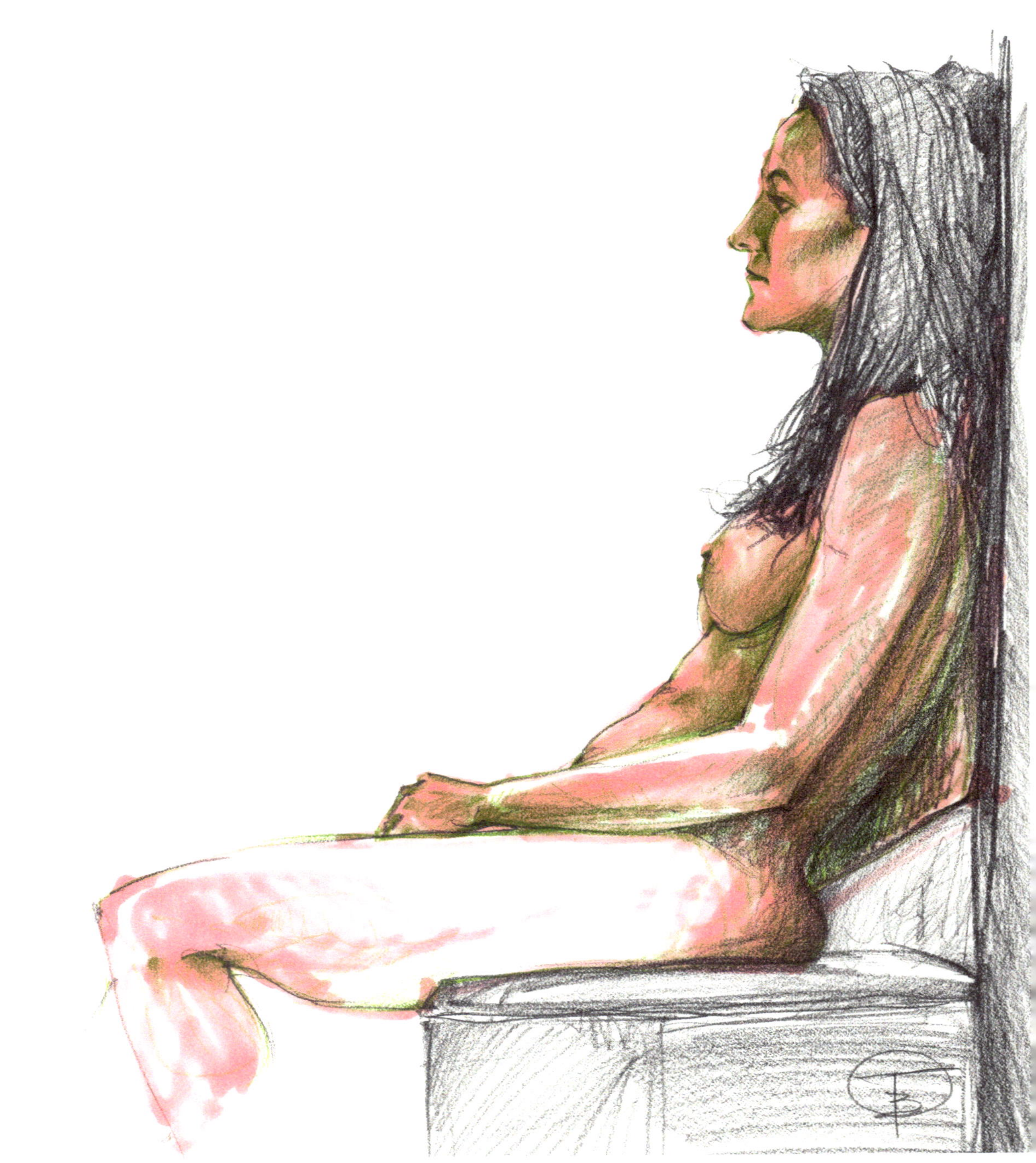

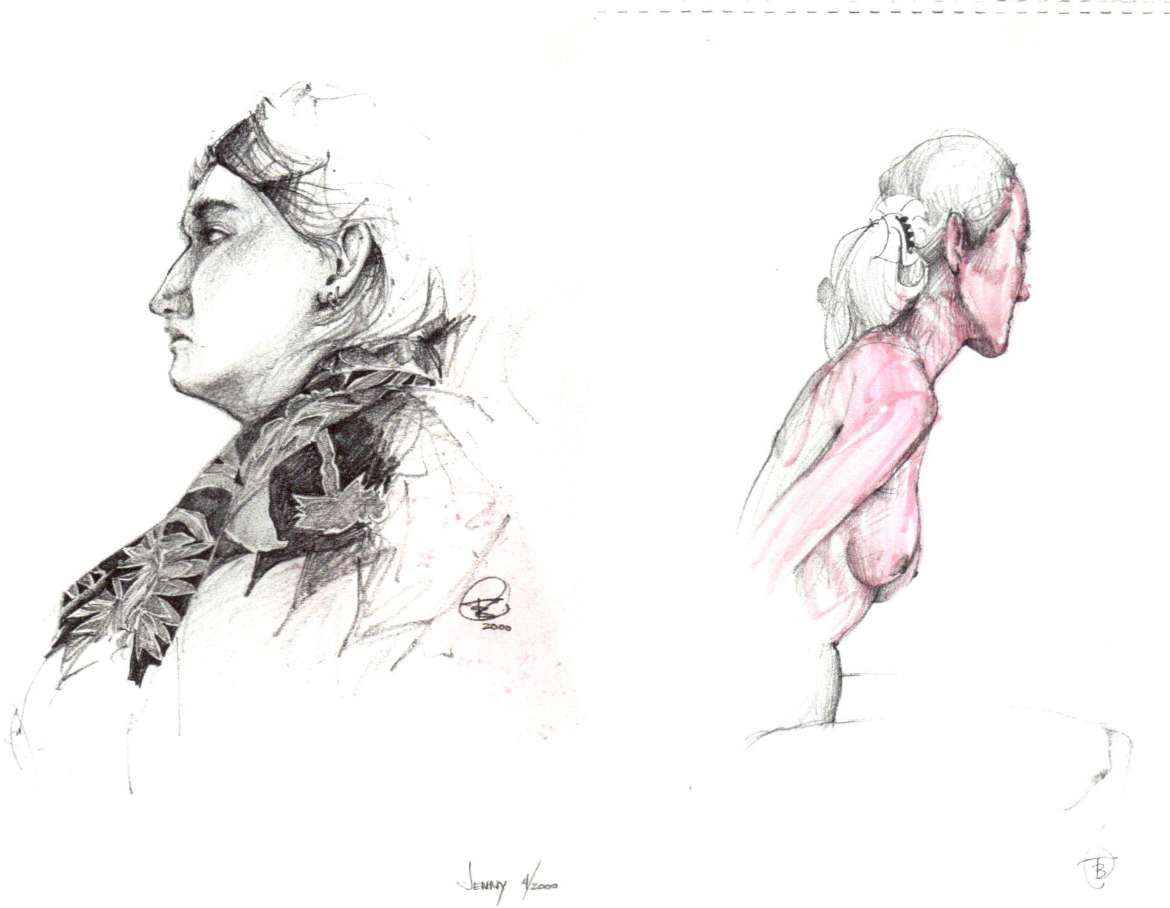

Left: Jenny's Blouse, Graphite

Left: Marker and graphite study

Above right: Graphite study on paper

Right: Fetal Nude
Charcole on newsprint

Right: Relaxed Gaze, Charcole

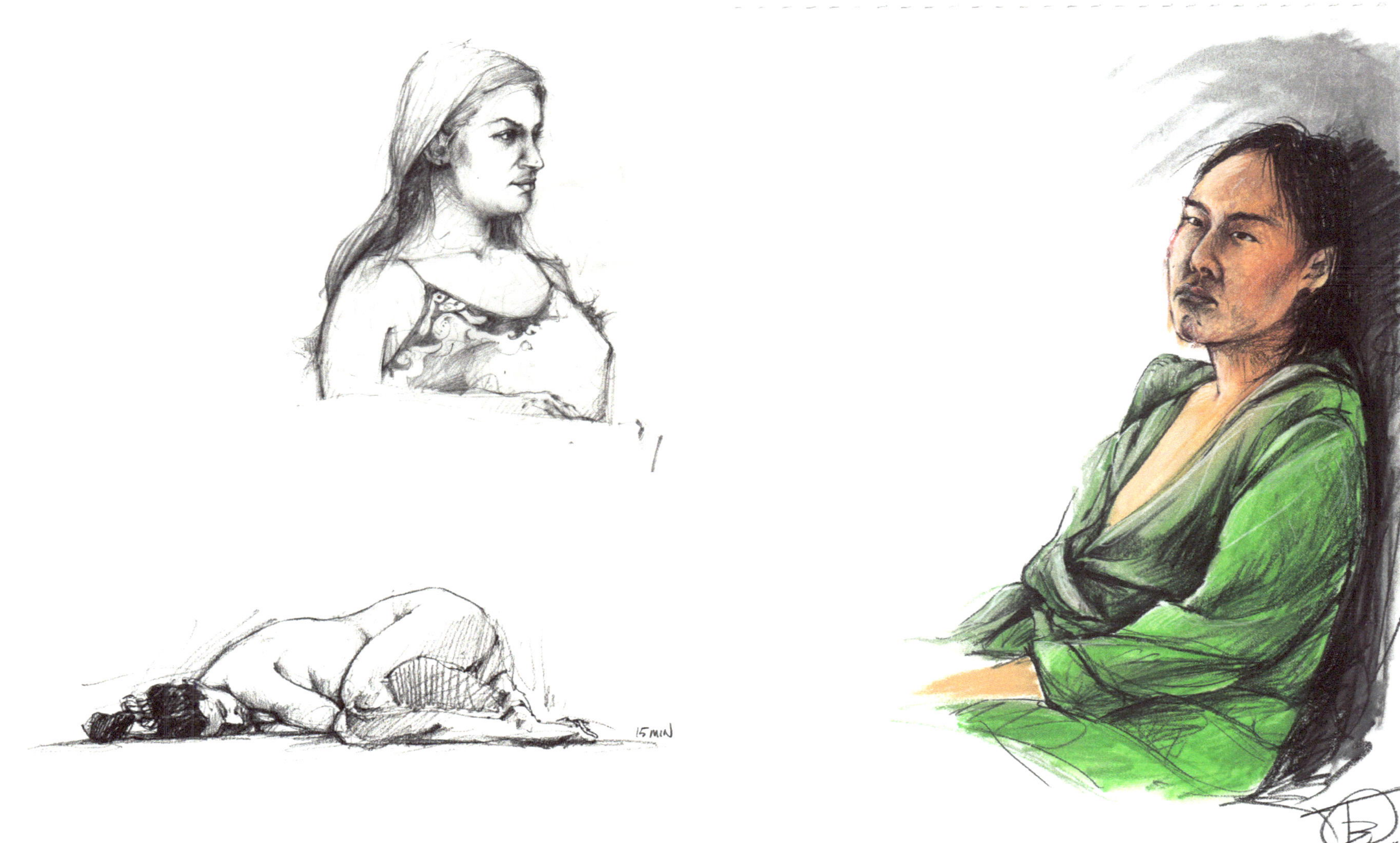
15 MIN

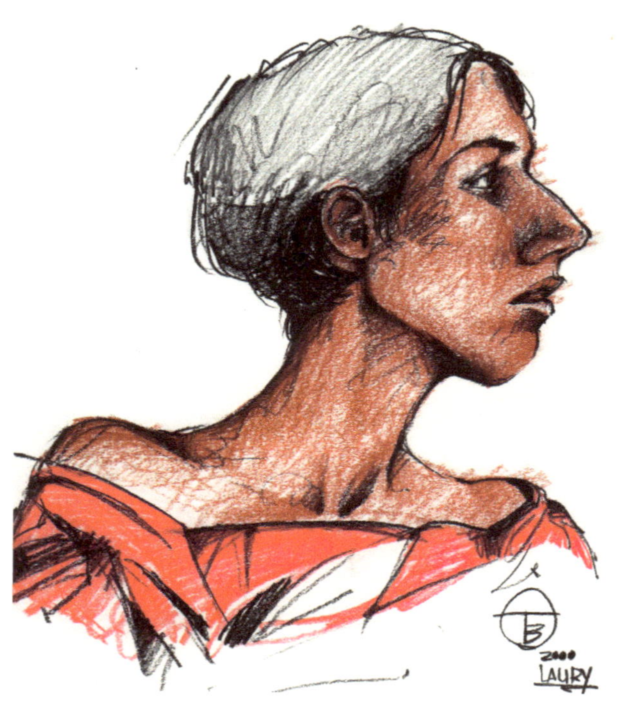

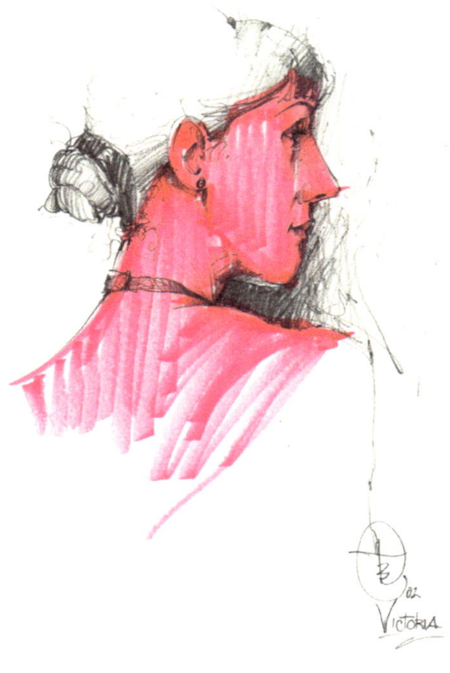

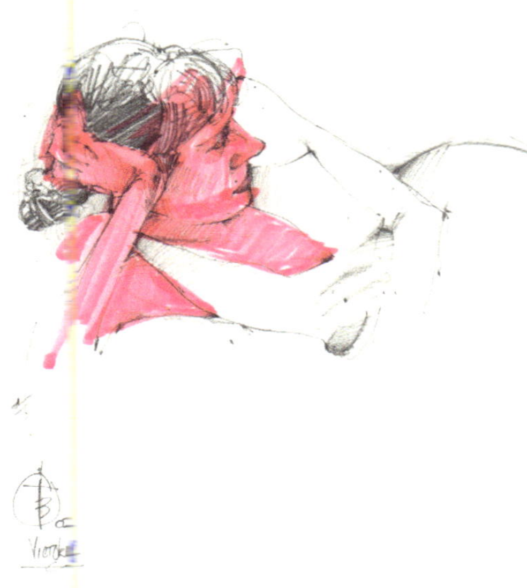

Left: Laura
Pastel study

Middle: Victoria
Marker and graphite

Top: Victoria relaxing
Marker and graphite

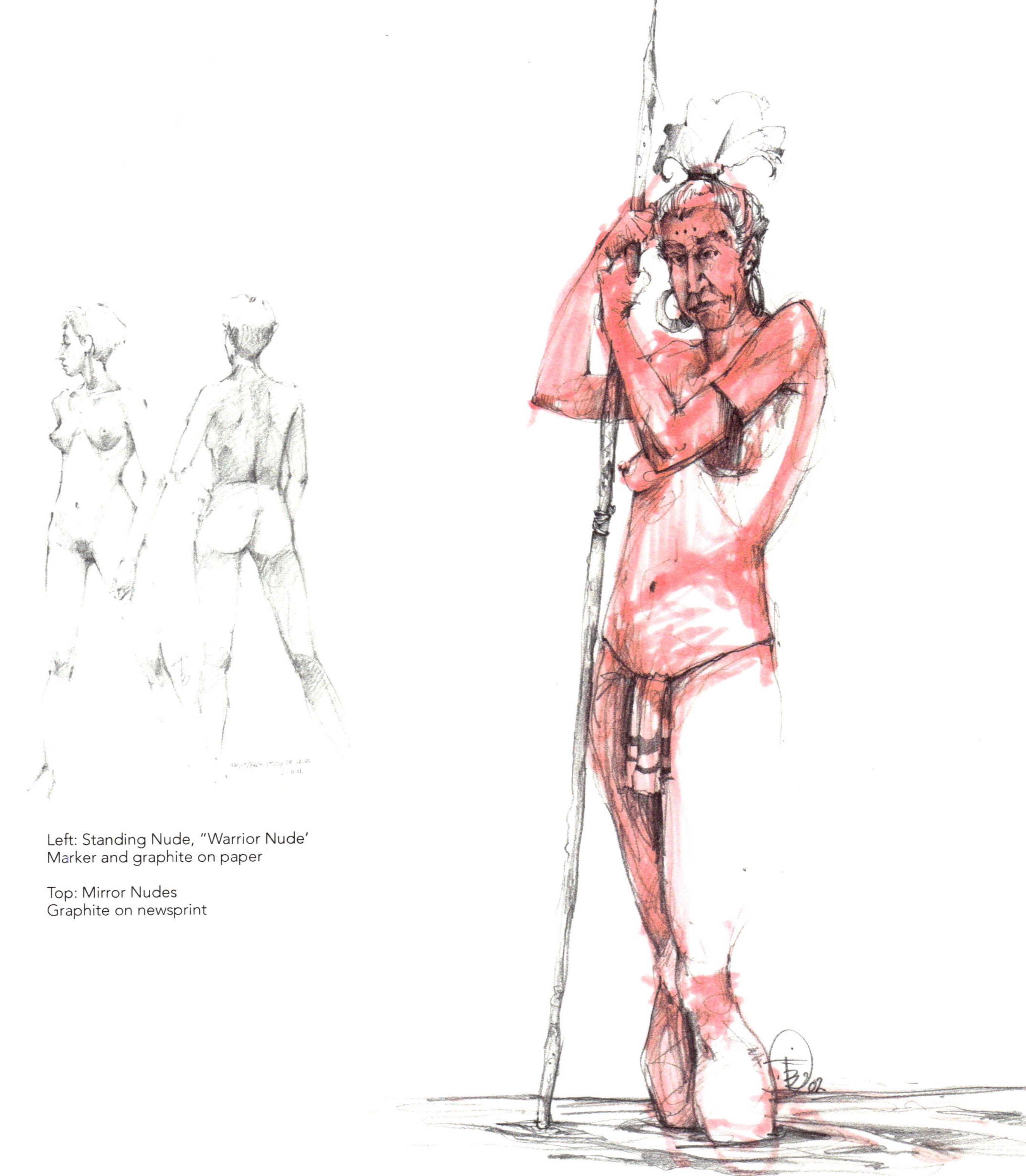

Left: Standing Nude, "Warrior Nude'
Marker and graphite on paper

Top: Mirror Nudes
Graphite on newsprint

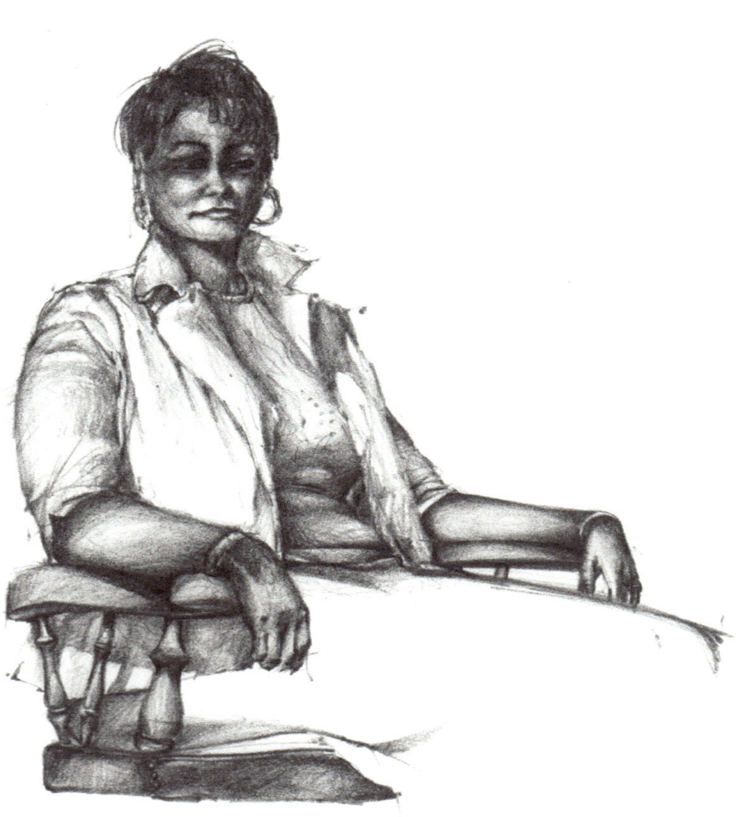

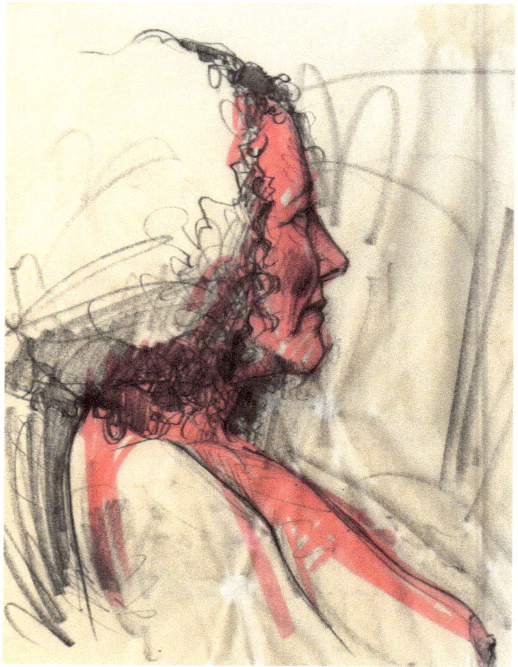

Figure drawing session sketches from an extremely rare African American and Asians model sitting while Troy was a membver of the Cincinnati Art Club in Mt. Adams.

Left: Connie Seated
graphite on paper

This Page Top: graphite study on tissue paper
Facing Page Right: Charcole study on newsprint

Facing Page Far Right: A black dude, pastel

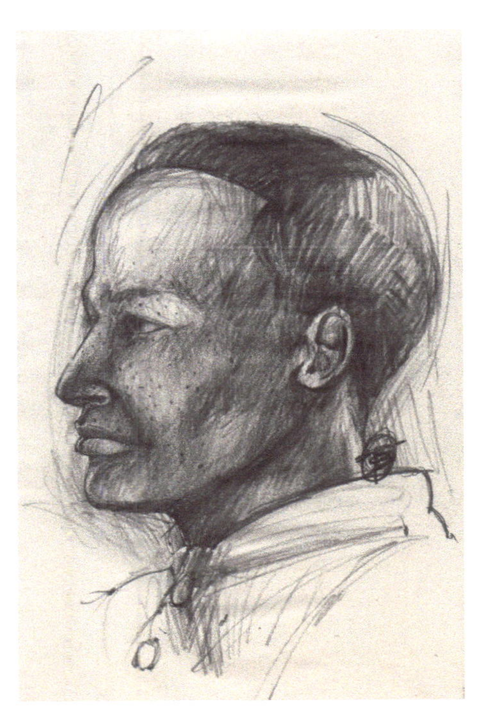
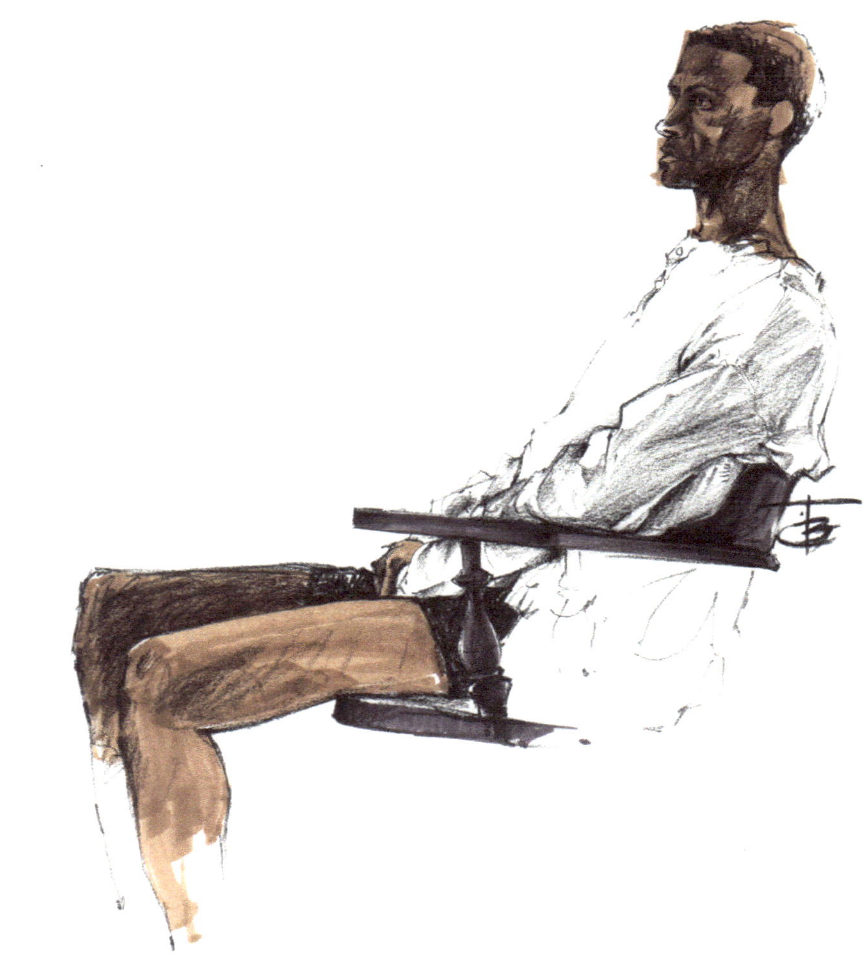

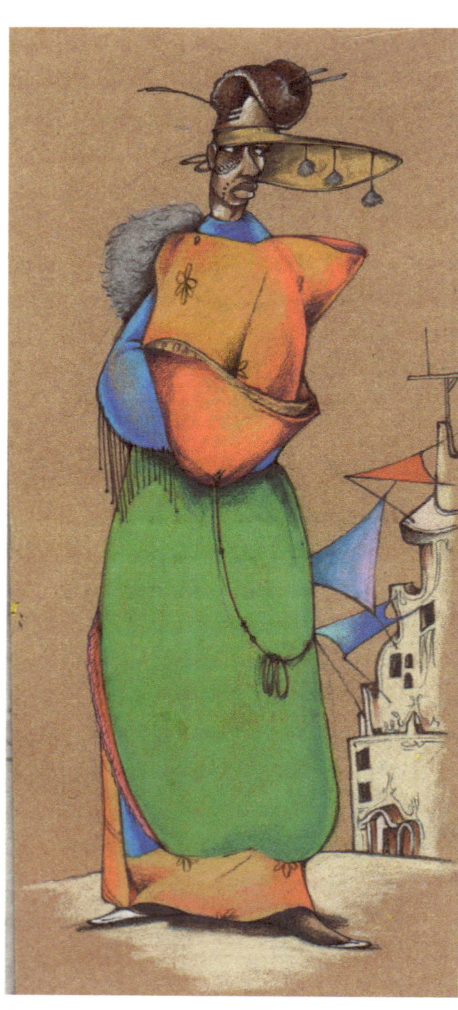

Artist Bio & CV

Troy's interpersonal communication skills have taken him from the classrooms of his alma mater. The Art Academy of Cincinnati, where he taught foundation and illustration courses for several years, to The School of the Art Institute of Chicago, where he used his skills to run SAIC's Summer Institute Residency Program, to his present location in his studio outside of Raleigh, North Carolina. Troy now focuses those interpersonal skills gained teaching and administrating programs to communicate complex emotional content in his illustrations and creative client-based projects. Currently, he moves between the worlds of children's book illustration and client-based illustration work.

In addition to his successful career in packaging design while working as an art director in his hometown of Cincinnati, T. Brown has a BFA in Communication Arts with an emphasis in illustration and graphic design. He also has a master's in Art Education from DAAP at the University of Cincinnati, where he focused on curriculum design and studio practice.

Artist Personal Statement

My work is narrowly focused on the emotional content of my characters. My goal is to allow the viewer to journey with my characters through the process of discovery. Stories happen on many levels, but my central goal is to push the emotional content hidden beneath the surface for the purpose of discovery beyond the basic story line. My images are direct and simplistic in composition to provide clarity for the viewer.

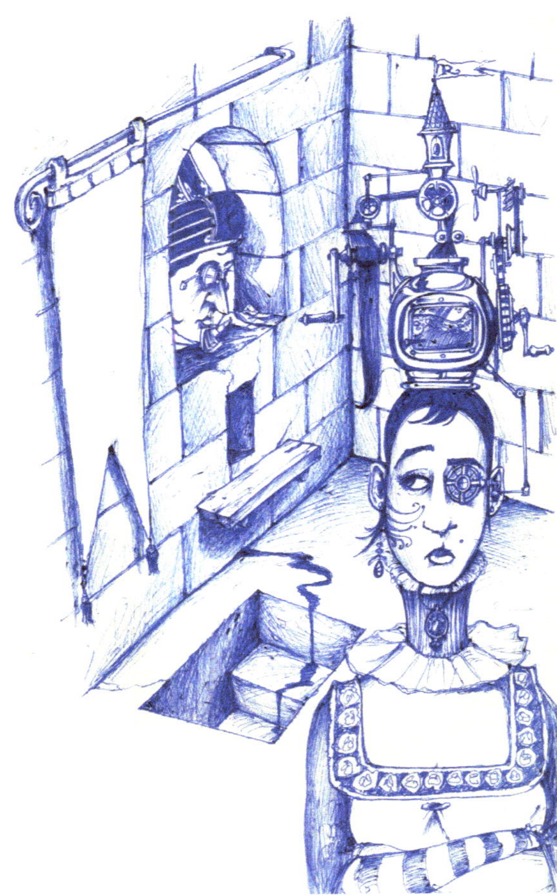

Left: Concept sketch for an upcoming book based loosely on Bible themes.

Above: Concept sketch for a children's book.

Exhibitions & Honors

2020	Studio Visit Magazine, Winter Edition #46
2018	Studio Visit Magazine, Winter Edition #44
2016	Studio Visit Magazine, Winter Edition #36
2014	Black Creativity Juried Art Exhibit, Chicago, IL
2012	US Air Force Artist Program Recipient/Southeast Region
2005	CMYK Magazine National Student Merit recipient/Illustration
2004	CMYK Magazine National Student Merit recipient/Illustration
2004	Excellence Award Winner, Art Academy Scholarship Competition
2004	Miller Gallery Scholarship recipient
2003	Tall Stacks Official Poster Contest Winner
2003	Top Scholarship Winner, Art Academy of Cincinnati

Exhibitions

2020	NCCU Faculty Exhibition/Carboro Arts Center, Chapel Hill, NC
2018	One Man Retrospective Exhibit & Residency/Maryville College, TN
2018	Studio Visit Magazine, Winter Edition #44
2018	AP Art Exhibit Curator 2018 AP Brochure/Exhibit
2018	One man Exhibition – Saul Alexander Gallery, Charleston, SC
2016	Studio Visit Magazine Exhibitor/Winter Edition #36
2016	Contemporary Art Museum Raleigh/CAMstellation Exhibition
2015	Black Creativity Exhibition Chicago
2013	School of the Art Institute of Chicago Faculty/Staff Exhibit
2011	AAC Community Education Faculty Exhibit

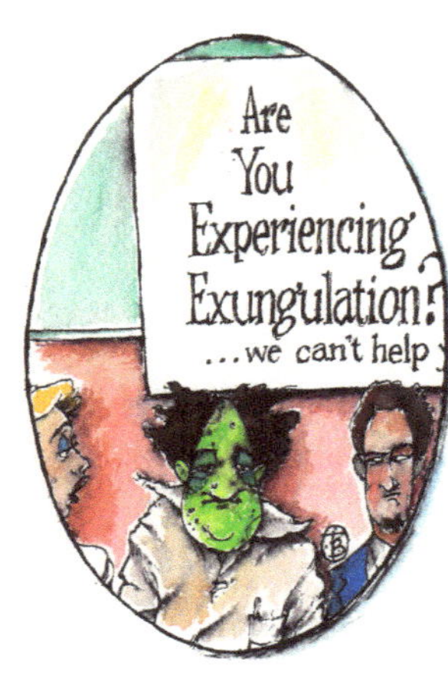

Exungulate.

Left: Exungulate illustrated, watercolor, 8' x 10'

Above: Concept sketch for a children's book.

2010	AAC Community Education Faculty Exhibit
2008	ARC Fundraising Exhibit
2008	AAC Community Education Faculty Exhibit
2007	Tiger Lilly Annual Exhibit
2005	Group Exhibit, Media Bridges, Cincinnati, OH.
2004	Chidlaw Gallery, Cincinnati, OH.
2002	Cincinnati Art Club Sketch Group Exhibit
2000	Cincinnati Art Club Sketch Group Exhibit
1998 - 2000	US Environmental Protection Agency, Black History Month Exhibit
1998	Freeman Gallery, Cincinnati, OH/One Man Show

Lectures

2016	North Carolina Central University, Art Department Durham, NC
2016	Cameron Library Guest Lecturer, Raleigh, NC
2010	Dater Montessori High School, Cincinnati, OH
	Lakota West High School, Fairfield, OH
	McAuley High School, Cincinnati, OH
2009	Covington Catholic High School, Covington, KY.
	Lakota East High School, Cincinnati, OH.
	Loveland High School, OH
2007	Newport Central Catholic
	Taylor High School
	McAuley High School

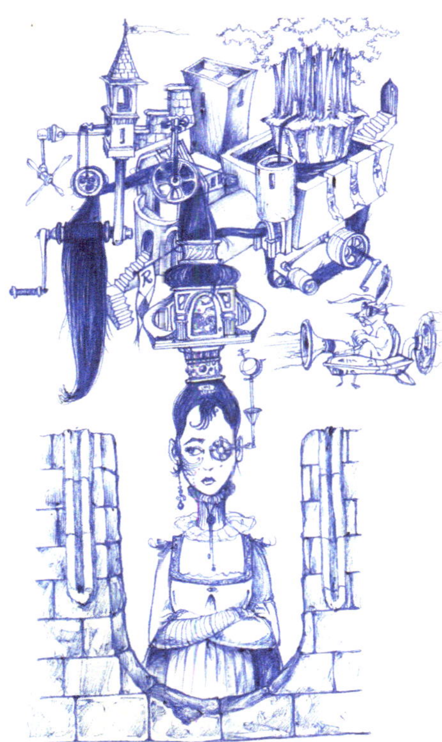

2006	J. F. Dulles Elementary School, Oak Hills, OH.
2005	William Henry Harrison High School, Harrison, OH.
	Loveland High School, Loveland, OH.
	Covington Catholic High School, Covington, KY.
	Villa Madonna Academy, Villa Hills, KY.
	J. F. Burns Elementary School, Maineville, OH.
2004	Clark Montessori School, Cincinnati, OH
	Options Academy, Hamilton, OH.
	Jacobs High School, Cincinnati, OH.
	Lakota East High School, Cincinnati, OH.

Commissions/Client List

1996 to Present	The Perfect Brew
2006 to 2009	Upstream Media
2007	Powers Agency
2006	Jetlag Productions Inc. Screening Room Mural
2004	Cincinnati Public Library, Mural for the Children's Department
2004	Art Academy of Cincinnati 2004 Graduation Invitation and Program design
2003	Margaritas Restaurant Group, illustrated 12 original prints for the 8th St. location
2002	Tower Place Mall, Margaritas Restaurant Mural Project, Cincinnati, OH
2001	Creative Department Design Studio, Cincinnati, OH. Illustrations for Planet Feedback Campaign

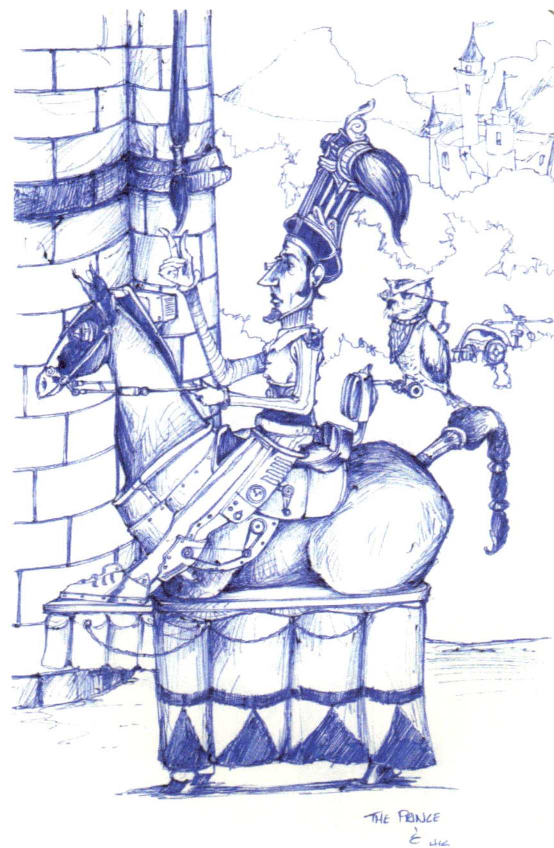

Above: Concept sketch for a children's book.

Right: Early concept, 'Steam Punk Pigs'

1999	Cincinnati Art Museum/Donald Sowell Endowment
	Design of the Black Film Festival Invitation and Program
1998	Otis Williams Limitless Enterprises, Victory for Youth Book Illustrations
1996	Cincinnati Ballet Kids' Wall Mural Project
1987-1996	Fifth Third Bank Jazz Series illustrations

Publications

| 2009 | Globalization Art & Education, Dr. Flavia Bastos Border Crossing Dialogues: Criti cally Preparing Art Educators for Participation in a Global Society |

Education

2018	K-12 Certification - SCAD/Savannah College Art Design
2005 – 2006	MAAE/DAAP University of Cincinnati, Cincinnati, OH
	Masters in Art Education
Summer 2006	Culmination/Study Abroad
	University of Cincinnati/DAAP – Sao Paulo, Brasil
	Museu Afro Brasil, Sao Paulo, Brasil
2003 – 2005	B.F.A. Art Academy of Cincinnati, Cincinnati, OH
2003	Virginia Commonwealth University, Richmond, VA
	Illustration Academy
1983 – 85	Cincinnati Academy of Design, Cincinnati, OH

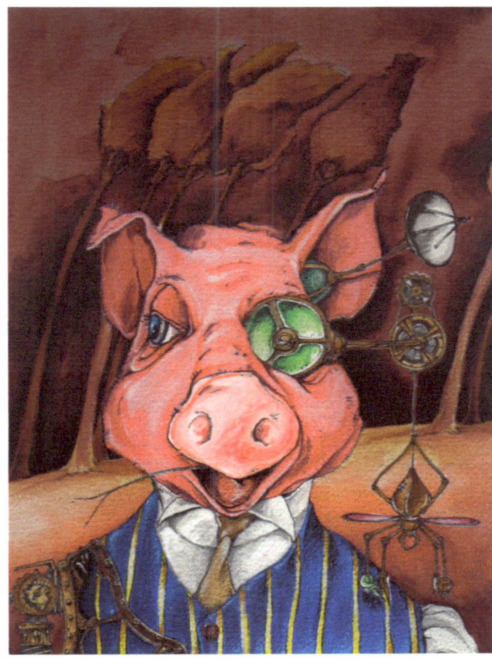

Areas of Specialization
Educator
Instructor/Lecturer: Illustration, Graphic Design, Drawing, Painting, Foundation Core, and Art History
Curriculum Development: Outreach Programs, Community and Continuing Education

Special Thanks:
My wife, Sherie, for her constant support and companionship. My many colleagues and mentors for their support over the years. To my mentors in education and illustration, Alex Bostic, Mark Thomas, Loren Long, Lydia Thompson, Flávia Bastos, and Matt Hart.

Maryville College and professor Carl Gombert
Special thanks to Maryville College student Sarah Cardall for the face-to-face interview that was included in the book.

This book is ultimately to my two sons, Quentin Lamar Brown & Xavier Sebastien Brown, as a testament to our legacy and to serve as a reminder for them that their destiny and purpose is even greater than their dad's.

Troy Brown
Contact: tbrown130@yahoo.com
www.artistrytbrown.com
www.brownsugarpress.com

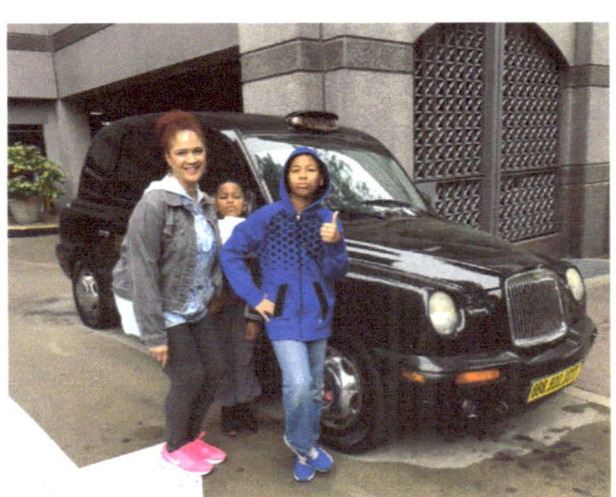

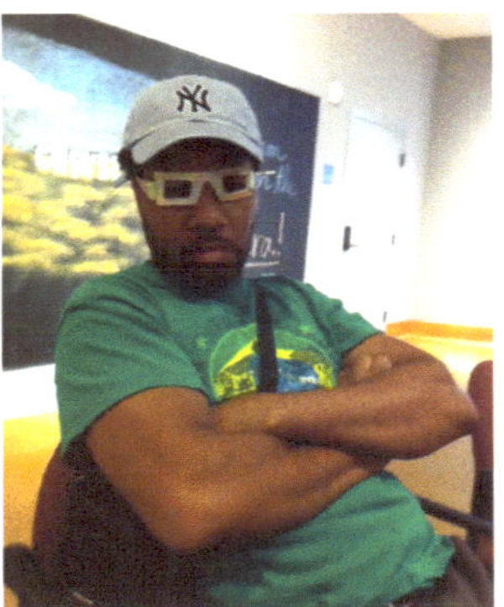

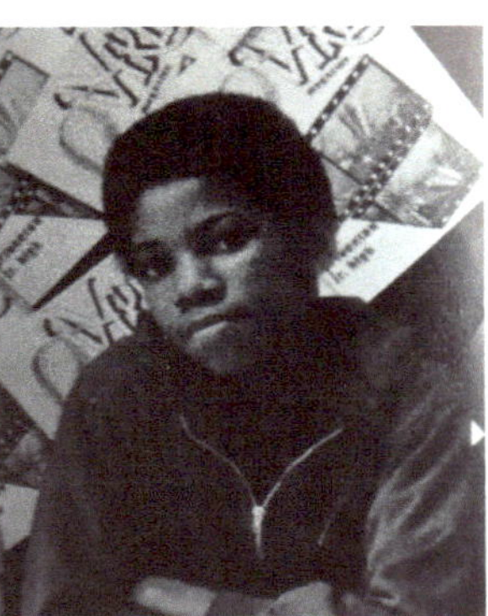

Thank You Contributors

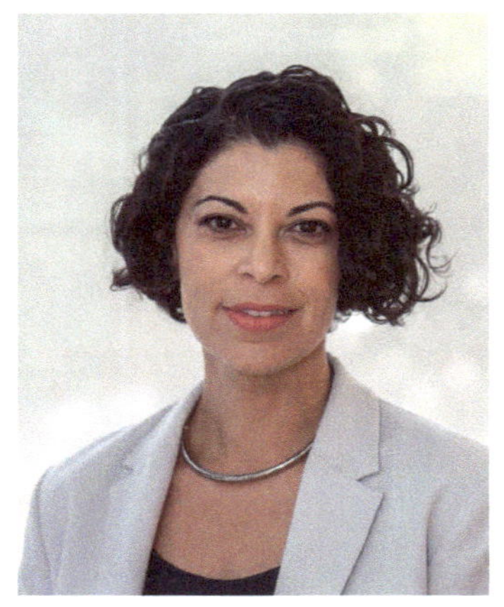

Dr. Flávia Bastos Ph.D.

Flávia Bastos, Ph.D., is professor in the School of Art, in the College of Design, Architecture, Art and Planning at the University of Cincinnati. Her research and scholarship are indebted to her Brazilian roots and her experiences with social and cultural diversity, and inspired by the educational philosophy of educator Paulo Freire. Her research and teaching honor diverse communities and celebrate creative potential of all people. Flávia is a Distinguished Fellow of the National Art Education Association, a Distinguished Research Professor at the University of Cincinnati, the chairperson for the Council of Policy Studies in Art Education, and former director of the Higher Education Division of the National Art Education Association. She received the 2009

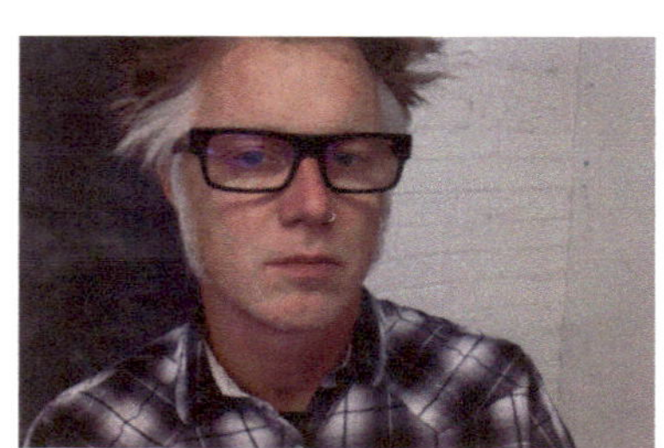

Ziegfeld Award of the International Society for Education through Art (InSEA) for her distinguished service in international art education and the Mary J. House Award of the National Art Education Association Women's Caucus in 2007. She is past senior editor of the Journal of Art Education and has published and lectured extensively in the United States and other countries, such as South Africa, Brazil, Chile, Indonesia, Spain, Portugal, and Canada. Her books include Transforming City Schools Through Art: Approaches to Meaningful K-12 Learning, a coedited volume published by Teachers College Press (2012), and the anthology Connecting Creativity Research and Practice in Art Education: Foundations, Pedagogies, and Contemporary Issues (2014), released by the National Art Education Association.

Matt Hart Ph.D.

Matt Hart is the author of nine books of poems, including most recently Everything Breaking/for Good (YesYes Books, 2019) and The Obliterations (Pickpocket Books, 2019). Additionally, his poems, reviews, and essays have appeared or are forthcoming in numerous print and online journals, including The Academy of American Poets online, Big Bell, Cincinnati Review, Columbia Poetry Review, Harvard Review, Jubilat, Kenyon Review online, Lungfull!, Mississippi Review, and POETRY, among others. His awards include a Pushcart Prize, a 2013 individual artist grant from The Shifting Foundation, and fellowships from both the Bread Loaf Writers' Conference and the Warren Wilson College MFA Program for Writers. A cofounder and the editor-in-chief of Forklift, Ohio: A Journal of Poetry, Cooking & Light Industrial Safety, he lives in Cincinnati where he teaches at the Art Academy of Cincinnati and plays in the band NEVERNEW.

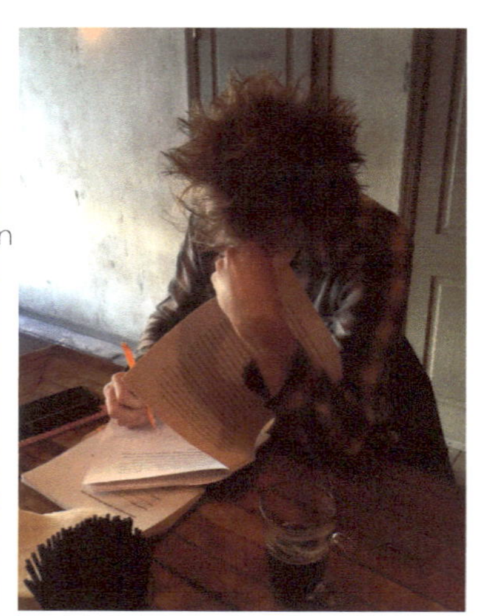

9 781735 261706